Promises Kept

EDITED BY HENRY C. FERRELL JR.

Promises Kept

East Carolina University,

1980–2007

East Carolina University   Greenville, North Carolina

Design and production by BW&A Books, Inc., Durham, N.C.
Printed in Canada by Friesens Corp.

Unless otherwise noted, all photographs are by Forrest Croce
or from the archives of East Carolina University

Library of Congress Cataloging-in-Publication Data
Ferrell, Henry C., 1934–
Promises kept / Henry C. Ferrell, Jr.—1st ed.
p. cm.
Includes bibliographical references and index.
ISBN-13: 978-0-9758874-3-1 (cloth : alk. paper)
1. East Carolina University – History. I. Title.
LD1741.E44 F472 2006   2006929936
378.756/44—dc22

For the faculty, staff, and employees
of East Carolina University

Contents

Preface

EDUCATIONAL INSTITUTIONS comprise some of the most successful inventions of humankind. Entrepreneurial establishments are only momentary organizations when compared with those of higher education. Some universities and colleges count their beginnings over seven hundred years in the past. Many have failed, sometimes owing to internal weaknesses or external events. Successful colleges and universities have depended upon skilled leadership, practiced faculty, competent staff, financial assets, and flexible responses to the change of the years to create and foster an environment of scholarship.

Institutional experiences differ within the framework of an encompassing pattern. East Carolina University, chartered in 1907, had determined to serve the community that created it. As the years passed, other groups and interests joined. Although based on a hundred-year-old concept, this youthful university journeyed beyond past practices and shunned ivory towers. Its motto, "To serve," reflected a commitment to change, if needed. It intended to serve as a repository of ancient learning, a laboratory for new understandings, and a projector of visions to benefit society.

By 1980, the university had assembled a body of intentions—promises —to cultivate. East Carolina had been successfully desegregated. Undergraduate degree programs won new students. Fine arts had obtained essential physical plants. Arts and sciences also benefited from construction and library expansion. The professional schools—business, allied health, and education—either had realized long-standing building goals or had plans to obtain them. The medical school partnered with Pitt Memorial Hospital and completed the last touches to its core campus. Other graduate programs, while postponed by the University of North Carolina system, made their way slowly and cautiously to reality.

To continue to advance required a fully supportive financial base from East Carolina's parent, the North Carolina General Assembly. Other fiscal sources included student tuition payments, patient fees, foundation grants, and individual contributions. Faculty members had carried heavy teaching and service assignments for the previous twenty years so that existing resources might support new programs. To achieve many of the university's promises, individual faculty would depend on more assigned time for research. Younger members must be recruited to help reach new academic heights. Required laboratory instruments and other resources had been too long deferred. Long-range plans were shaped to lead the university to new levels of achievement. During the next generation East Carolina would hurry to keep its commitments.

The university successfully spent the last third of its first century keeping promises made in the past. With the first century's conclusion, despite false starts and external interruptions, East Carolina prepared to greet its second.

Henry C. Ferrell Jr.
University Historian

Acknowledgments

THE APPROACH of East Carolina University's centennial celebration in 2007 prompted *Promises Kept: East Carolina University, 1980–2007.* Mary Jo Bratton's *East Carolina University: The Formative Years* had carried the university's history into the early 1980s. Chancellor William Muse proposed that a second volume be assembled that linked to the Bratton volume. It would complete a text survey of the university's first century. Muse's successors, William Shelton and Steven Ballard, endorsed continuation of the project.

Bob Thompson suggested that I furnish oversight for the undertaking. The administrative care of Austin Bunch and Jim Smith aided in its completion. University archivist Suellyn Lathrop provided in exceptional fashion her skills to assist the essay authors in their inquiry into the recent past.

Special appreciation for their assistance goes to Forrest Croce, Rebecca Futrell, Joe Gaddis, and Sage Rountree. Barbara Williams and Julie Allred at BW&A Books contributed valuable professional advice. Martha Smith Ferrell gave her understanding and the support needed to assemble *Promises Kept: East Carolina University, 1980–2007.*

The essays that follow are arranged topically. They inform a reader of the ways of a modern university. Each author has applied a personal perspective. Some essayists have chosen a narrative form. Others organized their chapters as memoirs. Sources are recorded within each essay.

The essay authors have given the university community a valuable review of East Carolina's immediate past. Using their knowledge, interviews with participants, and the resources of Joyner Library's Special Collections, they have left a record that future historians will reference profitably.

Introduction

HENRY C. FERRELL JR.

MANY GROUPS and people led in the formation of East Carolina University. The political atmosphere in 1890s North Carolina also influenced its establishment. Throughout this decade political collisions between Populists, Republicans, and Democrats spawned a move by the latter to restrict the voting franchise. They successfully required a state literacy test for voter eligibility. Democratic leaders such as Governor Charles Aycock promised to provide reading opportunities for both white and black voters. To grow, the public school system needed competent teachers across the state.

By 1900, teacher training schools for whites existed in Boone, Cullowhee, and Greensboro. Black schools emphasizing teacher education were located in Winston-Salem, Durham, Elizabeth City, and Fayetteville. Rural leaders of the eastern region insisted upon a white teacher training school. Not only did they see education as a key to its children's future, it was a political factor in the new electoral order.

Four people were critical in the placement of a teacher training school in Greenville: Sallie Southall Cotten, a well-to-do Pitt County reformer; William Henry Ragsdale, a teacher and educational administrator; James Lawson Fleming, a Greenville attorney and rising politician; and Thomas Jordan Jarvis, a lawyer and former North Carolina governor.

Fifty years old at the end of the nineteenth century, Virginian Sallie Cotten had cultivated a progressive view of the family. It did not stop at her garden's edge or the four walls of her plantation home. A well-traveled 1863 graduate of Greensboro Female College, she taught school before marrying Robert Randolph Cotten.

The couple moved to Pitt County, where they acquired land and had children. By the last decade of the century, Mrs. Cotten possessed a wide and positive reputation as an author and poet. She also belonged to what she and her associates labeled "the woman's movement." Campaigning for more public libraries, she sought expansion of women's legal rights and educational opportunities. Her husband, a member of the General Assembly, supported her reforms, including a proposal for an eastern teacher training school. In 1901, Cotten formed, along with other women, the North Carolina Federation of Women's Clubs, a statewide organization intent upon change.

William Ragsdale, ten years Cotten's junior, graduated from Wake Forest College and taught in Scotland Neck, North Carolina, before moving to Greenville to instruct at Greenville Male Academy. His standing as a teacher spread, and his students valued his friendship. In 1900, owing to a public school reorganization, Ragsdale became school superintendent for a second time.

Ragsdale's earlier youthful experience and teaching career had acquainted him with the poor educational opportunities among rural communities. A shortage of effective white teachers could lessen with a normal college in eastern North Carolina. The state Teacher's Assembly led a statewide campaign in 1902 to improve schools. Led by superintendents, they formed an energetic network aiming to convince politicians.

A student of Ragsdale's, James Fleming, a graduate of Wake Forest College and the University of North Carolina's School of Law, returned to Greenville in 1893. He opened a law practice and won a mayoral election. Chosen for the state senate, he introduced legislation to found a normal college somewhere in eastern North Carolina. Piedmont representatives feared a detour to the east of state funding and opposed the bill, which failed. In March 1907, bending to political reality, another Fleming bill reduced the suggested normal college to a teacher training school. This draft passed the legislature. Fleming and his associates had recruited Thomas Jarvis, an icon of North Carolina politics, to help carry the edited draft.

A native of Currituck County, born in 1836, Jarvis graduated with honors from Randolph-Macon College in 1860. He returned the next year and earned a master of arts degree. Intending to teach, he opened a school in Pasquotank County. The Civil War intruded. He joined the Confederate forces, fought in the Virginia campaigns, and, promoted to captain, was seriously wounded at Drewry's Bluff, where he lost full use of his right arm. Jarvis returned to North Carolina and started a general store. Becoming a lawyer, Jarvis won legal cases and the public's attention. Elected to the state's constitutional conventions of 1865–66 and 1875, he opposed elements of Reconstruction. In the General Assembly, he became speaker of the House of Representatives.

Jarvis moved to Greenville in 1872. He used his writing and speaking talents in the political wars of the next twenty-five years. Elected lieutenant governor in 1876 as a Democrat, he became governor three years later when the incumbent resigned. He also was a member of the Board of Trustees of the University of North Carolina. He accepted appointment in 1885 as ambassador to Brazil and in the mid-nineties briefly served in the U.S. Senate.

As governor, Jarvis endorsed public education, industrial development, and sanitariums. He instituted more reforms than did the General Assembly. In 1896, his backing of the presidential campaign of Democrat William Jennings Bryan placed him in the party's reform wing. He also participated in the franchise battles of the era. Although initially hesitant, he joined the maneuvers for a normal school in eastern North Carolina.

By July 1907, eastern towns had formulated plans to secure East Carolina Teachers Training School. Ragsdale made a presentation for Greenville before the selection committee. A willingness of the county and city to pledge $90,000, a well-connected railroad network, and the availability of elevated sites contributed to victory. At the moment, national and state trends, reform organizations, and aggressive public blessing for an eastern training school carried the day. On July 10, 1907, East Carolina Teachers Training School, the committee decided, would come to Greenville.

Until his death in 1915, Jarvis, as a member of the board of trustees, molded the course of the young school. Cotten, before her death in 1929, sustained through the Federation of Women's Clubs the new institution as she did other state teacher training schools and colleges. Fleming was killed in an auto wreck in 1909. Ragsdale became a faculty member of the new school while maintaining his superintendent's position until he died in 1914.

Of the four, Jarvis carried the greatest public influence. Portuguese mission-style architecture had impressed Jarvis during his stint as ambassador to Brazil. He argued successfully for its adoption in red brick construction and red tile roofs. In keeping with the practice of flying the North Carolina flag on state buildings, the state flag waved over the high cupola of the school's Administration Building. He also paid out of his pocket to gild the cupola. Sallie Cotten introduced him to a state meeting in 1912 of the women's club federation delegates. The assembly cheered. Jarvis rose and acknowledged their applause. At his suggestion, they then sang "Dixie."

Jarvis's long experience with command also led him to recommend Robert Herring Wright to the trustees as East Carolina's first president. Jarvis knew leadership when he saw it. A native of Sampson County and the son of a family dedicated to education, Wright had graduated from Oak Ridge Institute and entered the University of North Carolina as a sophomore. He won academic and leadership kudos that included an all-southern football award. After graduation in 1897, he taught in high schools, including three years at Oak Ridge. He attended Johns Hopkins University in history and instructed at City College before accepting a principal's position in one of Baltimore's two female high schools.

Wright's background in teaching and administration caught the East Carolina trustees' collective eye. Jarvis interviewed his fellow North Carolinian in Norfolk, safe from other prying eyes. The "Grand Old Man" was favorably impressed. Wright, a thirty-nine-year-old six-foot, four-inch athlete, accepted the board's offer, effective July 1, 1909. Wright would preside as East Carolina's president until his death in July 1934. Soft-spoken and determined, he led the infant institution toward maturity in remarkable fashion during his twenty-five years as chief executive.

Trustees also hired the first teachers. In the autumn of 1909, 11 instructors, 104 young women, and 19 young men began the first academic quarter. Summer classes from the first were heavily enrolled, as in-service teachers came to Greenville to burnish their skills and improve their erudition. In the first session in 1910, over 330 people enrolled, placing a strain on classrooms and rooming facilities. Local landowners and realtors discovered ready profits available in rental housing for East Carolina students.

Although most students came from eastern North Carolina, others traveled from across the state. Student fees and state appropriations would fund the school's operations. If a student agreed to teach for a certain number of years and achieved a degree, tuition, $45 a year, was waived. The first land was acquired with local contributions. Soon the school would turn away applicants owing to a lack of space. While the curriculum focused upon pedagogy—teacher training—most courses were set in arts and sciences and fine arts disciplines: English, history, foreign language, mathematics, geography, music, and art.

The buildings had a fresh paint and plaster smell about them. Only fifteen months earlier had Jarvis's long shovel broken ground for the new school. Placed on newly purchased acreage on Harrington Hill, it bordered Washington Road, eastward of Greenville. As a result, in September 1909 the first wagonloads of students took care to dodge scattered piles of building materials and cleared brush. Things were almost ready.

Six buildings, designed to house, feed, and instruct a planned 240 students, stood in order along what became Fifth Street. Moving eastward, a Girls Dormitory flanked the central Administration Building. There offices, a library, classrooms, and an auditorium carried the main burden of education. The building would be gradually enlarged. The Boys Dormitory completed the front campus. Behind stood the infirmary, refectory, and power plant. Only three would survive to the twenty-first century: the infirmary, the Boys Dorm, renamed for Thomas Jarvis, and the joined dining hall/power plant were altered to fit new necessities. The Girls Dormitory, named for Claude Wayland Wilson in 1920, was razed in 1968. Wilson had served as secretary to the board of trustees, and Wright considered him his primary assistant until Wilson's death in 1922. Only the infirmary, later named for English teacher Mamie Jenkins of the original faculty, retained its dimensions and design.

Students went to class early. They awoke by 6:00. Breakfast was served beginning at 7:30. Tennis and basketball games often caught their attention in these early hours. By midmorning they were busily giving recitations in classrooms. Lunch and another hour and a half of course work followed. Usually from 3:30 to 5:00 students could participate in organized hikes into forested grounds. (This may, however, have been the beginning of the tradition of the afternoon nap.) After an evening meal, studies, and socializing, lights were lowered at 10:00 p.m. Intramural games were popular, and in the early years, the young men organized baseball games with nearby teams.

Three ten-week quarters composed the academic year. The first began in September, followed by a winter quarter in December and then a spring one in March. The fifteen-week semester system did not appear until 1977. Wright met with students each week for announcements and a discourse. He usually used no notes, and his secretary recorded his comments for the record. A form of this practice lasted into the late 1950s.

Students were active and outspoken. Organized by classes, student committees oversaw dorm and behavior rules. In the 1920s, Wright believed East Carolina's students possessed more freedom than sister schools. Oversight, however, was persistent in the coming and going off-campus. With a student-drafted constitution approved in 1921, the Student Government Association (SGA) became a meaningful part of college governance. The SGA established many student fees and appropriated them for student organizations.

The two-year degree diploma, one-year certificate, and preparatory program gave way in that decade to two- and four-year degrees when in 1921 the school became East Carolina Teachers College. World War I had accelerated the idea of the four-year program. Teachers in North Carolina had left for well-paying wartime employment or other occupations that their disciplined education prepared them for, and teaching vacancies proliferated.

The war revealed low proficiency in both physical and mental abilities among many young Tar Heel males. In 1919, Wright pushed for improved high schools and sterner teacher certification. He joined a band of state educators and students to make changes. Four-year degrees became the desired diplomas. Both reforms, coupled with a fierce campaign at the state level for school bonds, led East Carolina beyond its earlier goals.

It also meant that whenever East Carolina adopted new or rearranged programs, a shuffling of current resources occurred. As a result, in the early 1920s faculty carried extra courses and preparations. Enrolled upperclass persons needed to adjust their schedules each quarter as teachers were assigned to where the largest student enrollments were. Smaller classes sometimes suffered cancellation or combinations. By the mid-twenties Wright, trustee board members, and political friends convinced the state to fund a set of buildings to answer some of the expanding college's requirements.

First, more land was needed. Looking eastward, trustees proposed doubling the campus along Fifth Street. Governor Cameron Morrison objected; he thought the acres overpriced. Again the East Carolina administration and boosters went to work and obtained the land. New facilities could now be authorized.

A new library building to house Joyner Library was opened in 1924 along a new entrance from Fifth Street. In 1954, it became home to the music department. In 1959, it was named for a longtime East Carolina advocate and the publisher of the Greenville *Daily Reflector,* David Julian Whichard. Three residence halls joined the row of buildings along Fifth Street: in 1923, Fleming and Ragsdale and, in 1929, Cotten. The trustees awarded the names with Wright's advice, honoring the influence of the founders.

In a campaign reminiscent of the original contest for the college charter, East Carolina advocates petitioned the General Assembly for the first of several large allocations. The center of activity shifted from the Administration Building upon completion in 1925 of the Social-Religious Building next to the new library. With a 1,500-seat auditorium that converted to a basketball court, it became the architectural centerpiece of East Carolina. At the end of the twenties, it assumed the name "Campus Building," and in 1936 it became Robert Wright Building. (Wright had long sought a freestanding gymnasium. Not until the late 1940s would one be funded.)

A new administration building was completed in 1930. In 1954, its name changed to honor East Carolina's first treasurer, John B. Spilman. The large former Administration Building was in 1929 named for Herbert E. Austin, the college's first scientist, who won the loyalty of students owing to his office's assistance in composing class schedules. In 1968, the building was demolished and replaced by a new Austin near Wright Building. In 1925, a student meeting building opened, snuggled among the trees of back campus. The Y-Hut would serve as a meeting place, a study hall, and a site for formal installations for student officers, games, and laughter. Torn down in 1952, its successor would become the Ledonia S. Wright Cultural Center in 1975, memorializing the respected professor of social work.

The circle before Wright Building—first named for the president—was renamed in honor of Martin L. Wright. This change honored the sociologist for his many years of campus landscaping. One of the last of those buildings constructed during Wright's presidency was a new classroom building in 1929 placed to the right of the Campus Building. Planned expansion later did not follow. In 1951, the trustees honored an original faculty member, mathematician Maria D. Graham, and named it for her.

Only one more building was built on campus until the late 1940s. Its design broke with the practice of the mission architecture and incorporated a neocolonial fashion. Cofinanced by the state and a New Deal work relief agency, the Public Works Administration, the four-story classroom building was named in 1941 for a Greenville politician and businessman, Edward Gaskill Flanagan. It would be renovated often in the future.

Wright suffered a fatal heart attack in April 1934 as the college approached its twenty-fifth anniversary. Working with trustees, administrators, faculty, and staff, he had brought the fledgling school to college status and to a high enrollment of 1,000 students in the late twenties. While he continued to emphasize the college's mission of training teachers, his flexibility had begun to allow people to take tracks based upon their interests. For example, business courses had attracted both men and, in increasing numbers, women. A growth in doctorates—Ph.D.s and Ed.D.s—had begun to alter the composition of the faculty. Although the Great Depression forced the third crisis of his presidency, Wright had faced it with innovation and courage. He urged the enrollment of men during the depression years and adopted an intercollegiate schedule for sports that included football.

Wright's successor, Leon Renfroe Meadows, had joined the school in 1910, becoming a popular English teacher and valued secretary of the board. He followed Wright's intentions, as he saw them. In 1941, after long debate, the college faculty adopted degree programs that did not require teacher certification. Meadows noted that no curriculum reform had been as significant. He proved a man slow to move and slower to articulate future plans. His actions would eventually split the faculty and the students. In 1944, he resigned, facing charges of embezzlement. Many Septembers would pass before the wounds cast by his exit would heal. In the midst of this uproar, World War II came to Greenville.

The student body saw most of its males withdraw owing to the war, but hundreds enrolled in 1946 with benefits from the G.I. Bill. By 1947, men outnumbered women for the first time. Older standards of behavior and permission slips, issued at the offices of lady principal Kate Beckwith and her successor, dean of women Annie L. Morton, had begun to melt before the hot flame of cultural change.

Clothing styles, as instruments of those young people seeking greater autonomy, would not completely be freely chosen by females until the 1970s. Dormitory visitation debates in the 1960s and 1970s joined the same currents. More students, male and female, preferred rooming off-campus.

Apartments spread across Greenville's landscape. Downtown moved from a commercial center to an entertainment commons. World politics that brought a new war to Harrington Hill—the Cold War—acted as a sobering force on young men as the draft in place until 1974 posed a hard reality.

While teacher education continued, World War II veterans moved to the ranks of the nonteaching professional degrees and those that would be labeled arts and sciences. After an interim president and two false starts, John Decatur Messick became president in 1947. He had big plans. Messick entered a building and land acquisition campaign to fit the emerging institution's requirements. When he first arrived on campus, the eastern North Carolina native intimated that the school should be East Carolina College to reflect its changing mission. In 1951, the General Assembly amended the charter to make it so.

Federal support of higher education expanded. More faculty and staff were recruited. The state treasury funded about half the cost of annual operations and salaries. Fees, sales, and tuition provided the remainder. A state bureau of the budget became a fiscal sieve through which college funding requests needed to pass.

Messick played catch-up with buildings. He obtained appropriations early during his term, but inflation forced postponement. The General Assembly passed more appropriations, and federal construction loans became available to the college.

Residence halls appeared in an almost constant stream: in 1949, one named for Dean Ronald Slay; in 1952, a faculty apartment building honoring veteran state superintendent and trustee chair Clyde Erwin; in 1955, another for recently deceased Governor William Umstead; in 1956, a structure along Fifth Street named for Greenville tobacconist and trustee Radford M. Garrett; in 1959, a residence hall honoring state senator Paul Jones; and in 1960, another for Governor Charles Brantley Aycock. Many of these buildings were made possible after acquisition of land beyond Tenth Street, in an area that became known as College Hill. Had not local leaders guaranteed options to buy, the acreage would have been lost. The legislature eventually purchased the land.

Working buildings also were a part of this vast construction. In 1952, Christenbury Gym was dedicated. In 1954, a new Joyner Library was erected. A classroom facility, named for Greenville leader Edwin Rawl, opened in 1959. College Stadium was completed in 1949, using contributions from businesspeople and other friends of East Carolina.

The college administration and trustees also moved to implement *Brown v. Board of Education* (1954). Quietly, the college charter was changed to remove whiteness as a provision for general enrollment. By the summer of

1957, African American teachers enrolled in summer school courses. In the early sixties, the first African American graduated with a four-year degree.

East Carolina awarded its first graduate degree in 1929. Messick and new dean Leo Jenkins led in the revision and development of more graduate degree programs in the late forties and early fifties. Faculty were recruited and new administrators hired to help in this evolution. Messick also boasted that East Carolina had the highest percentage of doctorates among its faculty among the state schools. The enrollment surged to over 2,000 students. Piedmont authorities formed a commission to survey what was labeled degree duplication and helter-skelter growth. A Board of Higher Education was formed to institutionalize such an opinion, requiring East Carolina and other state colleges to gain its approval for their funding requests.

In 1959, the three schools within the consolidated university system received $3.2 million in state funds, while the other nine schools' total reached only $1.39 million. Messick continued to seek equal treatment. Rumors of the Greenville school achieving university status were worrisome to authorities. Messick dissembled. The rumors continued. The new board gave evidence of its intention to restrict the surging college on Harrington Hill.

The issue of equity went to everyday operations. Student self-help wages at Piedmont schools were 75 cents an hour. At East Carolina they were 55 cents. Average class size at East Carolina was considerably larger than that of similar schools within the consolidated university. A request for grand pianos to support the music program was refused; the board suggested that uprights should suffice. Messick advised in 1959 that the state fund its colleges proportionally, as it did the consolidated university. At the heart of the problem lay a dual funding process: since the mid-1930s, the consolidated university had been financed apart from the other state colleges. To some observers, the only way to overcome this condition would be to elevate East Carolina to university status.

The Board of Higher Education, for example, delayed master's programs and the creation of a nursing school. Throughout the late fifties and until the late sixties, the college and its friends struggled to finesse the board to bring needed degree programs and support to the Greenville campus. In 1959, Messick resigned, leaving a legacy of community involvement, a pattern of activism, and a specific agenda to provide service for the region and state. The new president, Leo Jenkins, continued and expanded Messick's agendas.

The East Carolina faculty gained acceptance of a plan to broaden faculty involvement in shared governance at the college. Although he was counseled otherwise, Jenkins supported the first efforts of a new Faculty Senate and its system of academic committees. It marked a promising beginning.

In the sixties, construction continued. Jenkins, an experienced administrator at East Carolina, knew many political and business leaders in eastern North Carolina. In his inaugural address in 1960, the New Jersey native observed that East Carolina had made promises to the people and that to curtail these obligations would be harmful to the social progress of the state. He did not publicly seek to argue with opponents; he sought to attain East Carolina goals.

Jenkins found among the faculty ranks able and skilled associates. Veteran administrators, such as Robert Holt, gave continuity to the planning efforts. In the mid-sixties the college was reworked to resemble more closely a university structure. Schools were created, and new faculty were recruited. Baby boomers also had begun to appear, and their numbers increased state funds, garnering more student fees. New academic structures appeared, some of them made possible through government loans. State appropriations aided in the effort, and private donations became more frequent and larger. The region's politicians moved to accept the East Carolina agenda as it grew more diversified.

Land acquisition continued. Houses behind Garrett Dormitory to Tenth Street were acquired, sometimes with the threat of exercising the state's eminent domain laws. Additional acreage was added along both sides of Charles Boulevard to Tenth Street. Most of the seven high-rise residence halls built during Jenkins's tenure made use of these acquisitions. The buildings honored trustees, philanthropists, authors, faculty, and alumni: Kerr Scott, North Carolina governor (1962); Inglis Fletcher, North Carolina author (1963); Henry Belk, Goldsboro editor and East Carolina trustee (1966); Mary Hemphill Green, English professor (1966); Ruth Allen White, dean of women (1968); Sarah Clement, alumna, public school teacher, and philanthropist (1969); and Arthur M. Tyler, trustee and businessman (1969).

While these dormitories changed traffic patterns and walkways and brought more of the student body to campus, the academic construction occurred in the middle of the old campus. Bulldozers, graders, trucks, and construction crews provided a general air of progress afoot. Those who walked to class or work needed to watch their step, just as the original students had.

Eight major academic buildings were built during the era. They also gave credit to people who had supported East Carolina: classroom building, Herbert Austin, administrator and faculty member (1964); classroom building,

J. Brantley Speight, trustee and philanthropist, and Carrie Speight, philanthropist (1965); nursing and home economics classroom, Thomas Rivers, philanthropist (1968); science complex, John Howell, chancellor and faculty member, and Gladys Howell, faculty member (1969); classroom building, Lawrence Brewster, faculty member and philanthropist (1970); allied health science building, Carol Belk, philanthropist (1972); regional development center, Thomas Willis, institute director (1974); fine arts building, Leo Jenkins, president and chancellor (1977).

To add to the expansion, the move to join intercollegiate sports competition, begun by Robert Wright, found amplification during the Jenkins years. A new football stadium opened in 1962 and eventually would seat 43,000 spectators. In 1966, a new field house, swimming pool, and basketball arena opened, financed by state grants and private donations. Named in honor of M. O. Minges, a Greenville entrepreneur, the building also contained classrooms for physical education classes. The court in Christenbury Memorial Gym was kept for intramural games. A baseball field opened along Charles Boulevard in 1964. In 1971, an improved version was named for Milton Harrington, a Greenville tobacconist and corporate leader.

Using political alliances from both east and west, East Carolina leaders succeeded in elevating the college to university rank in 1967. At the same time, the whole of the public higher education system in the state was reformed into one system, the University of North Carolina. Jenkins also proposed that East Carolina would serve the state well if a medical school were established in Greenville to educate general physicians. The small places of the state, especially in eastern North Carolina, responded enthusiastically. Piedmont interests considered it a rambunctious proposal.

Governor Robert Scott, Lieutenant Governor Jim Hunt, state senator Robert Morgan, and state representative Horton Rountree, all politically adept, maneuvered with other talented politicians and leaders to bring a four-year medical school to Greenville. Jenkins had used East Carolina as his base of operations for this movement, ably sustained by an articulate Greenville physician, Edwin Monroe. Accomplishing this goal had required a legislative override of the new UNC governing board.

It remained to be seen how this new, centralized system would affect East Carolina University and its determination to serve the people. In 1978, Jenkins retired, revered as a tribune of the people, a man who had made startling promises to improve the quality of life and to assure higher education's benefits to the region and North Carolina. Thousands of enrolled students believed him.

REFERENCES

Bratton, Mary Jo Jackson. *East Carolina University: The Formative Years.* Greenville, NC: East Carolina University Alumni Association, 1986.

Cotten, Sallie Southall. *History of the North Carolina Federation of Women's Clubs, 1901–1925.* Raleigh, NC: Edwards and Broughton, 1925.

ECU Board of Trustees. Minutes and records. East Carolina University Archives.

ECU Chancellor's Office. Papers. East Carolina University Archives.

Escott, Paul D. "Thomas Jordan Jarvis," *American National Biography,* Vol. 11. New York: Oxford University Press, 1999.

Jenkins, Mamie E., et al. "Robert Herring Wright," *East Carolina Teachers College Bulletin,* 29, no. 4, December 1938.

Link, A. William. *William Friday: Power, Purpose, and American Higher Education.* Chapel Hill: University of North Carolina Press, 1992.

Williams, Wayne C. *Beginning of the School of Medicine at East Carolina University, 1964–1977.* Greenville, NC: Brookliff, 1998.

CHAPTER ONE

The Planning Process at East Carolina University, 1974–2005

GEORGE BAILEY

IN APRIL 1974, East Carolina University provost John Howell reported to the ECU Board of Trustees that the General Administration of the University of North Carolina expected each UNC campus to submit a 1975–80 planning document. The deadline for submission was September 1974. The provost indicated that ECU's planning document should "list programs by year and in priority rank." Howell also indicated that two new procedures for program development were being required. Institutions must request from the General Administration authorization to plan new degree programs. After planning, institutions must request authorization to establish new degree programs.

In October 1974, Howell provided a copy of the "1975–1980 Long-Range Plan" to deans and chairs in the Division of Academic Affairs. This thirty-three-page document contained three sections: a description of the present state of the institution, enrollment projections, and academic program planning.

Section 1 noted that "the programs proposed in this five-year plan remain within the scope and mission described in the memorandum of October 30." This refers to the October 30, 1973, memorandum from UNC president William Friday on the scope and mission of East Carolina University. This memorandum described, in part, "At this stage of our development of a comprehensive plan, programs which effectively change the authorized scope and mission of your institution should not be submitted. . . . In addition, East Carolina University is authorized a one-year medical program in cooperation with the University of North Carolina at Chapel Hill."

Section 3 indicated that academic program planning would include improving and expanding existing programs, with considerable emphasis placed on the health sciences. Thirty-six new programs were proposed (four undergraduate, twenty-two graduate) for the years 1975–80, including a master of administrative services in 1974–75, an M.S. in nursing, a B.A. in communication, and an M.A. in historical administration for 1975–76, a B.S. in political science for 1976–77, an M.F.A. in theatre for 1977–78, a master of social work for 1978–79, and an M.A. in anthropology for 1979–80. Thirty-one new faculty members would be needed, at an average cost of $17,900 each, to accomplish these goals.

In August 1979, during the last year covered by the 1975–80 plan, the East Carolina Board of Trustees created the 1982–1992 Long-Range Planning Commission. This commission was charged to review academic programs, service areas, and support components of the university. This effectively expanded long-range planning to include each area of the university. The board instructed the commission to divide its recommendations into six categories: academic programs, academic support, organization, institutional support, student service, and public service. The commission's report also would serve as the ten-year self-study required by the Southern Association of Colleges and Schools for their visit in the spring of 1982. This in part explained why a good portion of the 1982–92 long-range plan described the university's accomplishments in the prior ten years.

The 1982–1992 document was a "bottom-up" plan. As such, it compiled the individual reports of eighty-four task forces under three subcommissions involving nine hundred people from the faculty, staff, alumni, students, and trustees. Most of these reports were completed during March 1980. The public service subcommission report was the first of its kind for ECU.

Chancellor Thomas B. Brewer appointed history professor and general faculty poo-bah Henry Ferrell as coordinator for the planning commission. The commission consisted of five members of the trustees' executive committee, the chancellor, four vice chancellors, the dean of the medical school, the president of the alumni association, three members of the senate's executive committee, two representatives of the graduate council, three representatives of the academic council, two deans, three student government association representatives, three representatives from the senate's educational policies and planning committee, and three representatives of the university staff (nonfaculty SPA employees). Membership on subcommissions and task forces was determined by each subcommission's charge.

The commission's report was structured to address six broad areas of university activity: academic programs, academic support, organization, institutional support, student service, and public service. The task forces within each area mirrored the structure of both the units and the tasks within that area. For example, under academic programs, there was a task force for each degree-granting unit. These task forces were charged to address faculty scholarship, recruitment, compensation, and evaluation. A general faculty task force was charged to consider personnel policies. Analogously, the task forces under academic support addressed libraries, general college, records, academic advising, and academic personnel development. Under institutional support there were task forces for financial resources, alumni, institutional research, the computing center, and similar areas.

The commission was charged to review the recommendations and suggested priorities of the reports of the six subcommissions, compose and circulate a draft report throughout the different components of the university, and submit in late 1981 a final draft for the approval of the chancellor and the Board of Trustees. The final report, "Long-Range Planning 1982–1992, East Carolina University," contained an introduction stating East Carolina University's philosophy and goals. The first paragraph of the two-page statement of ECU's philosophy reads, "The University is a community of scholars who discover, create and disseminate knowledge; who believe in the power of knowledge to provide a synthesis that enhances personal experience and the quality of life; who foster personal discernment and informed commitment; who challenge assumptions and encourage conclusions; who seek to liberate individuals from the limitations of ignorance, prejudice, place and time through enlargement of mind and spirit by exposure to differing ideas and ways of thinking."

The statement continues that as a community of scholars, ECU seeks to promote understanding through effective teaching, seeks to "create awareness of the major areas of human knowledge and to deepen that knowledge in one or more areas," and otherwise is "committed to the life of the mind" and "the development of intellectual, physical and moral sensibilities of students in order that they may become self-sufficient, sensitive, contributing members of society." Finally, as part of its philosophy ECU accepted an obligation to society "to promote the common good by providing an environment that encourages the formulation of a lifelong habit of mind—the attributes of which are equity, calmness, moderation, and wisdom—and that is conductive to learning, understanding and complete development of self-determining individuals."

The report recommended that the university adopt goals in these four areas: student, institution/faculty, research/creative activity, and services. Paraphrased, the goals listed under "student" were: sustain and improve the living and learning environment, attract disadvantaged students, ensure equal access, support programs of financial aid, provide guidance to students in selecting areas of study, and provide for students to progress to postgraduate education. Primary proposals for "institution/faculty" were to develop and maintain high-quality academic programs; monitor and balance what students want to study with what society needs, continuously evaluate programs, faculty, and staff; provide dynamic leadership for obtaining the resources needed for academic programs, research, and support services; recognize faculty and staff achievement; participate in shared governance; promote alumni development; and support excellence in athletics. Under "research/creative activity," items included promoting research and creative activities, seeking grants, encouraging students to become involved in research, and providing faculty members with opportunities to develop the skills necessary for research or creative activity. Under "services," goals would make academic accomplishments available to the public; provide public services of high ethical and professional quality; enhance the campus as a cultural and recreational center; extend education by community development, conferences, workshops, and institutes; and expand cooperative relations with other institutions.

Academic programs comprised the report's first chapter. The introduction listed four goals addressed by each of the task force reports that make up the rest of the text of the chapter. This chapter was generated first as a review of academic progress and suggestions for continued growth, sophistication, and diversity. A second general intention establishes priorities for this development in order to respond in the best and most useful fashion even in the event of diminishing resources and steady or declining enrollments. A third objective is to identify advanced programs needed by society and capable of being implemented at East Carolina University at the doctoral level. Finally, recommendations are offered to stabilize, combine, or concentrate parallel programs or to delete those no longer pertinent or possible of effective and/or certifiable realization.

The chapter presented reports of the individual task forces of eighteen departments and nine professional schools, as well as those from task forces on general education, the general faculty, the honors program, the multidisciplinary degree programs, and the special studies program. Each academic unit (departments and schools) followed the same format, though the contents varied from report to report in the other task forces in this and other chapters. In the introduction to chapter 1, the recommendations presented in task force reports are referred to as planning objectives. It is noted that "besides the School of Medicine, six units qualify for highest consideration in resource allocation. They are the Schools of Business and Education and the Departments of biology, English, geology and psychology."

The format for academic unit reports required three to four pages with an introduction highlighting the unit's accomplishments over the last ten years, a section titled "Curriculum" describing the unit's curriculum, and a list of possible changes. Sections titled "Faculty," "Support," "Special Concerns," and "Opportunities" were also included, each containing descriptions of the unit's current status and suggestions for change. These proposed reducing class size or increasing the number of faculty in the unit, for example. The last page of each report contains a chart covering three areas: curriculum, faculty and staff, and support. The recommendations are prioritized from level 1 to level 4. Presumably, these charts provide ready access to the information the university needed to set its priorities for the next decade. There are twenty-two of these charts, each containing about fifty recommendations. That averages a bit more than four recommendations per level per category (curriculum, faculty and staff, and support). The introduction states, "These levels should not be seen as specific time frames but rather as steps to achieve planning objectives over a decade."

Some illustrations of level 1 recommendations under "Curriculum" were to review undergraduate and graduate degree programs, plan an undergraduate honors track, discontinue the B.S. in teaching, review service courses, appoint area curriculum coordinators, monitor class enrollments, and modify quantitative courses. Under "Faculty" were to propose a unit code, increase grant activity, review course assignments, review and improve teaching techniques, review and improve computer capabilities, emphasize creative activity, and consider adjunct appointments. Under "Staff and Support," requests included equipment needs, reviewing library requirements, increasing secretarial aid, proposing graduate assistant aid, evaluating relationships with the Regional Development Institute, reviewing office arrangements, and reviewing software support needs. (Given that an eight-course-per-year load was a full-time load, an interesting level 2 recommendation from one unit was "reassign course responsibilities to permit no more than eight courses per faculty member.")

The general faculty report described the past and present situation of the faculty, making recommendations here and there as it proceeded. Approximately fifty unprioritized recommendations were made in this section. These recommendations are not numbered or otherwise distinguished from the text surrounding them that aims, in part, to justify the recommendations. This section is divided into five parts: monetary considerations, faculty development, personnel policies, continuing education considerations, and general considerations. Recommendations made in the first part propose that faculty should receive an equity adjustment to their salaries and that the university develop "a more reasoned remunerative policy." Faculty development asked that faculty acquaint themselves with innovative instructional techniques such as computer-assisted instruction.

Special attention was to be given to facilitating faculty research and creative activity. A nine-hour teaching load per semester should become the norm for faculty members doing research. The other sections of chapter 1 also each contain a large number of recommendations narrow and specific in scope.

Chapter 2 of the 1982–92 report addressed academic support. Its introduction said, "The major goal for academic support units and activities during the decade is to maintain efficient service despite increasing demands upon time, energy, and resources. The means to meet this goal are four: improved technology, reorganization, personnel development, and increased and/or reallocated funding support."

Twelve task force reports followed. Among these were academic advising, academic personnel, continuing education, curriculum development and review, the general college, the graduate school, and the libraries. Examples of recommendations stated in some of these reports are academic advising: coordination of responsibility for academic advising through a central agency; academic personnel: maintenance of staff morale; curriculum development and review: maintenance of quality in curriculum through encouragement of innovation and flexibility; the graduate school: designation of the graduate school as the coordinating agency for the promotion and development of research; libraries: increased efficiency, particularly through innovative technology.

Chapter 3 evaluated university organization. These suggestions drew on the goals and recommendations found in other chapters of the report. This chapter had three sections, program services, support services, and governance instruments, and it contained various organizational suggestions:

Section 1, "Program Services," suggested the College of Arts and Sciences establish an Army ROTC program; the School of Business should be renamed the School of Management; student services should establish an office of off-campus housing; the university should establish a student foundation for fund-raising; and philosophy move to the second new classroom building located in the Eighth and Ninth street areas. In section 2, "Support Services," objectives mentioned were establishing an office of academic computing with a full-time administrator and moving the functions of the General College to an academic advising office under the vice chancellor for academic affairs. Section 3, "Governance Instruments," said the faculty organization should continue to improve the relations between the general faculty and the university administration.

Chapter 4 addressed institutional support. Among its fourteen subsections are alumni affairs; custodial personnel; grounds, parking, and traffic; and university printing. In the introduction, although specific goals were lacking, a variety of items were mentioned that provided a basis for goals, recommendations, or suggestions made in a subsection of the chapter. For example, chapter 4 observed that financial support for data processing was far lower than it should be and that "a desperately needed data base . . . is hampered by the lack of programmers and analysts. . . . Improvement in data processing is needed in virtually every support area reviewed." The next point stressed that the activities covered by this section of the report "suffer from a general lack of institution wide planning," since academic planning did not take into account financial support for support areas. The introduction noted that "budgeting is an area where creative improvements would be especially useful." Some specific recommendations in the reports were: increase funding to computing and information systems; improve data systems; correlate unit plans with institutional goals; and no longer consider "nontraditional" a viable term.

Chapter 5 reviewed student services. This chapter had fifteen subsections, covering topics such as handicapped students, intercollegiate athletics, and student financial aid. Its introduction stated that the primary goal of student life administration was enhancing the quality of the total education environment. Planning objectives for the next ten years included maintaining the university's commitment to shared responsibility in governance and identifying committed students for service on university committees. Providing funds to achieve the student service goals was recommended as a long-range objective.

The last chapter in the 1982–92 long-range plan addressed public services. This chapter had ten subjections, such as consulting, public entertainment, and public information. Its introduction notes that "with appropriate foresight, public services shall contribute substantially to the strengthening of a productive and growing institution."

The plan also contained ten appendices, including appendix C, prediction of enrollment; appendix F, charge of the subcommission on public service; and appendix I, charge of the subcommission on organization.

In December 1984, Chancellor John Howell provided President Friday with a three-page biennial revision of what he now referred to as the "1982–1987 Long-Range Plan." Howell stated that "the proposals included have been developed and/or reviewed by unit faculty committees, administrators, and the East Carolina University Planning Commission and are consistent with our commitment to the goals of the Consent Decree."

The chancellor continued, "In view of the level of doctoral granting activity and the level of research, library, and grant resources, East Carolina University proposes a reclassification as a Doctoral-Granting University II." Howell argued that "current enrollment in the five Ph.D. programs is 27, which projects a productivity well in excess of the required number." He continued with a prioritized listing of new degree programs. First priority was a B.S. in communications submitted to the UNC General Administration in March 1981. Also requested were new B.A. degrees in biotechnology, statistics, and mathematics. As the top priority in medical education, Howell requested authorization to plan a Ph.D. program in pathology. The report requested permission to establish new degrees, among them a B.S. in applied sociology and a B.S. in applied anthropology and an M.A. in technical and professional writing. A request was made to change the name of the B.S. track in correctional services to criminal justice. The report had eight appendices describing the status of programs authorized for planning or establishment and providing supporting information for the report's recommendations.

On February 9, 1987, Chancellor Howell forwarded to UNC president C. D. Spangler a biennial revision of what he now labeled the "1984–1989 Long-Range Plan" for the 1986–1991 UNC General Administration planning period. Howell again requested that ECU be reclassified as a doctoral-granting University II, citing the awarding of sixty-two M.D.s and three Ph.D.s in 1985–86 and the current enrollment of thirty-three students in five Ph.D. programs. Authorization to plan was requested for four M.S. and two M.A. degrees, including an M.S. in accounting and M.A.s in French and Spanish. A number of name changes were requested, including renaming the School of Technology as the School of Industry and Technology. A request was made to plan a multidisciplinary public service center for the study of gerontology. The report had six appendices, listing requests for authorization to plan and supporting materials and reporting on the status of new degree programs.

In July 1987, Roy Carroll, vice president for planning of the University of North Carolina General Administration, informed the new ECU chancellor, Richard R. Eakin, that the UNC president would recommend the Board of Governors approve some of the requests to plan new degree programs made by ECU in February. This included the M.S. degrees in accounting and physical therapy. The name change for the School of Technology to the School of Industry and Technology was approved, along with permission to plan a gerontology center. The requests to plan masters programs in French and Spanish were not approved. Carroll noted that "considerations of any new programs in Foreign languages should be deferred until completion of a Board-mandated review of all programs in that discipline division." Regarding ECU's request that its status be changed to doctoral-granting II, Carroll hesitated: "We also want to discuss with you further the proposal to change the institutional classification. At its last meeting, the Board of Governors approved an additional Ph.D. program . . . and it is clear that East Carolina is moving toward the status of a doctoral-granting institution. The relatively small number of Ph.D.'s being conferred annually up to this time does raise questions. Later this summer we will meet with you on this matter."

In November 1987, Carroll notified Eakin that the Board of Governors had approved permission to plan an M.S. in accounting (but not in physical therapy), the name change for the School of Technology and several other name changes, as well as the gerontology center.

In the autumn of 1988, Chancellor Eakin initiated a new "strategic planning" process designed to enable a set of university goals. The previous major planning event initiated under Chancellor Brewer in the late 1970s was a bottom-up process that resulted in a vast number of plans containing a large number of very localized goals. The 1990–95 planning event was structured to be a top-down process based on ten university goals (six basic goals and four supporting goals). For the preliminary and advisory phase of the strategic planning process, four work groups were created: the external environmental analysis work group, the strengths and weaknesses work group, the institutional values assessment work group, and the strategic planning advisory group (SPAG). The reports of the first three work-groups were presented to the chancellor in April 1989. In November 1989, the chancellor received the SPAG report, which was based in part on the reports of the other three work groups.

Janice H. Faulkner chaired the external environmental analysis work group. Its report cited competitive forces challenging the university, demographic trends, economic forces affecting the university, legal forces to which the university responds, and political forces and technological forces that affect the university's mission. Competitive forces discussed included "the diminishing number of qualified faculty available for employment." Under demographic trends, it was noted that fewer black males sought higher education. Political forces predicted a shift in the balance of political power within the state to the Piedmont crescent. Under social forces, the report noted that eastern North Carolina "often is characterized as having alarmingly high rates of poverty, illiteracy, and marginally adequate schools." Technological forces on the mission were seen as both an opportunity and a threat, namely, the opportunity to expand technologically but at an "astronomical" cost.

The strengths and weaknesses work group was chaired by Richard A. Edwards, executive assistant to the chancellor. A "strengths and weaknesses identification, executive summary" in the work group's report found eight strengths and nine weaknesses. Among ECU's perceived strengths were "scope and diversity of undergraduate and graduate programs," "history, reputation, and nature of the School of Medicine," and "quality and character of East Carolina University faculty and staff." The perceived weaknesses identified were:

A university image with serious shortcomings, as perceived both internally and externally, absence of a clear-cut commitment and support system for teaching, research, and faculty and staff development, no strategy or systematic effort to manage enrollments, to enhance student quality, and to promote geographic and cultural diversity, insufficient numbers of minorities and women in faculty and staff positions, and the absence of a significant number of persons within the campus community from different cultural and ethnic backgrounds, absence of a university-wide plan for new construction, building renovations, and improvements; preventive and deferred maintenance; campus beautification and safety, university's organizational character and structure including patterns of communication and line responsibilities needing further delineation, clarification and refinement, absence of clearly defined processes for budget planning and program evaluation and absence of a clearly defined student life mission which addresses quality of student life and student learning experiences.

The institutional values assessment work group described twelve categories valued by East Carolina University. These included ECU's heritage; the development of human ability; offering a wide range of academic programs; ethnic, gender, and cultural diversity; admitting students with a wide range of academic capabilities from diverse origins; and fair and rigorous academic standards that foster communication and analytical skills.

The major document generated in the initial phase of the strategic planning process for 1990–95 was "Strategies for Distinction: Final Report of the Strategic Planning Advisory Group." SPAG, a fifteen-member committee, was chaired by William A. Bloodworth, vice chancellor for academic affairs. Sue A. Hodges, director of the office of planning and institutional research, served as an ex officio member of the committee and of the other three work groups.

SPAG began its work by identifying twenty "elements of distinction" that it recommended for underpinning the development of the strategic plan. Among these were "a small-college atmosphere in a major university and a tradition of individual, caring attention to students, a growing national reputation in medical education, an individual faculty and faculty groups of national distinction, recent recognition for international programs, a commitment to strategic planning."

As a preface to its final report to Chancellor Eakin in November 1989, SPAG concluded that "the members of the Advisory Group believe that there is considerable support within the university for the recommendations in this report . . . we hope that our efforts will help East Carolina University to move forward with confidence, its efforts founded on the accomplishments of its past and a clear, distinctive vision of its future."

The SPAG report's major recommendation was that "the University chart its future in the direction of five basic and interrelated goals." Namely, "achieve distinction in undergraduate education, develop a pluralistic academic culture based on respect for individual rights and human diversity, expand Doctoral programs, strengthen the commitment to productive research, scholarship and creative activity, improve teacher education and public schools." SPAG also recommended four supporting goals: "Recruit and support academically proficient and talented students, promote the university effectively to external publics, develop and use expanded information resources and library services, provide effective stewardship of the University."

In the SPAG report, some of the basic and supporting goals were expanded with the addition of lists of objectives. For example, under "Achieve distinction in undergraduate education," we find "c. Appropriately small classes at the freshman and sophomore levels," and "e. Undergraduate research and independent learning programs." Likewise, under supporting goal 1, "Recruit and support academically proficient and talented students," was a list of five objectives, including "increase emphasis on the recruiting and retention of minority and non-traditional students" and "commitment to a strong honors program."

The SPAG report was revised by Eakin and his staff and published as "University Directions, 1990–1995." This document contained seventeen elements of distinction but otherwise was much the same as the list recommended by SPAG. For example, the report described ECU as "a large university with a small-college atmosphere, a long institutional history of teacher education, educational programs that have responded to regional needs and a strong and widely recognized tradition of faculty governance."

A sixth basic goal was added: "Strengthen the commitment to excellence in teaching." The SPAG report's "develop a pluralistic academic culture" was changed to "develop a university culture." "Improve teacher education and public schools" was revised to "improve teacher education and stimulate improvement in public schooling." The third supporting goal recommended by SPAG was changed by eliminating the words "and library services."

The publication of "University Directions, 1990–1995" in November 1989 initiated the second stage of the strategic planning process. During the spring semester twenty-nine university organizations (from Enrollment Management to the Division of Student Life) created plans for realizing the goals and objectives stated in "University Directions." These twenty-nine plans, together with "University Directions," constituted the document titled "Strategies for Distinction, 1990–1995."

The document began with the general goals and objectives section. Three others followed: implementation plans, academic unit plans and support unit plans. The plans in these sections set objectives to be accomplished in order to achieve the general goals and objectives stated in "University Directions."

In "University Directions, 1990–1995," basic and supporting goals were supplemented with from four to eleven objectives. The twenty-nine unit plans addressed each of the goals and objectives in "University Directions" appropriate to the unit. Each unit plan begins with the unit's vision statement. Next, some units listed "elements of distinction," while some did not. In the last section of the plan, titled "Priorities for Action," some or all of the goals stated in "University Directions" and some of the objectives listed under these goals were listed, as appropriate to the function of each individual unit. Although the wording of the goals in each unit plan mirrored the text in "University Directions," each unit reworded the objectives from "University Directions" that best fit the unit's mission. Units combined parts of some of the separate objectives presented under a given goal and also added new objectives. For example, "University Directions" states: "Goal 1: Achieve distinction in undergraduate education. A. Strengthen the commitment to the overall development of students, with particular emphasis on academic achievement, intellectual curiosity and endeavor, self-confidence, and integrity," and "G. Offer undergraduate instruction that includes the following emphasis throughout the curricula. (2) the ethical dimensions of decision making and behavior; and (3) the development of communication skills, analytical ability, and critical reflection."

The "Priorities for Action" section of the "College of Arts and Sciences Unit Plan, 1990–1993," stated: "1: Achieve distinction in undergraduate education. a. In all courses where such emphases are pedagogically sound, particularly in general education courses, develop curricula which emphasize writing, critical thinking, reading, oral communication, mathematical skills, the ethical dimension of decision-making, the acquisition of knowledge, and lifelong learning."

An example of a new objective not found under goal 1 in "University Directions" appeared in the College of Arts and Sciences plan: "b. Integrate information technology into the structure of all courses where such emphasis is appropriate."

Allowing individual units the flexibility to create new objectives for achieving the goals stated in "University Directions" challenged units to set additional objectives uniquely fitting each unit's specific ability to contribute to accomplishing the university's six basic and four supporting goals.

The resulting long-range planning document was approved by the Faculty Senate on September 11, 1990, and by the ECU Board of Trustees a month later.

Approval initiated the third stage of the strategic planning process. The twenty-nine units having strategic plans in "Strategies for Distinction, 1990–1995," and in addition, the individual departments in the College of Arts and Sciences and the professional schools containing departments, created in the fall of 1990 individual plans for achieving the goals and objectives stated in the unit plans in "Strategies for Distinction." These planning documents were called operational plans.

Each operational plan had two sections. The first section presented the unit's vision statement. The second, "Objectives," listed the objectives that the unit aimed to achieve. The dual structure—strategic planning units, such as the College of Arts and Sciences, operated alongside other planning units containing departments as lower-level operational planning units— involved creating two types of operational plans. For example, the administrators and staff of the college dean's office created an operational plan that addressed the goals and objectives stated in the "College of Arts and Sciences Unit Plan, 1990–1993" from the perspective of the dean's office. This was called the "Dean's Office Operational Plan." Second, the faculty of each department in the college created departmental operational plans that addressed the goals and objectives stated in the "College of Arts and Sciences Unit Plan" from its perspective. The titles of these plans were specific to each department, such as the "Department of Physics Operational Plan, 1990–1993."

The "Objectives" section of each unit organizational plan listed verbatim some or all of the goals from either the unit's strategic plan or its parent unit's strategic plan. For example, when the operational planning unit was a strategic planning one, such as the dean's office in the College of Arts and Sciences, the goals listed came from the College of Arts and Sciences. When the unit was an operational planning unit that was not one of the twenty-nine strategic planning units such as the physics department in the College of Arts and Sciences, the goals came from the College of Arts and Sciences unit strategic plan. Thus the college had an operational plan responding to its strategic planning goals, and the departments in the college had operational plans addressing the college's strategic planning goals.

Second, under each goal in each unit, the operational plan was repeated as a verbatim or reworded version of one or more of the objectives from the parent unit's or a higher level unit's strategic plan. These items were not labeled objectives. Instead, they were named by the letter used in the parent unit's strategic planning document. Under each such item was listed one or more actions that were to be taken by the operational planning unit. These descriptions were titled "Objectives" and were numbered. Three more items occurred under each statement of an operational plan objective: a description of how results would be measured, a statement of how measured results would be used, and a time frame for meeting the objective.

An example from the "Department of Physics Operational Plan, 1990–1993" illustrates the format outlined above:

> Objectives. (1) ACHIEVE DISTINCTION IN UNDERGRADUATE EDUCATION, a) Develop curricula which emphasize writing, critical thinking, reading, oral communication, mathematical skills and the ethical dimension of decision-making in all courses, particularly those in general education, where such emphases are pedagogically sound. *Objective 1:* In addition to our Advanced Laboratory . . . expand our introductory course offerings to include an introductory laboratory to stress physics skills in critical thinking and mathematics. . . . Students will be required to analyze and write lab reports on significant problems in physics using only geometry, trigonometry, and algebra with the aid of an advanced software program which incorporates a word processor. *Evaluation:* The writing portion of the laboratory will require the students to present an original draft to the Writing Center for its signed comments. The effectiveness of the course will be further evaluated not only in the course itself, but also in all future physics courses where these applied mathematics, critical thinking, and expository skills will be used (providing for corrective feedback). *Results:* Information from the evaluation will be used to change, or otherwise update, the course as needed. *Time Frame:* Fall 1992–Spring 1993.

Item "(1)" duplicates what is found in the "College of Arts and Sciences Unit Plan, 1990–1993" under "Priorities for Action." This statement, in turn, copies "Goal 1" in "University Directions" in "Strategies for Distinction, 1990–1995." Item "a." in the above is a partial paraphrase of "a." in the college unit plan, which in turn is a composite of some parts of some of the objectives stated under "Goal 1" in "University Directions."

Each unit operational plan thus addressed from five to all ten of the goals listed in either the unit's strategic plan or the parent unit's strategic plan. Each unit responds to from five to thirty of the objectives from the relevant strategic plan falling under each of the goals. Each unit listed one or more of its own objectives under each of the objectives taken from the strategic plan, using the format illustrated above. The resulting set of 1990–93 operational plans and the 1990–95 strategic plans for the twenty-nine planning units fills eight 8.5" by 11" binders. This is without the unit strategic plans and the operational plans for enrollment management, facilities, faculty and staff development, financial, information resources, organization, and public outreach and without the operational plan for athletics. It would appear that these units either did not turn in plans or that the plans they turned in were not made a part of the university's strategic planning document.

Each operational planning unit reported its progress on its 1990–93 operational planning objectives in its May 1991 unit 1990–91 annual report. Reports were in narrative form. Here is an example of a portion of the report from the philosophy department:

> v. ASSESSMENT OF PROGRESS TOWARD UNIT GOALS: During the Spring Semester 1991 the Philosophy Department will establish a Departmental Curriculum Committee (hereafter "the committee"). (i) The committee shall examine course proposals, program proposals for the minor or minor tracks, program proposals for the major, institute proposals, center proposals, and any other proposal that may affect the Philosophy Department's curriculum. (ii) Based on the College's and the University's goal statements currently contained in the College's Unit Planning document, and the University Directions document, the committee shall evaluate and, if required, recommend revisions to (a) the course objectives currently contained in Departmental course syllabi, (b) the Philosophy Department's vision statement, and (c) the Philosophy Department's operational objectives.

In 1992 this rather informally structured reporting process was replaced by a format that directly linked each action reported to the relevant objective in the unit operational plan as well as to the objective and goal in the relevant strategic plan. The May 1992 physics department operational planning progress report contained: "Physics: Goal 4.a Seek permission to plan Ph.D. program in Medical Biophysics. Objective 1. Continue to seek support for permission to plan. This objective was a total success and planning is on schedule."

This format continued to be used for reporting progress on operational planning objectives for the 1992–1993 academic year.

In September 1992 a new Advisory Committee of Strategic Planning (ACSP) was created. This committee was chaired by Robert J. Thompson, acting director of the office of planning and institutional research. In fall 1992, strategic planning units revised their strategic plans for 1993–95. Concurrently, the ACSP initiated work on the reporting formats to be used for the 1993–95 priorities for action and the operational plans and progress reports based on these strategic plans. Planning units were to use the format of the original strategic planning documents. A March 1, 1993, memo from Thompson to ACSP members notes, "Each operational plan should identify the University Goal, the planning unit Priority for Actions (PFA), the operational objective, means of evaluation, expected result, and time frame for each operational objective." This further formalized the reporting process initiated in 1991–92.

On April 30, 1993, Thompson sent a memo to vice chancellors, deans, directors, and other planning unit and subunit administrators describing the final format for the planning period. The format followed the 1990–93 model, except that each planning unit progress report would now contain new sections: deletions, priorities for action that were in the unit's 1990–93 plan but were being deleted from the unit's 1993–95 plan; revisions, revised priorities for action listed by number and letter but not text; additions, new priorities for action listed by number and letter only; and a summary, a full listing of priorities for action for 1993–95. The instructions read, "In your summary, please place an asterisk in the left margin directly adjacent to each revised PFA included in your proposal and two asterisks by each new PFA. Original 1990–1993 PFAs that have not been modified will be apparent by the absence of asterisks and therefore will not require any special identifiers. Enumerate your resulting 1993–1995 PFA list consecutively, i.e., 1.a., 1.b., 1.c., etc, 2.a., 2.b., 2.c., etc."

Thompson's April 30 memo also described how units were to fill out operational planning worksheets. These worksheets were in the style of spreadsheets and were sent to units on computer disks. The newly required format was similar to the format of the 1990–93 plans and the 1992 and 1993 progress reports. Since the information was to be entered on the spreadsheets in a horizontal rather than a vertical fashion, some new information was required, and the names for the categories of activities being reported had changed, the instructions on reporting went into considerable detail. One change from past practice was that units would now report on progress only on their top five priorities for action. These five priorities were identified in the initial operational objectives section of the operational planning worksheet in columns one through three. Another change would link a unit's priorities for action to the unit's funding priorities. The following instructions give the format for reporting a planning unit's top five priorities for action:

2. Use the following method to indicate the top 5 PFAs in each of the categories of funding and overall importance for your planning unit during this planning period: a) Place a dollar sign ($) to the right of each of the top five funding priorities. b) Place an asterisk (*) to the right of each of the top five priorities of overall importance. c) Place both a dollar sign ($) and an asterisk (*) to the right of those PFAs that you have determined to be in the top 5 priorities for both funding and overall importance.

These instructions were followed by examples.

This format contained three major sections: operational objectives, planned objectives, and implemented objectives. The operational objective section was subdivided into two subsections. The first subsection was the label/priority section where the operational objective's identifier was stated and the top five priorities for action identified. The second subsection was the focus section, indicating the topic being addressed by the operational objective. The planned section, the second major section, was subdivided into two subsections that were further subdivided into two sections. There were planned scheduling, with a beginning and completion date, and planned funding, with source and amount. The last section, the implemented section, indicated progress. Employing electronic submittal on computer disks of planning and subunit materials via spreadsheet-style worksheets while excluding descriptions of goals and objectives made reporting plans and progress *much* less time consuming.

An April 23, 1993, memo from Vice Chancellor for Academic Affairs Marlene Springer to deans and directors stated that Chancellor Eakin had approved the new and revised 1993–95 unit strategic plans. This memo included Eakin's criticism of some of the terms used in the new plans. He complained that "terms like 'continue,' 'ensure,' 'monitor,' are not strategically oriented verbs. They imply Standard Operating Procedures and/or continuation functions which should not be the focus of a strategic or operational plan." Despite this accurate assessment, the verbs mentioned above and like verbs were used in all subsequent strategic plans.

The strategic planning process at ECU in the late 1980s into the early 2000s rewarded only new activities. There was no place for and no reward for doing well the essential, core, continuing educational, research, and service activities of the university. This might not have mattered if only a few units had been targeted to address new initiatives. But every unit in the university had to devise new objectives that addressed some of the university's new goals. At the same time, each unit had to continue working to accomplish standing unit missions that were not addressed in the planning process. This approach to long-range planning had an interesting effect on what is, by all external appearances, a top-down planning process. Since units were allowed to create operational objectives under university planning goals that had, at best, only a very tangential relation to the university goals, what appeared to be a top-down planning process actually evolved into, for practical purposes, a bottom-up planning process.

Springer's April memo stated the deadline for submission of the 1993–95 unit operational plans as May 1993. During the period from April 23 to May 14, academic faculty members gave final exams, and unit administrators prepared faculty evaluations and unit annual reports. Some operational planning units had not received their parent unit's 1993–95 strategic plans. These units had nothing to build their operational plans. The final deadline for submission of unit operational plans was changed to October 1993. Units reported their progress on 1993–94 operational plans in the May 1994 unit annual reports and reported progress on 1994–95 operational plans in the May 1995 unit annual reports. Reports were filed electronically using the format described previously.

The ACSP prepared a strategic planning workbook. This workbook was distributed to all strategic and operational planning units in January 1994. In a meeting held on March 2, 1993, ACSP suggested that "planning unit administrators be asked to ensure that constituent planning units and subunits have opportunity for input on PFA revisions in their parent planning unit." At this time ACSP also began discussion of the nature and structure of the 1995–2000 planning process. The committee discussed: "#1—the wisdom of having subcommittees which matched the five major areas of the SACS criteria in order to ensure that self-study conclusions are included as 'givens.' #2—the appropriateness of starting again with the three initial committees: Internal Strengths and Weaknesses; External Analysis; and Values analysis. #3—closer linking of PFA's between parent planning units and constitutive planning units." The committee expressed a consensus on #1 and #3, and suggestions were made to try to combine elements of #2 into #1. ACSP implemented these decisions.

Public forums were held in early April 1994 on new university goals. Reports from the external environmental analysis committee, the institutional values assessment committee, and the internal strengths and challenges assessment committee were provided to the university community before the forums. On May 5, 1994, Chancellor Eakin presented the reports to the Board of Trustees.

The external environmental analysis committee report read:

The projected decline in freshmen enrollments will compel the University to pursue more aggressively student recruitment strategies. Competition for qualified faculty will increase as the University moves toward doctoral-granting status. The number of potential students in NC in the traditional age bracket will decline by approximately six percent over the planning period. Successful development of the Global Transpark will eventually have substantial economic effects on the region. Pressures for educational accountability for the legislature likely will increase. Further improvements in SAT profiles and overall strengthening of academic standards will continue to erode the "party school" image. Integration of the University's fiber optic network with the State digital communication system will lower the long run cost of pursuing all of the University's missions.

The institutional values assessment committee built an information base from three sources: the findings of the 1989 institutional values work group, the institutional goals inventory survey, and the 1994 committee deliberations. Rather than tender a list of institutional values, the committee's fifty-page report included this database (forty-three pages), summarized the data (three pages), and provided an analysis section (one page). Beginning its "Statement of Values and IGI Survey Findings," the committee noted that "even though Heritage is not covered by the IGI, it remains an important value at East Carolina University." After expanding this claim, the report provided a summary of the IGI conclusions:

> The rank order of the goal areas in any one year indicates, in general terms, the relative importance of the separate goal areas as perceived by the respondents. Major changes in rank ordering of the separate goal areas from 1989 to 1994 would thus allow one to conclude that the goals of the institution, as perceived by the current respondents, have changed substantially from the perception of the earlier respondents.
>
> In the current survey, the highest "Is" means were [in rank order]: 1. Academic Training 2. Advanced Training 3. Research 4. Intellectual Orientation 5. Freedom of Expression and Life Style.
>
> In 1989 these same areas were ranked as highest with one exception. Intellectual orientation was ranked eighth in the previous survey and moved to fourth on the current survey. Community was the fourth ranked goal area in the previous study, and it moved to the seventh position in 1994.

This continued for two more pages, moving from the highest "is" means to the highest "should be" means (in rank order, community, academic development, intellectual orientation, advanced training, and vocational preparation) to the lowest "is" and "should be" means (notably, 18. humanism/altruism, and 19. off-campus learning for "is" valued and 17. social egalitarianism, 18. cultural/aesthetic awareness and 19. off-campus learning for "should be" valued). The last four paragraphs of the summary report contained a brief "analysis" of these results. Finally, conflating institutional values with the opinions of the individuals who took the relevant surveys, the analysis concludes: "An examination of the results indicates that there is a substantial consensus on the overall values of the university between the two surveys as they are measured by the IGI instrument and the locally added items. Some shifts occurred with the separate respondent groups, but in general the results remained consistent. This is not an unexpected finding as five years is a relatively brief time in which to change the values of an institution."

Highlights from the internal strengths and challenges assessment committee report include: "Strengths: Strong historical commitment of service to the region of Eastern North Carolina, scope and diversity of undergraduate and graduate programs, quality and character of faculty and staff, and university commitment to advancing information technology. Challenges: Staff morale, faculty morale, public relations issues, campus signage and parking."

In April 1994, the ACSP produced the first draft of university goals. The eight goals in the report were: "Distinction in Undergraduate education, excellence in teaching, respect for individual rights and human diversity, progressive graduate programs, excellence in research and creative activity, academically proficient and talented students, expanded information resource management capabilities, and effective stewardship of the University." Under each goal were from six to twelve strategies, bringing the draft document to seven pages.

Individuals across campus submitted to the ACSP comments on its draft. Carson Bays, economics chair, suggested the words "and its strong curricular foundation for teacher education" be changed to "and its strong academic foundations for professional education" since *academic* and *professional* are both more general than the words they replace. He also suggested changing "in keeping with the mission of East Carolina University, the faculty are committed to research and creative activity that is appropriate to the expectations of their respective disciplines" to "in keeping with the mission of East Carolina University, the faculty are committed to research and creative activity," since the first wording "provides a basis for units to evade the general expectation for productivity in research and creative activity. The applications of these goals will surely vary between units . . . but the general goal statement of the University is an inappropriate place to articulate such details."

Vice Chancellor for Academic Affairs Springer wrote ACSP:

Under goal 1: Achieve distinction in undergraduate education, I suggest that we state more emphatically our commitment to "improving retention and graduation rates," as follows: Implement the Plan to Improve Graduation Rates, especially as measure by the four-year graduation rate of first-time, full time freshmen, Encourage and enable full-time students to maintain course loads of at least 15 credit hours per semester, Monitor the four year graduation rate . . . and use the results to revise academic policies and procedures as indicated, and Assess the effectiveness of academic programs, including general education, against their established goals.

By August 1994, the ACSP developed a second draft of nine university goals plus numerous strategies for 1995–2000. These aspirations, adopted as the university planning goals for the 1995–2000 strategic plan, read:

Goal 1: Demonstrate excellence in Undergraduate education, Goal 2: Offer outstanding and distinctive graduate programs, Goal 3: Promote excellence in teaching, Goal 4: Expand excellence in research and creative productivity, Goal 5: Recruit, retain, and graduate academically proficient and talented students, Goal 6: Ensure respect for individual rights and human diversity, Goal 7: Provide effective University leadership in public education, health care, and regional development, Goal 8: Pursue state of the art information resource management capabilities and Goal 9: Ensure effective and efficient stewardship of the University.

Public forums were held on these goals in September.

Concerns raised by Chancellor Eakin in April 1993 were not addressed in the new goals statement. In the final version, three strategic planning goals were slightly revised. Under goal 1 there were five strategies lettered A–E—for example, "A. strengthen the academic and personal development of our students" and "C. refine assessment strategies for general education program and courses." There were four strategies under goal 2, including "increase the number of candidates and the graduation rates in existing doctoral programs." Goal 3 included six strategies, among them "refine effectiveness of teaching and advising effectiveness" and "expand the University's and the faculty's ability to engage effectively in distance learning programs." The four strategies under goal 4 included "promote policies, procedures, and resources that support faculty research and creative productivity" and "encourage collaborative research and creative productivity by faculty from different disciplines and institutions." Goal 5 contained seven strategies, goal 6 contained six strategies, goal 7 contained five strategies, goal 8 contained six strategies, and goal 9 contained thirteen strategies.

The 1995–2000 strategic plan, as previous strategic plans, established as the university's new top priorities a large number of aims for implementation by divisions, colleges, schools, and departments and by the support units of the university. In this case, a total of fifty-six separate aims (strategies) were presented under nine separate goals. As with the previous strategic plan, any one of the strategies listed under each goal could be the focus of as many as twenty or more unit operational planning objectives. In addition, units lower in the hierarchy also would be creating operational objectives to address the plans of their school, college, or division.

In October 1994, Chancellor Eakin presented the ACSP's recommended university strategic planning goals for 1995–2000 to the Board of Trustees. The board adopted the new university directions document with its nine goals and fifty-six strategies. In January 1995, Thompson sent a memo from SPAG to vice chancellors, deans, and directors containing guidelines for preparation of the next round of strategic plans and noting:

> The linkage you should make between the current strategic and operational plans and new ones that will begin on July 1, 1995 is a simple one. You should review your current plans . . . and determine how much progress you have made toward their accomplishment. You may wish to reconfigure some of those PFAs and objectives using new standards of measurement. You may wish to drop some of those that you did not accomplish because you now question their utility. . . . Whatever approach you take with the previous PFAs and objectives, they are the appropriate starting point for the development of new plans. By taking such action, you will help make the point to your faculty and staff that progress on the plans does make a difference.

Having made it clear that goals and objectives from the previous university strategic plan can be carried over to the operational plans for the 1995–2000 planning period, the memo continued:

> *University Directions,* the statement of university-wide goals and strategies [for 1995–2000] . . . should now be the basis for the strategic plans developed at the level of the professional schools, the College of Arts and Sciences, and the libraries. The priorities-for-action of these units should be directly derived from the university goals and strategies as well as the division priorities-for-action. . . . The university goals and strategies and the various PFAs that are in the process of being written are for the 1995–2000 period. Operational Objectives, however, will be for the 1995–1998 period. In 1998, at the end of this period, the operational objectives will be revised to cover the final two years of the 1995–2000 planning cycle.

The memo also alerted its readers that they would be required to indicate the resources needed to achieve their operational objectives. This was "because our new resources are likely to be very limited." The planning documents should be built "on the assumption that there is a competition for resources." The College of Arts and Sciences and the professional schools were required to complete their strategic plans (vision statements and priorities for action) by March 3, 1995. All other strategic and operational planning units were expected to complete their operational plans by April 30, 1995.

On January 19, 1995, Chancellor Eakin sent a memo to the Leadership Forum Members titled "Personal Comments on Strategic Planning Process." In this memo, Eakin explained that the reason that the goals and strategies in the 1995–2000 strategic plan (which now was being called "University Directions") were so "broadly cast" is because ECU is a "large, complex institution." The chancellor went on to say that "conflicts over their implementation will inevitably arise as they compete for our time and resources."

Eakin emphasized certain areas: retaining and graduating students; improving student facilities, programs, and support services; effectively using and expanding new computer capabilities (the new fiber-optic network); making clear to faculty the basis for personnel decisions (using the newly approved appendix D of the *Faculty Manual*); improving training and support for faculty and staff; increasing diversity of faculty, staff, and student body; developing approved academic programs; broadening student recruitment; integrating public outreach; and developing the athletics program.

Three months later Thompson notified university administrators that the Divisions of Academic Affairs, Health Sciences, and Student Life had "completed their strategic plans and that it was now time for the operational units to develop their plans." He scheduled two informational meetings to be attended by a representative from each unit, noting that the meeting would cover the process for developing and reporting operational plans and that he had held off sending this information until the PFAs were finalized.

The initial timeline to realize the 1995–2000 strategic plan called for units to create 1995–98 unit operational plans during April 1995. These plans were to contain a unit vision statement and a unit operational plan for the academic years 1995–98. Beginning July 1, 1995, units were to begin fulfilling their operational objectives. Unit annual progress reports on operational objectives for 1995–96 operational plans were due May 1, 1996.

The 1995–96 unit operational plans differed widely from one another. The Department of Psychology's operational plan contained eight operational objectives. The Department of Philosophy's plan incorporated thirteen objectives. English's plan employed twenty-five operational objectives. Industrial Technology's plan comprised seventy-five operational objectives.

Unit operational planning objectives varied. The psychology department's included: "1.B.0.0.4, Renovate Rawl 303 and 304 for use as experimental psychology labs. (To be completed by Fall of 1997 at as cost of $50,000.00 to be paid for by Business Affairs.) 2.A.1.0.1, Seek permission to plan a Ph.D. program. (To be completed by Fall 1998 at a cost of zero dollars.)"

Philosophy's plan stated: "1.A.1.0.4, Publish the philosophy major/ M.B.A. Flexible Careers Option by providing a description of the option with required philosophy courses for inclusion in the Business School section of the Graduate Catalog. (To be completed by Spring 1996 at a cost of zero dollars.) 8.D.0.0.2, Integrate information technology into the classroom by purchasing a roll-around security cart to continue implementation of philosophy's Portable Master Classroom project. (To be completed by Fall 1998 at an estimated cost of $600.00.)"

The English department proposed:

2.A.1.2.1, Prepare and submit a proposal to secure authorization to plan a Ph.D. program in Rhetoric, Composition and Professional Writing. (To be completed by Fall 1998 at a cost of zero dollars.) 4.A.1.0.1, Support faculty research and creativity through awarding reassigned time to faculty for mentoring Graduate Teaching Assistants and directing theses, as well as for advising and for research per se. (To be completed by Spring 1996 at a cost of zero dollars.) 4.A.1.0.3, Consider idea of creating and awarding an English Department Excellence in Research Award. (To be completed by Spring of 1997 at a cost of zero collars.) 8.E.1.1.3, Submit proposal to fund networking of newly-installed computer labs in GCB 2017 and 2018. (To be completed by Spring 1998 at an estimated cost of $71,200.00 to be funded from the student computer and technology fee.) 9.C.0.0.3, Establish criteria and procedures for reappointing fixed-term faculty beyond a sixth year of service, not that the six-year cap is removed. (To be completed by Spring 1996 as a cost of zero dollars.)

Industrial Technology's plan included: "1.B.0.0.5, Review and revise the Industrial Technology curriculum to be current, dynamic and continuously responsive to industrial needs. (To be completed by Spring of 1998 at an estimated cost of $100.00.) 3.A.0.0.2, Ensure that adequate and timely advising and counseling services are available to students. (To be accomplished by Spring 1998 at a cost of $300.00.) 3.C.0.0.3, Employ appropriate incentives to motivate students to excel in their undertakings. (To be accomplished by Spring 1998 at a cost of $7200.00, University and external funds.)"

At the August 1995 East Carolina convocation, Chancellor Eakin presented his goals for 1995–2005:

Contain student enrollment at 20,000 students. 2. Continue improvement in student quality. 3. Continue improvement of facilities, including a new science and technology building on the East Campus and the establishment of the East Campus as an integrated, pedestrian campus. 4. Significantly improve grant and sponsored programs activity. 5. Attain Doctoral II Carnegie classification. 6. Consolidate Health Sciences on the West Campus. 7. Establish ECU as a national leader in public school education and training. 8. Establish ECU as the technological hub of eastern NC. 9. Establish ECU as the leader in outreach activities in our region. 10. Position ECU for a $100 million campaign in 2007. 11. Obtain a Phi Beta Kappa Chapter for ECU. 12. Add a Ph.D. program in maritime studies. 13. Place ECU in a major Division 1-A football conference and expand the stadium to 46,000 seats.

During the next three academic years, planning units annually reported progress on their operational planning objectives from their 1995–98 operational plans. These reports were made using electronic submission of the operational planning progress worksheet. Tables 1.1 and 1.2 are an example from the Department of Philosophy's spring 1996 report:

TABLE 1.1   Operational Planning Report, Philosophy, 1996

Reference					Status of Objective	Estimated Expenditures
UG [1]	US [2]	PFA1 [3]	PFA2 [4]	OBJ [5]	[6]	[7]
1	A	1	0	1	continued	$100
1	A	1	0	2	continued	none
1	A	1	0	3	continued	none
1	A	1	0	4	continued	none
1	B	0	0	1	continued	none
1	B	0	0	2	continued	$100
1	B	0	0	3	Accomplished	none
1	B	0	0	4	Accomplished	$100
1	B	0	0	5	Continued	none
1	B	0	0	6	Continued	$100
8	D	0	0	1	Continued	$750
8	D	0	0	2	Accomplished	none
8	D	0	0	3	Continuing	$650

TABLE 1.2   Progress Narrative, Philosophy, 1996

Brochures are being provided to potential 5th year MBA students identified
during class based on their performance in the class.

Curriculum Committee working to structure "Flexible Careers" track to
add to the Undergraduate Catalog. Committee also reviewing possible
changes in course descriptions, though so far the committee finds current
descriptions satisfactory.

Writing of the new text for the Undergraduate Catalog is underway.

Revisions are before committee.

Instructors contacted students; mailing lists set up to automate.

Acquired mailing lists from General College. Will acquire again for Summer
1996.

Dr. Miller is the Pre-Law advisor; appropriate university offices informed;
General College assigns Dr. Miller as advisor to students declaring pre-
law interests.

Brochure used in approximately ten orientation sessions, will be used in
seven more by August 1996.

Text before committee (should be ready for first Freshman Orientation for
Summer 1996.

Initial brochure under revision by committee for Freshman Orientation
Summer 1996.

Department purchased SuperCard and RamDoubler, which are being used to
produce software for the classroom MultiMedia project.

College provided cart it was no longer using for philosophy multimedia
project.

College and department provided funds for CD-Rom drive. Will aim to
purchase SyQuest next year.

Beginning in August 1997, strategic and operational planning units began revising their plans for 1998–2000. They followed the format used for
the 1995–98 plans, continuing the implementation of the goals and strategies in the 1995–2000 strategic plan. Implementation of these revised plans
began July 1, 1998.

In January 1999, the university began development of its third strategic plan for 2000–2005. At the same time, the university prepared for the
2002 reaccreditation visit from the Southern Association of Colleges and
Schools. Implementation of the 2000–2005 plan was scheduled for July 1,
2000.

Changing previous planning cycles, Chancellor Eakin conducted more
than a dozen focus group sessions. These included the Board of Trustees,

alumni, the board of visitors, the board of public school superintendents, the city council, the county commission, community college presidents, and local mayors. The findings that resulted "became the basis for revising the university's mission statement and developing a new set of strategic planning goals."

The March 1999 report of the external environmental analysis committee discusses in detail competitive forces (such as virtual universities, private universities, corporations teaching students, and so on), demographic forces, economic forces, health care forces, political forces, technological forces, and social and educational forces effecting ECU. This report furnished accessible, useful information in each of its areas. For example, the section dealing with political forces concludes, "ECU will also need to work with the local governmental agencies of Greenville, Pitt County, and the surrounding region. This cooperation will focus on issues such as: future ECU growth will boost demands for parking, water and sanitation services, and other needs. Cooperation with local agencies is essential in meeting these needs; and enrollment projections indicate that ECU will have to fund new classroom space, dormitories, and other physical facilities, as well as additional teaching and support staff."

The March 1999 internal strengths and challenges assessment committee report identified progress toward resolving challenges listed in the 1994 committee report. It also noted areas in which progress was made. For example, the report states that "in most ECU units, faculty morale appears to be improved over that evidenced in 1994." Among the current strengths listed are: "The university fosters strong academic programs, the quality of human resources is excellent, campus physical facilities are exceptional and positive efforts have been made to increase cultural diversity on the university campus." Among the challenges listed are: "Recruiting superior undergraduate and graduate students, maintaining the quality of existing academic programs in the face of significant and rapid growth, developing campus information technology and distance education and enhancing external support."

In addition to these reports, the 2000–2005 strategic planning process used a number of other planning committees issuing reports prepared during 1998–99. One such report was the academic program development implementation plan that addressed leadership and procedural issues, such as fostering strong leadership in academic program development and streamlining procedures for development of new programs. The diversity implementation committee report recommended that East Carolina's strategic plan should encompass such things as establishing diversity and excellence as complementary and compelling goals for the university and increasing student, staff, and faculty understanding of multicultural communities.

The enrollment management implementation plan listed goals such as the need for a comprehensive plan for enrollment management. The external support implementation committee report recommended, among other things, that ECU establish clear university unit fund-raising priorities and increase participation and visibility of the university's trustees in the fund-raising process. The facilities implementation committee recommended a proactive, comprehensive space management program and developing and improving transportation. The faculty-staff development implementation plan advised that the university refocus or revitalize socialization and inclusion efforts through which new and existing faculty and staff develop a sense of community. The university should develop appropriate policies, procedures, and practices that will redevelop inclusiveness and eliminate perceived barriers to communication that fostered mistrust. The information technology committee report identified issues for the Academic Affairs and Health Sciences divisions. The report suggested that "based upon a comprehensive funding model for information technology initiatives," ECU should "create a culture that provides incentives for superior achievement by providing and supporting an advanced information technology infrastructure to achieve redesign of administrative processes for more efficient operation."

The marketing and public outreach university-wide implementation committee favored that "East Carolina's leadership team clearly state the university's vision and the image to be built on that vision." It recommended that "an office or individual should be designated to coordinate, enhance and fund public service." The organizational implementation committee proposed that "a chief of staff will be created" and "an institutional effectiveness committee will be established." Some of the financial implementation plan's recommendations were "engage the campus in a conversation and analysis of the changing nature of the academic enterprise and its implications for resource allocation decisions" and "institute a rolling multi-year financial planning process with fiscal year budgeting." Among the recommendations from the student support services implementation committee were "enhance student access to services and activities, faculty and staff be trained to provide informed, quality services" and "monitoring and coordination of course scheduling for adequacy and availability."

In spring 1999, the university reviewed its mission, and an emended mission statement was presented to the campus for discussion. This new statement was presented to the trustees in May 1999. New strategic planning goals were created during the summer of 1999 and were approved by the Board of Trustees in October 1999. While these goals were in the development stage, eleven implementation committees reviewed the university's operations and made recommendations on steps needed to achieve the goals. As in previous planning cycles, each implementation committee was asked to review the appropriate SACS criteria and to recommend the appropriate changes in policy necessary to strengthen the university's compliance with the SACS criteria.

"University Directions, 2000–2005" resulted from the planning process outlined above. The new ECU vision statement read: "East Carolina University is a public, doctoral institution distinguished by excellence in teaching and research and committed to serving the people of North Carolina and beyond." Chancellor Eakin then introduced the new ECU mission statement:

Our mission: to serve through education, to serve through research and creative activity, to serve through leadership and partnership.

East Carolina University, a constituent institution of the University of North Carolina, is a public, doctoral university committed to meeting the educational needs of North Carolina. It offers baccalaureate, master's, specialist, and doctoral degrees in the liberal arts, sciences, and professional fields, including medicine. East Carolina University is dedicated to educational excellence, responsible stewardship of the public trust, and academic freedom. The university values the contributions of a diverse community, supports shared governance, and guarantees equality of opportunity. East Carolina University's motto is "Servire," meaning "To Serve," and it seeks to meet that obligation through the following interrelated components of its mission.

"University Directions" listed ECU's elements of distinction, examples of which were:

A highly visible athletics program committed to academic excellence, an expanding base and rapidly growing levels of private financial support, the maintenance of a small-college atmosphere and a tradition of individual, caring attention to students while increasing student enrollment, a breadth of strong academic offerings at the undergraduate and master's level amid a vigorous, thriving liberal arts program and nationally accredited professional schools, emerging doctoral strengths in the biomedical sciences, communication sciences and disorders, coastal resources management and maritime studies, and educational leadership, service as the cultural center of eastern North Carolina through critically acclaimed programs in music, art, theatre, and dance.

Various challenges faced by ECU included "increased competition for highly qualified students, high quality faculty and staff and new academic programs." Emphasis was given to "alternative patterns of campus space utilization." A closer working relationship "with city, county, and other regional government and non-government agencies" was required.

Six 2000–2005 strategic planning goals developed the planning response from the various studies and reports cited above: "1. Expand the educational opportunities provided on and off campus by 20 percent. 2. Enrich the learning environment of students. 3. Increase the productivity of faculty, staff, and students in research and creative activity. 4. Extend external leadership and partnership roles in eastern North Carolina. 5. Be a leader in the application and development of information technology in higher education. 6. Improve the quality and efficiency of services and operations."

Under each goal listed were from eight to ten subgoals (identified as "strategies" in the two earlier strategic plans). Examples included:

Goal 1: B. Identify and prioritize for development new and existing programs that meet the needs of students and the state
   C. Improve its competitiveness for superior undergraduate and graduate students
   E. Improve recruitment, retention, and graduation rates
   F. Ensure that academic programs are appropriate to accommodate both the expected enrollment increase and the institution's new doctoral status
   G. Expand distance education offerings to meet the changing needs of students and the state.
Goal 2: A. Preserve ECU's tradition of being a large institution with a small campus feel
   B. Raise the academic quality of the incoming classes
   C. Create an environment that fosters the recruitment and retention of a more diverse student.
Goal 3: A. Develop selected, new, interdisciplinary doctoral programs
   B. Encourage the development of university and system wide collaborative and interdisciplinary research programs in bringing information and expertise to bear on regional concerns
   F. Increase by 50 percent the grant and contract dollars secured over the next five years
   G. Strengthen the campus infrastructure that supports the application for and implementation of grants and contracts.
Goal 4: B. Provide leadership and information for sustainable economic development and improvements in education, health care, social and human services, and the natural and cultural environ-

ment of the region, especially for underserved populations and rural communities

C. Develop partnerships with health care, education, government, public service agencies, and industry for the coordination and application of information technologies to their needs

D. Explore how to better link people in the region with others outside the region who have successfully dealt with comparable concerns.

Goal 5: C. Redesign its administrative processes to be electronic-based rather than paper-based

D. Provide faculty, students, and staff with appropriate access to state-of-the-art services and technological infrastructure

E. Enhance support services for high-performance computing, networking, and information technology the challenge of focusing its resources to create "centers of excellence" and to provide the infrastructure for continued growth of educational programs and scholarly activity.

Goal 6: D. Develop and implement a multiyear financial planning process

E. Establish clear priorities for the focused investment of existing and new resources

F. Explore and implement alternative work styles, evaluation criteria, and rewards for its employees.

The last two sections of "University Directions" presented ECU's 2000–2005 funding goals and described ECU's students and other clientele.

ECU planning units created strategic plans containing the unit vision statement, the goals and subgoals from "University Directions," and, in addition, listed under specific subgoals, the action to be taken by the planning unit to implement the subgoal. These actions were called "priorities," while in previous plans they were called "priorities-for-action." When one planning unit reported to another planning unit, as in the case of the College of Arts and Sciences reporting to the Division of Academic Affairs, the college strategic plan duplicated the academic affairs strategic plan, adding under some of the priorities stated in the academic affairs plan a statement presenting the action the college would take to support a priority. These were referred to as the college's strategic planning priorities.

In operational planning units, the operational plans duplicated the strategic plans of their parent unit, adding one or more operational objectives under some or all of the priorities stated in the parent unit's strategic plan.

As an example, the College of Arts And Sciences strategic plan presented:

Goal 1: Expand the educational opportunities provided on and off
campus by 20 percent.
   D. Increase the proportion of in-state enrollment from the Pied-
      mont and western sectors of North Carolina.
      1. (Academic Affairs priority) Ensure enrollment expansion con-
         sistent with the mission and goals of the university.
         a. (College priority) Maximize efficiency in utilizing available
            resources to best meet the challenges of teaching more stu-
            dents while at the same time trying to increase research/
            creative productivity and expand research commitments.

Each of the other college priorities came under academic affairs priorities.

In February 2000, the Advisory Committee on Strategic Planning and the Office of Planning and Institutional Research issued "Implementing Strategic Planning: A Handbook for the Development of the 2000–2005 Plan." This handbook contained instructions on how to plan, listed materials to be used for developing plans, and included ECU's vision and mission statements, a statement on resource allocation connection, and a timetable, as well as the reports of the external environmental analysis committee, the internal strengths and challenges committee, and the institutional values committee. It contained reports and plans of the implementation committees and ECU's SACS alternate self-study proposal and, in the final section, the appropriate division, college, school, or library vision statement and strategic plan for 2000–2005. (Recipients of the handbook had the strategic planning document appropriate to their unit.)

ECU's alternate self-study proposal is titled "Growth and Quality: Excelling as an Emerging Doctoral University." This proposal was submitted to SACS in October 1999. It outlined ECU's strategic planning process, emphasizing the ongoing assessment activities and their use both in academic programs and in administrative and support services. The stated goals of the self-study were to "1. Develop strategies to manage up to a 40–50% enrollment increase over a 9-year period, 2. Develop strategies to enhance quality undergraduate education, while increasing research and doctoral programs, 3. Develop strategies to respond to changes in course delivery and teaching methods as a result of technology, 4. Develop strategies to respond to changes in how scholarly activity is undertaken and how resources are managed, and 5. Develop strategies to facilitate the delivery of service and support functions through the use of technology."

The implementing strategic planning workbook explained the differences between strategic planning units and operational planning units. The former units are charged to create priorities in their plans that address the goals and strategies of the 2000–2005 strategic plan. Strategic planning units had to create plans containing priorities that could be used by units that report to the strategic planning unit (this was not a strict requirement on operational planning units; see below). Strategic planning units also had to prepare their own operational plans presenting how they would play their part in operationalizing their strategic plans. Operational planning units were to create plans that addressed some of the priorities for action of their parent unit (for example, the philosophy department's plan was expected to operationalize some of the priorities of the College of Arts and Sciences strategic plan). As with previous cycles of the strategic planning process, operational planning units did not create strategic plans.

In discussing operational objectives to be created for the 2000–2003 portion of the 2000–2005 planning period, the workbook stated:

> As each strategic planning unit and its related operational planning units determine how they can work together to achieve their priorities, they will develop more specific objectives that they will seek to complete during the planning cycle. Those specific objectives are referred to as operational objectives. In writing these operational objectives, both strategic and operational planning units seek to identify key aspects of their operational activities to more effectively fulfill their own vision statements. If the appropriate linkages have been made between the various planning levels, the fulfillment of these operational plans will lead to the university, as a whole, achieving its goals.

The workbook also noted:

> The designation of departments and offices as operational planning units is not intended to diminish the significance of their work or in any way affect their governance status. It is simply a reflection of the fact that the resource decisions made at the departmental or office level primarily concern a single academic discipline, function, or service activity of a single division. One of the purposes of strategic planning is to help us, as a university, division, or college/school, make more effective resource allocation decisions. That perspective is not particularly feasible at the departmental/office level.

This format for strategic planning effectively shifted some of the responsibility for identifying the range of priorities that would be operationalized by a specific operational planning unit such as the Department of Chemistry to this department's parent strategic planning unit, the College of Arts and Sciences. This approach unsuccessfully aimed to ensure that planning at ECU would finally be top-down.

The workbook makes it clear that the operational planning units were responsible for evaluating their previous planning efforts, establishing operational objectives that were consistent with their strategic planning unit's priorities, achieving these objectives, and assessing and reporting on their progress toward these objectives. Among other things, the workbook states that operational planning units were to develop priorities "in a manner consistent with their strategic planning unit's priorities." Strategic planning units were to supervise the operational planning of the units that report to them and ensure assessment and reporting of their own progress and the progress of the units reporting them. The strategic planning units would do the same to their own plans.

The handbook also allows that "if any unit desires to work on an operational objective for which it cannot find an obvious priority [in its parent unit's priorities] it should consult its next higher strategic planning unit administrator before including the objective." In addition, the handbook warns that "an operational planning unit *cannot commit resources* to objectives outside those established by the strategic planning unit without the concurrence of the appropriate strategic planning unit administrator."

On April 14, 2000, Thompson sent a memo to operational planning units that moved the date for submitting operational plans from the departments in the College of Arts and Sciences to June 15, 2000. Thompson explained that the planning office was "trying to bring more focus to the priorities and operational objectives of the units this time around; consequently, the number of priorities and operational objectives is being limited. The College and professional schools will be limited to 5 priorities and *operational planning units (departments and others) will be limited to 10 ranked objectives.*"

Thompson's memo also instructed that

in developing your department's operational objectives, you . . . should review . . . the department's previous operational plan . . . the previous strategic planning efforts of the College, your unit's Five Year Unit Evaluation Report as well as the responses of your Dean, Vice Chancellor, and the Chancellor; the 1998 SACS Criteria for Accreditation; and the university and divisions strategic planning documents. Of particular importance for SACS and most professional accreditation reviews is the topic of institutional effectiveness. We will be called upon to demonstrate that the University has in place methods of assessing the institutional effectiveness of each unit and can document how it *has utilized* the results of those assessments in making improvements in its operations.

Operational planning units used the opportunity to operationalize priorities not in the parent unit's strategic plan. Some operational planning units did not operationalize any of the priorities of their parent unit. Other operational planning units created some objectives addressing priorities of their parent planning units and some objectives addressing priorities in higher-level plans. A few operational planning units addressed only the priorities of the parent planning unit. This was the case, even though Thompson's memo also stated that "each operational objective may be linked to only *one* College priority."

Wide variety in operational objectives created by operational planning units resulted:

University Directions Goal 3. Increase the productivity of faculty, staff, and students in research and creative activity.

Priority F. Increase by 50% the grant and contract dollars secured over the next five years.

Academic Affairs Priority 5. Increase the level of research and creative activity.

College of Arts and Sciences Priority 3. Identify and develop concrete types of support for research.

Department of Chemistry operational objective: Increase funding for graduate education.

University Directions Goal 1. Expand the educational opportunities provided on and off campus by 20 percent.

School of Social Work and Criminal Justice operational objective: Develop the human resources of the School by exploring alternative organizational structures and increasing staff and administrative positions commensurate with the existing and anticipated workload of the school.

University Directions Goal 6. Improve the quality and efficiency of services and operations.

Priority C. Establish benchmarks and targets for improvements of its various activities.

School of Education Priority 1. Create a unit restructuring process as part of the larger movement to become a College of Education.

School of Education operational objective: Establish at least one new doctorial program.

For the 2000–2003 planning period, the unit operational plans were submitted electronically on computer-generated spreadsheets. As with previous operational plans, each unit's progress to date on its operational objectives was reported during May of 2001, 2002, and 2003. Each objective's status usually was ranked as accomplished, not-completed/ongoing, or discontinued. Costs to date were stated, along with indication whether the reporting unit wanted any accomplished objectives described in the campus-wide report that highlighted some of the university's accomplishments for the year.

For example, in 2001 the Department of Psychology reported that none of its five objectives were completed. It had expended $74,900 to date, and it did not want this information included in the campuswide report. In 2001, the economics department reported that four of its objectives were accomplished, three were not completed, and one was discontinued. Costs were reported as $4,000, and three objectives were to be included in the campuswide report: "Post senior research papers of students who complete the economics Honors sequence on the Economics homepage, require oral presentations in those courses where pedagogically appropriate, increase external research support for research."

On August 1, 2001, Chancellor Eakin, the individual behind the planning effort at ECU since the late 1980s, resigned.

With the arrival of Chancellor William Muse in the summer of 2002, new planning initiatives were introduced. In his August convocation address Muse introduced his "Four Pillars," that foundation on which ECU's future would be built: international prominence in education, international prominence in the arts, achievement in health care, and regional economic development. In his inaugural speech on March 8, 2002, Muse stated that ECU needed to attain:

1. A highly effective undergraduate educational program as measured by appropriate student outcomes such as job placement, entry into graduate school, and success on qualifying exams. This program should be composed of a sound foundation in the liberal arts and sciences and opportunities to obtain specialization in fields that are in high demand.
2. A growing graduate program, particularly at the doctoral level, in areas of faculty strength and where there is a demonstrated need for the graduates.
3. A research program that is focused on areas that are consistent with the university's strengths and directed toward the needs of the constituency we serve and the region where we are located. An emphasis should also be placed on projects for which external funding is available and where the opportunities for application of the results are high. A movement from research-intensive toward research-extensive status should be our direction.
4. A heightened emphasis on engagement with the external community, particularly eastern North Carolina, providing the opportunities and

the structure for faculty, staff, and students to use their knowledge and skills to effect positive change in the region we serve.

5. The development of a "community of scholars" among our faculty that will allow individuals to focus their efforts on their strengths, consistent with unit priorities, and that will reward performance, both quantitatively and qualitatively.

6. A student life program that provides students with significant opportunities to develop the skills they will need to be successful, to become fully engaged in the life of the University, and to form life-long friendships in an environment that fosters and values diversity.

7. An athletic program that is a dominant force at the Conference USA level and reflects positively on the University in terms of both the on-field and off-the-field performances of those student-athletes and coaches involved.

8. A dedicated team of administrators and support staff that provides the facilities, finances, and services that are so essential to performance of the institution's academic mission.

9. A commitment to diversity and equal opportunity throughout our organization, developing programs and structures that nurture talent and reward performance.

10. A greater international presence in terms of student enrollment from other countries, student involvement in study abroad programs, and faculty and staff participation in programs of an international nature. We are part of a global community and must act and think as such.

The presentation of the new chancellor's ten goals did not affect the existing strategic and operational plans or objectives. What was reported on the May 2002 and 2003 operational planning reports continued to reflect operational planning units responses to the goals and priorities contained in "University Directions, 2000–2005." The following are examples from the operational planning reports for the academic years ending in 2002 and 2003.

In May 2002, the School of Business reported that it had accomplished four of its objectives, was continuing four of its objectives, and had discontinued one objective. It reported that this was done at no cost in some cases, entered a question mark in the relevant box on the form in two cases, and left the cost box blank in three cases. The school indicated that it did not want its accomplishments reported in the university report. In 2001, academic library services reported that it had not completed any of its ten objectives. Costs to date were reported as $1,165,300, and it did not want anything listed in the campus report.

In May 2003, business services reported that it had accomplished two of its four objectives, was continuing one objective, and had transferred one objective to campus operations. Costs reported were $19,021,898. No accomplishments were submitted for the campus report.

During the 2002–3 academic year, while strategic and operational planning units were continuing to implement plans created before Chancellor Muse's arrival, ECU's new provost, William Swart, proposed wide-ranging changes for the university, including three-year degree options, a new engineering school, and the rearranging of departments and schools to create six colleges. These initiatives, announced on January 16 at the Provost's Convocation, were "part of a three-year action plan that includes expanding educational opportunities, increasing productivity and increasing the efficiency of university services and operations. Academic changes would include: The creation of three-year bachelor's programs and the establishment of a combination bachelor's/master's program, the creation of an engineering program, the re-establishment of an honor code and enhancement of diversity."

In autumn 2002, Provost Swart established a number of task forces, which issued reports in the spring of 2003. There were task forces on each of the four pillars identified by Chancellor Muse during his convocation address, as well as many other task forces that produced reports on what ECU should do in the immediate future. The motto adopted for ECU during Muse's chancellorship was "Tomorrow starts here."

During the June 19–20, 2003, administrative retreat, Chancellor Muse identified two principles important to ECU as an institution:

PRINCIPLE 1: A public university that desires public support must have a "sense of place"—i.e., it must remember where it is located and it must be responsive to the needs of the market or area it serves. . . . In our case, our primary market is eastern North Carolina. . . . this is the area that identifies us as "their university," and that this is the primary area we should serve. Distinguished public universities, in their desire to achieve national or international acclaim, sometimes neglect their primary market, often to their peril. . . . increasingly in the future, public universities that do the best job of serving their constituencies will enjoy the greatest public support.

PRINCIPLE 2: In order to achieve distinction beyond its primary market, universities need to identify a few areas where it has the greatest potential to excel and, therefore, receive national recognition.

Muse then identified four categories of "needs," or areas in which ECU has the greatest potential to excel and, therefore, receive national recognition: education, health, economic growth and development, and cultural enrichment. These four items were presented as the new four pillars for planning at ECU.

In mid-September 2003, Muse resigned and was replaced by William Shelton, who served as interim chancellor until June 2004. Shortly after Muse resigned, Provost Swart was reassigned to faculty status in the School of Business. James LeRoy Smith was appointed interim vice chancellor for academic affairs on September 26, 2003, leaving the provost's position unoccupied until April 2, 2005.

In November 2003, Interim Chancellor Shelton defended the four pillars approach to planning Muse introduced and Provost Swart had begun implementing. Under Shelton, the four pillars to be used for planning purposes were health care, performing arts, education, and economic development.

In preparation for the 2004–9 planning period, in November 2003 a report titled "Critical Issues for East Carolina University General Themes" was published. The report emphasized ten areas of concern, including:

Leadership: both interim and future permanent campus leaders (Chancellor, Vice Chancellors, etc.) must not only demonstrate vision, enthusiasm and energy but also a high level of integrity and a love for this university. Mission: We must realistically assess our ability to grow total enrollments to the level projected and the implications that will have on quality of the "student experience," budgetary resources, facilities/ space, faculty and staff support, curriculum, organization, etc. Personnel Compensation: in light of no or only negligible permanent salary increases for most employees in the last several years, compensation issues are directly impacting our ability to recruit and retain a highly motivated and competent workforce. Diversity: there continues to be a need for a clear and well-focused diversity initiative that is comprehensive in nature, improves communication and unites the campus community.

On November 23, 2003, "Strategies for Distinction, University Directions, 2004–2009" was presented. In addition to repeating the mission statement from "University Directions, 2000–2005," this document reaffirmed Muse's August 2001 four pillars as ECU's current "Areas of Emphasis."

"University Directions, 2004–2009" then presented six new strategic planning goals with twenty-four priorities spread under these goals.

Goal 1. Expand and enrich access to learning. Priorities: a. Promote access to ECU to a broader audience; b. Increase learning opportunities using diverse instructional methods and contexts; c. Provide expanded lifelong learning opportunities; d. Fund more merit and need-based scholarships; e. Ensure that its graduates excel in communicating and working effectively in contemporary environments; f. Increase campus retention and graduation rates; g. Enhance student participation in professional development programs and activities; h. Implement an organizational structure to support and enhance interdisciplinary programs.

Goal 2. Integrate more fully and effectively the activities of the university and the broader community. Priorities: a. Integrate community-based learning experiences into the curriculum, especially in ways that have a direct regional impact; b. Increase the transfer and application of knowledge to the community to aid the development of eastern North Carolina; c. Support and reward faculty efforts in community engagement; d. Expand the university involvement in planning and economic development activities within eastern North Carolina.

Goal 3. Create and sustain an environment conducive to scholarly and creative activity consistent with ECU's development as a research university. Priorities: a. Increase undergraduate and graduate student involvement in faculty scholarly activities; b. Create more researcher-friendly administrative support systems; c. Support research/scholarly projects that have a direct regional impact; d. Seek expanded external funding to support faculty scholarly efforts; e. Create an ongoing process to identify a select number of existing and emerging Peaks of Excellence supportive of the university's Pillars; f. Recruit students, faculty, and staff with the necessary skills and experience to enhance the development of campus scholarly activity.

Goal 4. Promote and sustain an environment of diversity, equity, respect and inclusiveness for all members of the university community. Priorities: a. Develop and sustain a shared, inclusive understanding of diversity on campus; b. Recruit and retain a more diverse student body, including more international students; c. Recruit, retain, and promote a more diverse university workforce at all levels; d. Develop an expanded culturally pluralistic curriculum; e. Strive to raise the university community's respect for diverse perspectives and people.

Goal 5. Excel in the application of information technology in support of the university's mission. Priorities: a. Forge a campus culture that readily accepts and adapts technological changes; b. Develop a comprehensive long range planning and funding system to meet campus information technology needs; c. Use information technology to enhance instructional, administrative and communication process improvements; d. Promote the ability of the university community to learn and work in a forward-thinking information technology environment; e. Be a recognized leader in the application of information technology to the activities of higher education.

Goal 6. Improve and enhance the quality of university services. Priorities: a. Improve staff/faculty development program with the aim of recruiting, training, and retaining the best possible employees; b. Implement administrative processes that are integrated, efficient, and cost effective; c. Ensure that university services are of quality, accessible, and easy to use; d. Integrate administrative functions and student support services across East and West campuses when applicable.

The timeline presented in table 1.3 also was published for the 2004–9 strategic planning process.

On December 18, 2003, a diversity task force report was issued. This report detailed the university's obligation as well as the evolution and context of the issues involved. Recognizing that progress had been made, it listed four areas of "targeted diversity programming": "1. Initiated Chancellor Funded Initiative on Race; 2. Awarded $70,000 Z. Smith Reynolds Grant to fund Race Relations Program; 3. A well-funded, well-staffed Cultural Center with one of the largest programming budgets in the UNC system; and 4. Attendance at 2003 Minority Family Weekend increases by nearly 130%."

The report highlighted minority faculty and student recruitment and recommended developing an ECU diversity framework. This involved recommending this university diversity vision: "East Carolina University recognizes that diversity and respect for human difference within the academe is a key source of intellectual vitality and innovative spirit. The Office of Institutional Diversity (OID) seeks to promote diversity on campus, nurture it and realize its full benefits within the context of teaching, learning and living. ECU will focus on diversity not as an end unto itself, but rather as a means to an end of respect for and unity among members of our University community."

The report also recommended a university diversity goal:

East Carolina University is committed to enriching the lives of students, faculty and staff by providing a diverse academic community where the exchange of ideas, knowledge and perspectives is an active part of living and learning. The University seeks to create an environment that fosters the recruitment and retention of a more diverse student body, faculty, staff and administration. The University defines diversity in a broad context to include the representation, integration and interaction of different races, ethnicities, cultures, national origins, abilities, religions, orientations, intellectual positions and perspectives. The University desires a pluralistic academic community where teaching, learning and living occurs in an atmosphere of mutual respect in pursuit of the excellence. The University considers diversity, the opportunities afforded by a diverse learning environment, and the authentic interac-

TABLE 1.3 Revised Strategic Planning Timetable, November 2003–July 2004

2003 November	December	2004 January	February	March	April	May	June	July
Academic Affairs prepares its 2004–9 strategic plan by January 31			Colleges prepare their strategic plans based on university strategic plan and Academic Affairs strategic plan by March 1	Schools/departments prepare their operational plans based on University strategic plan, Academic Affairs strategic plan, and College strategic plan by May 15			Units report progress on 2003–4 strategic plan objectives	New 2004–9 strategic plan becomes effective on July 1
			Academic Affairs support units prepare their operational plans based on university strategic plan and Academic Affairs strategic plan by April 1					
		Health Sciences prepares its strategic plan based on draft goals by January 31	Schools prepare their strategic and operational plans based on university strategic plan and Health Sciences strategic plan by March 1	Departments prepare their operational plans based on university strategic plan, Health Sciences strategic plan by May 15				
		Remaining divisions and chancellor's area prepare their strategic plans by February 15		Individual offices and units prepare their operational plans by April 15				

tion among people from various backgrounds and persuasions to be essential elements in achieving excellence in education.

The report then stated five diversity goals:

Goal 1: Develop and sustain a shared, inclusive understanding of diversity on campus.

Goal 2: Recruit and retain a more diverse student body, including more international students.

Goal 3: Recruit, retain and promote a more diverse University workforce at all levels.

Goal 4: Develop an expanded culturally pluralistic curriculum.

Goal 5: Strive to raise the University community's respect for diverse perspectives.

The report concluded by presenting detailed plans and timelines for accomplishing the five goals. One strategy for success in the plan for goal 1, for example, was "Develop 3–5 year plans for diversity objectives and long term, sustainable projects that are collaborative in nature and promote relationships for and between students from majority, minority, and international groups. Provide monetary incentives for such projects. Chancellor to allocate budget dollars for monetary incentives. End of Fall 2004, Dean of each college and school to provide an Annual Report to OID from each college and school dean indicating plan outcomes in relation to stated objectives and projects."

From January 2004 though April 14, 2004, strategic planning and operational planning units did not engage in new planning activities. During this time discussion centered on whether or not to begin the new planning cycle before the arrival of the new chancellor, Steven Ballard. Thompson sent planning units a memo stating that "the current strategic planning timeline and process is suspended." Thompson explained that the Office of Institutional Planning, Research, and Effectiveness recommended to Ballard "that we suspend the conclusion of the current process to permit him time to understand more fully the reasoning behind the choices the plan represents and to have more opportunity to influence the preparation of the university's plans."

Steven Ballard assumed his duties as chancellor on July 1, 2004. In his convocation speech on August 23, 2004, Ballard emphasized focusing on what the campus community can create by working together. He noted that in his first ninety days as chancellor his focus would be internal. "We must get the right people on the bus and then make sure those people are working together with each other, with the faculty, and with our community and constituents." Ballard noted things ECU values: ECU's strong spirit and its commitment to students, learning, and strong values. He then noted four things he values: community, people, quality, and aspirations. On community, he explained, "What really makes a difference to organizational performance is how we work together." Emphasizing people meant being sure that ECU's employees are valued. The reference to quality addressed ECU's products and services and the role they play in achieving ECU's future. "Aspirations" focused on the recognition that "who we are depends in part on who we want to be." Ballard stressed the following in presenting his vision for ECU:

> First, our vision is about us and our role in our state and the nation. We need not define ourselves by the definition of others. Second, our vision must be bold. We must be known for our aspirations, not our fears. . . . I see a pathbreaking public university that improves the lives of its constituents and ignites their spirits. I see a public university that is engaged throughout society and an effective partner with its community, its region, and its state. I see a university that is not only the most important institution east of I-95, but is recognized among all universities for its commitment to its society. We will be the catalyst for growth, economic development and a better quality of life in eastern North Carolina. I see a university that is the hub of its region, a vibrant community, known for its ideas, resourcefulness and creativity. I see a campus that people seek out to visit because of its spirit and because it is welcoming and friendly. I see a university that is a mandatory stop on any tour of institutions that know who they are, what they value and where they are headed.

Ballard affirmed that "the future—tomorrow—starts here!" He reviewed ECU's major challenges: money (state financial support for higher education is decreasing), accountability (ECU will be publicly accountable), diversity (ECU must recognize the nature of our world and evolve accordingly) and growth (ECU has an obligation to provide access to our programs and eastern North Carolina depends on ECU).

In February 2005, Thompson issued a report that reviewed the current state of the planning process at ECU. This report observed that the current strategic plan would expire on July 1, 2005. A new Advisory Committee on Strategic Planning was formed. This committee was charged to recommend draft vision and values statements be followed by draft university goals. The target for values and vision statements was March 1, 2005. The date for university strategic planning goals was May 1, 2005. Divisions were to complete their strategic plans by August 1, 2005. Colleges would finish their strategic plans by October 15, 2005. Departments and schools were expected to complete their operational plans by December 1, 2005.

Thompson's report then identified the following planning process needs: "A strategic plan that integrates and coordinates the following planning dimensions according to established university mission and priorities, a multi-year academic program development plan, a long range enrollment management plan, a multi-year technology plan, multi-year plan on research development, a multi-year plan on student services, a comprehensive campus master plan and planning process, a fund-raising campaign planning process (private and federal dollars) that supports the above and a rolling multi-year business and budget plan."

In his installation speech on March 31, 2005, Chancellor Ballard emphasized that "ECU will not be deterred from its vision; ECU will be recognized for our performance; ECU will realize our aspirations." He then said, "Our commitment to our state can be summarized in three words: relevance, responsiveness, and respect." Turning to the quality of ECU, he noted that we have very high standards. He described the strengths of ECU's health education and science programs, performing arts programs, and teacher preparation programs. Ballard then focused on what ECU should be like in the future. He stressed leadership, athletics and academics, service and engagement, access and diversity, and ECU's role as an economic catalyst, partner, and center for innovation and health technology"

Leadership: In 2015, ECU will be recognized as "The Leadership University," where each member of our community is empowered to achieve his or her aspirations. Athletics and academics: Our goal by 2015 is to not just meet the NCAA Academic Progress Rates, but for all 20 Division I sports at ECU to have graduation rates higher than the general student body. Service and engagement: Just imagine ECU in 2015 as the university that re-defined the notion of public service, making it among the highest honors of the university. Access and diversity: Imagine a university that lives its values related to access and diversity. By 2015, we intend to be known for ending the tyranny of admissions processes biased by income and race and to be first in the nation in minority graduation rates. Economic catalyst and partner: Imagine a university recognized as the best economic development partner in North Carolina and the very best collaborator and friend of the community college system. Center for innovation and health technology: imagine ECU in 2015 as a national leader in the innovation and application of medical technology, as the first medical school to not only cure diabetes but the place where the molecular trigger for diabetes is identified and inhibited, as a national center for technologies dealing with speech impediments and speech pathologies and as a world center for research and technology transfer related to minimally invasive surgical technology.

On April 2, 2005, Chancellor Ballard appointed James LeRoy Smith ECU's new provost. This significantly expanded Smith's role in the ongoing strategic planning process.

At the end of July 2005, the advisory committee on strategic planning presented Ballard with a strategic planning report and a 2005–15 strategic planning draft containing six strategic planning goals for 2005–10, many subgoals, and three alternatives for the university's new vision statement. At the beginning of August, Thompson resigned as director of institutional planning, research, and effectiveness and from his post as chair of the Advisory Committee on Strategic Planning.

The strategic planning report recommended that the chancellor discuss the draft strategic plan in his convocation address and then have six weeks of public discussion of the document. The report suggested a timeline for proceeding:

> August 22–September 30, 2005, time for public discussion and Executive Council consideration; October 1–21, 2005, revision of draft document based on public comments; October 24–December 16, Academic Affairs and Health Sciences Division complete develop of their divisional plans; January 2–February 24, 2006, Colleges develop their college-wide plans; February 27–April 14, Schools and departments develop their unit plans; January 2–March 1, 2005, have the other divisions (University Advancement, Research and Graduate Studies, Student Life, Administration and Finance) complete their strategic plans in response to the overall university plan and those of Academic Affairs and Health Sciences.

The suggested timeline was not implemented by the university.

The potential vision statements recommended by the Advisory Committee on Strategic Planning were: "East Carolina University—a legacy of service and determination, a commitment to leadership and innovation for a brighter tomorrow"; "ECU—Leading, teaching, discovering, and serving for a better tomorrow"; and "East Carolina University—a university for the people of North Carolina. Their potential is our passion."

The six recommended strategic planning goals were: (1) enrich the quality of student learning experiences—in and out of the classroom, (2) provide leadership in economic development and improving the quality of life for Eastern North Carolina, (3) position the university's academic programs for national recognition, (4) achieve national recognition of our research and creative activities, (5) create a diverse and inclusive campus, (6) create a culture of leadership—of shared responsibility—for the future development of East Carolina University. Six to eight subgoals were listed under each major goal area. Under goal 2 was found "a. become a role model for public university leadership in improving the quality of life and economic development of their home communities and region," under goal 3, "f. ensure that faculty tenure and promotion criteria recognize and reward the full diversity of scholarly activities," and under 4, "b. increase faculty scholarly productivity in top tiered research journals, academic presses, and juried national venues."

In his convocation speech on August 22, 2005, Chancellor Ballard stressed that ECU must clearly define its future, understand challenges, identify goals that will make the most difference, and invest its resources wisely in those goals. He stated:

> The next step is for the entire campus is to identify *our most significant* opportunities and use them to define our future. I am fully aware that this will require that most dreaded of all activities foisted upon the campus by the central administration. Exactly, the dreaded "P" word is emerging. *PLANNING,* the most boring, most easily forgotten aspect of our work. However, *integrated planning* has been identified by our Board of Trustees as one of two top priorities. *More importantly,* a real strategic plan is in our self-interest. A useful strategic plan begins with three elements: a bold vision, strategic challenges, and strategic directions.

In addressing the university's new vision, Ballard emphasized that "we are ready to be the university *FOR* North Carolina." He then listed five strategic challenges immediately confronting the university: growth (imagining ECU's future without losing its core), faculty success (balancing opportunities for faculty growth with the need to build the infrastructure to ensure the success of ECU's new faculty), status (being true to ourselves and establishing the right values for who we are), student access (the economic plight of ECU's students), and ECU's research profile (defining ECU's goals for research productivity). This was followed with a listing of ECU's strategic opportunities. This list began, "Our challenges, while real and formidable, pale in comparison to our opportunities. Developing and investing in our most significant *strategic opportunities* cannot be an exercise or an attempt to reward some programs while others are neglected. Rather, real Strategic Planning will: define our place *in the system, inspire us* to greater accomplishments and create new opportunities *throughout campus,* for growth, funding and collaboration. A rising tide lifts all boats."

The five strategic opportunities were (1) at ECU, students come first; (2) ECU provides educators for the twenty-first century; (3) ECU leads culturally and artistically; (4) ECU will transform the economy of our region; and (5) medical innovation. Ballard concluded, "Our future is incredibly bright and compelling. The foundation is here and the opportunities abound. It will require a strategic approach, ownership throughout the campus, and aggressiveness. As in every endeavor of a great university, the faculty will be at the center of what we do. This will be a tremendously exciting year. I am very happy to be a part of it."

In September 2005, Provost Smith appointed Associate Provost Henry Peel interim director of institutional planning. During the meeting of the ECU Faculty Senate on November 8, Peel introduced the faculty senators to a new planning model: "integrated planning." It was an attempt to incorporate all aspects of the university into one comprehensive, integrated plan, using strategic directions as the basis for the plan. This new approach was grounded in five assumptions: Planning should consider all aspects of an organization relating to operations; any factors impacting operations should be considered; planning should be ongoing and dynamic; individual unit planning should follow the unit's planning cycle (program review and so on); unit planning entry into the model should be open.

The new integrated planning model was intended to encourage simultaneous unit planning. Unit plans in an integrated planning model were to address benchmarks and assessment and evaluation. Assessment and evaluation was to be tied to criteria such as the Southern Association of Colleges and Schools accreditation requirements, professional program accreditation outcome measures, and program review outcome measures.

At the senate meeting, Peel presented an outline of the new planning process and a timeline. The planning process was proceeding by analyzing existing artifacts for ECU, sharing possible strategic directions with various stakeholders and receiving input, facilitating college and unit planning, analyzing input from all groups and determining university-wide strategic directions, determining college and unit directions aligned with or in addition to university strategic directions, creating appropriate data analysis informing the strategic planning process, creating budget and enrollment projections and identifying needs in various areas, determining resource shortfalls and identifying potential resources, and returning to stakeholders to discuss strategic directions and accompanying resource needs.

Peel reviewed the UNC Board of Governors draft of seven strategic directions for the University of North Carolina system for the planning period 2006–11. These strategic directions were:

1. Access and Student Success: Ensure affordability and access to higher education for all who qualify, and embrace a vision of lifelong learning, and promote student success. 2. Intellectual Capital Formation: Through high quality and relevant undergraduate, graduate, and professional programs, develop an educated citizenry that will enable North Carolina to flourish. 3. K-16 Education: Continue to propose and support initiatives to serve the needs of the State's public schools. 4. Creation, Transfer and Application of Knowledge: Expand the frontiers of knowl-

edge through innovation and scholarly activities, basic and applied research, technology transfer, outreach, and public service activities. 5. Internationalization: Promote an international perspective throughout the University community to prepare citizens to become leaders in a multi-ethnic and global society. 6. Leveraging Information and Knowledge Management: Use the power of information technology guided by strategic IT planning for and more effective educational, administrative, and business practices to that will enable the University to respond to the competitive global environment of the 21st century. 7. Economic Transformation: Promote higher education transforming North Carolina's economy through high quality degree programs, basic and applied research, creativity and innovation, transfer of new knowledge, the application of best practices, and an understanding of the economic needs and directions of the state.

The UNC Board of Governors draft was followed by a draft of the university's five potential strategic planning directions. A set of goals was listed under each objective, along with examples of how progress on goals would be assessed and examples of university development priorities. The five directions, along with an example of a goal, assessment objective, and development priority falling under each were:

ECU will prepare tomorrow's leaders: we will distinguish ourselves among large, national universities by becoming the model for the modern leadership university; assessment: be in the top 10% on student surveys; university development priority: endowments for student support —$40 million.

ECU will generate the ideas and innovations that define our future: through an active research agenda, ECU will address the social and economic development challenges and problems of our region and thus contribute to the quality of life of its people; assessment: promote and support the highest levels of scholarship, creative activity, and research by increasing external funding from $10 million to $50 million in 5 years; development priority: endowments for research program/research infrastructure—$140 million.

ECU will grow its academic health science center into a world class center matched to regional needs: ECU will enhance the health of North Carolina's people; assessment: be ranked in the top five nationally recognized academic health science centers for regional care; development priority: health sciences—$____ million.

ECU will enhance the cultural life of the region, state, and nation: we will contribute to the economic, social, and cultural progress of

North Carolina and to the enrichment of the quality of life of its citizens through encouraging excellence in artistic and athletic achievement; assessment: be ranked in the top five nationally of programs in the arts; development priority: visual and performing arts center—$85 million.

ECU will prepare an educated citizenry that will contribute to the overall development of our state: ECU will contribute to an enhanced overall quality of life in North Carolina by graduating citizens who are responsive to our state's economic, social, and intellectual needs; assessment: become the undergraduate institution of choice in NC with excellent baccalaureate offerings (in the top 10% of appropriate student surveys); Development priority: endowments for student support—$40 million.

The senate also was provided with samples of integrated planning flowcharts. These flowcharts presented the university's potential vision statement (ECU is the intellectual and cultural capital of eastern North Carolina), mission statement (ECU will engage the region, state, and nation as a significant national university focusing on the quality of life in eastern North Carolina), and strategic directions. The flowcharts illustrated the relationship between these items and the plans of the Division of Academic Affairs and other major planning units in the university.

The proposed timeline for implementing the new integrated planning model after presenting it to the senate involved a November meeting with faculty officers and senate committee chairs, a review of the draft plan by the ad hoc advisory group on strategic planning, input from faculty members to deans, input from community groups, and input from university divisions. The new university plan was to be completed in fall 2006.

REFERENCES

ECU Chancellor's Office. John Howell Papers. East Carolina University Archives.

ECU Chancellor's Office. Richard Eakin Papers. East Carolina University Archives.

ECU Chancellor's Office. Steven Ballard Papers. East Carolina University Archives.

ECU Chancellor's Office. Thomas Brewer Papers. East Carolina University Archives.

ECU Chancellor's Office. William Muse Papers. East Carolina University Archives.

ECU Chancellor's Office. William Shelton Papers. East Carolina University
Archives.
ECU Diversity Office. Papers. East Carolina University Archives.
ECU Institutional Planning, Research & Effectiveness Office. Papers. East
Carolina University Archives.
ECU Provost Office. Papers. East Carolina University Archives.
ECU Vice Chancellor of Academic Affairs Office. Papers. East Carolina
University Archives.
UNC General Administration. Papers. East Carolina University Archives.

## CHAPTER TWO

Campus Development:
A Fundamental Change of Direction

BRUCE L. FLYE JR. AND ROBERT J. THOMPSON

WHEN MARY JO BRATTON concluded her history of East Carolina University's first seventy-five years, she wrote at the end of a major period of expansion of student enrollment, faculty, range of academic programs, and campus facilities. The three decades since have also seen tremendous increases in enrollment, faculty, and programs—all of which are reflected in the physical embodiment of that growth—the campus. A survey of the physical development of East Carolina University from 1982 to the present, a résumé of future needs, and a review of the evolving processes for decisions reveals the dynamics of this metamorphosis.

A university campus reflects many of an institution's attributes. These include available funding, academic programs, the student experience, accumulated capital needs, future aspirations, and the pride its employees, students, and alumni invest in the institution. According to one authority, "*Campus* sums up the distinctive physical qualities of the American college, but also its integrity as a self-contained community and its architectural expression of educational and social ideals."[1] An understanding of the extent and context of changes aids in appreciating the significance of the changes in both university and state decision-making processes evident in the campus's development. It also sets the basis for understanding how the university has matured.

In the autumn of 1982, East Carolina University's head-count enrollment was 13,311 students taking a total of 159,340 credit hours of classes. The faculty numbered 854, with the university employing another 1,486 people. The campus consisted of 73 buildings with a total gross square footage of

3,255,670. Estimated replacement value of the university's buildings and land stood at $235,293,495. The total land mass of the campus consisted of 275 acres. Students, faculty, and staff registered 10,088 cars for parking on campus that term.[2]

Table 2.1, ECU in 1982 and 2004, contrasts the growth of the campus in these dimensions. Map 2.1, ECU Property, 1982–2005, shows the physical layout of the campus in 1982 and the changes that have occurred since then. Student enrollment increased by over 9,400 students taking almost 500,000 credit hours worth of classes. Faculty serving those additional students grew by more than 600, and the university's total employment grew by more than 2,000. Buildings increased by more than 100 with almost 2,400,000 new square feet of added space and more than 800 new acres of land.[3] Some aspects of the campus did not increase as one might expect at first glance. For example, students living on campus in university housing actually dropped by a bit more than 500.[4] Similarly, the number of cars registered to park on campus increased only by about 800.[5] In both student housing and parking, other means were used to accommodate the growth.

ECU no longer is a comparatively small regionally based undergraduate institution with associated professional master's level graduate education. In the years after 1982 it became a complex nationally recognized research institution offering its undergraduate and graduate students, both on and off campus, a wide array of excellent educational opportunities.

In a comparative sense, the 1980s produced a period of slower development in campus facilities. A backlog was created. The funding processes in use by the state of North Carolina also greatly affected the ability of the campus to add additional facilities and to provide adequate care of its existing facilities. The basic process then in place for funding new academic or administrative buildings, buying land, or repairing and renovating existing space was for the university to submit budget requests to the president and the general administration of the University of North Carolina. The budget became part of the overall state higher education request. ECU's ability to secure funding for these purposes, as with any other university, depended upon the availability of state funds, which varied from legislative session to session. Universities were not permitted to carry unspent money from one budget year to the next. There were strict and low limitations on the amounts of appropriated state dollars that could be redirected in a fiscal year from one budget purpose to another to meet unexpected campus needs.

One consequence of this system was inadequate funding of campus repair and renovation needs that formed a backlog of projects. Another was the tendency to focus on the project of the moment as opposed to developing a longer-term perspective on overall campus facilities requirements.

TABLE 2.1 ECU in 1982 & 2004

	1982[1]	2004[2]	Difference	% Change
Total Student Enrollment	13,311	22,766	9,455	71.0%
FTE Student Enrollment	12,241	18,573	6,332	51.7%
Undergraduate Enrollment	11,273	17,408	6,135	54.4%
Graduate Enrollment	2,038	5,258	3,220	158.0%
Fall Credit Hours Taught	159,340	283,052	123,712	77.6%
# Students Housed on Campus	5,514	4,980[3]	−534	−9.7%
# Faculty	854	1,529	675	79.0%
Total Employees	2,340	4,525	2,185	93.4%
# Buildings	73	230	157	215.1%
Total Square Footage	3,255,670	5,679,908	2,424,238	74.5%
# Acres	275	1,376	1,101	400.4%
Replacement Value— Buildings & Land[4]	$235,293,495	$19,640,763,758	NA	NA
# Cars Registered	10,088	10,900[5]	812	8.0%

[1] *1982–1983 Fact Book,* East Carolina University, Office of Institutional Research, March 1983.

[2] *2004–2005 Fact Book,* East Carolina University, Office of Institutional Planning, Research & Effectiveness, March 2005.

[3] Personal communication, Todd Johnson, ECU Housing and Dining Services, November 2004.

[4] The methods used for calculating replacement value have changed such that a direct comparison is no longer feasible.

[5] Personal communication, Mike Vanderven, ECU Office of Parking and Traffic, November 3, 2004.

Supplementing state funds with private funding in support of campus projects, while becoming important, was not sufficient to initiate and complete a construction project. They could and did enhance the nature of some of the buildings, but state funding was necessary for their completion. In a similar way, the ability of the campus to use its private foundations as a means of funding additional facilities through either secured bonds or direct expenditures was also limited by the comparatively low level of available resources. Several of these funding practices and operational policies changed in the 1990s, thereby enabling the subsequent expansion.

In contrast to instructional or administrative facilities, successful funding for auxiliary operations such as health care clinics, student life facilities, athletics fields, and parking derived from money raised through student fees, ticket sales, private donations, or parking registrations and fines. Some special state appropriations would occasionally be secured that supported individual projects. By and large, the auxiliary enterprise then and now is still responsible for self-funding its projects. Thus, the means for such new facilities is tied directly to the amounts of money that can be raised from these sources. The distinction between the funding of academic space and student activity space became important in the early 1990s. The development of the new Student Recreation Center advanced, while the planned expansion of Joyner Library was impeded by limited state-appropriated funding. Many faculty and students could not comprehend why the university was making such a choice in its priorities. They did not understand the student fees would pay for the recreation center but could not be used for the library.

With these processes in mind, several major additions to the campus occurred in the 1980s. Work on the Brody Building was completed in 1982, as was an addition to McGinnis Theatre and the scene shop. These were followed by an addition in 1984 to the Jenkins Cancer Center on the medical campus. No new construction was begun for another four years. In 1988, the first major academic addition to the east campus, the General Classroom Building (now named the Bate Building), opened. This new building enabled the first major relocation of academic units in almost twenty years. The School of Business, the Departments of English and Foreign Languages and Literature, the administrative offices of the College of Arts and Sciences, and cooperative education were moved to the new building. Many other shifts in unit locations followed in the space left vacant in Rawl, Speight, and Brewster. The following year, the Ward Sports Medicine Building opened to provide space for both the Departments of Athletics and Health and Physical Education.

During the period from 1982 to 2004, no single element of change at East Carolina University attracted as much public attention as the change in campus grounds and buildings. A phrase often repeated was "I used to go school here, but it never looked this good!" As the university sought a greater recognition of its role in the state's higher education system and recognized the importance of the quality of its campus in attracting new students and faculty, it began to value its sense of physical place, acquired new skills in creating resources, and matured its institutional planning processes.

During this twenty-two-year period, overall enrollment increased by 71 percent. Although this rate of change paled in comparison to the growth experienced between 1945 and 1965, the increase of nearly 9,450 students

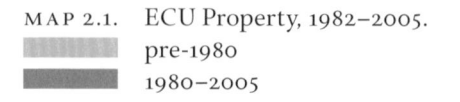

MAP 2.1. ECU Property, 1982–2005.
pre-1980
1980–2005

exceeded any similar period in the institution's history. The construction, acquisition, and refurbishment of buildings and land accelerated. Nearly 2 million square feet of space were added to the 3.3 million square feet that had taken seventy-five years to accumulate.

The shift in the university's concept of its physical self is best marked by two events: the chancellorship of Richard R. Eakin and the preparation of the 1992 comprehensive facilities master plan. Although these were brought about by separate needs and energies, the two events produced new ways of thinking about the campus. Chancellor Eakin arrived in March 1987, fascinated by the potential of the campus and shrewdly aware of the importance of seemingly minor facilities details in fulfilling that potential. Soon after his arrival, the campus needed to hire a new director of the physical plant. The chancellor stipulated that the position should be filled by an architect if at all possible, and subsequently, Robert C. Webb was hired from Western Carolina University. Between the two of them, they implemented subtle changes that improved the ambience of the campus. For example, if windows could be painted with a color other than the traditional stark white, building exteriors could assume a much warmer appearance.

Another important but little-recognized participant in this transformation at the detail level was Chancellor Eakin's wife, Jo Ann. The two of them would regularly walk the campus, sometimes alone, sometimes with Bob Webb. Questions about why things were as they were and numerous suggestions for improvements in campus aesthetics were the products of these casual strolls. Gradually, subtle improvements evolved, such as the planting of perennials here and there, screens around an unsightly utility apparatus, and changes in the way service vehicles parked. Over time the grounds department, led by Douglas Caldwell, began to realize the appreciation being shown for their role and for what they could do. They contributed their own improvisations: flower baskets hung from lampposts are one example of a small, low-cost element that brought significant charm to the campus.

Another more expansive opportunity for improvement Eakin recognized was the necessity for a formal campus master plan. Part of the background work done in 1988–90 in preparation for a new strategic plan was a general assessment of campus facility conditions and needs. It was clear to Eakin and others that the university required a more detailed assessment of campus needs and a plan to meet those needs. The initial analysis laid the groundwork but could not go far enough. This challenge and opportunity also became an obligation, however, as a functioning campus master plan was an essential component for a successful Southern Association of Colleges and Schools (SACS) reaccreditation process. The next SACS accreditation site visit was scheduled for spring 1992. Work began on the self-study in 1990.

The firm of O'Brien/Atkins Associates from the Research Triangle Park led this master planning effort. The intention of the plan was to guide and facilitate growth of the university through the year 2000 and beyond. In addition to diagrams prescribing circulation patterns, building locations, and land use, two technical, detailed areas of study emerged: assessments for future building space and for parking. The scheme contained a long list of needs and projects, many of which were implemented by the turn of the century. Its essential worth, in retrospect, lay in various planning principles that took on lives of their own.[6]

Some of the plan's concepts could be considered de rigueur to contemporary campus planning. A goal to "reinforce the core campus" was a typical recommendation, along with the idea that the campus must strengthen its edges, gateways, and other identifying elements. The "development of a central Landscape Pedestrian Spine" was diagrammed in a manner that was relatively Beaux-Arts and consequently difficult to visualize and implement.

Other concepts were grasped immediately as fitting ECU's context, and they became permanent and well-known guideposts for both major and minor improvements to the campus. The campus was to be pedestrian-friendly; vehicles would not be totally eliminated, but the safe and easy movement of walking students, staff, and faculty would take priority. Owing to the limited land area, the core campus should be restricted as much as possible to academic uses, whereas support and administrative functions —and parking—should be relocated to the perimeter. Such ideas became part of the campus lexicon because their value could be immediately visualized and understood. They also took a firm grip of the campus consciousness in the way of most successful ideas—through the active and vocal leadership of the chancellor.

This was the first formally adopted master plan for East Carolina University; however, it was not the first effort of this kind during this same period. The Campus Beautification Committee, chaired by John Bell, consisted of eighteen members representing a comprehensive mix of staff, faculty, alumni, trustees, and influential citizens. Among its recommendations was the creation of a formal campus master plan, but at the same time it suggested that many improvements could be made without waiting for a completed plan. Their seminal report makes for interesting reading, all the more so given the years that have passed since its publication. Seeds for many of the proposals of the 1992 master plan can be found here: "Centralize the academic function on the main campus"; "Manage vehicular traffic flow to limit vehicular access to the campus"; "Upgrade appearance of existing campus boundaries and entrances." All such recommendations were well supported with lengthy lists of specific tasks to be undertaken.

There is also an element of prescience in the 1988 report. At present, planners in universities and their professional associations are developing and advocating methodologies that variously describe planning as "comprehensive," "integrated," and "continuous," among other terms. Anyone interested can take advantage of innumerable workshops, institutes, and publications on the subject. It is not necessarily a unique or new idea, however, as its value was recognized in the 1988 document: "The most important lesson for us from this pattern of growth is that physical planning cannot be a one-time effort, but must be a continuing process based on well-defined policies and goals, supported by all components of the University, supported by adequate funding, and carried out in accordance with a comprehensive University-wide planning effort. *Responsibility and accountability for planning must be incorporated into the administrative process.*"[7]

By 1992, when the master plan was adopted, the 165,000-square-foot addition to Joyner Library had been designed and awaited funding. In November of that year, the voters of North Carolina approved a bond referendum for higher education facilities that included $31 million to construct the Joyner addition and renovate almost all of the existing building. This was a monumental project unto itself, but it would have plenty of company.

The Division of Student Life had three significant works on the boards: Todd Dining Hall began construction in 1992; the Student Recreation Center broke ground in 1993, within weeks of the start of the library expansion; and renovations to Slay and Umstead Residence Halls commenced in 1994. The campus soon appeared overwhelmed with construction workers, barricades, heavy equipment, and building material. Emotions were split, with high excitement and anticipation on one side and a fair amount of annoyance on the other. There were challenges to the process, asserting that this much construction should not be occurring at once because of its negative impact on students and faculty. Other observers shrewdly pointed out that when opportunity knocks, it is best to throw the door wide open.

Dreams of such improvements had been building for some time, but the visions took on a higher degree of focus during the process of recruiting Eakin. As part of the candidate evaluations, a visiting team from ECU made a trip to Bowling Green State University, where Eakin was vice president for student life. While there, they had the opportunity to visit a recently constructed student recreation center. Christenbury Memorial Gym had seemed a little rough around the edges before this trip, but in light of the new Bowling Green facility, it was plainly well below new and growing expectations. The bar was raised further when, during his candidate visit to ECU, Eakin commented not only on the essential need for a new recreation center but also on the poor state of on-campus dining. At that time, both food service and food service facilities were so meager that many students preferred to cook in their dormitory rooms.

Dreaming was one thing, but implementation was quite another. The key was the hiring for two critical positions. Dr. Alfred Matthews arrived on campus as vice chancellor for student life in 1988. He brought to the campus a high level of energy committed to a quality environment for students and a powerful expectation that the campus should acquire a new mindset about the importance of the physical environment in the student experience. Richard Brown arrived as vice chancellor for finance and administration in the next year, bringing to ECU a highly evolved financial acumen coupled with a can-do attitude. In conjunction with the chancellor, these two new leaders, unencumbered by previous institutional habits, took the first steps in one of the largest ongoing construction programs the campus had ever seen.

Todd Dining Hall opened in 1992. With an architecture intended to recall the forms of the early ECU campus, it proclaimed campus dining a significant experience. A timely change in food service contractors completed a campus commitment to make nutrition an important element in the total student experience. Construction of the Student Recreation Center commenced the following year and immediately became the centerpiece of ECU's televised advertising and student recruitment. Six basketball courts, an indoor pool, an indoor running track, and other accoutrements assembled in a building designed to generate excitement upon entrance.

After renovations to Slay and Umstead Residence Halls began in 1994, significantly higher-than-expected costs resulted in the projects being scaled back. Even with those modifications, here again was the delivery of yet another improvement to meet growing student expectations. Air conditioning and elevators were added, as were cable television and Internet service. All rooms were upgraded, bath facilities were enhanced, and meeting and activity spaces were added.

As a result of this combination of leadership and new construction, the campus culture changed. An awareness of the inability of ECU's campus and grounds to pass "the drive-by" test spurred renewed attention to landscaping, building repairs, and signage. Much of this was aided by legislation passed in 1991 that established annual allocations of state funds for purposes of repairs and renovations for all state buildings. At the same time, attentive ingenuity showed that much curb appeal could often be gained by small investments. A few perennials around a stop sign cost next to nothing, but this evidence that the campus cared about its staff and its students was of inordinate value.

Administrative changes that occurred in the early 1990s also had a major impact on campus facilities. In 1992, Richard Brown created a position for an assistant vice chancellor for facilities to meet the ever-increasing need for expertise in that area. George Harrell, a senior-level administrator at Florida State University, filled the position in 1993. The state of North Carolina made a major change in its provision for application of repair and renovation funds shortly after Dr. Harrell's arrival. Previously these funds had been included (though not necessarily provided) as part of the capital planning process. The net result was that every campus developed a backlog of repairs and renovations but little consistent funding with which to address them. Recognizing the growing problem this was creating statewide, the General Assembly enacted legislation that mandated annual appropriations of funds for the repair and renovation of all state buildings. This provided ECU with $4–6 million per year for about five years beginning in the late 1990s. With the benefit of this new funding stream in place, Facilities Services made considerable progress on the backlogged repairs and renovations. In addition, the increased funding compelled a more consistent planning than had ever been feasible before. A great deal of work was done each summer to improve classrooms in a number of buildings, including Rawl, Austin, Brewster, and Speight. Campus heating, ventilation, and air conditioning systems were also greatly improved. After 2000, the state's financial difficulties prevented this arrangement from continuing, but it may begin again once the state budget situation improves.

Another major change occurred in the hidden infrastructure—the campus information technology systems. ECU was the first University of North Carolina campus to commit to developing its own fiber-optic computing network. The decision made in the early 1990s proceeded with funds largely drawn from student fees and phone charges. This set the stage for major advances in the use of information technology in the classroom and in campus communications. This decision was later followed in the late 1990s to develop a wireless network on campus that is still being extended in 2005.

As the main campus underwent a transformation, a complete face-lift had already begun in the vicinity of Minges Coliseum, with completion in 1990 of the Ward Sports Medicine Building. No longer would athletics and the School of Health and Human Performance be crowded together in Minges Coliseum and Scales Field House with this new space available to expand to new offices, weight rooms, and classrooms. Of singular significance was the ability to further legitimize the sports medicine program, at that time the first of its kind in the United States.

Dave Hart, the director of athletics, had only started with the completion of the Ward Building. Ideas were beginning to brew for a major step forward for the basketball program: Minges Coliseum needed expansion.

Early design studies indicated that this high school–type basketball arena could be reconfigured for seating in the round, a pattern far more common on other college campuses.[8] Financing to accomplish the first hurdle was arranged through a creative combination of student fees, philanthropy, and receipts.

The project entailed a near total demolition of the building's interior as well as most of its exterior. Only the structural frame would remain. Most of the existing walls would be removed to expand the envelope of the coliseum itself. In addition, structural elements on the perimeter of the roof would be raised to improve sightlines for the uppermost of the new seats. Seating could be created that would surround the basketball playing floor. Shrewdly recognizing the value of engaged students in the competition, the designers planned to include court-level bleachers.

The next challenge lay in completing the building between basketball seasons. NCAA regulations placed restrictions on a Division I team to play "home games" in locations other than on its home court. Late December marked the end of renovations for any given calendar year. Minges Coliseum was, however, also used for academic purposes. Therefore, construction could not begin until the end of the school year in late April. This left a scant eight months for completion of the work.

It is difficult to describe this undertaking to anyone who was not there at the time. The best picture is painted by the fact that, while the renovation was in progress in September 1994, a small airplane could have flown in one side of the coliseum and out the other. The extent of the reconfiguration was that complete. In hindsight, there were probably few institutions— and even fewer architects and contractors—who would have thought about attempting work of this nature within such a compressed timeline. Only through the energies of the architect, Haken-Corley and Associates, and the general contractor, J. H. Hudson Construction Co. of Greenville, and a sense of expediency did it prove to be possible. As improbable as it was beginning to seem by October and November of that year, a renovated coliseum opened for its first game against the Catamounts of Western Carolina on December 19, 1995.

Most athletic programs would have breathed a sigh of relief and called for a long hold on everyone's ambitions upon completion of such a project. But Dave Hart now turned to expand Ficklen Stadium. As originally conceived, the enlargement of the stadium on its south side would provide box seating and significantly enhanced press box facilities. Provisions would be made for an upper seating deck of approximately 10,000 seats as a second phase of the work.

Concurrently, in 1995, Hart moved to the athletic director's position at Florida State University. As is often the case during leadership change at high levels, priorities shifted within the Department of Athletics, and the value of additional public seating weighed more heavily than the importance of improving the press box. (In addition, there was a certain amount of resistance to the idea of box seating coming from the University of North Carolina General Administration.) With these thoughts in mind, the south-side additions were temporarily set aside, and a plan for the addition of 10,000 upper deck seats was created for the north stands.

The north-side expansion began in late 1997, with the hope of being completed for a home opener against Wake Forest University in September 1998. Unfortunately, as is sometimes the case, this was a project in which everything that could go wrong did. The cost of precast concrete increased significantly owing to production shortages, and labor shortages made it difficult to keep skilled workmen on the job site. These and other factors postponed completion until the fall of 1999. By then, new athletic director Michael Hamrick continued momentum to move forward with design and construction of club-level seating—again on the south side—subsequently completed in 2000.[9]

By this time, millions of dollars had been spent on this portion of the campus, and the effect was staggering. Minges Coliseum was enlarged. The football stadium became a veritable edifice; chain-link fences and dirt paths had yielded to iron and masonry perimeter walls and landscaping. Ironically, one of the features that generated the most conversation actually cost a relatively modest amount. In an effort to make some improvements in portions of the stadium not directly affected by these additions, the cast-in-place, painted concrete walls on the faces of the stadium along the playing field were covered with red brick. Of all the improvements made, this single addition generated more conversation, more phone calls, and more exclamations than all of the other additions and improvements put together. "Now this feels like a real campus!" became a virtual mantra.

Hamrick once remarked that one day East Carolina would awaken to realize that the total makeover of its facilities for Pirate athletics was brought about by a pair of graduates from two rival institutions: West Virginia University and North Carolina State University. The Mountaineer-bred athletics director pointed the university architect toward the design and construction of the Murphy Center at about this point.

Nationally many critics in the country felt that college athletics had begun to be involved in an arms race, making ever more significant facility investments to recruit and win. Whether this was true or not, ECU did not intend to be left behind. How a university presented itself to prospective athletes and what it could offer those young adults in terms of their development and their future were becoming strategic issues. Hamrick conceived a facility built to impress prospective athletes with the importance of their chosen sport. The result evolved into what was at that time the second-largest strength-training facility in the entire country. It was to be joined by a trophy lobby to celebrate the history of Pirate athletics. Completing the scheme were banquet facilities for recruits on one side and Pirate Club activities on the other side. The result was one of the most exclamatorily ebullient architectural statements on campus, now known as the Murphy Center.[10]

Once again, athletics continued to invest in its program with another facility expansion. A woefully inadequate Harrington Baseball Field underwent renovation, featuring a totally new grandstand and team facility on the same site. The new steel-and-concrete structure included seats for approximately 5,000 fans. An additional 3,000 seats can be added with bleachers for significant events such as regional baseball competitions. This work began in the spring of 2004 and was opened for use with the start of the 2005 season.

The Division of Student Life was able to expand the campus's intramural activity support space. The first expansion came with a financial donation that enabled the development of the Blount Intramural Fields by the Belk Building. Made possible by the purchase of over 100 acres on the northeast side of Greenville by Highway 33, a second expansion is now under way. Once these fields are developed, they will become the primary intramural sites for the campus and greatly expand the services available to students through the inclusion of outdoor running and walking paths and more fields for soccer and softball.

In addition, Jarvis Residence Hall was extensively renovated. As one of the oldest remaining campus building, it was gutted and then renovated. Another recent project expanding the infrastructure for student services is the West End Dining Hall. This new facility will come online in later spring 2005 and will replace the dining facilities in Mendenhall. Also, for the first time in over thirty years a new dorm is being constructed on College Hill, and plans are being reviewed for the further expansion and renovation of student housing on campus.

In 1997, the Office of the President added a new committee activity to the responsibility of the university's planning staff. The effort at hand was simple enough and even routine, but as it turned out the University of North Carolina took its first steps in a major series of planning initiatives that three years later would make available the largest amount of capital funding the university had ever enjoyed.

During the 1990s, the University of North Carolina and the North Carolina General Assembly had sought means to develop better ways of funding the university system and allocating capital dollars. Thanks to the recommendations of a state government performance audit, a steady stream of funding was legislated for repairs and renovations for all state buildings. A modest process for prioritizing capital projects was exchanged back and forth between the university system and the legislature. Still, the capital budget organization process was not necessarily scientific. There was significant ambiguity of roles among the three parties involved in funding capital projects for the university: the legislature, the University of North Carolina, and the sixteen individual campuses. All had roles, sometimes in cooperation, most often in competition. To give some order to the process, a framework was put in place using a set of prioritization criteria agreed upon by the legislature with which the university system might develop its capital priorities. Among the factors included were enrollment growth, the creation of new programs, and campuses' ability to maintain their current missions.

In 1997, the prioritization standards were drafted with a methodology for determining space needs in university buildings. The Office of the President contacted each campus and requested specific individuals to participate in a committee to write space-planning standards under the leadership of independent consultant Eva Klein. The consequent methodology relied on a benchmark derived from the practices of other universities and other university systems, as well as extensive data available within the University of North Carolina and the constituent campuses. Together, this committee crafted a set of planning standards, specific to North Carolina, for the most enrollment-critical spaces.[11]

Coincidentally with this effort, the legislature was also engaged with the issues of equity and adequacy among the North Carolina campuses. Two separate studies were subsequently commissioned. The first, conducted by MGT of America, Inc., was directed to examine the overall financial resources provided to the individual campuses for operating dollars. The study would make recommendations for possible revisions to the full-time student equivalent enrollment change funding formula then in use. It concluded that various adjustments were needed in the base operating budgets of many of the system's individual campuses and recommended a new enrollment funding model based on differences in program costs and levels of instruction.[12]

Eva Klein and Associates also produced a second study drawn from their earlier work. The report compared the capital resources and allocations among the sixteen UNC campuses. Of particular interest to a number of legislators were the historically black universities and the extent to which they were or were not being supported at a level comparable with the other campuses in the system.[13]

Initially, the assumption was that the study would compare levels of capital funding from their initial creation. As a result of the scarcity of records and the difficulty in locating meaningful information, it was tentatively agreed that the study would begin with the 1965 fiscal year. Even with that shortened range, meaningful data that would truly offer an accurate cross section of the system's funding was not readily available. Finally agreed upon, the various campuses would be evaluated on the ability of their facilities to meet their current missions.

The space planning standards under development would be the immediate tool in comparing this assessment. Enrollment capacities would be analyzed and compared across institutions. It would also be appropriate, however, to consider the condition and the quality of the campuses, and an appropriate discipline for evaluating this data would also be adopted. As the study unfolded, these dimensions were to become parallel tracks. The capacity analysis would use data on enrollment, student contact hours, personnel, and other factors that were collected both from the system and from the individual campuses. With this information, it was then possible to calculate the surpluses and deficits of mission-critical space on each campus.

Just as planning standards had been written for the capacity analysis, standards now had to be prepared for condition and quality. Condition information was available from the state of North Carolina's routine biennial assessments of all state facilities. What needed to accompany this information, however, was an evaluation of the quality of existing facilities and their continuing ability to meet their intended purpose. With the prospect of potentially immediate legislation dictating a policy change, the quality standards were quickly developed and endorsed. Next, the consultants presented an Internet-based assessment instrument by which each campus could then conduct a self-evaluation of their facilities. Uniform reliability across the institutions was maintained as the members of the consultant team spent two days on each campus familiarizing themselves with the facilities as well as local perception of institution-specific capital issues.

Further fuel for these activities was the 1999 long-range enrollment forecast from the Office of the President, which projected that the system would grow by one-third over the next decade. This created immediate and extreme concern in the legislature, where it was believed that the state would be building many new and expensive classrooms and that a funding mechanism would need to be in place immediately. At the same time, those legislators whose prime concerns were of equity and adequacy among the institutions began to understand that funding the enrollment growth could be a tool to bring uniformity in resources to each institution.

As it turned out, the legislature was amazed and, in some instances, pleasantly surprised by the findings of the study. First, it was found that the system had an adequate supply of classrooms to meet the pending enrollment growth; on the other hand, there was an extensive need for new science laboratories. Although there was a significant amount of additional space requested to meet future growth, there were also opportunities to meet most of these needs by renovating buildings, both to correct deteriorating conditions and to modernize for the current and projected patterns of use.

The Office of the President and the legislature were determined to find a way to fund these needs. This was yet another example of the new methodologies being developed that had never been used in the state of North Carolina—never had so many aspects of planning been brought together at one time. Discussions led a state bond referendum that would provide the necessary funding. The question was how much funding would be required.

The findings of the equity and adequacy study gave a snapshot of where the institutions were at that particular time. By applying the campuses' enrollment projections to the findings of the study, it was possible to then forecast both the space needs and the renovation and modernization necessities for the next ten years. The data produced indicated that the cost of a higher education capital plan for the state of North Carolina would be approximately $6 billion. A first phase of funding was proposed in the amount of $2.5 billion, and the university system was instructed to prepare campus-by-campus plans. Never before had the North Carolina system been able to undertake capital planning in so holistic a manner.

University of North Carolina administrators as well as local campus leaders now had reliable data for renovations, for new construction, for high-quality campus grounds, and for infrastructure. These ten-year plans were to be prepared comprehensively for each campus, regardless of the source of funds appropriate to the individual projects; in other words, projects that would be supported by student fees or by revenues would be compiled along with projects that would be funded by state appropriations. Again, the value in this process was that it caused each campus to think about the entire campus as its ten-year plans were being developed. This process change not only illuminated constructive linkages among projects but also enabled more creative thought for the resulting proposed projects.

The initial phase's bond funding was proposed for $2.5 billion. Each campus received an apportionment match to its total need. The leadership on each campus, in conjunction with its planning staffs, the Office of the President, and Eva Klein and Associates, then developed the specific line-item projects to be funded on each campus. Following an extensive public relations campaign, this groundbreaking planning effort culminated in voter approval in November 2000. This approval was in itself historic, with 76 percent of the voters supporting the bond program.

For East Carolina University, the top priority in its ten-year plan centered upon additional science labs. Accordingly, the Science and Technology Building was funded at $65 million. Upon completion, the Department of Chemistry and the then School of Industry and Technology (now the College of Computer Science and Technology) moved from Flanagan Building. Additional funds were directed to completely renovate that building. The bond bill included funds for new facilities construction for the Schools of Allied Health and Nursing and for the Health Sciences Library on the health sciences campus. Comprehensive planning enabled this project to be fully realized in providing this new space. On the main campus, other departments used the available space to meet additional growth needs. Logically, renovation funds for these older facilities were also included in the bond bill. To complete the program, funds were used for the renovation of the old cafeteria building and for the modernization of various campus classrooms. The campus information technology and computing services offices moved downtown after these funds also made possible the purchase and renovation of the old Daily Reflector building.

The campus moved aggressively to complete the bond projects. A confident Eakin took a chance and spent some of the money that had previously been authorized for planning a new science and technology building to begin site preparation for the new building in anticipation of the bond program's approval by the voters. This move gave the project a six- to nine-month head start. While the Science and Technology Building[14] was under construction, an addition to the Rivers Building began. The Science and Technology Building was completed in the summer of 2003. Thereafter work began to completely renovate the original three wings of Flanagan Building. The Rivers addition was finished in the summer of 2004 along with Flanagan in the autumn.

In the meantime, work began on a new allied health sciences/nursing/health sciences building on the west campus. This project intended to place the various health sciences closer to one another and the School of Medicine. This project should be completed in summer 2006. On the east campus, the next major project is the refurbishment of the old cafeteria building. The building will house a number of student services and faculty offices. Accompanying this project, a small expansion of the Fletcher Music Building will also be under way. Aside from some additional renovation work, these projects will basically complete ECU's bond-funded construction. The bond referendum also provided funding for property acquisition, which eventually was used to acquire various pieces of property supporting future campus expansion. The principal area of land acquired was approximately 20 acres of land south of Tenth Street and west of Evans Street and east of the railroad tracks.

In total, the bond bill provided for East Carolina $190 million in capital funding, an amount never before imagined. The value of the current facility planning to the university, however, should continue long beyond the expenditure of these funds. From now on, data would become the backbone of planning; the methodologies for space needs assessments, planning, and resource management would continue; and planning would be accomplished comprehensively as opposed to one project at a time. Most important, the value of collaboration between different elements of the campus and iteration would be remembered.

In recognition that the 1992 campus master plan was already out of date, and in anticipation of the likely arrival of another bond referendum and the development of a new university strategic plan in 2000, Eakin accepted a recommendation that a new master plan be developed for the main campus. The authors, Mr. Bruce Flye Jr., then university architect, and Dr. Robert J. Thompson, then director of planning and institutional research, served as codirectors of this new plan. Flye and Thompson had exchanged information and ideas informally since the beginning of the Eva Klein study. This new assigned collaboration became the campus's first official response to a mandate of the university's 1990 strategic plan: "Align academic planning with facilities planning." One of the master plan's consulting architects, Krisan Osterby of Ellerbe Becket Architects, would note that this kind of relationship, although seemingly obvious, was extremely unusual on university campuses.

The same enrollment growth data and facilities needs data generated via the ongoing Eva Klein study served as the basis for the campus master plan and the university's requests for funding through the bond program. Concurrent to the Office of the President developing its estimates for the entire University of North Carolina, East Carolina University moved ahead of the curve by developing its own detailed campus master plan for the coming years.

ECU eventually found itself developing not one but two master plans. The health sciences campus lies two miles from the main campus and immediately adjoins Pitt County Memorial Hospital (PCMH). The School of Medicine currently enrolls over 360 students. An additional 1,100 students are expected upon the move of the Schools of Allied Health and Nursing to that campus in 2006. That building will provide 300,000 square feet of new instructional space.

A primary challenge for the main campus resides in the limited availability of land for building expansion. In particular, the main academic campus is landlocked in an urban and residential setting. The relationship with local government was generally free of serious difficulties, but the relationship with the residential and business community had never developed into an active and ongoing dialogue; property acquisition would be necessary, but would prove to be difficult in part due to this lack of ongoing partnerships. In contrast, the School of Medicine Foundation had slowly acquired land over a period of many years, and as expansion became possible the university had approximately 175 acres of land adjoining this campus.

The health sciences campus had never had a land-use plan that would not fit on the back of a napkin. Now, timing played an important role. The Schools of Allied Health and Nursing could move from the main campus. In addition, a new family practice center was accumulating funding, and conversations began about a new outpatient center. PCMH was considering its own growth requirements as well as significant modernizations. As PCMH's new facilities master plan developed, the university was invited to participate in a joint hospital/university plan. This, too, became the first formal master planning effort ever done for the health sciences campus. The two institutions had collaborated on issues of mutual interest. For the health sciences campus plan, a joint steering committee selected HDR as the planning consultant firm. By using extensive focus groups in a comparatively smaller academic community, there was a higher level of participation throughout the School of Medicine on this plan on the main campus. At the same time, HDR and the steering committee never succeeded in creating a high level of awareness of the common issues faced by the two organizations, and the plan quickly evolved into two separate plans.

The critical moment for the health sciences campus appeared a few months later. Although this campus was free of neighborhood issues by virtue of its location, the hospital's near-term and immediate tactical issues created a growing focus on the hospital's aspects of the plans at the expense of progress on the university's planning. (This was exacerbated in part by the fact that issues common to the two institutions did not compete well with their respective individual urgencies.) In August 2000, the joint planning agreement and planning for the university's property assigned the project to another firm, NBBJ, which had already become involved in the design of a new building for that campus. Vice Chancellor for Health Sciences James Hallock assembled his staff as a steering committee and committed to attending and actively participating in each working session. A forty-five-day working period was established for data gathering and for design. This included three three-hour working sessions for the vice chancellor, his staff, and NBBJ.

Some campus planners believe any plan hinges on the presence of a "big idea" at its center. On the health sciences campus, the "big idea" differed from the stereotypical notion of an academic medical center. Rather than stacking space into a single megastructure that requires construction of parking decks and roadways, this plan would take advantage of ample and available land to create a campus of human-scale buildings connected by a network of outdoor spaces. Eventually, it became known as the Learning Village. It would seek to take the better attributes of the Main Campus and restate them in a manner consistent with the mission and programs of the Health Sciences curriculum. The plan was received enthusiastically by the Health Sciences faculty and staff. Its subsequent presentation to the Board of Trustees went smoothly and earned immediate acceptance.[15]

On the main campus, the "big idea" was a significantly expanded campus, carefully crafted to respond to the constraints of an existing city network and to support the notion of "a major university with a small campus feel." The value of the old campus core to the undergraduate experience would be preserved and built upon. Graduate and other components were to be located next to this nucleus, depending on type of program and expected frequency of contact with the core. In general, the resulting plan was highly compact, an aspect that was at least initially well received by city government.

After the architect was selected to prepare the main campus plan in April 1999, a steering committee was organized around individuals who had previously served as chairs of various working groups for the strategic planning process. This committee would in turn report recommendations to the chancellor. In addition, a representative from the adjacent residential neighborhoods and a representative from city government were added to the steering committee. Each of the chairs subsequently organized one of a series of focus groups that contributed to the planning process. This arrangement worked well during the data gathering and conditions analysis phases.

Many campus and community planning sessions were held in 1999, and overall campus space needs were estimated. These included both academic, administrative, and student support requests that included land for intramural activities and physical education. The plan looked beyond five or six years out, focusing on the campus's needs over the next ten to fifteen years. It also included consideration of some projects that could not be directly tied to enrollment growth projections. The concept was to develop a full outline of the campus's space requirements. It would serve as both a decision process for the bond program and an educational process for the campus and community future priorities.

Inevitably, these estimates of space needs described the real estate required by the university in order to expand. The plan envisioned acquiring property between its existing eastern property lines and Evans Street, the former Rose High School property on Elm Street (now Eppes Middle School), as well as various other sections of property on the perimeters of the campus. The intention was to firm up the existing campus boundaries and to acquire sufficient space for the expansion of the eastern academic core. The plan contained a delineation referencing not property recommended for acquisition, but rather areas of the city in which the university was particularly concerned. Several areas were residential, and the plan hoped they would remain so in the future. As alternatives unfolded, the steering committee role shifted to the chancellor and his cabinet, with periodic updates to the Board of Trustees. Once prepared, the alternatives were made available for public viewing. The campus open house was not very well attended, but the community open house was standing-room-only. Although the planning process had been relatively open through the focus groups, there were no expressions of disagreement until the public meeting occurred. An overflow crowd was vocal about its homes and the apparent arrogance of the university. Within a very few days, yard signs and bumper stickers appeared in front of houses around campus. SAVE OUR NEIGHBORHOODS, they proclaimed. Inset in a corner of the signs and stickers was a red circle and slash over the words NEIGHBORHOOD DESTRUCTION. The focal point of the community opposition became the property between the east border of campus and Elm Street. Local neighborhoods organized against the proposed plan. They effectively mobilized residents, local legislators, and even initial backers of the plan to modify what they deemed offensive sections. (Up to and during this time, the trustees' interest in acquiring these adjacent properties had been restricted to the issue of timing—acquiring them as they became available—as opposed to questions of propriety or community sentiment.)

As the board prepared to meet in May 2000, legislators who had been contacted by adjacent neighborhoods complained about the proposed acquisition of their homes by the university. Under the threat that this issue could compromise the entire $3.1 billion bond bill then in discussion and especially the university's portion for land acquisition, the trustees retreated from the Elm Street neighborhood. The trustees ordered the removal of this section of the plan and subsequent revision of the overall plan. No bond funds were to be used to acquire property in the Elm Street area.[16]

Sensing that changes were nonimperative, the university removed the plan proposed for property acquisitions, instead tabulating unmet needs and detailing an organized process for investigating and acquiring additional property. Given the most recent enrollment forecasts as well as the slow rate at which the state would actually fund expansion, this ongoing process was more appropriate in 2000 than would have been thought a year beforehand. The university had experienced success over the preceding years by gradually and quietly acquiring strategically located parcels of land as they became available, and this practice would now be continued into the future.

The completed plan obscured the "big idea" for the main campus as additional land remained necessary to give the ideas physical form. Accordingly, an observer would not easily determine what progress actually occurred by studying only the maps. Even though those most familiar with the details and the context believed what was being proposed was the best alternative for the campus, the subsequent public reaction was not anticipated. That opposition ultimately detracted from one of the major objectives of the planning process: to educate the campus and community about the longer-term space issues facing the university. Discussion focused almost solely on one portion of the proposed plan. The reaction also hardened some community concerns about the university at precisely the time when the university needed public understanding of its land requirements.[17] At the same time the experience reinforced the intention to expect closer planning cooperation between university and city officials. Both city and university came to a greater recognition of their mutual dependency. This experience contributed to subsequent cooperative ventures such as the joint investment in the Tenth Street project, the various proposals concerning university investment bordering downtown Greenville, and even the establishment of the Greenville Redevelopment Commission.[18]

Campus facilities have undergone significant changes in the past twenty-five years. Construction has moved from a long, drawn-out, project-to-project focus dependent on specific legislative support to a more comprehensive approach based on campus needs. This is best exemplified by the 2000 bond referendum. The projects proposed for East Carolina University as part of the referendum are now nearly complete. Those not completed remain in various stages of construction and will be available by the end of the 2007–8 academic year. After that, no new academic facilities for the east campus have been funded behind them.

The campus and, indeed, the other University of North Carolina institutions are at a critical juncture. The 2000 bond referendum dealt only with roughly the first half of the project needs to meet the projected enrollment identified in 1999. Moreover, changes in programs and the unanticipated distance education enrollment growth have added greatly to the university's requirements.

One unanticipated change brought about by ECU's experience with the bond referendum and its campus master planning process was in future facilities planning. As a consequence, East Carolina University may now analyze and articulate its space needs. An Office of Campus Space Planning was created in 2002 and placed within the overall planning office, now identified as the Office of Institutional Planning, Research, and Effectiveness. This is the first time the university has had a full-time staff member responsible for analyzing campus facility needs in terms of current and future program requirements and anticipated enrollment growth.

There are also several sets of projects under way that are not dependent on bond funding, but which possess substantial implications for the future of the university. Two of these involve partnerships with other public entities. In 2004, ECU received a $60 million appropriation from the General Assembly to build a joint cardiovascular center with University Health Systems. This partnership will permit construction of a $210 million center dedicated to teaching, treating, and researching cardiovascular diseases. The second partnership involves ECU's relationship with Greenville. At present a joint enterprise is being developed that will permit the building of a hotel/alumni center/office building in the downtown area. The city will provide the land and assist with parking facilities, while the university, funded through one of its foundations, will build the complex. The project is part of both the city's and the university's effort to help rejuvenate Greenville's downtown area. Both projects will have important economic development implications for the community and symbolize a new willingness to build partnerships. In a similar development, the university has leased a significant amount of space in the newly renovated Self-Help Building (formerly the old Proctor Hotel or Minges Building). This leased space was needed both to move people out of the Old Cafeteria Building so that its renovation could take place and to accommodate the increased numbers of new faculty being hired. The move also continued the campus trend of moving administrative and auxiliary offices to the perimeter of campus. Student Media/Publications and the Division of Continuing Studies and Summer School were among the units removed to the Self-Help Building.

In addition, the Division of Student Life is advancing on several projects. Two have already been mentioned, the West End Dining Hall and the new residence hall. The other principal project is a proposed renovation and expansion of Mendenhall Student Center. The project, estimated at roughly $30 million, when funded will add significant area to the facilities for various student organizations and involve the development of a new cultural center.

One additional prospect that has been in the works for several years is the old Voice of America site, known colloquially as the west research campus. The rights to use this site were acquired in 2000 in pieces from the U.S. Department of Education. Over 580 acres compose this site. Initially a submission was made for a small section of the land on which the main buildings are located with a second request for the remaining larger parcel. The university indicated its intention to use this land for educational purposes and demonstrated how the land could be secured without cost. If the university met its general commitments in fairly good and consistent order, then the federal government would deed the land to the state in thirty years. This arrangement meant, however, that the university would report annually and progress would be evaluated. In 2003 it became apparent that the amount of suitable land on which permanent buildings could be located was actually small and scattered over the total land area. The university then began exploring the possibility of buying the land outright, and those negotiations are ongoing as of spring 2005. This site has considerable potential for outdoor classroom/laboratory facilities, including a university garden. The planning and funding necessary to chart the realistic use of this area has not yet materialized, but the site does have significant instructional and research potential that will need to be addressed once the university's rights over the land are settled and now that the details of the wetlands designation are understood.[19]

These projects, however, only partially address all of the campus's needs. For example, the medical school requires new, expanded clinical facilities to adequately handle its patients. The east campus is short of office space. More than 300 new faculty will soon be added. There will also be additional administrators and support staff hired. To accommodate this growth in personnel, Slay Hall will be leased from Student Life for offices. This action, though, will only meet the campus faculty office need through the 2007–2008 academic year. Expanded research facilities on both the east and west campuses must occur if the university is to expand its externally funded research. Other programs such as music, art, and theatre and dance need updated, expanded space.

These few examples illustrate the fundamental necessity for the university to continue to develop its planning capacity and to consider its facility projections in an open, comprehensive, and integrated manner. East Carolina has matured beyond the point of being able to develop each project one at a time. It has become a complex, nationally recognized research institution offering its undergraduate and graduate students, on and off campus, a wide array of excellent educational opportunities.

1. Paul Venable Turner, *Campus: An American Planning Tradition* (New York: Architectural History Foundation, 1984).
2. East Carolina University, Office of Institutional Research, *1982–1983 Fact Book*, March 1983.
3. East Carolina University, Office of Institutional Planning, Research, and Effectiveness, *2004–2005 Fact Book*, March 2005.
4. Todd Johnson, ECU Housing and Dining Services, personal communication, November 2004.
5. Mike Vanderven, ECU Office of Parking and Traffic, personal communication, November 3, 2004.
6. O'Brien/Atkins Associates, HNTB, and Stanton Leggett and Associates, "East Carolina University Comprehensive Facilities Master Plan," July 1992.
7. East Carolina University, "Report of the Campus Beautification Committee, Planning for an Academic Environment . . . Toward the Year 2007," April 1988. All emphasis is in the original report.
8. The architect for the renovation of Minges Coliseum was Hakan-Corley of Chapel Hill. This firm also designed the Student Recreation Center, mentioned elsewhere.
9. Walter, Robbs, Callahan, and Pierce were the architects for the stadium expansion. Other referenced projects for which they were the designer are the expansion of Joyner Library, the renovation of Harrington Field, the Schools of Allied Health and Nursing, and the Health Sciences Library.
10. Lee Nichols Hepler of Charlotte were the architects. In addition, this firm designed the renovations for Jarvis Residence Hall.
11. Eva Klein and Associates, "University of North Carolina Space Planning Standards," October 1998.
12. J. Kent Caruthers, MGT of America, Inc., "An Analysis of Funding Equity in the University of North Carolina, Phase I Final Report," March 27, 1996.
13. Eva Klein and Associates, "Capital Equity and Adequacy Study and Preliminary 10-Year Capital Needs, the University of North Carolina," April 1999.
14. The architect was NBBJ, Morrisville, North Carolina.
15. NBBJ, "The Learning Village, East Carolina University," February 9, 2001.
16. Ellerbe Beckett, "Campus Master Plan," East Carolina University, December 7, 2000.
17. Bruce L. Flye Jr., AIA, "A Tale of Two Plans," a case study proposal made to the Association of University Architects, April 2001.
18. "The Center City—West Greenville Revitalization Plan," prepared for the Redevelopment Commission, City of Greenville, North Carolina, March

2005 draft. This plan is working its way through the formal adoption process at the time of writing.

19. Application for Public Benefit Allowance Acquisition of Surplus Federal Property for Educational Purposes, Voice of American Relay Station, Site C, Greenville, NC, GSA Property Number: 4-GR-NC-721B, Undeveloped Land, 581 Acres, more or less, East Carolina University, 12/15/00.

REFERENCES

City of Greenville. Papers. Greenville, North Carolina.

ECU Facilities Services. Papers. East Carolina University.

ECU Institutional Planning, Research & Effectiveness Office. Papers. East Carolina University Archives.

Johnson, Todd, personal interview with author, November 2004.

Turner, Paul Venable. *Campus: An American Planning Tradition*, New York: Architectural History Foundation, 1984.

UNC General Administration. Papers. University of North Carolina General Administration.

Vanderven, Mike, personal interview with author, November 2004.

CHAPTER THREE

Support Staff

RALPH SCOTT

SUNDAY EVENING, March 1, 1980, had a strange stillness on the campus of East Carolina University. Students were in their dorms and the library, working on the upcoming week's assignments, and support staff were home with their families enjoying a quiet evening. At first a few snowflakes fell on the campus, then, as the night and next morning progressed, the snow fell at increasingly heavy rates. By March 3, twenty to twenty-five inches of snow, sleet, and freezing rain had fallen on eastern North Carolina, and high winds had piled the snow into three- and four-foot-high drifts, making travel virtually impossible in the area. Throughout the "blizzard of 1980," support staff found a way to get to the campus to work at essential duties. Housekeepers had to be available, plumbers and electricians were on call, police made their rounds, nurses treated patients, and cooks and servers provided food to those stranded in their dorm rooms.

Jim Westmoreland, a Scott Residence Hall counselor, reported a few problems: the cafeteria was serving hamburgers on English muffins or French bread, and there was nary a hot dog to be found in the meat lockers. Ira Simon, director of the cafeteria contract agency, Servomation, reported that they had not received deliveries of bread or milk for several days. Of course, local markets, in true eastern North Carolina fashion, were striped bare of foodstuffs by early Monday. Some support staff reported walking several miles around four-foot drifts to get to their work stations. The ECU Police had to borrow four-wheel-drive research vehicles from the geology department just to get around the campus. The few highway graders available in eastern North Carolina were plowing the main federal highways in the region. It was several days before the first plows could make the trip down even major Greenville thoroughfares such as Tenth Street.

Classes were canceled Monday and Tuesday, and university officials decided to reopen the university on Wednesday, March 4, following a major rise in temperatures. Long-time support staff member Agnes Barrett, administrative assistant to the chancellor, noted that this was the first time since Hurricane Hazel in 1954 that the governor had officially closed the university. One staff member commented that the storm could have been worse: the blizzard could have happened during spring break. While some support staff were stranded at home, many others walked or got rides to work at essential campus duties. In a few short days, the storm was just a memory, and many students and faculty scattered to warmer climates for spring break.

In 1980, East Carolina University had 1,014 support staff in a wide range of roles including nurses, police, painters, roofers, locksmiths, administrative assistants, clerk-typists, and housekeepers. Of the 458 secretarial positions, 445 were held by women, while 49 of the 51 skilled craft positions were held by men. Since the early 1970s, the University of North Carolina system had been under a judicial consent degree from Federal Office of Civil Rights to increase the number of both student and staff minorities at the university. By 1980 some progress in this integration had been made, but staff in categories such as housekeeping and secretarial/clerical jobs were still largely composed of single racial groups. Exact racial data are sketchy before the early 1990s, and memorandums as early as 1975 allude to the fact that the new "automated data systems" were unable to capture the federally required "racial/ethnic and Occupational activity."

The earliest data categorized by race available indicates that in 1993 there were 1,904 white employees, while minorities comprised 502 members. This amounts to about a 79 percent to 21 percent ratio. Ten years later, in 2003, there were 2,153 white employees, while minorities totaled 777. This increase in minority hiring led to a 5 percent increase in the number of minorities being hired by East Carolina University and resulted in a 74 percent to 26 percent ratio of whites to minorities.

In 1988 East Carolina hired its first director of minority affairs, Larry T. Smith. A cum laude graduate of Johnson C. Smith University in Charlotte who also held a doctorate in higher education administration and supervision from Bowling Green State University, Smith came from a post at Galesburg College in Illinois, where he was director of minority affairs. He assumed the title of assistant vice chancellor for student life and director of minority student affairs in August of 1988. Smith's new post involved "developing programs and activities of interest to minority students, advising student organizations and assisting with orientation." Smith held this key minority recruitment position for the next five years, until 1992.

A number of other individuals held this position during the 1990s. In the autumn of 1999, Chancellor Richard Eakin appointed Nell Lewis to head a new initiative featuring an expanded role for the Ledonia Wright Multi-Cultural Center. Nell soon made a name for herself with her bright, smiling, and upbeat personality. The center became a focal point for new campus multicultural initiatives. Having laid the foundations for a number of very active center programs, Nell was transferred by Provost William Swart in the fall of 2002 to Joyner Library to start yet another East Carolina initiative with the public schools in Eastern North Carolina. She retired in December 2003.

Throughout the 1980s and 1990s, the university tried various means to increase employment of minorities among the State Personnel Act (SPA) staff. This initiative culminated in the award in the summer of 2000 of the special Z. Smith Reynolds Foundation $70,000 grant to conduct the "Coffee in the Kitchen" project. This was part of a special "Race Will Not Divide Us" initiative on the part of the executive director of the foundation, Thomas W. Lambeth. He noted that "for much of the Foundation's history we have been concerned about the race relations in North Carolina and we believe that this grant to East Carolina University will make a difference in how people of different races interact with one another in eastern North Carolina." The project was a continuation of Chancellor Eakin's Initiative on Race and was a collaborative effort on the part of the ECU Office of Equal Employment Opportunity, the Ledonia Wright Cultural Center, the ECU Division of Student Life, the ECU Department of Intercultural Affairs, and the ECU Minority Student Coalition.

The "Coffee Project" occurred in three phases. The first took place during October–December 2000, the second between February and April 2001, and the final phase, which involved community leaders, concluded during the June–August 2001 time period. Participants gathered together in a study circle for two hours a week for a set number of weeks, after having attended an initial two-day workshop with a dynamic professional diversity trainer. The Coffee Project objectives aimed to improve communication between diverse campus groups, to share historical issues regarding race, to discuss open and frank difficult racial topics, to increase awareness and interaction among diverse campus groups, to enhance the appreciation of cultural differences, and to increase the probability that these focus groups would continue in the future.

While these study circles were the main group interactions, other events such as official lectures, cultural arts activities, and panel discussions were held. The project started a yearlong initiative on race during the 1999–2000 school year. It featured a lecture by Dr. Christopher Edley Jr., senior adviser to President Bill Clinton on race, a U.S. Civil Rights Commission appointee, and Harvard law school professor, followed by a second presentation by Dr. Mary Frances Berry, chair of the U.S. Civil Rights Commission, and a theatrical production of *Let My People Go*, a North Carolina–based slave revelation. The beginning of phase I started the following September with another theatrical presentation of the choreopoem *One Race, One People, One Peace*, by James Chapmyn. The opening ceremonies featured speeches by U.S. Representative Eva Clayton, N.C. Senator Frank Ballance, N.C. Representative Marian McGlohon, and Ramsey Connor, president of the ECU chapter of the NAACP. Throughout the project, participants in each of the earlier phases obtained an opportunity to meet with later participants at social luncheons. Following the end of the project in the summer of 2001, a number of project members continued to meet for lunch at the Todd Dining Hall. Overall, the project was very successful and helped to increase awareness of the racial divide on campus. Participants committed themselves to a lifelong goal of improving the racial climate on the East Carolina campus and in Greenville and Pitt County.

The support staff at East Carolina University has been majority female for most of its existence. In 1976, 56 percent of the support staff were female. At that time, there were 402 male support staff members and 522 females. By 2003, the figure for females had risen to 67 percent. While the overall support staff numbers had risen to 2,934, there were 1,989 females and 945 males employed. However, specific occupational activities still are gender-based. For example, in 1976 the secretarial/clerical support staff members were 349 females and 17 males, 95.4 percent to 4.6 percent ratio. By 2002 there were 1005 females and 75 males in these positions, still a 93.5 percent to 6.5 percent ratio. Similarly in the skilled crafts in 1976 there were 43 males and 1 female, a 97.7 percent to 2.3 percent ratio. By 2002 this had changed some, to 169 males and 9 females, a 94.9 percent to 5.1 percent ratio. In the technical/professional area, gender has changed from majority male to majority female. In 1976 there were 35 males and 30 females in this category, while in 2002 there were 193 females and 81 males. This resulted in a change in ratio of 54 percent male to 46 percent female in 1976 to 70 percent female to 30 percent male in 2002. This probably reflected the addition of more females to what were previously largely male-dominated occupations such as information technology and laboratory technology.

Support staff salaries rose very slowly during the period 1980–2004. In recent years, with a variety of state budget crises facing lawmakers in Raleigh, the increases have been nonexistent and failed to track consumer price increases. For example, in 1979, a Clerk-Typist III, now called Office Assistant III (Grade 57), started at a hiring rate of $8,364. The 2004 hiring rate for Office Assistant III stood at $18,479. In that year if a person had not been promoted in rank and had reached the end of the so-called old step increases (which were eliminated in the mid 1980s), they would have received $28,426. During this period, the purchasing power of the dollar fell for these employees by a significant amount. Owing to a decline in the value of the dollar, the 1979 salary of $8,364 would require $21,663 in 2004 dollars to match the earlier salary. Similarly, those hired in 1979 who had topped out in grade at $11,316 would actually need a salary of $29,308 in 2004 to equal their 1979 purchasing power. During this time period, the costs of items such as benefit packages (health care) and parking had risen substantially. In the late 1970s, parking fees almost doubled, to $25 a year. By 2004, prime-location parking space at East Carolina had risen to nearly $400 a year.

Parking charges, of course, vary in the UNC system for support staff. Current parking rates for support staff at UNC-Asheville were pegged at $70 a year. Generally speaking, support staff throughout the state receive the same salary grade levels. The increased cost of living differentials in areas such as the Research Triangle and Greenville is especially regressive for support staff in the lower pay grades. Under Chancellor William Shelton, some support staff employees in the lower salary grades received reductions in campus parking permit charges. Recent initiatives by the University of North Carolina Office of the President to attempt to secure even modest increases in support staff salaries were rejected by the N.C. General Assembly in Raleigh.

Among the most visible support staff members of the university have been the East Carolina University Police. Visitors, students, and staff often relied upon them for directions, traffic control, opening locked cars, jump-starting dead batteries, and, on occassion, removing them from burning buildings. On October 29, 1988, passing ECU police officers spotted smoke coming from a neighborhood apartment house. Corporal Lawrence Watson and Lieutenant Joseph Pollack quickly gave the alarm. Together with Greenville police, the two officers evacuated the students who were asleep in the building. In April 1989, the two officers received a certificate of appreciation from the North Carolina Association of Campus Law Enforcement Administrators.

These brave men and women seek to protect thousands of individuals from many walks of life who work and study on an increasingly large urban campus. Looking at the career history of a number of support staff can show how issues such as salary equity and grade position changes have affected both these individuals and the university as a whole.

Pat Elks

Support staff today come from all over the world, although the majority still have eastern North Carolina roots. Some came to East Carolina as students and have remained. Pat Elks's career path is typical of support staff. She came to East Carolina in July 1978, when she was twenty-one years old, as a clerk-typist making $6,000 a year. Before coming to ECU, the Greenville native worked in a local retail store. She wanted to come to ECU because of the benefits package, especially the state retirement plan. Elks came to ECU at twenty-one with retirement in mind. She has a goal of retiring at fifty-one.

Elks first worked in the Computer Center. At that time, in 1978, the director of the Computer Center was Richard Lennon. Pat Spain was Elks's supervisor. Elks worked primarily on the Computer Center payroll from 1978 to 1983. Soon the center had a new director, Glenn Crowe, whom Elks worked under for the rest of her time at the center. The Computer Center staff grew from twenty-five when Elks came to seventy-five when she left in 1983.

More people in the center required more staff in the payroll section to maintain the increased payrolls. At this time there were conflicting missions of the center, which served both administrative and academic computing needs. There were conflicts between the two groups over scarce computing resources. In general, the academic side claimed that they needed more staff support and facilities to provide quality computing for faculty and students. In Southern Association of Colleges and Schools self-studies and other assessment documents, faculty and students frequently complained of a lack of resources. On the other hand, as the administrative and finance needs expanded, they also required attention.

At times the air conditioning for the computer in the Austin Building failed, and the whole computing center shut down until repairs were made. Director Crowe's agenda included funding for a new air conditioning system as soon as possible. The Computer Center in Austin expanded by removing partitions between classrooms on the northeast side of the first floor. One of the first major mainframe computers at ECU was an IBM 360/30 system. By the time Director Crowe arrived, it had become outdated and too small for the emerging "giant of the east." At Crowe's insistence it was replaced by a Burroughs B5500. While the Burroughs B5500 was a more modern computer, it was not by any means the latest model, and it caused considerable controversy on the campus.

A number of academic applications would not run on the Burroughs because it used non–industry standard tape drives. But the administrative side of the center, which purchased the new computer, was very pleased with the system. Programmers were able to write code to handle business applications including payroll, accounts payable, and student accounts.

The academic community clamored for more and better computers capable of handling standardized software packages then in common usage at other academic institutions. This need was partially met when the system was upgraded to a Burroughs B6600, a later but, alas, again not state-of-the-art computer. Some departments, such as the library, physics, and chemistry, bought their own computer systems to handle specific applications that the mainframe could not.

When Pat Elks came in 1978, most data were input into the mainframe computers by means of punched cards. The university had a large staff of keypunch operators. When keypunch machines were phased out in the 1980s, these SPA staff members were retrained to handle other duties in the center. Input on the later computers was by means of magnetic tapes and "dumb" terminal-type workstations. There was a dispatch window in Austin where faculty and staff brought their punched cards and tapes. The worker would return the next day to pick up the paper output that the computer had produced after running the input against software on the mainframe. While other offices on campus had purchased workstations to input records into the computer, the Computer Center lacked these machines' staff. The business office installed the IBM Displaywriter systems for some staff. Other staff had Sperry terminals on their desks. A lot of faculty, students, and staff wanted to support IBM software such as Displaywriter, which was becoming standard in modern business offices.

Pat Elks left the Computing Center in 1983 to work at the new medical school. For her, this was a lateral move that resulted in neither increased pay nor a higher classification. She felt, however, that if she was to move up, a change had to be made. This reflected a typical advancement pattern followed by many support staff—transfer to a different position to gain added work skills. She worked for Dr. Walter Pories for approximately three months. Dr. Pories helped many patients in eastern North Carolina who could not afford to pay for their medical care. When people could not pay their bills, he said, "Bring me a cake sometime." Elks noted that she ate a lot of cake when she worked for Pories. At the medical school, her position was upgraded to Secretary IV.

In 1983, Pat Elks transferred to the Recreational Services Division, again to continue the advancement of her career. She worked in Christenbury Gym until she moved again in 1988. While Elks worked at the division, plans emerged for a Recreational Center on the west end of campus. The Student Government Association decided to refinish the floors of Christenbury Gym, even though a new center was being built. Shortly after Elks came to Recreational Services, the center needed a new director, and she became involved in this search, just as she had in the search for the new Computer Center director. She helped train the replacement director in the Recreation Center when she moved to Joyner Library in 1988. It was then that she learned that her replacement, who was a Clerk-Typist III working in Mendenhall, was actually making more than Elks was as a Secretary IV in the Recreation Center. (SPA staff working at the same classification in different ECU divisions can make different salaries.)

At Joyner Library as an Administrative Assistant I, Elks again sought to advance her career. She was asked by the personnel director Richard Ferris to come for an interview. She had never been interviewed before by a group of faculty. Don Lennon, a faculty member in the library, put her at ease by asking her if she always had "this sense of humor." Elks stated that she found that humor always helped out in a tense situation. She got the job.

Elks found the world of librarianship fast-paced. Comparing it to the other divisions where she worked, Business and Recreational Services, she found activities at the library changing at an ever-increasing pace. Elks came to Joyner in March 1988, and the director of Joyner Library, Ruth Katz, resigned in June 1988. The new administrative assistant became involved in yet another director search.

Elks's job in the library consisted of many parts. A major task was operating one of the largest departments on campus. Joyner had become a fast-paced portal to the Internet and not just a quiet place to study and read. In 1988, computerization consisted of one "dumb" Sperry terminal that interfaced with the university purchase order system. Lou Rook typed orders on the terminal, and they were then placed with university-approved vendors. At the time the library administration did not know anything about other uses for workstations. Elks knew from her work at Recreational Services that even the Sperry terminals could do things other than just purchase orders. She persuaded the then–associate director, Marilyn Miller, to allow her to use the workstation. Soon a second terminal was purchased and Joyner Library joined the age of electronic word processors.

Again Elks had to more or less learn her job on her own, as her predecessor had left for the vice chancellor for academic affairs office. Elks found that according to her job description as an Administrative Assistant I, she was supposed to supervise the other SPA staff in the director's office. Elks assumed this new role and continued to enhance the use of technology in the library. The telephone system connected with the library was very outdated. As an example of the use of new technology, the university bought a new computerized Centrex branch exchange and placed it in the library shortly after Elks came to Joyner.

When Elks started in Joyner Library, no workstations existed in the library. The first automated project in Joyner was the microcomputer-based LS2000 Integrated Library System sold by the Ohio College Library Center. As a new administrative assistant, one of her first jobs was to establish policies and procedures in the administrative office. Prior administrations had left few operational documents. With the help of human resources and the Equal Employment Opportunity Commission office, Elks developed and implemented many administrative policies. These policies had to be integrated with the faculty manual and Academic Library Services' unit code. Elks asked around to learn what had been done in the past in the library and more generally on campus, and in some cases she had to develop policies that were entirely new.

Elks's job description stated that she would approve SPA leave records and supervise the other SPAs in the administrative office of the library. Elks was also assigned to handle the assessment procedures for the library. She became responsible for collecting and submitting standardized assessment reports such as those required under the Integrated Postsecondary Educational Data System (IPEDS), the Association for College and Research Libraries (ACCRL), Southern Association of Colleges and Schools (SACS), and curriculum-based reports (such as the Association of Colleges with Graduate Schools of Business [ACGSB]). Elks later found that only she and one other SPA staff member in the state possessed this level of responsibility.

Technology led to large changes for the SPA personnel. Job descriptions did not reflect new technologies; they still spoke of World War I–era tasks such as filing, typing, and answering the telephone. When Elks started working at ECU, managers would provide written notes or tape recordings of letters and documents to be typed. Eventually she handled everything from composing the information to mailing the letter. She does the actual work, rather than processing what others have done. In the early 1980s, North Carolina acknowledged the role technology played in clerk-typist positions by upgrading positions one step. Since then no upgrades have occurred. The specifications for most jobs were written in the 1970s using 1920s technology. While North Carolina in many way leads in technology, it did not lead in modern job descriptions.

Recently Elks joined the administrator's advisory group, which consists of administrative assistants from various campus units. Through the efforts of this group, the Excel-based system that Elks helped develop became the university standard by 2003. Elks has also developed a computerized spreadsheet-based tracking system to manage EPA funds allocated to the library. She feels that it is her job to take technology to the maximum level, and she has tried to do this throughout her career here. Elks and other SPA people discovered that one may do many more tasks with automation.

Elks has also observed changes in the way SPA incentives are awarded. In the past SPA staff had received an automatic annual salary increase, calculated using a step-based system. In 1983, these steps were reduced to half steps, then later quarter steps, and finally they were removed. Staff in the past tried to give an extra effort because there was a monetary incentive to work harder than coworkers: the step increases were given to those employees who had received good job evaluations. Now the only way to advance in ranking is to change to a higher-classified job. The old system gave a pay incentive to keep good people working at the same job. Now there is constant hiring and rehiring and the training of new people to do the same work. SPA staff no longer receive longevity pay, which has also had an effect on morale among the professional staff.

Elks is a Pitt County native, married with two children. She likes writing and research and plans to write editorials when she retires. Her personal hobbies are fishing, snow skiing, overseeing her grandfather's home, NASCAR, water sports, and most recently deer hunting.

Judy Tucker

In 1978, Judy Tucker, R.N., began her career as a graduate of the Rex Hospital School of Nursing. She started working as a nurse part-time and in 1979 became the first nurse hired by the new ECU School of Medicine, with an assignment to work in the obstetrics and gynecology clinic. The clinic was first held in the teaching annex to the Pitt County Memorial Hospital, near the entrance to the hospital. At first she had a small office, which soon became an examining room. When the Family Practice Center was constructed, the clinic moved into one of the hospital pods. Tucker did general nursing for expectant mothers but soon moved into what became the high-risk pregnancy center for eastern North Carolina. She often, however, took care of "anything else that came along." She traveled around the twenty-nine counties of eastern North Carolina, working with high-risk pregnancies. Tucker was instrumental in introducing new technologies such as ultrasound and fetal monitoring. As would be the case in other positions she has held, Tucker trained people to do the work she was doing and then moved to other assignments.

During this period, Tucker worked for Dr. Robert Brame. Under his leadership, she hired two additional nurses to help out with the clinic. A lot of her work included teaching others about outreach, teaching local health staff new technologies, and improving diabetic care standards throughout eastern North Carolina.

Tucker found this an exciting time to learn in the School of Medicine. The school was growing, and with this growth came new knowledge and skills. Tucker recalls that during this period the school led in neonatal care in eastern North Carolina under faculty such as deans Edwin Monroe and William Laupus, and physicians such as Jon Tingelstad and Stephen Engle-key. All of these faculty members were located in offices in the old hospital.

The clinic expanded with many new nurses and added patients in the 1980s. In 1990, Tucker became the manager for the department, a position she held until 1998. In short, Tucker managed those people managed by the neonatal clinics. At this time the clinics were housed in Brody, the ECU Women's Center, and the Jenkins Cancer Center. Judy Tucker was ready for more change and challenge, just as Pat Elks has experienced.

In 1998 Tucker went to work for Dennis Sinar in medical informatics. She had the clinical background that was needed to help transfer the paper clinical records to digital records. The concept of digital clinical records intrigued her. Using many of the skills of an obstetrics nurse, she was able to bridge the gap between patient and doctor and return to the patient via the digital record. In short, she became a broker/interpreter between the various medical/computer doctors and support staff that interfaced with electronic medical records. Two people started on this project in 1998. The group grew again and again, and soon Tucker was training her replacement as she moved to yet another challenge. She would now design customized templates for inputting the medical records. Tucker conducted the medical informatics training of the entire Brody School of Medicine as well as training her two replacements. For a person with no computer background, she had learned the computer and its nature from the ground up.

Tucker became a part of the Clinical Support Staff (CSS) at the Brody School of Medicine. (The difference between SPA and CSS is largely the funding source.) CSS was first introduced in the mid-1980s, when legislation was enacted on the state level to provide for a flexible hiring practice within the School of Medicine. The University of North Carolina at Chapel Hill School of Medicine and the ECU Brody School of Medicine both have CSS staff. Legislation has also allowed for flexible bidding, which provides for the purchase of supplies outside the normal state contract bid system.

Joseph Walas

Joseph Walas serves as the chemistry department glassblower in the Academic Affairs Division of the Harriot College of Arts and Sciences. He came to ECU in 1996 with thirty-five years' experience in private commercial and academic glassblowing. About half of his work experience before coming to ECU was spent in chemical glassblowing, the other half in engineering glassblowing. The university glassblower must support the research of the entire university. Walas fabricates assemblies for use in university laboratories as well as conducting educational classes in glassblowing for interested eastern North Carolinians. His specialty is lamp working rather than traditional glassblowing. Lamp working uses a gas burner (natural gas or butane), as opposed to glassblowing, which uses a large open-air furnace.

The first glassblower at ECU was Owen Kingsbury Jr. He began in 1971 and worked in the chemistry department until his death in 1995. Kingsbury pioneered the use of glassmaking as instructional support for chemistry classes. Starting in 1996, under Walas, the mission of the glassblower became larger along with the expanding research mission in the sciences. An important component of this scientific glassblowing is that it required a person to perform a function rather than ornamental or artistic glassblowing, which appeals primarily to the eye. All glassblowing involves hazardous materials heated to high temperatures. Safety instructions are an important component of any instruction Joe provides. When you visit his shop, you will notice safety valves and cut-offs critical to secure handling of glass. The ECU glassblower receives inquiries from around the world about this craft. Walas is glad to exchange information with those who are interested.

While his work has not changed much over time, the scope of the work has changed. Most of the current work is 60–70 percent high vacuum fabrication. Work in quartz glass constitutes 80–90 percent of Walas's work. A lot of this glass was used in the production of computer chips. Some of the work at East Carolina will in the future be more of an engineering nature rather than fabrication of assemblies for chemistry. Walas also fabricates assemblies for use in research at the Brody Medical School and the Harriot College of Arts and Sciences biology department, and the College of Technology and Computer Science also uses his glass fabrication services. The technology faculty members were unaware of Walas's work with composite materials and were happy to learn that he had experience in this area. He was able to show them the use of ultrasonic machine devices used in the construction of composite material. Walas works to break down barriers between people and departments, and remove compartmentalized thinking. When people work in isolation in very specialized areas, he says, someone like a glassblower can come in, look at their problem, and perhaps come up with a better idea to meet their need.

Rhonda Brown

Rhonda Brown began working in the School of Education as a temporary secretary for Dr. Clinton Downing in 1980. She had just graduated in May of 1980 from North Carolina Agricultural and Technical State University with a B.A. degree in business management. She applied for a permanent

SPA position in Joyner Library as a Clerk-Typist II. Brown secured a position in Joyner, where she worked with building maintenance work orders, greeting people in the administrative suite as they entered the area, and doing such other odd jobs as the director and associate director assigned her. Two years later she was promoted to a Secretary III position, where she prepared supply requisition orders, worked on the library budget, and prepared the student payroll. She also processed correspondence for the director, reviewed faculty and staff travel forms, initially screened student applicants, and provided secretarial assistance to the Friends of the Library organization. At that time, 1981, she processed time sheets by hand on a electric typewriter. Budget information for the entire library budget was kept in a manual handwritten ledger.

In the mid-1980s, Brown moved to the Division of Academic Affairs in Spilman, where she worked as an Accounting Technician I. She handled travel and reviewed applications for research and teaching grants. Her first assignment in Academic Affairs was supporting the office of William Bloodworth, and later she worked with Marlene Springer. Working at the division level was different from working in Joyner Library. In her new position, Brown gained a larger perspective of the university as a whole. She certified state travel application forms were accurate and had to deal with each division's activities with regard to budget and personnel.

In 1992, Brown became the Immigration Officer (Administrative Officer II) for the university's international programs. Here she worked with students, faculty, and staff under the direction of Lucy Wright. Other directors of international programs Rhonda has worked with are John Hiese, James Van Fleet, and Charles Lyons. Currently Brown does the paperwork for visas (J1, F1, and permanent resident). She reviews students at the interview stage and files paperwork with the authorities, who determine the status of the applicant. Some of the applications for status forms are online, others are on paper. These petitions for entry are adjudicated at a regional INS service center. If a visa is granted, the information is then sent to the U.S. embassy overseas, where the applicant goes to receive the student visa.

Brown has been active at the professional level since 1992, with the National Association of Foreign Students Advisers and the Association of International Educators. She has presented papers at regional, state, and national conferences on international education. Most recently she has been accepted into the ECU Leadership Academy. This academy, spearheaded by interim chancellor William Shelton, trains a new generation of in-house leaders for East Carolina. She was chosen as one of fourteen people to be appointed to this academy and only one of few SPA personnel appointed.

Brown works with SEVIS, the Student and Exchange Visitor Information System, which tracks foreign nationals following the events of 9/11. Under SEVIS the university obtains annual certification for each foreign national and is subject to site visits by INS. When Brown started out in 1980 in a clerical position, she saw the potential for a career at ECU, and people at ECU saw the potential in her. She was able to move from a clerical job into a more professional position with many new opportunities.

Lydia Woolard

Lydia "K" Woolard coordinates the East Carolina University Office of Special Events and Protocol. This office assists in the planning and production of university-wide executive-level events that use the fiscal and human resources of the various upper-level administrative offices of the university. Such events serve to market the division and the institution to the general public. These events include members of the executive division of the university who serve as speakers when they travel, when their attendance is required by university protocol, such as the chancellor attending commencement ceremonies, groundbreaking ceremonies, and inauguration, and when they host dignitaries, such as the president of the United States. The Special Events Division incorporates a variety of university services and facilities: catering, grounds, housekeeping, moving services, audiovisual services, electricians, security, parking services and transportation, university printing and graphics, and news and communication services. While Woolard now uses computers to perform her work, when she began all of special events' lists were handwritten, and invitations were hand-addressed.

Each scheduled event is unique. The Office of Special Events and Protocol maintains a donor's database arranged by interest. This way workers can quickly determine who should be invited to a specific event. Woolard must rely on voice mail and computer forms to remain in touch with the myriad of people attending various events, including special events, luncheons, and social and academic events. Event organizers specify whom to invite and what type of event they desire, and develop a specific checklist of activities that should take place. Woolard also works with groups such as Phi Beta Kappa, Friends of the Library, Friends of the Theatre, and others across the university to organize the events.

Woolard began work in 1969 at East Carolina as a support staff member in the admissions office. She worked for five deans, including deans Wellington "Bud" Gray and Albert Lang, while working in the School of Art from 1973 to 1987. In 1987–88, Woolard moved to a part-time position in the School of Technology under Dean Darryl Davis. In February 1988, Diana Lowe asked her to join the Office of the Vice Chancellor for Academic Affairs with Vice Chancellor Marlene Springer.

In the early 1990s, Woolard assumed duties with the special events office in the chancellor's office. When Chancellor Richard Eakin came to ECU in 1987, there was a major renovation of the chancellor's home. The new chancellor gave additional money to entertain university guests at special events. Woolard's office expanded to provide the many current services that it offers today.

Woolard recalls many exciting stories from the history of the Office of Special Events and Protocol, from the time when the flower arrangements blew off the stage during a sudden windstorm that came up during a commencement to the time a sudden bolt of lightning struck very close to the stage where the chancellor and guests were sitting. This ceremony came to a rather quick and sudden conclusion. Her job varies from placing programs on chairs at 2:30 a.m. for a chancellor inauguration to the mundane assignment of ordering supplies and housekeeping for the university guesthouse on Fifth Street. Woolard described her charge as doing anything that needed doing, that no one else wanted to do, or that no one had the time or skills to do.

Janice Harris

In 1980, Janice Harris, a native of Charleston, South Carolina, started working at East Carolina University with Servomation. She began as a cashier in the snack bar in Jones Dormitory. The bar serves short-order items and snacks to students living in the dormitories on the "Hill." In 1985, Harris moved to being a line server in Jones Cafeteria, where she progressed through cook's helper to cook. She worked in Jones for about ten years before coming to Todd Dining Hall.

Harris notes that cooking techniques have changed over time, and more staff help with the tasks than used to be the case. In Jones she served five to six hundred people each day, preparing each item by herself. Several assistant cooks aid her in order preparation today. They have received instruction on food safety, including procedures like cutting-board cleaning to eliminate cross-contamination of foods and holding and serving hot and cold foods at the correct temperatures. In the early 1990s, the Jones staff received all new equipment, uniforms, dishes, and tableware, which made them more efficient and helped to improve the dining atmosphere for students.

The construction of Todd Dining Hall in the 1990s, during the Eakin administration, advanced dining facilities on the Hill at Jones Dining Hall. Trucks come every other day with the needed foodstuffs, and appropriate quantities are stored under climate-controlled conditions in the walk-in freezers. Cooks prepare what is needed today and leave some of the entrées for the night shift to exhaust the supply.

Now lines have three choices at each meal, usually a "normal" entrée for those not on a diet and a fat-free entrée for those students watching their weight, plus one other entrée to fill out the meal line. The cafeterias now feature what is called "AFF," or "All Foods Fit," to introduce students to a variety of cuisines. This enables diners to have a choice of a familiar entrée as well as something from another culture that they might not have experienced. One complaint that students have about cafeteria food is that is not like what Mother fixes at home. The AFF program enables students to explore the dining alternatives that they will face as they go into the wider world. Another change Harris notes is the all-you-can-eat program. When Harris came to ECU in 1980, there was only one entrée per customer, and diners were discouraged from asking for additional portions. Meal planning now allows for diners to have two-thirds of their meal consisting of vegetables and starches. Dining menu schedules are planned in cycles, and Harris helps plan the menus and subsequent ordering of provisions.

Most cooking is done on large gas grills. A new innovation in cooking is lava rocks, which give a charbroiled flavor to grilled meats and vegetables. To cook vegetables and starches such as rice, cooks use steam kettles buried in the floor. An automatic feeder brings the food up to table level for preparation for serving, reducing some of the heavy work involved in lifting the food out of the cooking vessels. The new Todd Dining Hall has even-tilt skillets, which enable the large quantities of prepared food to be tilted into the serving trays rather than lifted separately, piece by piece. For baking and broiling, the new cafeteria uses the same type of ovens as did Jones, but Harris notes they are a more modern convection oven rather than the older, traditional stacked oven.

During the 2004 snow and ice storms, administrators brought the cooking staff to work in four-wheel-drive vehicles. This marked a change from the old way of doing things when the cooks walked through the snow to work. Staff member George Jones became famous for walking a long distance in heavy snows over the years to cook and prepare food in the Mendenhall Dining Hall. During Hurricane Floyd in 1999, Harris remembers that she cooked for all the police (including highway patrol and sheriff's officers), relief workers, and university staff who came for meals during the flood.

When Harris retires, she is looking forward to spending time on hobbies she loves, such as fishing.

Janice Rice

Janice Rice joined ECU in 1976 as a Clerk-Typist III in Joyner's reference department. She typed, filed loose-leaf reference services, and assisted with questions on the reference desk. Rice experienced the computer revolution when word processing was introduced via a stand-alone TRS 80 microcomputer. A few years later, the department library ordered IBM AT-model personal computers, and her work consisted of creating needed department spreadsheets and word-processing documents. Moving to microforms, she became overseer for the area, hiring students, operating the public-service desk, and helping patrons and staff with reference questions involving department microforms. An important part of her position was the selection, use, and maintenance of the many different types of viewing and copying equipment that the department possessed. Material appeared in a variety of formats: microfilm, microfiche, microprint, microcard, and ultrafiche. Each format required a different machine for viewing. Often users required substantial help with using the equipment.

When the periodicals/microforms department head Janet Kilpatrick retired, Rice moved downstairs to work with the newly combined microforms and documents department. Rice observed, as do many others on the support staff, that computer technology had become a part of about every aspect of her work. The first totally integrated automation system used in the library was the Online Computer Library Center's LS/2000 terminal-based system. This Integrated Library System (ILS) was used for a number of years in conjunction with a paper card catalog. The online catalog, Horizon, replaced the card catalog and LS/2000. Recently a large portion of the microforms and documents collections have been incorporated into the catalog records in the Horizon system. Even today, however, the microforms and documents department still uses a card-based shelf list to help staff locate material in the collections.

Generations of East Carolina students and faculty used the reader printers to make copies of articles on microform. With the introduction of the Internet, the use of the paper-based technology declined. Students do not make copies of microfilm as frequently nowadays, Rice believes, because of the widespread use of home computers that connect online to computer databases. Also, Rice says, people use scanners to scan in material. In the past Rice's staff made copies of needed microform journal articles for patrons. A few years ago the library shifted to a copy system where patrons make their own "self-service" copies. This has resulted in a large decline in number of copies being made from microformatted materials. To counter this trend, copies are now free in microforms.

R. V. Parker

Robert "R. V." Parker came to work at ECU in 1982. The eastern North Carolina native's first position was working on the construction of the Brody

School of Medicine building. He did the framing on the outside and interior of the building and became foreman with a local scientific company. Soon, however, East Carolina offered him a carpenter position in the building trades section. He has worked for fourteen years with the building trades support staff, which consists of carpenters, locksmiths, painters, roofers, and masons. Their jobs help maintain the quality of physical plant eastern North Carolinians have come to expect of their university. Parker became manager of the building department, then assistant director of facilities services.

For the last few years Parker helped build a new building or renovated an old one each year. As a novice he worked with Perry Ennis and Dean Richard Hayek. During this period, as the Brody Medical School grew, the physical plant also expanded. Parker moved to the Fifth Street campus, where he worked with George Harrell, Ken Kisida, and Vice Chancellor Richard Brown in the Business and Finance Division.

Computer technology helped move the building trades department into the twenty-first century, incorporating technology. Parker manages the university garage as well as all carpenters, masons, locksmiths, painters, and roofers. He has a support staff of around forty-five, depending on hiring levels. New vehicles have been purchased over the last few years under the direction of Vice Chancellor Richard Brown. This has improved morale in the workplace. A recent survey by the UNC Office of the President voted East Carolina University building facilities as an "outstanding" facility in the university system.

Parker's connections go deep in East Carolina. A native of Ahoskie, he counts two sisters as East Carolina alumnae, and his daughter is enrolled at ECU. Parker has pride in the work he and his craftspeople do as part of the biggest state agency in the east. With the recent hurricanes and the decline in manufacturing and farming operations in the east, Parker feels special empathy with and pride in being from eastern North Carolina.

Outsourcing, the hiring of local contractors for repair and renovation work on buildings, is a recent innovation at East Carolina. Parker counts the move as a mixed blessing. At times there is too much work for his staff, and the university needs some help with repair and renovation needs. The university has been subject to the effects of six major hurricanes over the last few years, and after each one, Parker's staff certified the buildings on campus as safe.

To help with any eventuality, Parker has established a computer roofing database that allows tracking of roofs' needs for replacement or repair. Now the university does not have as many leaky roofs as it did in the past. Having dry roofs makes certain that the walls, floors, lights, and other fixtures remain secure.

Painting illustrates the way Parker manages his department. He allows painters to use their initiative. An example can be found in the windows in Wright Auditorium, which have been replaced with lower-maintenance components to conserve both money and labor. Another example can be found in the clay-tiled roofs on the original campus structures. The introduction of these architectural details aid the shaping as a distinct East Carolina architectural style. The tiled roofs also last longer. Original drawings from the past allowed for the use of the mutton bar sight lines on the Wright Auditorium renovation.

Parker's sense of the historic East Carolina also results in hiring true craftspeople. He thinks that if one looks hard enough, true craftsmen can be found. He tells the brick masons, for example, that "you can bring your grandchildren to see the work you did. You can have a piece in the history of the university. Put things in correctly."

At one point the university had a two-class system of workers: craftspeople and helpers. The permanent class of "helpers" has been eliminated in the building trades at East Carolina, and craftspeople now advance along the same career path. No longer does a novice work in the building trade.

Douglas Caldwell

Douglas Caldwell moved to East Carolina University from Charlotte in 1968 to assume the duties of head of buildings and grounds. He is a 1948 graduate of the University of North Carolina at Charlotte, but after thirty-five years at East Carolina, he is a tried and true Pirate fan. Doug thought he would stay only two years, as he was considering a position at the Smithsonian Institution in Washington, D.C., but was unable to negotiate the salary that he thought he was worth at the time.

At ECU, Caldwell was basically responsible for everything outside of buildings on the east and west campuses. This includes grass, shrubs, trees, walkways, steps, streets, moving services, and collecting the garbage. Caldwell served under the administrations of chancellors Jenkins, Brewer, Howell, and Eakin. One of the first things he did when he arrived was to install an underground irrigation system on the lawn of Chancellor Leo Jenkins's home. Lillian Jenkins, the chancellor's wife, did not want the system turned on, however, because she thought that neighbors would not approve of what was actually a rather inexpensive system. Caldwell would turn the system on to water the chancellor's lawn during dry periods, and just as soon he left, Mrs. Jenkins would rush out and turn it off. Mrs. Jenkins also did not approve of state grounds workers spending time in their yard maintaining the lawn, bushes, and shrubs. Betty Brewer, the wife of Chancellor Brewer, on the other hand, was a very active gardener and enjoyed directing the re-landscaping of the chancellor's compound on Fifth Street. Caldwell noted that "she wanted to dig things." This also led to improvements in natural areas on campus during the Brewer administration. Caldwell also liked to work with Gladys Howell, wife of Chancellor John M. Howell, who more or less let him do what he wanted to with the landscaping of the chancellor's residence. Jo Eakin, wife of Chancellor Richard Eakin, also was interested in improving the appearance of the East Carolina campus. Eakin thought that improving the buildings and grounds of the university would make the campus more appealing to parents and students during a period of rapid enrollment expansion. Caldwell also worked with a number of other administrators, including James "Jim" Lowry, director of the physical plant; William "Bill" Whitehurst, director of buildings, and Larry Snyder, director of utilities.

Caldwell noted that when he arrived at ECU, there were no campus irrigation systems installed. The chancellor's residence received the first one in the late 1960s. Before the campus was irrigated, grounds workers had to haul and struggle with garden hoses during periods of drought. This was very labor intensive and did not help much. The number of places workers could use hoses during a given period was limited, and everywhere needed water. Caldwell suggested that the university take the overtime pay he would be due for the extra watering time and begin to purchase irrigation systems with these funds. After discussing his scheme with his superiors, Caldwell found out that he was not eligible for overtime as a manager. After a long summer struggling with hoses on the football field, Caldwell finally convinced the athletic department to let him install a sprinkler system on the Pirate field. After the last fall game was over, he purchased parts for the system—which cost at that time around $4,000 or $5,000—dug up the field, and installed the sprinklers. In the fall he had a turf that was the envy of other state institutions. Duke and Wake Forest had similar systems, but East Carolina was the first state-supported school to install one. Athletic officials and buildings and grounds staff from North Carolina State University and the University of North Carolina came to examine the East Carolina installation, which Doug was very proud of.

The next task was to install similar systems on the baseball and intramural fields, which was done as funds permitted. At the height of the women's movement in the early 1970s, when a local business owner saw the men's softball field had a sprinkler system but the women's didn't, the owner funded a similar system on the women's field. Now the turf on all fields looks like someone cares about it, and it is well maintained. The nursing project, now the Rivers Building, was the first building to come with sprinkler systems written into the design specifications. Caldwell recalls working with Dean Evelyn Perry on the landscaping. Perry knew exactly what she wanted and told Caldwell where it should go. He enjoyed working with her because she showed an interest in plants and making her new facility look attractive. Now buildings are built with underground systems connected by wire and fiber optics to a weather station at the building and grounds office near the Irons Building. Here staff monitor the transpiration rates of plants and apply moisture as needed. About one-third of these systems are completely computer controlled.

During his tenure at ECU, Caldwell added to the variety of campus flora. East Carolina had since its inception in 1907 strived to have an attractive campus and had planted specimen shrubs and trees in many pleasant groupings. During the energy crisis, emphasis was placed on low-maintenance varieties, many of which are native to eastern North Carolina. Caldwell noted that he was sorry to see the old arboretum removed for the construction of the Howell Science Complex. He made efforts to make sure that as few trees as possible were removed during later construction projects. He moved quite a few trees from the allied health project (now the Belk Building) to areas on the main campus near where the present Joyner library addition is situated. These trees were dug up by hand and moved to large holes that were manually excavated—a very hard and hot task in the humid climate of eastern North Carolina. Nowadays, of course, large powered scoops come and dig the trees up and move them to a new location. When the Brody School of Medicine came into being, Doug was also responsible for the landscaping and maintenance of those buildings.

Trash on campus is a big issue and includes not only garbage from offices and dorms but also materials eastern North Carolinians discard along walkways, streets, fields, and hedges. A number of newly constructed dorms, including high-rise dorms, had trash chutes located in the middle of the building. Grounds workers had to manually haul the trash outside to areas where side-loading garbage trucks could pick it up. This was a health hazard and not a very good situation. Garrett Dorm was particularly problematic in this regard. Tyler Dorm had the same sort of problems. Caldwell spoke with a consultant who was a state sanitarian and had him to come look over the garbage situation at East Carolina. He was so upset that he immediately ran to the Dowdy Student Stores and purchased a camera to record the situation for his report.

In response to his report, the university purchased the large garbage bins scattered around campus for housekeeping to place trash in. Along with the bins, the university purchased a front-loader garbage truck. When it was bought in 1974, the only other truck of that type nearby was in Beaufort County. This meant that if the truck was down, there was no easy way to empty the garbage bins. Unfortunately, this gasoline-engine truck proved to be less than satisfactory. In addition to having a gasoline engine that used two thirty-five-gallon tanks of fuel a day, the truck had a weak frame, and it was always breaking down. Caldwell had to contract with a company in Raleigh to come on the weekends to empty the trash bins when the ECU truck was down. Needless to say, the weekends were long in coming. During move-in and move-out times in the dormitories, trash bins had to be emptied several times a day, with the trash transported to the county landfill on Allen Road. Along the way the truck had to pick up waste at the medical school.

The front-loader simply did not have a frame capable of supporting the weight on the trash bins while loading. In addition, mechanical breakdowns were common. The Ford dealer in Bethel, North Carolina, F & D Motors, who had supplied the vehicle, had to keep a constant stock of water pumps, front axles, and springs, all of which failed regularly on the old truck. Caldwell had to have the truck towed to Bethel for repairs, not a long but a bothersome task. After messing with the truck for a number of years, Caldwell decided to replace it with a more modern and strong diesel vehicle that uses about seventy gallons of fuel a week, instead of the seventy gallons a day the old truck used. The new truck proved a dream come true and was down or out of service very little. Caldwell decided to place the trucks on a seven-year replacement cycle, which helped insure that up-to-date trucks were always in use on campus. He also had the bright idea of keeping the replaced truck around to use as a backup when repairs or maintenance were needed on the prime garbage truck.

In addition to garbage, Caldwell was responsible for removing ice and snow from campus walks and steps. In the winter, it seemed to him that architects always placed the handicapped ramps on the north sides of buildings, where the ice and snow buildup was greatest. These areas often did not receive solar radiation during the day and consequently were the last areas to melt on campus. A large snowstorm hit Greenville in 1979, dumping eighteen inches of snow on the ground. East Carolina did not have any means to remove that amount of snow, and their small plows were unable to make a dent in the drifts.

The university contracted to use grader equipment from Barrus Construction to clear the campus streets and parking lots. Manual and small plows were used to clear sidewalks and steps. Unfortunately, on College Hill one of the Barrus graders hit a manhole cover and broke in two parts, with the blade snapping off. Caldwell knew a welder who lived near Fifth and Eastern streets and usually carried his portable service welding truck home from work. He called the welder, Edgar Cox, and asked him if he would help weld the grader back together. Cox had the typical attitude of the day to major snowstorms, asking why anyone would want to clear snow from the campus when it would soon melt! Caldwell soon worked out a deal with Cox: if his driveway was cleared so he could move his truck into position, he would work on the Barrus grader. The drive was shoveled, and Cox laid down on the cold ground and welded the two portions of the broken grader back together. Then he had to reattach the blade to the scraper control mechanism. Caldwell's men then worked twenty-four hours in a row clearing streets and lots of the accumulated snow. He piled the snow up into mounds, where he left it to melt. This is an example of the way local Greenville citizens pitch in and help out the university community when it is in a tough spot. This can-do attitude has been evident since the founding of the university and helps explain why the university is so highly valued among residents of eastern North Carolina.

Caldwell also recalled the devastation Hurricanes Bertha, Fran, and Floyd caused on campus. During Bertha and Fran as well as Hurricane Connie, water backed up to the loading dock at the Howell Science Complex. Of course, Floyd was much worse, and the entire basement of Howell was flooded. This was where the HVAC and telecommunications switches were located. During many of these storms, water came waist-deep on Tenth Street. Caldwell's workers tried to do what they could with the onrushing waters. Many of his staff lost all they had during Floyd. When the Greenville Utilities pumping station at the east end of Fifth Street failed during Floyd, raw sewage began backing up on Tenth Street in front of what was then Darryl's restaurant. Caldwell had never dealt with this situation before and at first did not realize what was happening. He could only sit by and watch the sewage rise after sending his workers first to the hospital for hepatitis A and C vaccines and then home to look after their families. The university had to contract with a firm out of Charlotte to come and disinfect the area and clean up the debris. During this period, the main steam lines for the campus were under several feet of sewage. During Hurricane Bertha, Caldwell's staff kept the streets clean as best they could. All of their vehicles had open cabs at this period, and he had to borrow an enclosed cab vehicle from the city of Greenville to remove debris.

During Hurricane Fran, Caldwell was concerned about a tree on the chancellor's grounds. Jo Eakin came out and asked Caldwell what he was doing looking at a tree in their yard. She told him to go on home. Instead, he went down to the Rivers Building to check on the situation there, and shortly he received a police radio call that the tree had fallen into the chancellor's upstairs bedroom. Fortunately there were no injuries, and Jo was left to remark, "I see what you were looking at." Fran created a huge mess of debris, more than Caldwell's staff could handle. This time the university had to hire a private contractor to remove the limbs and other accumulated materials. A contractor from Columbia, North Carolina, was selected but proved to be a rip-off, performing less than satisfactory work. (It seemed that the only thing they were good at removing was the funds they were given for debris removal.) The university had to contract a second time with E. R. Lewis, a firm that actually came and did the work.

Caldwell recalled that during the 1973 addition to Joyner Library the contractor was very strict about requiring workers to wear hard hats. If you didn't want to wear a hat, he pulled out from under his desk an aluminum hard hat that had a steel bolt going right through it. The bolt had fallen from an upper story during construction and went through the aluminum hat and into a worker's head. Workers soon got the message after seeing the hat.

A number of contractors went bankrupt during or soon after major university building projects. Contractors failed as a result of the Joyner addition, Howell Science Complex, Jenkins Art Phase I, the medical school addition, and the student recreation projects. In some cases the contractor failed to understand the size of the project or simply had problems in general with other contracts.

Caldwell recalled, for instance, that with the construction of the Brody Building, the contractor poured the foundation in the wrong place. They had to tear it up and pour the large area over again, costing them funds they had not planned on using. Caldwell recalled the removal of the old power plant in the 1970s. Big Chief Demolition out of Orlando, Florida, got the contract for the removal of the plant. All went well until they got to the foundation of the steam plant chimney, which simply would not come out of the ground. The company was prohibited from using dynamite on the project because of the danger to students living in nearby Slay Dorm and elsewhere on campus. Finally, after many days of frustrating work, early one Sunday morning there was a muffled explosion at the site at the base of the chimney. Suddenly the base was in small pieces that could be hauled off. Big Chief went next off to Greenville, South Carolina, to demolish a hotel there. During the demolition the entire working force of the company, save one foreman who was elsewhere, perished as the hotel collapsed around them.

Caldwell recalled the speed with which the renovation of Williams Arena took place. It was a job that should have taken about three years to complete, but it was done in nine months, between basketball seasons! Caldwell also remembers that he was in charge of parking lot construction, which could be a challenge during rainy periods. During the paving of the College Hill Drive parking lots, the grading of the lots had been completed but eastern North Carolina had an unusually long rainy period that prohibited finishing the job. The contractor was eager to pave the lots and get his money. Caldwell was told that the contractor's home office had ruled that there would be "no such thing as a rain delay" in completing the contract.

The on-site contractor paved during the rain. Despite misgivings on the part of university officials, the paving has held up to this day.

Caldwell remembers the service his grounds crew gave during commencements. One time during a strong gust of wind, the flag almost fell on the mace bearer, Marguerite Perry. On one commencement day when it rained very hard, the only thing the commencement speaker said was, "My mama didn't raise no fool, let's all go home!" That was the end of the speech. President Leo Jenkins was mortified and stood up and gave a rousing speech while everyone sat in the rain. Sometimes the media would give the commencement times wrong in their messages to the public. Parents and graduates would come to Ficklen Stadium and Williams Arena, only to find Doug's people folding up the chairs and stacking them for removal. These people were often quite upset and took their frustrations out on the poor grounds crew members who were just trying to clean up after the ceremony!

University budgets in the old days had more management flexibility than they do today. Caldwell recalls ordering some fertilizer. After a certain period it was getting late to apply the fertilizer, so he made inquiries up the line. Julian Vainright knew nothing about the fertilizer order, and neither did Jim Lowry. Caldwell decided to go ask F. D. Duncan about his fertilizer. Duncan was in his office, with many files surrounding his desk. He quickly pulled out an order ledger and scanned pending orders. He stopped his finger at one place, where Wendell Smiley had ordered some needed movable storage units for the Joyner Library. Duncan remarked that he did not think Smiley needed the storage units that badly that year. Doug soon got his needed fertilizer, and Smiley was left to wait another year for funds. Such was the old management budget flexibility at East Carolina University.

SUPPORT STAFF MEMBERS have a number of organizations that provide group cohesiveness. A large number of support staff belong to the State Employees' Association of North Carolina (SEANC). This group, headquartered in Raleigh and divided into a number of regional districts, provides group buying opportunities and lobbying efforts on behalf of its members with the General Assembly and capital agency headquarters. A number of East Carolina University support staff leaders have chaired the SEANC Greenville District.

Another opportunity for support staff group action derives from the East Carolina University Chancellor's Staff Senate. This group, founded in January 1999 by Chancellor Richard Eakin, replaced a number of previous staff consulting groups going back to a "Captain's Mast"–type group that met to advise Chancellor Leo Warren Jenkins in the 1960s. During the period between Jenkins and Eakin, these groups met at the chancellor's pleasure, a time period that varied with each chancellor. Some chancellors did not regularly consider the suggestions from the staff. Chancellor Eakin revived the practice and regularized the meetings, bylaws, committees, and formalized agendas of the Staff Senate.

This new Staff Senate consists of senators and alternates elected from the various university divisions. Each division has a staff senator and alternate for every one hundred SPA employees in that division. The Staff Senate currently consists of twenty-eight members and eight ex-officio "advisers." Senators must be full-time staff from the university's eight divisions: "Chancellor's Area," Academic Affairs, Administration and Finance, Athletics, Health Sciences, Institutional Advancement and Research, Economic Development and Community Engagement, and Student Life. The Staff Senate's goal is "to provide communication between [the] staff of East Carolina University and the administration as well as faculty and students where appropriate." Specifically the Staff Senate is charged with reviewing procedures and making "recommendations regarding interests and concerns that effect staff members." Assisting with communication of directives that relate to support staff, serving as liaison between the chancellor and his or her staff, promoting staff participation in the university community, and encouraging "a sense of community among all university employees."

The Staff Senate meetings begin with reports by the executive committee members on their activities. Meetings last about an hour, from 4 to 5 p.m. The Staff Senate does most of its work through its seven subcommittees: Executive, Bylaws, Communications, Compensation and Benefits, Diversity, Personnel Policies, and Recognition and Rewards. These committees make monthly reports of activities to the Staff Senate meetings concerning committee activities and recommendations. Officers of the executive committee include the chair, the vice chair, the secretary, the treasurer, and the vice chancellor of human resources who serves in an ex-officio non-voting advisory capacity. The bylaws allow one ex-officio member, who is required to attend the monthly meetings of the executive committee and Staff Senate. This individual has power to appoint an unlimited number of ex-officio members to both the Staff Senate and any standing committee "as he or she sees fit." Currently there are eight ex-officio advisers in the Staff Senate. The bylaws also address member attendance, duties, vacancies, and removal of members from office. As an administration-authorized committee, the Staff Senate's procedures and powers are delegated by the chancellor.

The 1999 support staff focus group was created as the East Carolina University Staff Forum in part as a result of an administrative memorandum from the Office of the President of the University of North Carolina. On June 30, 1998, President Molly Corbett Broad wrote in her memo to system chancellors: "Each campus will have in operation by the end of the fall 1998 academic term a consultative body representing staff employees with which you or your designee will meet on a regular basis. We will not establish a system-wide staff assembly comparable to the [UNC] Faculty Assembly."

The first meeting of the East Carolina University Staff Forum was held on January 12, 1999—just barely past the "end of the fall 1998 academic term"—at which time the group was congratulated by and received its charge from Chancellor Richard Eakin. Willie Lee (University Printing and Graphics) was elected chair, Margarete Boyd (University Health Systems of Eastern North Carolina) vice chair, and Beth Furlough secretary. The 1999 Staff Forum met twelve times, with the July 1999 meeting an executive committee retreat held at the Brody School of Medicine.

Among the accomplishments of the Staff Forum in 1999 were recommendations on promotion restrictions for probationary-term staff, who were prohibited from applying for other positions at ECU; release time for staff to attend forum meetings; a blue-ribbon "Who I Am Makes a Difference" campaign; a report on salary inequities; and a staff computer loan program. As we have seen, high on the agenda for staff members are issues such as diversity, salary inequities, and benefits packages. Among the unfinished business of this first Staff Forum at East Carolina were concerns such as summer school tuition waivers, access to university personnel policy manuals (often difficult for staff to access in the past), and short-term no-interest payroll deduction loans.

The 2000 Staff Forum retained Willie Lee as chair and elected Phillip Lewis (EHS) as vice chair and Pam Lanier (Facilities Services) as secretary. The 2000 forum also met twelve times (including the now annual executive board retreat). Key issues were a textbook loan program, attendance at meetings (attendance was low at times), and a "perceived inequity study." At this time the forum accomplished increased coverage of staff activities in *Pieces of Eight*. Special emphasis was placed on recognitions and rewards with refreshments being served and door prizes awarded at Staff Appreciation Week; a review of employee-suggested bonus incentives; November "Praise Committee" service awards; and visibility of the Staff Forum at new employee orientation. During the year the forum saw the printing of a series of "Diversity Yes!" brochures, and involvement of forum members in the "Coffee in the Kitchen" project. Carryover issues were almost the same as the previous year: a computer loan program, summer school tuition waivers, Personnel Policy Manual access, and Web page presence for the forum.

In 2001, new officers took over the helm of the Staff Forum: David Batts, (Research and Graduate Studies) chair, Edna Hodges (Health Sciences), vice chair, and Connie Blake (Academic Affairs), secretary. Seventeen meetings of the Staff Forum were held between January 2001 and May 2002. That year the annual retreat for the executive committee was held in early August instead of the traditional July. One of the first challenges of the new forum was the organizing of "official documents in a consistent manner." Forum records apparently were an issue, and the secretary was charged with collecting these materials and placing them in order for use. The by-laws of the forum were also revised this year. The chair of the forum spoke on the stage at a memorial service for victims of 9/11. Major recommendations for 2001 revolved around diversity issues. Each division or school was urged to develop a plan for growth in this area. The university was urged to "address the historical perspective of employment" with respect to underrepresented groups. Additional training for supervisors, along with the establishment of a diversity officer for the university, was urged upon the administration.

Two suggestion boxes were placed in strategic locations on east and west campus, and a benefits fair was also promoted on both campuses. Three forum members attended a Senate Forum at North Carolina State University. Members brought back new initiatives for the East Carolina Staff Forum from this systemwide meeting. The Compensation and Benefits Committee researched such issues as telecommuting, scholarships, pay equity, tuition payroll deduction, and expansion of the textbook loan programs to summer school during the 2001 year. The Personnel and Policies Committee looked at a Staff Forum flyer, supervisor evaluations, the west campus smoking policy, personal use of cell phones, and speed bumps on the west campus. The Recognition and Rewards Committee posted billboards at various Trade Mart locations during Excellence in State Government Week and suggested that employees receive birthday cards signed by the chancellor and that an Employee of the Quarter award be given.

The 2002 term Staff Forum saw the same executive board serving the second half of what had become a traditional two-year term. The forum met nine times during 2002–3. The first thing the Staff Forum did that year was to change its name to Staff Senate. It was noted in the annual report for the year that "this change produced a more positive atmosphere in our meetings, among our members, and how people viewed the Senate." The new Staff Senate proposed that the Staff Senate be created systemwide. It was also suggested that tuition waivers be made available at both all UNC system universities and at community colleges in North Carolina.

Other issues discussed during the year were allowing staff to take classes outside their lunch hours (a previous restriction on staff attendance), securing area business discounts, an increase of the tuition waiver from six to nine hours a year, the development of a liaison to the East Carolina University Faculty Senate, and "support and recognition of" U.S. military personnel at the university. Other concerns were salary compression, telecommuting, a location on OneStop for the Staff Senate, computer loans, health benefits, Performance Evaluation System glitches, vacation bonus leave, the adverse weather policy, volunteers being listed in *Pieces of Eight,* receiving discount athletic tickets, the noontime employee fitness program, and diversity.

The 2003–4 Staff Senate got off to a challenging start when the previous chair, David Batts, accepted a faculty position and Pat Brown (Education), the secretary, had to limit activities due to a broken elbow. Batts called an emergency meeting in July 2003, where Carolus Brown (Student Life) was elected chair, Kris Holly (Health Sciences) vice chair, and Christy Duke (Health Sciences) secretary. This team filled out the 2003 calendar year, at which point both Brown and Holly resigned. The remaining members of the Staff Senate executive committee assumed the key leadership positions and, with the help of Human Resources, the Staff Senate continued on following the cancellation of the February and March 2004 Staff Senate meetings. In April and May 2004, the Staff Senate adopted emergency provisions to the bylaws and allowed for a new executive board to the elected midterm. Rebecca Bizzell (Campus Operations) was elected chair, Kim Wilson (Academic Outreach) vice chair, Amanda Turner (Group Practice Administration) secretary, and Alan Bailey (Academic Library Services) treasurer. New standing committee members were elected in June of 2004 to replace those who had resigned or whose terms had expired.

Much of the year of 2003–4 was spent with membership issues, and the chair (Bizzell) expressed the hope in her annual report that a revitalized Staff Senate could focus on the positive aspects of their work and not on the difficulties suffered during the recent unpleasantness. The Staff Senate recommended in their annual report that the connection with the administration be "developed and improved" and that the new chancellor and human resources support the work of the Staff Senate. Issues that concerned the Staff Senate during 2003–4, besides organizational ones, were familiar support staff issues: the benefits fair, health benefit improvements, Pirate Perks with local business discounts, salary equity, Employee Appreciation Week, and spotlighting support staff in *Pieces of Eight.* Dress codes and new employee orientation as well as administration support through "providing an engaging environment that makes members feel comfortable, respected and valued" were also major themes of the Staff Senate during this period. The Staff Senate met nine times in 2003–4, with the August meeting being again the traditional executive committee retreat. While the

Staff Senate was now back on its feet again, all in all the year proved a challenging one from an organizational perspective. The Staff Senate moved on to 2004–5 with a renewed hope for meaningful and valued input into university affairs.

The participation of support staff in the chancellor's Staff Senate typifies the commitment among employees toward the well-being and thriving of East Carolina University. Support staff are among the most enthusiastic of Pirate fans, and the quality of their daily work demonstrates a similar commitment. As we can see through the concerns expressed in this chapter, staff members can and do make a difference in the quality of our students' educational experience. These individuals represent the hopes, wishes, and spirits of the thousands of support staff workers that through the years have made East Carolina University what it is in this centennial year.

NOTE

The author wishes to especially thank Layla Edwards Floyd, systems coordinator, ECU Financial Services, and Vira Hogan, human resources associate, North Carolina Office of State Personnel Compensation Program Team, for their help with historical statistical information. Rebecca Bizzell was also very helpful in supplying Annual Reports of the Staff Senate for 1999–2005.

REFERENCES

"Acquisitions: Large Operations Growing Larger," *Vending and OCS: A National Journal of Industry Information*. September–October 1998.

Aramark Corporation. *Our History,* http://www.aramark.com/aboutaramark. asp, Philadelphia: Aramark Corporation, 2006.

Caldwell, Douglas, personal interview with author, August 2005.

Daily Reflector, 1980–2004, Greenville, NC: Cox North Carolina Publications, Inc.

ECU Chancellor's Office. Leo Jenkins Papers. East Carolina University Archives.

ECU Equal Employment Opportunity Office. Papers. East Carolina University.

ECU Human Resources Office. Statistical Reports. East Carolina University.

ECU Media Board. *East Carolinian,* 1965–1973; 1980–2004, Greenville, NC: East Carolina University.

ECU Media Board. *Fountainhead,* 1974–1979, Greenville, NC: East Carolina University.

ECU News & Communications Services. *Pieces of Eight,* 1976–2004, Greenville, NC: East Carolina University.

ECU Institutional Planning, Research & Effectiveness Office. *Fact Book*, 1976–2003, Greenville, NC: East Carolina University.

ECU Special Events & Protocol Office. Papers. East Carolina University.

ECU Staff Forum. Papers. East Carolina University.

ECU Staff Senate. Papers. East Carolina University.

Lawson, Craig. "Food Fight," *Peak*, September 18, 1995, Burnaby, British Columbia: Simon Fraser University.

North Carolina State Personnel Office. *State of North Carolina Salary Schedule*, 1976–2004.

Parker, R.V., personal interview with author, April 2004.

Rice, Janice, personal interview with author, March 2004.

Tucker, Judy, personal interview with author, March 2004.

United States Bureau of the Census. *Statistical Abstract of the United States— The National Data Book*, 2003.

Wallas, Joseph, personal interview with author, March 2004.

Woolard, Lydia "K," personal interview with author, April 2004.

## CHAPTER FOUR

East Carolina University's Programs

BRENDA KILLINGSWORTH

ACADEMICS and its environment have changed considerably over the past twenty-five years. The types of academic programs offered have evolved to continue to serve the needs and interests of the students and region. The rise in the number of students served and the corresponding number of faculty has been breathtaking. Given the tight federal and state budgets of recent years, the costs of obtaining a degree have increased significantly due to increases in tuition and fees. Academic support programs have expanded and evolved to meet student needs. The facilities required to support the influx of students and new degree programs have had tremendous impact on the campus learning environment. Technology has influenced virtually every dimension of campus, from the delivery of support services such as advising and registration to the means and methods of learning, both with the use of technology in the classroom and with the use of technology for distance learning.

FACULTY, STUDENTS, AND ACADEMIC PROGRAMS

East Carolina University has evolved from a comprehensive university in the early 1980s to a research-intensive university in the early 2000s. In fall 1980, there were 628 faculty members serving 13,165 students. The budgeted student/faculty ratio was 15.4. The university offered 104 baccalaureate degree program tracks, 70 graduate degree program tracks, 1 professional program track, and 5 doctorate degree program tracks. The university also offered preprofessional courses qualifying students for admission to schools of cytotechnology, dentistry, engineering, law, medicine, optome-

TABLE 4.1   Fall Head-count Enrollment, 2004–5

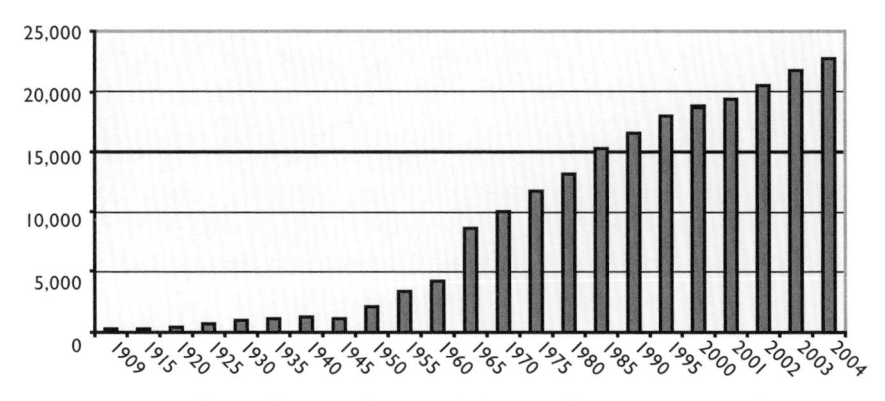

Source: East Carolina College Catalog, UNC-OP enrollment report, and Institutional Planning, Research, and Effectiveness data files.

Note: Beginning in 1983, head-count enrollment includes both on-campus and distance education enrollment; before 1983, data include on-campus enrollment only.

try, and pharmacy; two-year curricula in forestry, agriculture, wood technology, and pulp and paper technology, qualifying students for transfer to other colleges; and a Certificate of American Studies for foreign students.

Over the last two and a half decades, there have been significant increases in the number of academic programs, faculty, and students enrolled. In the early 2000s, the University of North Carolina projected a huge influx of students in the system over the next decade. In an effort to prepare for serving the students, the university identified several targeted growth campuses. East Carolina University was one of the universities designated as a targeted growth university with expected on-campus enrollment of between 25,000 and 27,000 by 2010. Since that time, enrollment has steadily climbed. In fall 2002, the campus enrollment surpassed 20,000 with an enrollment of 20,577 students. Enrollment continues to climb, with the fall 2003 enrollment at 22,802. At the same time, the number of faculty at the university has also grown; in fall 2003 ECU employed 1,380 faculty.

Since 1980, several changes have been made in the preprofessional curriculums available to students. Preprofessional training for the field of cytotechnology was no longer an option. However, two additional preprofessional training curricula had been added: a three-year preveterinary curriculum and a pretheology curriculum. Beginning in fall 2004, students interested in pursuing a bachelor of science in engineering with a concentration in systems engineering finally had an option to complete the degree at East Carolina University. As in 1980, students interested in other engineering programs could follow a preengineering curriculum and transfer to another school to complete their degrees.

While the number of baccalaureate degree programs offered has been relatively steady over the past two and a half decades, the number of graduate and doctoral degree programs has increased. An increasing emphasis in graduate programs and research resulted in the university being granted Doctoral II status in 1998 by the Carnegie Foundation, a designation later reclassified as Research-Intensive. The university has continued to place increased emphasis in graduate programs and research, fostering growth in its library collections and research support for its academic programs.

East Carolina University's academic programs have evolved over the past twenty-five years with the development of new graduate programs and expanded library resources. Its nationally recognized, four-year medical school began in the autumn of 1977. Quickly following the establishment of the medical school in the spring of 1979 was the development of five Ph.D. degree programs in sciences basic to medicine—pharmacology, physiology, microbiology, anatomy, and biochemistry. Four years later the first Ph.D. (in anatomy) was awarded to Thomas Edward Curry Jr. Soon a doctoral program in pathology was authorized, which in 1999 was combined with other research programs in the Brody School of Medicine clinical departments, and the molecular and cellular programs of the Department of Biology and the neuroscience program to become a Ph.D. in interdisciplinary biological sciences.

In 1987, East Carolina University and North Carolina State University embarked on a cooperative doctoral program in educational administration. In 1990, East Carolina University received approval for an Ed.D. program in educational leadership and enrolled its first students that fall. Over the next fifteen years, another nine doctoral programs were added —communication sciences and disorders (1996), coastal resources management (1998), medical biophysics (1998), bioenergetics (2000–1), nursing (2001), medical family therapy (2003–4), technical and professional discourse (2003–4), rehabilitation counseling and administration (2003–4), and physical therapy (2004). By the 2004–5 academic year, the university offered 107 baccalaureate degree programs, 86 master's degree programs, 2 certificates of advanced study, 2 educational specialist degrees, and 15 doctoral programs.

In 1980, the university had one college (College of Arts and Sciences) and nine professional schools (School of Allied Health and Social Professions, School of Art, School of Business, School of Education, School of Home Economics, School of Medicine, School of Music, School of Nursing, and School of Technology).

Many changes have occurred over the past twenty-five years that reflect the changes in economic and societal needs as well as interests of students. In the early 2000s, the university underwent a major reorganization that consolidated schools and created six professional colleges. In 2004, the university's academic structure included seven colleges, the Thomas Harriott College of Arts and Sciences, College of Business, College of Education, College of Fine Arts and Communication, College of Health and Human Performance, College of Human Ecology, College of Technology and Computer Science, and three professional schools, the School of Allied Health Sciences, Brody School of Medicine, and School of Nursing.

In 1980, East Carolina University was a member of or accredited by twenty-eight associations. With the expansion of academic programs offered and rigorous pursuit of quality, the number of associations the university is a member of or accredited by has increased almost six-fold to 154, not counting the membership of individual disciplines in other organizations.

The cost of an undergraduate education has significantly risen over the past twenty-five years. According to the 1980–81 undergraduate catalog, applicants for admission to the university were required to pay a $10 nondeductible, nonrefundable application fee in 1980. The average in-state student incurred necessary expenses of approximately $2,200 for room, meals, tuition, fees, and books during an academic year of two semesters. In-state tuition was just $260 per semester, while out-of-state tuition was $1,120 per semester. Health fees ($24) and other required fees ($81) totaled $105 per semester. Room rent was $238 per semester, meals were estimated to cost approximately $500 per semester, and $90 was considered a reasonable estimate for books per semester. The university maintained a depository, the Student Supply Store, for students to purchase their textbooks and supplies.

In contrast, applicants for admission to the university were required to pay a $50 application fee for the 2004–5 academic year. The current in-state student incurs necessary expenses of approximately $8,500 during an academic year of two semesters. In-state tuition has risen to $909 per semester, while out-of-state tuition has risen to $5,737 per semester. Health fees, the educational/technology fee, and other required fees have risen even more dramatically than in-state tuition, to a total of $610 per semester. Room rent varies depending on the location and ranges from $2,750 to $3,690 per academic year. Meals are estimated to cost approximately $1,100 per semester. While the cost of textbooks and supplies varies with the different curricula, $400 to $600 is considered a reasonable estimate for books per semester. The Ronald E. Dowdy Student Stores continues to serve students as a location for purchasing books and supplies and donates a portion of the sales to student scholarships. While students also have the option to purchase textbooks at the local book exchange, the Internet has also opened up new avenues for acquiring textbooks. A growing percentage of students now use the Internet to search for and purchase discounted new and used books.

In an effort to encourage students to complete their academic work in a succinct time frame, the legislature also imposed a 25 percent tuition surcharge beginning in the 1990s for all undergraduate students seeking a baccalaureate degree who exceed a specific credit-hour threshold (which depends on the number of hours required to earn the degree). Effectively, the surcharge affected students who exceed 110 percent of the minimum hours needed to earn a baccalaureate degree or a program involving a double major or combined bachelor's/master's degree program.

Further, the university has designated portions of the tuition-based increases over the past few years to financial-based assistance programs to support students adversely affected by the tuition increases who qualify for assistance. This designation has helped ensure that students on financial aid are held harmless by the fee.

ACADEMIC SUPPORT PROGRAMS

A number of programs were initiated or strengthened during the 1990s and early 2000s to attract and retain high-caliber students. Over the last fifteen years, an increased emphasis has been placed on offering accelerated degree programs and enhanced scholarship opportunities. The honors program has been greatly expanded to serve the overall university, providing students with increased academic challenges through research and service opportunities. In addition, seven accelerated degree programs have been designed and implemented to assist students in completing their academic degrees in a shorter time frame. Further, the East Carolina Scholars campaign was undertaken to promote the establishment of additional scholarships for highly qualified students.

The honors program at East Carolina University has significantly expanded over the past two and a half decades. In 1980, the honors program was open only to freshmen and sophomores who were judged to be qualified. These students were invited to participate in the Freshman and Sophomore Honors Program, which consisted of seminars in the Great Books presented by two senior faculty members. There were six seminars in the curriculum, including Tragedy (HSEM 2010), Politics (HSEM 2020), Scientific Method (HSEM 2030), Philosophy (HSEM 2040), Comedy (HSEM 2050), and Some Human Lives (HSEM 2060).

In 1984, the honors program became a university-wide endeavor, span-ning across disciplines and providing courses into the junior and senior years. In addition to admitting interested freshmen and sophomores currently enrolled with a 3.5 average, high school students already admitted to the university were contacted and invited to participate. The breadth of the courses offered to students expanded beyond the seminar programs previously offered. Now the university offered honors sections in many of the regular introductory courses in disciplines such as English, history, anthropology, and psychology. In the academic year 2002–3, an entire residence hall on central campus was designated for honors students. That same academic year, the first annual Undergraduate Research Symposium was held. And in January 2003, the Honors College was established to house the honors program, the EC Scholars program, and Undergraduate Research.

Mirroring a national trend, the ECU honors program initiated a new requirement in fall 2004 that embodies the intent of the university to serve. A community-service learning component, referred to as academic service learning, was introduced. Before graduation, honors students are required to complete at least three semester hours of service learning. This program was implemented through a partnership with the ECU Volunteer Center. Service learning combines academics with community service in an effort to provide students with experiential education opportunities to develop civic responsibility while improving critical and reflective thinking skills.

By 2005, the university honors program had grown to approximately 1,250 students. The honors program has also expanded its Undergraduate Research Assistant awards, which currently provide eighty-five honors students with a $500 research stipend and the opportunity to learn research techniques while working closely with faculty.

Over the past few years, seven accelerated degree programs have been introduced. These programs include Degree in Three, Summer Scholars, M.D. in Seven, J.D. in Six, D.D.S. in Seven, and Integrated Bachelor's and Master's. The Degree in Three Program, established in the summer of 2003, provided an opportunity for highly motivated and highly qualified students to complete their undergraduate degrees in three years. Students admitted through this program could begin during the second summer session before their freshman year. Students were assigned special advisers to assist them in customizing their program of study. These students could also receive priority registration during the three-year program and met with advisers and graduate program coordinators to discuss the professional school admission requirements. The Summer Scholars program, implemented the following year, was an extension of the program to allow rising high school seniors to participate in enrichment programs and attend second summer session along with entering Degree in Three students.

The M.D. in Seven is available to a limited number of students in each incoming class of the Brody School of Medicine. The J.D. in Six program and the D.D.S. in Seven program involve partnerships with other universities to allow undergraduate students to be admitted to graduate programs earlier in their undergraduate studies.

Established in 1998, the EC Scholars awards program was designed to attract entering freshmen with the greatest potential to become scholars and leaders. The Campaign for East Carolina Scholars lasted two and a half years, surpassed its original goal of $12 million, and generated a total of $15.3 million in gifts and pledges, creating 182 new merit scholarships for undergraduate and graduate students.

In conjunction with the introduction of the EC Scholars awards, four Early Assurance Awards were offered to the Brody School of Medicine along with four alternate Early Assurance Awards. In 2005, twenty scholars were selected, each receiving a full scholarship award for four years.

In 1980, the main campus encompassed approximately 340 acres adjacent to downtown Greenville. East Carolina University served an enrollment of 12,874 with a physical plant that was valued at more than $80 million. Many of the classroom buildings, dormitories, and facilities were less than ten years old. Most classes were located within walking distance of the dormitories. A wing had just been added to Joyner Library, doubling its capacity. The library could seat 1,800 students and house 800,000 volumes. Its collection contained approximately 465,000 bound volumes, 530,000 pieces of microtext, and more than 6,000 serial titles. The new campus for the School of Medicine encompassed approximately 40 acres of land next to the Pitt County Memorial Hospital.

Over the past decade, the university has spent over $350 million on capital expansion to enhance the educational environment. Now, East Carolina University's academic programs reside across 3 separate campuses totaling over 920 acres of land. The main campus, located near the downtown area and shopping centers, has grown from 340 acres in 1980 to over 400 acres in 2004. Passage of the higher education bond referendum in November 2000 made available funding that permitted the long-awaited expanded health sciences campus to become a reality. The health sciences campus has expanded to 70 acres of land and has become the hub of the university's health sciences program, housing the Brody School of Medicine, the School of Allied Health Sciences, and the School of Nursing. In the late 1990s, the university acquired over 450 acres of land to create a third campus, the west research campus, housing a number of research and graduate programs.

While students still meet with advisers before registering for classes, how students register for their courses has changed dramatically since 1980. In 1980, students would register and wait months to find out if they received the classes they requested. If any changes or additions needed to be made to their schedules, students stood in long lines at Wright Auditorium in hopes of obtaining a coveted "punched card" that represented a seat in a given course and section.

In the late 1980s, a phone registration system was implemented with some success. Online registration became an option for students in 1985. With the early version of online registration, students could register for classes at an adviser's office or using one of fifty-four personal computer terminals located across campus instead of standing in line at a central site. Students knew immediately whether seats were available in a given course. In the late 1990s and early 2000s, effort was directed at developing a one-stop university portal that would provide students and faculty with a central location to retrieve and manage their university information dynamically online. With the introduction of OneStop, online registration was expanded to include a Web-based platform, permitting students to register online anywhere. Today students have three options to register for courses—online terminal registration, Web registration through One-Stop, and telephonic registration through Automated Voice Response System (AVRS).

In addition to procedural and technological changes, organizational changes in academic advising have been implemented to provide more seamless advising for students. Together, these changes over the past two decades have dramatically transformed the manner in which students are advised. In an effort to improve academic advising in the first two years of a student's college experience, the Academic Advising and Support Center was created in the early 2000s. The center was designed to support undecided majors, transfer students, and students considering a change in major. In addition, advising centers were created in the colleges and schools to better serve declared majors.

Over the past generation, technology has had considerable influence on how the university delivers academic programs to off-campus students as well as classes taught on campus. Distance learning has opened up opportunities for students not located near campus as well as nontraditional students who are juggling work schedules, family, and civic responsibilities while trying to obtain a degree. Technology has also changed the way faculty members deliver information in the classroom as well as how they communicate with students.

While the basic goal of distance education has not changed over the past twenty-five years, the manner in which the education has been delivered and the student population effectively served has dramatically changed. With the advent of the Internet, the focus of distance education has evolved from serving groups of students residing near the campus or established centers located at several military bases in the east to serving students across the state and beyond.

In the early 1980s, the Division of Continuing Education operated the University College to provide opportunities for students to take college work on campus during the evening on a part-time basis. Off-campus undergraduate centers at Camp Lejeune and the Marine Corps Air Station at Cherry Point offered all courses required for a degree in five areas. The program was organized around five eight-week terms, with most classes meeting at night. The division also operated graduate centers at Fort Bragg, Camp Lejeune, Cherry Point, and Fayetteville State University. Off-campus freshman- and sophomore-level courses were offered at Carteret Technical College and Johnston Technical Institute. Students could receive resident credit for undergraduate courses taken through the Division of Continuing Education, with no limit on the number of hours a student could earn through continuing education. However, for a student to receive an undergraduate degree from East Carolina University, the student must have completed at least one scholastic year's work in residence at East Carolina University.

Over the past two and a half decades, the college's focus has evolved to supporting two groups of students—nondegree students who do not hold a baccalaureate degree and nontraditional students admitted through the performance-based admission policy. The college's function is to support these students as they work to meet the retention stipulations specified in their letters of admission. Once these retention stipulations are met, the students then transfer to the general college or apply for a specific academic degree program. Currently, the East Carolina University Office of Military Programs provides outreach services to the military bases in North Carolina. The office delivers courses and degree programs to the Armed Forces community through a variety of methods, including on-site and online. The office is comprised of the Department of Aerospace Studies and the Department of Military Sciences.

Many academic programs are seeing an increase in the number of distance learning students, especially in graduate programs. East Carolina University has been a leader in the implementation of technology to support distance learning in the state and in the nation. It has received many awards, including the first award for excellence given to a university by the North Carolina chapter of the U.S. Distance Learning Association in

TABLE 4.2　Head count, 2000–2004

Year	On Campus Head Count	% change from previous year	Distance Education Only Head Count	% change from previous year	Total Head Count	% change from previous year
2000	17,851	−2.0%	899	52.9%	18,750	2.9%
2001	18,174	1.8%	1,238	37.7%	19,412	3.5%
2002	18,955	4.3%	1,622	31.0%	20,577	6.0%
2003	19,374	2.2%	2,382	46.9%	21,756	5.7%
2004	19,570	1.0%	3,197	34.2%	22,767	4.6%

Source: Student data file, fall 2000–fall 2004.

Note: Head-count calculations in previous fact books were based on on-campus enrollment only.

2001. The award recognized the university's leadership in distance learning. In just a little over five years, the distance education headcount at East Carolina University has grown at a rapid rate from 899 in fall 2000 to 3,197 in fall 2004. East Carolina University is the leading provider of distance learning in the University of North Carolina.

Computing facilities to support course work have also changed dramatically over the past twenty-five years. In 1980, the Computing Center, located in the Austin Building, used a Burroughs B6800 computer and remote access to dual IBM 370-165 computers to support instruction, research, and administration. Staff at the Computing Center consisted of twenty-six full-time data processing personnel, augmented with part-time graduate and undergraduate student assistants. The center's remote batch teleprocessing link to the Triangle Universities Computation Center (TUCC) in the Research Triangle Park provided access to a variety of instructional software.

Today, students carry their own laptops to class and can access course material using Blackboard software from home, their dorm, or personal computer labs on campus. Technical support has adapted to meet the changes in computing needs. An ACE Student Computer Support program has been established to provide training, support, and service to students using computers in their academic degree programs. RezNet provides residence hall students with in-room Ethernet connections to the campus network and Internet. Faculty has access to many support facilities to assist in developing technology-enhanced course material. Information Technology and Computing Services assists faculty and students in a wide array of services—from how to set up e-mail accounts to software support. The Technology Advancement Center is a learning laboratory that researches, tests, and applies technology with a goal of improving learning, organizational effectiveness, and the economic well-being of citizens. The Center for Health Sciences and Communication provides support on the west campus for photography, video, and multimedia projects. There is also a university multimedia center that supports academic unit instructional technology consultants as well as faculty in the development of multimedia course offerings.

LIBRARIES

When East Carolina Teachers' Training School opened in 1909, the school founders understood the need for a library and created an initial library plan, which consisted of a room allotted in the original administration building and no provision for books. In 1910, President Robert Wright made a formal appeal to the Board of Trustees for books and shelving. The trustees appropriated $1,000, and by December 1912, East Carolina's library had a small collection of 1,080 volumes. With the General Assembly's authorization for the development of four-year degree programs, the college developed plans for a new library building to be designed by H. A. Underwood. The new library, located in the Whichard Building, was completed in the early 1920s.

The first professional librarian, Helen G. Gray, was hired in 1923. Miss Gray organized the collection by Dewey Decimal classification during her tenure. At the time she was hired, the library contained seating for 150 and room for growth with stack space for 66,000 volumes. After the Board of Trustees allocated $10,000 to the library, the collection expanded to 17,000 volumes. The enlarged collection, while exceeding the collections of other teacher colleges in the state, did not meet American Library Association standards.

Later, two other notable librarians, James R. Gulledge and Felix Eugene Snider, addressed the challenges involved in expanding the library collection by obtaining grants from the Carnegie Foundation and soliciting for additional university funding. Through their efforts the upper floor of the library was completed in 1939, the library staff was enlarged through the hiring of a trained cataloger, a Department of Library Science was established, and materials were acquired to support the fledgling graduate department. By 1943, the library collection had increased to over 43,000 volumes with a capacity for 80,000. The library staff consisted of three full-time employees and seventeen student assistants who provided service seventy hours per week. The facility could accommodate approximately 250 visitors.

The next thirty years of library development were influenced by librarian Wendell W. Smiley. Smiley's most significant accomplishments included library staff growth to twenty-eight faculty members and forty support staff, increasing library operation hours to ninety per week, and structuring the library to become a U.S. government document depository. Accepting East Carolina's inability to compete with major research libraries in print-based resources, he explored other less expensive avenues for collection expansion, settling on microforms. At Smiley's retirement, the library budget exceeded $1 million and the collection included over 400,000 volumes, 400,000 microforms, and 5,000 periodicals.

Smiley's tenure witnessed the building of a new library facility. James Yadkin Joyner, a former educator and North Carolina state superintendent for public instruction who successfully passed legislation to establish teacher training schools in Greenville and Boone, was posthumously honored by having the newly expanded facility named for him. The library was dedicated to Joyner's memory on March 8, 1955. The facility housed a curriculum laboratory, a broadcasting studio, an audiovisual laboratory, a projection auditorium, a library science department, stacks for 117,000 books, and the capacity to accommodate five hundred visitors.

Despite the library's progress, East Carolina's rapid student population growth kept the new library from adequately meeting student and faculty needs. Smiley understood the library's shortcomings. He envisioned the creation of a west wing with space for 250,000 volumes and 900 visitors. The west wing opened in 1975. Under Smiley's guidance, Joyner Library outpaced every regional university in the University of North Carolina system.

Although the older section of the library was renovated in 1976, inflation affected further expansion of the library during the seventies. While the collection made the transition from Dewey Decimal classification to Library of Congress classification, it was unable to acquire additional resources due to lack of revenue during a difficult recession. To counter the deficiency in funding, the library canceled periodical subscriptions, developed more extensive interlibrary services, and offered a system of online searching known as Dialog.

During the 1980s, ECU's growing student population increased demand for library resources. Space to house the library's steadily increasing number of volumes, microfilm, manuscripts, and other documents as well as space to support the library's patrons became critically short. University patrons became aware of the need for further expansion of Joyner Library. Although plans were developed, the state economy was struggling, and money was not available to fund the renovation and expansion until 1993. On November 1, 1993, North Carolina passed a statewide university construction bond referendum containing $33.5 million dedicated to addressing the need for extensive renovation and construction at Joyner Library. The expansion would be the largest building project ECU had ever undertaken.

After a decade of planning and waiting, construction of the new library began with the first of three phases. Under the oversight of Dr. Kenneth Marks, ground was broken for phase 1 of the library expansion. This expansion provided for the construction of a major addition on the south side of Joyner Library. Phase 1 was completed in the fall of 1996. Phases 2 and 3 of the project involved extensive renovation of the old east and west wings of Joyner Library during the period 1996–98. Overall, the project provided the library with the space to expand holdings to 1.5 million volumes. The net square footage of the library was increased by 49 percent, adding 17 miles of additional shelving. In addition to space for an expanding collection, the project provided 250 computer workstations for accessing library resources, 100 graduate student study carrels, 75 faculty study carrels, 36 group study rooms, a television studio, 5 interactive media classrooms and conference rooms, and a state-of-the-art conservation and preservation laboratory. In August 1998, Dr. Carroll Varner became the director of Academic Library Services. The official dedication of the new and renovated Joyner Library was celebrated on March 8, 1999.

The completion of phase 3 brought significant improvements in library services. As the final section of the building was renovated, several library departments were relocated, and new furniture and shelving were purchased. The Media Teaching Resources Center and an eighty-station computer lab were transferred to the ground floor. Government documents moved to the second floor. The third floor contained general stacks and the campus' copier service, Rapid Copy. An additional department was added to the basement in the phase 3 section, the periodicals department. Ceased journals were moved from the periodicals department to compact shelving accessible only to staff. The compact shelving, which doubled the storage capability of regular shelving, was designed to eventually hold nearly 60,000 ceased journal volumes. Library staffing was increased to provide adequate service in the reorganized departments.

In addition to the expanded space and functions of the internal portion of Joyner Library, attention was given to landscaping the exterior of the building for use by the library patrons. An interior courtyard was designed for the east wing and was in 2003–4 complimented by Java City, a coffee shop housed directly in front of the courtyard. The second and most extensive landscaping initiative was the design of the Sonic Plaza, a 300-foot mall area located between the library and Joyner East.

Further enhancement of the new library came about when Artworks for State Buildings legislation allowed for the development of a multimedia display, Sonic Plaza. Funding for the plaza came from the allocation of 0.5–1 percent of the state building construction budget from 1989 to 1995 for the creation of public artworks. A national competition was held in 1991 to determine the designer for the project. A preselection committee consisting of library architect Larry Robbs of Walter, Robbs, Callahan, and Pierce; Dr. Ken Marks, former director of Joyner Library; Pat Guyette, head of Interlibrary Services; and others who were affiliated with Joyner Library was formed to narrow the field of prospective designers. After examining over one hundred applications, the preselection committee chose three finalists, whose applications were reviewed by the Artworks for State Buildings Committee. Based on their findings, Christopher Janney, a sound and environmental artist, was commissioned to design the plaza.

Janney's concept for Sonic Plaza integrates four design elements into the architecture of Joyner Library Plaza. Each element allows visitors to interact with light, mist, and music. The classic columns that originally stood in front of Joyner are now the "Sonic Gates" and serve as the entrance to Sonic Plaza. An electronic sensor detects anyone who walks past the gates and melodic tones are played from an overhead speaker. The second element is the Percussion Water Wall located near the front door of Joyner Library. Fifteen feet tall and forty feet wide, the wall contains sixty-four water jets that spray water at various intervals to the accompaniment of Janney's percussive musical composition. The Media Glockenspiel element forms a part of Joyner Library's clock tower. Abstract videos play on a ring of the Glockenspiel's video monitors throughout the day. The final element, the Ground Cloud, is located in front of the Media Glockenspiel. Mist rises from a circular grate, forming a cloud that dances in the plaza. At night the cloud is illuminated. Janney designed the plaza for continual change, envisioning it as a place where East Carolina's students could develop new designs for the video monitors and compose original musical works for the Percussion Water Wall. At the completion of the project, the cost for Sonic Plaza totaled $116,235. The plaza was dedicated by East Carolina University Chancellor Richard Eakin during a ceremony held on Friday, December 11, 1998, in front of the plaza's clock tower.

Behind many of Joyner Library's successes was a group of library advocates called the Friends of Joyner Library at East Carolina University. Founded in 1978 and originally known as the Friends of the ECU Library, the group has provided enhanced financial support for the library through fund-raising endeavors. One significant estate contribution came from a founder of the organization, Dr. Virginia Herrin. Dr. Herrin was a member of the English faculty and a longtime supporter of the library. She donated her estate, worth approximately $500,000, to benefit the library upon her death on December 15, 1997.

In addition to endowment initiatives, the Friends of the Library have participated in programs to share Joyner's resources with eastern North Carolina. In 1994, the Friends of the Library collaborated with Sheppard Memorial Library to provide Celebrity Readers Theatre. Attendance and revenues from this venture have been high since its inception. Another event was "A Convergence of Worlds and Ideas: An Evening in Washington." The event was organized as a series of trips to bring the 1775 Mouzon Map to various communities in eastern North Carolina.

Friends of Joyner Library, under the leadership of past presidents Kitty Joyner, Dave Stevens, and Steve Smiley, started the Endow Joyner Library project to raise $10 million for the library by 2007. In the spring of 2000, Friends of the Joyner Library dedicated a Patrons' Wall in memory of former Joyner librarian Wendell Smiley. As a centerpiece of the endowment project, the wall was created to enable devoted ECU patrons of the endowment project to have their names inscribed in the building.

Joyner Library has seen significant change in its collections over the past twenty-five years. In 1980, Joyner Library maintained a collection of 600,338 volumes, 8,452 periodical subscriptions, 349,634 government documents, and 402,691 microforms. A significant milestone reached was the acquisition of the library's millionth volume. By 2003, Joyner Library's collection had grown to 1,183,729 volumes, 14,964 e-journal and in-print periodical subscriptions, 522,794 government documents, and 2,369,336 microforms. In addition to growth, the library has also seen other significant changes in each of its major collections: government documents/microforms, special collections, and the music library.

On April 28, 1995, shortly after the initiation of a major construction and renovation project, the Joyner Library reached a milestone when it acquired its millionth volume, presented by the Friends of Joyner Library. The Friends of Joyner Library presented a copy of the three-volume 1598–1600 *The Principal Navigations, Voiages, Traffiques, and Discoveries of the English Nation* by Richard Hakluyt. On that day, Joyner Library held a one-day symposium that focused on the future of information distribution and on Richard Hakluyt "as an information expert in his own age."

In 1980, the library housed 349,634 government documents and 402,691 microforms. The government documents collection has since grown by almost 50 percent and now houses 525,000 print volumes, 565,000 pieces of microfiche, over 103,000 sheet maps, and more than 4,700 CD-ROM and DVD-ROM products. The General Microforms Collection has grown to over 1.75 million items on microfilm, microfiche, ultrafiche, microprint, and microcard. Over 90,000 maps published by the U.S. government are now available in the documents and microforms department. Joyner Library staff have used the World Wide Web to open up resources for library patrons, including an extensive list of Web pages on government publications and access to over 250,000 online government titles available through the Government Information Web Directory.

The Teaching Resources Center was established in 1988 to support the School of Education and North Carolina teachers. The center contains children and young adult materials, K–12 North Carolina state-adopted textbooks, audiovisual materials, and reference resources. Since its creation, there have been several key expansions to the center's collections. In 2000, a fund-raising initiative by the Joyner Library Development Office successfully resulted in the establishment of a Center for Children's Literature to promote the importance of books, reading, and oral stories in the lives of children. A kickoff event was held on February 11, 2000, with a storytelling conference featuring Donald Davis, North Carolina master storyteller. On March 8, 2002, the Ronnie Barnes African American Resource Collection was dedicated. This collection focuses on significant works written by or about African Americans, including award-winning juvenile books such as the Coretta Scott King Award books, and biographies of African Americans. Most recently, the Debnam Resource Center for Family Literacy was dedicated on March 24, 2004, by Betty Debnam Hunt and Richard M. Hunt in memory of Mrs. Hunt's parents, W. E. and Stella Glass Debnam. (In 1970, Betty Debnam created and has continued to be the editor of the *Minipage*, a newspaper insert for children.)

The university bond referendum generated great excitement for patrons of the special collections department. A newly expanded and very elegant space occupying the third and fourth floors of the circular end of the library's addition was provided for special collections. The new space was designed to assist the staff in long-term preservation of collections and improved access to them in an environment conducive to research. It provided a closed stack area for rare books and maps as well as a dedicated room to house all of the library's North Carolina–related microforms. The department, which includes the East Carolina Manuscript Collection, the University Archives, the North Carolina Collection, the Rare Book Collection, and the Hoover Collection on International Communism, has continued to expand its preservation of a variety of archival, manuscript, and published materials focused on eastern North Carolina history.

In 1999, in the aftermath of Hurricane Floyd, individuals, churches, and libraries around the region sought assistance from Joyner's preservation and conservation department to help save damaged books and documents.

While neither Joyner Library nor the music library lost materials or equipment on-site as a result of the floodwaters, students, faculty, and libraries around the region were not spared the flood's wrath. Many students lost all of their possessions, including textbooks and library materials. Libraries around the region experienced damage to their collections. In an effort to support students, the library identified over two hundred currently adopted university textbooks in its general circulating collection and placed them on reserve for use by students and faculty who had lost their personal copies. The libraries also suspended overdue fines assessment throughout the fall of 1999. For the next couple of years, working with flood-damaged materials remained one of the major activities of the department. Many requests were made for cleaning and repair of family Bibles as well as church record books that needed to be disassembled and repaired. Flood-damaged books were placed in the freezer/dryer, with an average drying time of twelve to fourteen months, with books made of coated papers or bound with thick covers requiring longer time to dry than those books without covers or made of porous paper.

The Manuscript Collection, originally established by the Department of History in 1966, became a unit of Joyner Library academic services in 1976. This collection has grown to over 4,500 cubic feet of documentary materials with 4,649 individual collections covering 1800 to the present. Since its beginning, the collection has focused on solicitation of manuscripts focusing on five basic categories: North Carolina history, naval and maritime history, American military history, the tobacco industry, and worldwide missionary activities. A variety of unpublished historical works, including financial and legal records, letters, diaries, photographs, genealogical notes, reports, speeches, and approximately five hundred hours of oral histories, are available for patron use.

Several exhibits and collections have been established since the early 1980s, including the Edward Moseley Map of North Carolina, the O. W. "Sonny" Martin Jr. Coast Guard Auxiliary Records Collection, and the Flood of the Century Collection. The Edward Moseley Map of North Carolina was donated by Mrs. John W. Graham of Edenton in 1983. This map was published in London in 1733 and is the only original copy known to exist in the United States. The first accurate map of the Carolinas, the Edward Moseley Map of North Carolina had significant influence on the development of eighteenth-century maps for the region. The O. W. "Sonny" Martin Jr. Coast Guard Auxiliary Records Collection was established in 1988. The collection houses over 225 cubic feet of materials documenting the auxiliary's activities from 1939 to the present. The Flood of the Century Collection was established in 2000 to document the devastation of Hurricanes Dennis and Floyd on eastern North Carolina as well as to document the recovery by the region in the aftermath of $6 billion in property damages and displacement of over 4,200 people. The collection contains photographs, oral interviews, and written statements by people affected by the hurricanes documenting their memories and personal stories.

The University Archives and Records Center was established in 1982 as a permanent depository for university records. A comprehensive initiative was undertaken that year to develop records schedules for all offices within the university. Through the collection and preservation of administrative papers, newspapers, minutes, departmental files, university publications, photographs, and memorabilia, the archives has served as ECU's collective memory and provided a resource for historical, administrative, legal, and record management needs. The center currently maintains approximately 3,500 cubic feet of records and, based on the records schedules, destroys or orders destroyed almost 500 cubic feet of nonpermanent records in the offices of origin. The archives department is currently in the process of creating a Web feature called "ECU Memories" to provide historical information about the university.

Suellyn Lathrop, East Carolina University's archivist and records manager, describes her job as the university's "cradle-to-grave records caretaker."

The North Carolina Collection was started shortly after ECU opened in 1909. The collection was moved from the Whichard Building to Joyner Library in the late 1960s. In 2000, the name of the collection was changed to honor Verona Joyner Langford, an ECU benefactor. From the collection's inception, the library has collected materials pertaining to the entire state, with an emphasis placed on acquiring materials that reflect the history of eastern North Carolina. The collection's concentration on the eastern part of the state reflects and strengthens Joyner Library's mission to be the most important research facility available to the people of eastern North Carolina.

Significant contributions from individual benefactors that have helped the North Carolina Collection expand over the past decade. In May 2001, the collection received a valuable gift of over 1,100 North Carolina–related works of fiction from Snow L. and B. W. C. Roberts of Durham. The extensive scope and rarities in the gift prompted the North Carolina Literary Review to feature the donation in its 2002 edition.

The Minnie Marguerite Wiggins Endowment Fund provides additional funds for acquisitions to the North Carolina Collection. Upon her death in 1999, Miss Wiggins, a former ECU librarian, funded an $80,000 endowment to the collection through her estate. Funds from the endowment have been used to further the library's goal of developing a comprehensive collection about eastern North Carolina. Because of Miss Wiggins's devotion to Joyner Library, she was recently awarded posthumously the first Friend of the Verona Joyner Langford North Carolina Collection Award.

Today over 25,000 volumes can be found in the North Carolina Collection. Approximately 40 periodicals, 4,500 cartographic pieces, 13,000 reels of microfilm, and 37,000 pieces of microfiche are housed in the North Carolina Collection. A small collection of rare books and an extensive vertical file with newspaper articles and other information about Tar Heel people, places, and events can be found in the collection. The department also created the N.C. Periodicals Index, an online index of forty-five periodicals published in the state.

The Rare Book Collection, established in 1992, focuses on collecting print works on maritime history, voyages of exploration, and pre-1865 works regarding slavery. The small collection continues to grow and contains rare published works dating from the sixteenth century to the current time.

The special collections department was awarded two grants from 2001 through 2002 to develop a search guide for rare documents. The grant was awarded through North Carolina's "Exploring Cultural Heritage Online" (ECHO) program and the Library Services Technology Act, a federally funded initiative. The initial grant for $26,000 was awarded in 2001 for the library to demonstrate how well the process works. After a successful first phase, the second grant for $50,000 was awarded. The completed searchable guide allows patrons to locate valuable handwritten manuscripts from the eighteenth, nineteenth, and twentieth centuries that are too fragile for normal library browsing.

The Hoover Collection on International Communism, donated by Dr. J. C. Peele in 1968, contains monographs, serials, pamphlets, leaflets, and other materials relating to communism around the world. Procommunist and anticommunist views of various organizations are available in the collection. At the present time, the collection has more than 5,000 titles.

Joyner Library has made major strides in facilities, staffing, and technology over the past twenty-five years, even in the face of budget reversions and increasing costs. In 1980, Joyner Library was open only ninety-five hours a week. Looking to improve access to patrons, the library pursued technological avenues in addition to expanding hours. The library has continued to expand its virtual library, available 24/7, while increasing its operating hours by 21 hours a week since 1980 for a total of 116 hours each week.

With a peak of in-print periodical subscriptions of 6,120 in 1997, the double-digit increases in subscription fees and the continued tightening of the state budget forced the library to drastically cut its periodical holdings over the next four years. The library undertook a realignment task that reduced the library's reliance upon print journals while increasing the availability of periodicals through electronic sources. By 2001, the library's in-print periodical subscriptions had been reduced to only 2,706. By 2002, electronic journal databases were operational, providing library patrons with access to 10,076 e-journals in addition to the 2,771 in-print periodical subscriptions.

The library currently has over 265,000 square feet of new and renovated space with adequate room for expansion within the next few years. The research collections of the library are continuing to expand at a rapid pace. A major aspect of this expansion includes improvements in the collections supporting doctoral-level programs. The door to expansion of doctoral level resources was opened in 1998 when the University of North Carolina General Administration approved the university's request for reclassification as a Doctoral II institution. The reclassification enabled Joyner Library to obtain additional funding to expand its research collections and staff.

In December 1998, Joyner Library established its first fund-raising development office. Dr. Carroll Varner, director of Joyner Library, saw the need for a full-time development officer and appointed Dwain Teague to the position. Since its establishment, the Joyner Library development office has added an additional staff member to promote library-related events and relocated the office to make it more accessible to patrons. The office sponsors an annual patrons and benefactors' dinner in the library and helps execute other campus events such as the Chancellor's Society, ECU open houses, and homecoming activities. The staff members serve as library liaisons for their benefactor organization, the Friends of Joyner Library at East Carolina University.

In the last two decades, there has been increased emphasis on library development through endowments. Before the 1980s, only two endowments had been established—the Manuscript Endowment Fund and the Special Manuscripts Fund. Since that time, twelve additional endowments have been created, including the Coast Guard Auxiliary Endowment in 1993, the Elizabeth Price Crockford Missionary and Church History Endowment in 1989, the Friends of the Joyner Library Endowment in 1996, the Friends of Joyner Library Patron's Wall Endowment in the mid-1990s, the George C. Smith Library Enrichment Fund in November 1986, the Herrin Endowment in June 2000, the Langford Endowment in October 2000, the Minnie Marguerite Wiggins Endowment in May 2001, the Naval History Endowment in 1996, the Professor Bodo Nischan Manuscript Endowment in August 2002, the Ronnie Barnes African American Resource Center Endowment in March 2002, and the Sarah Batten Endowment in 1995.

In addition to obtaining library resources through endowments, efforts have been made to increase grant acquisitions for the library. The university has pursued individual grant efforts as well as collaborative efforts involving partnerships between the university and institutions throughout the state. One such partnership involved the Joyner Library collaboration with the Outer Banks History Center, a part of the North Carolina Division of Archives and History, to acquire a $10,000 grant from Apex ePublishing for underwriting the Dare County component of the North Carolina History and Digital Library. In 2003, Joyner Library also received a North Carolina Exploring Cultural Heritage Online (NC ECHO) Digitization Grant totaling $49,954. The grant was used to support the digitization of local history titles representing twenty-six eastern North Carolina counties. It also supported the digitization of fiction relating to at least thirteen counties in the eastern part of the state. The digitized collection, known as the Eastern North Carolina Digital History Exhibits, has been developed by the Digitization Center. The center, established in 2001 as a unit of Joyner Library's systems department, is responsible for selecting documents for digitization and writing introductory material to display with exhibits. As of December 2003, the center had developed digitized exhibits on the ECU Centennial, steamboating on rivers feeding the Albemarle Sound, the rise of the tobacco industry at the beginning of the twentieth century, "John Lawson: Imaging a Life," and the Wright Brothers Centennial digital exhibit. In addition to continually expanding the ECU Centennial Digital Exhibit, plans are underway for future exhibits to commemorate the founding of Bath, New Bern, and Edenton.

The music library, housed in the A. J. Fletcher Music Center, is a department of Joyner Library. Created in the early 1960s, it consolidated with Joyner Library on July 1, 1974. In the 1999–2000 academic year, the music library celebrated its twenty-fifth anniversary. Since the music library's inception, the staff and collection have both experienced strong growth. It is the largest music library in eastern North Carolina.

The music library's collection has grown considerably from the 30,000 volumes it held in the early 1980s. In 1990, the music library's collection included 42,000 volumes and could no longer house the music library's complete collection. The library was forced to transfer items to an off-site storage facility. Only after the completion of Joyner Library's expansion and renovation project in 1999 were all of the music library's volumes stored off-site relocated to Joyner. In 1992–93, the music library was renovated. It now contains approximately 73,000 books, scores, periodicals, and media materials on various types and periods of music in 2004.

Paralleling advances in technology, the music library has undergone many changes over the past twenty-five years. In the early 1980s, when overdue items were still posted as a list each week in the hall outside the library, the first computer was acquired for the library, and, in anticipation of online cataloging, a smart bar coding project was implemented. In the late 1980s, the online catalog and circulation system was implemented.

In 1992–93, the library began converting its LP collection to CDs, the first CD-ROM music indexes were purchased, and the library's workstations were connected to Joyner's local area network. In 1993–94, the music library gopher was created, and in the following year it was converted to the music library home page. In 1996–97, the library purchased its first Web-based music index.

The music library has continued to stay abreast of the latest music formats and technologies, as has been reflected by its expanding staff and computing lab support. In 1980, the music library staff consisted of two faculty music librarians and two paraprofessional positions, a library clerk and an information specialist. In the late 1980s, a media technician was also added to the staff. Having acquired its first computer in the early 1980s, the library now houses a thirteen-workstation computer lab and equipment to support a wide range of sound recordings (LP and 45 rpm records, analog and DAT cassette tapes, and CDs), videos (VHS videocassettes and laser discs), minidisks, DVDs, and interactive multimedia discs.

Another significant change has been the introduction of digital exhibits, and the music library has been at the forefront of this technology. In 2004, the music library received two awards from the North Carolina Society of Historians for the digital exhibit "Alice Person: Good Medicine and Good Music," available at http://www.lib.ecu.edu/digital/music/person/. This exhibit presented the life of Alice Person, a nineteenth-century folk musician who was a women's rights advocate as well as a patent medicine entrepreneur. The story of her life was presented online through a compilation of her sheet music arrangements with links to interpretations of her work in audio files, an autobiography, and newspaper and journal articles. The exhibit was awarded the Paul Green Multimedia Award, recognizing the promotion of state history through creative and artistic methods, and the Paul Jehu Barringer Award, one of only two given out of eight hundred entries. The exhibit was described by judges as "one of the finest digital exhibits we have ever had the pleasure of judging. It is a magnificent achievement that has already had a profound effect on North Carolina history."

Through generous contributions, the music library has expanded its resources. A recent acquisition was an eight-hundred-title CD collection donated by Joan and Scott Respess in memory of their father and grandfather, David Serrins. Mr. Serrins was a former ECU professor who established a quality orchestral program at the university during his five-year tenure. His collection contains multiple interpretations of major orchestral works and highlighted Mr. Serrins's favorite composers, Mahler and Mozart.

The Health Sciences Library was created in 1969, one year after the School of Allied Health Sciences was established in response to the growing demand for allied health professionals and health care services in eastern North Carolina as well as for the state as a whole. The school hired its first librarian, Dr. Jo Ann Bell, to serve the needs of the faculty and students in allied health sciences and the medical school. Originally housed in a room in Joyner and later moved to the Old Cafeteria, the library's collection consisted primarily of twelve tons of donated books. Both the University of Kentucky and the Bowman Gray School of Medicine provided duplicate volumes from their collections to assist the fledgling library in its quest. Dr. Robert Phillips of Greensboro and Mrs. Donnell Cobb of Goldsboro also provided significant contributions. Facilities to stack the books for easy access were not available, so the library's books were stacked on a steam table in the back of the cafeteria room. One year later, the library moved to the Biology Building in the science complex.

In 1971, the General Assembly appropriated $1.4 million to create a one-year medical school at East Carolina. It also appropriated $350,000 to establish the Health Affairs Library to serve students and faculty in allied health, nursing, and medicine. Construction of the Carol Belk Building was completed in 1972, and the library was moved to its new facilities. The collection had grown to include 12,683 volumes and was managed by three librarians and one support staff worker. Over the next few years, several significant grants and contracts made possible new library services for its patrons. The Health Affairs Library was approved by the National Library of Medicine as a MEDLINE center in 1973. In the same year, the library was awarded a Regional Medical Library grant for working with community hospitals in eastern North Carolina. In 1974, the library received a contract from Eastern Area Health Education Centers to operate as the learning resource center for eastern North Carolina.

The long-awaited School of Medicine was officially established by the North Carolina General Assembly (Act 116–40.4) in 1975. As a result, the library would experience a rapid growth over the next five years. Technology would also begin to play a more significant role in the management of library resources. In 1978, the library implemented a terminal-based network for cataloging and two years later purchased two TRS-80 microcomputers to automate the current journal list. In 1980, the Health Affairs Library was renamed the Health Sciences Library to more appropriately reflect its mission. In 1981, the library moved into the newly constructed Brody Medical Sciences Building. Within just 12 years, the library had acquired 87,550 volumes and increased its support personnel to 13 librarians and 18 support staff.

Over the next few years the library introduced many technological advances to improve its services. All library functions were automated in 1984 with the installation of an LS/2000 Integrated Library System. The library's first computer lab, consisting of six IBM PCs and three Apple IIes, was introduced in the audiovisuals department in 1985. To commemorate the retirement of the card catalog, a New Orleans–style "funeral" was held in 1987 when the card catalog was removed. By 1992, all library employees had been provided a desktop PC that was linked to a local network and had access to remote information resources.

In 1993, the library was renamed William E. Laupus Health Science Library in honor of a former dean of the East Carolina University School of Medicine. The library continued to implement leading-edge technologies to improve its services. The library, in conjunction with East Carolina University's Joyner Library, implemented the first client-server integrated library system in the state of North Carolina, replacing its LS/2000 with the Marquis Integrated Library System.

In 1997, Dr. Jo Ann Bell retired and Dr. Dorothy A. Spencer was hired as the library's second director in its history. In 1999, the university-wide bond referendum was passed. It included funding for a new health sciences library facility as a part of the Learning Village project for the Division of Health Sciences. In 2001, wireless computer access was established for patrons visiting the library. In the summer of 2002, the library transferred its social work and criminal justice collections to the Joyner Library to facilitate support of these academic programs. In 2003, the library was once again renamed, this time its name was shortened to Laupus Library, to parallel the shortened name of Joyner Library. Also in 2003, the Country Doctor Museum and its collections were donated to the university, citing the university's focus on rural primary health care. The Country Doctor Museum, established in 1967, includes artifacts pertaining to nursing, pharmacy, homeopathy, and dentistry. The Health Sciences Library has come far from its origins of donated books and one librarian to be a state-of-the-art library facility with over 48,000 monographs, 29,147 microforms, 846 print periodicals, 8,111 e-journals (jointly held with Joyner Library), an 83-station computer lab, 16 librarians, and 24 support staff.

REFERENCE

ECU Academic Library Services. Papers. East Carolina University Archives.

## CHAPTER FIVE

Resources

FREDERICK NISWANDER

EAST CAROLINA UNIVERSITY is an academic enterprise that educates over 20,000 students. It is also a food-service business that serves over 15,000 meals each day, a multiple-location housing operation that accommodates 5,000 students, a medical clinic with revenues of almost $100 million, an NCAA Division I athletic program fielding 20 teams with over 400 student-athletes, an employer of more than 4,500 individuals, and a faculty that performs basic and applied research ranging from computational chemistry to studying entrepreneurship in a rural setting.

ECU is a complex university in the fullest sense of that word. The manner in which the university funds its diverse operations is also complex and has changed over time.

ECU obtains financial resources from five primary sources: tuition and fees, appropriations from the state of North Carolina, grants and contracts, the medical practice plan, and auxiliaries. Table 5.1 details the amounts and proportions of each source for fiscal year 2004.[1]

Tuition and fees: In 2004–5, in-state tuition amounted to $2,135 per student (it was $12,349 for out-of-state residents) and fees were $1,319 for a total of $3,454 for the academic year per in-state student. Student fees were assessed to support the operation of the Mendenhall Student Center, student recreational facilities and operations, intercollegiate athletics, the student newspaper, student health service, student government, and similar activities.

State appropriations: Public higher education is sold at a price far less than its cost. In other words, the amount paid by in-state students for tuition and fees does not approach the cost of that education. For universities

TABLE 5.1   Revenue Sources for Fiscal Year 2004

Revenue Category	Amount	Percentage
Tuition and fees	$80,094,000	17%
State appropriations	171,008,000	36%
Grants and contracts	58,748,000	12%
Medical Faculty Practice Plan	93,318,000	20%
Auxiliaries	56,740,000	12%
Other	13,761,000	3%
Total	$473,669,000	100%

such as ECU, the state provides a considerable portion of the funding necessary to operate the university enterprise. ECU is, thus, a "state-supported" university. As shown above, state appropriations are the largest single component of total university revenue at 36 percent.

Grants and contracts: Universities are a significant store of intellectual capacity. Universities contract with federal, state, corporate, and foundation entities to discover new knowledge; improve and expand existing ideas, processes, or products; and perform other agreed-upon work.

Medical Faculty Practice Plan (MFPP): One of ECU's academic units is the Brody School of Medicine. Through its faculty, the Brody School operates a medical clinic that serves the community and region. The amount noted above represents the net patient revenues from the operation of the clinic.

Auxiliaries: Auxiliaries are the nonacademic operations of the university that generate revenue. The primarily auxiliaries are student housing, dining, and the bookstore. These three operations account for almost 75 percent of the auxiliary revenue in FY 2004.

Other revenue: This category is predominately investment income and noncapital gifts to the university.

Most of this chapter will focus on tuition and fees and state appropriations, the two largest components of annual operations, with some discussion related to grants and contracts. National statistics and comparisons generally exclude medical practice plans and auxiliaries primarily because these activities are not designed to support the basic academic mission of the university. In effect, they are self-contained and support themselves. For example, revenues generated by housing support the operation of the dormitory system. Excess revenue (if any) is generally not used to support faculty salaries or classroom building operations or other academic operations.

TABLE 5.2   Expenses in Fiscal Year 2003–2004

Expense Category	Amount	Percentage
Salaries and benefits	$310,849,000	66%
Supplies and materials	51,219,000	11%
Services	73,219,000	15%
Scholarships and fellowships	11,009,000	2%
Utilities	13,082,000	3%
Depreciation	14,134,000	3%
Total	$473,512,000	100%

TABLE 5.3   Information Related to Physical Property

	Fall 2004	Fall 1980
Property, buildings, and equipment, at original cost	$601,719,000	$104,639,000
Estimated replacement cost	930,740,000	Unknown
Acres of land owned	1,376	411
Number of buildings	230	76
Square feet of buildings	5,680,000	2,825,926
Number of classrooms	240	Unknown
Number of labs	686	Unknown
Number of computers and servers	8,395	< 100

EXPENSES

East Carolina University spends its financial resources primarily on salaries and benefits for its 4,500 employees. FY 2004 operating expenses are outlined in table 5.2.

FACILITIES

East Carolina University is a large enterprise in terms of the property, buildings, and equipment it has accumulated over the last hundred years. It has grown substantially since 1980.

ECU received almost $200 million from the systemwide $3 billion bond package for higher education capital improvements passed by North Carolina voters in November 2000. This funding has accelerated the construc-

TABLE 5.4   State Appropriations to Education, FY 2004–2005

	Dollars	Percentage
Public schools	$6.3 billion	71%
UNC system	1.9 billion	21%
Community colleges	0.7 billion	8%
Total	$8.9 billion	100%

tion and renovation of buildings at a rapid pace. Since 2000, construction activities include a new Science and Technology building, a new Allied Health building, and renovations of Flanagan, Rivers, Howell, and Old Cafeteria.

Some of the major sources of annual revenue have changed over the last two decades. Because of the long time horizon, some dollar amounts have been adjusted for inflation. In the twenty-five years since 1981, inflation has increased by a total of over 120 percent. For many comparisons, inflation-adjusted numbers are more meaningful. To adjust for inflation, we use the consumer price index for all urban consumers from the U.S. Bureau of Labor Statistics. Inflation-adjusted numbers are stated in terms of 2004 dollars.

It is also important to note that information becomes available at different times. Some comparisons that follow will be through FY 2004, while other analyses will have data through FY 2005. The ending date used does not affect the observations and trends noted in the data.

STATE APPROPRIATIONS

General State Appropriations

The state of North Carolina has a long history of financially supporting education. Since 1980, funding for education grew from $2.1 billion to $8.9 billion, an increase of 325 percent. Adjusted for inflation, the growth was from $4.6 billion to $8.9 billion, or 93 percent.

In FY 2005, this $8.9 billion was allocated to public schools, community colleges, and higher education as shown in table 5.4.

Figure 5.1 illustrates the change in education funding in North Carolina since FY 1981.

Funding for public schools increased from about $1.4 billion to $6.3 billion, an increase of 350 percent, while the UNC system recorded a 270 percent increase from $515 million to $1.9 billion.

FIGURE 5.1   State Appropriations for Education (not adjusted for inflation)

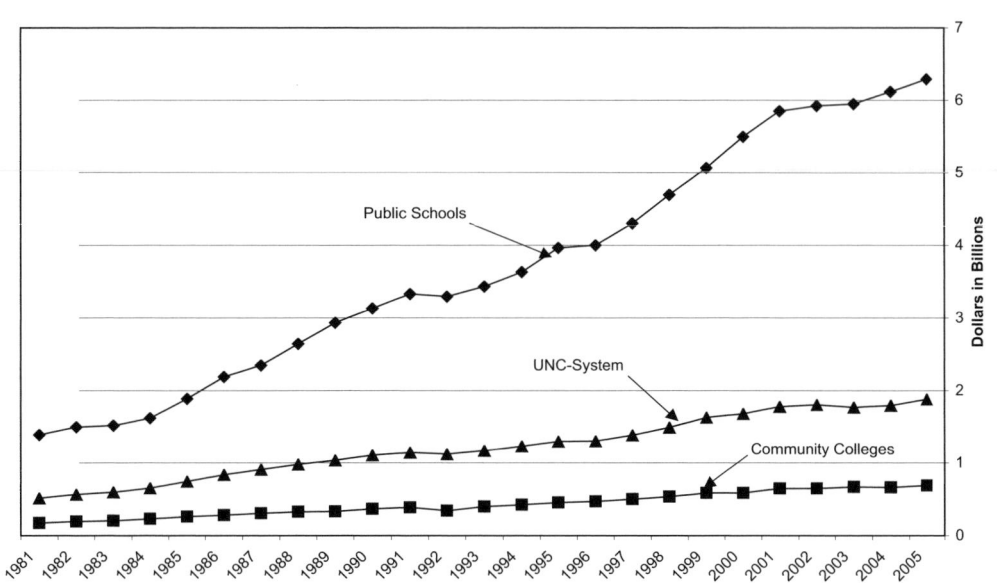

State Appropriations for Education (not adjusted for inflation)

Although education funding increased in total over the FY 1981 to FY 2005 period, education received a smaller and smaller portion of the current operations budget of the state.

In FY 1981, state funding for education was 66 percent of operating appropriations. In FY 2005, the proportion dropped ten percentage points, to 56 percent. Each of the three components of education funding lost ground —public schools and the UNC system lost 4 percent each, and the community college system lost 2 percent.

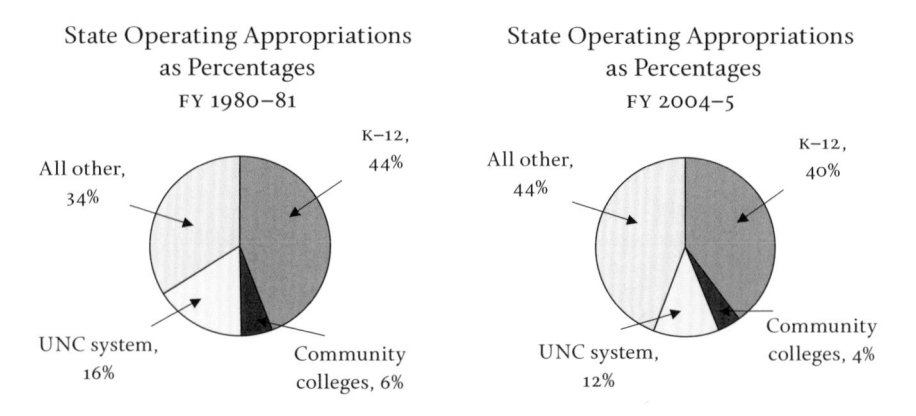

State Operating Appropriations as Percentages FY 1980–81

K–12, 44%
All other, 34%
UNC system, 16%
Community colleges, 6%

State Operating Appropriations as Percentages FY 2004–5

K–12, 40%
All other, 44%
UNC system, 12%
Community colleges, 4%

While the loss of 10 percent may not seem like much, if education were to be funded in FY 2005 at the same proportion that existed in FY 1981, total funding for education would have been $10.5 billion rather than $8.9 billion, a $1.6 billion difference.

UNC System Appropriations

As noted, the UNC system has seen its state appropriations grow from $515 million to $1.9 billion over the FY 1981 to FY 2005 period. Adjusted to 2004 dollars, appropriations grew from a base of $1.1 billion to the current $1.9 billion, around a 70 percent jump. Growth in state appropriations, adjusted and unadjusted, is shown in figure 5.2.

Both adjusted and unadjusted appropriations show a steady upward trend. Missing from the analysis is the growth in the systemwide student population, which climbed from 116,588 in fall 1980 to 189,615 in fall 2004, an increase of 63 percent. As shown in figure 5.3, while unadjusted appropriations per student increased from $4,419 to $9,909, the inflation-adjusted per-student amount is virtually the same in FY 2005 as it was in FY 1981. Adjusted for inflation, per-student appropriations have varied between $10,000 and $12,000 for the last twenty-five years and are currently on the low end of that range.

FIGURE 5.2   State Appropriations for the UNC System

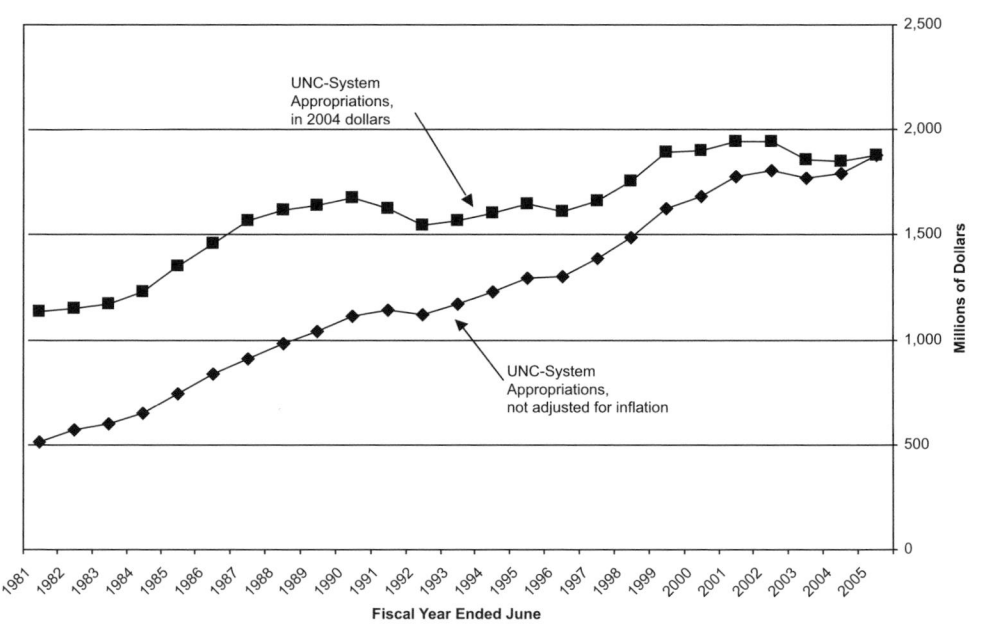

FIGURE 5.3   State Appropriations per Student for the UNC System

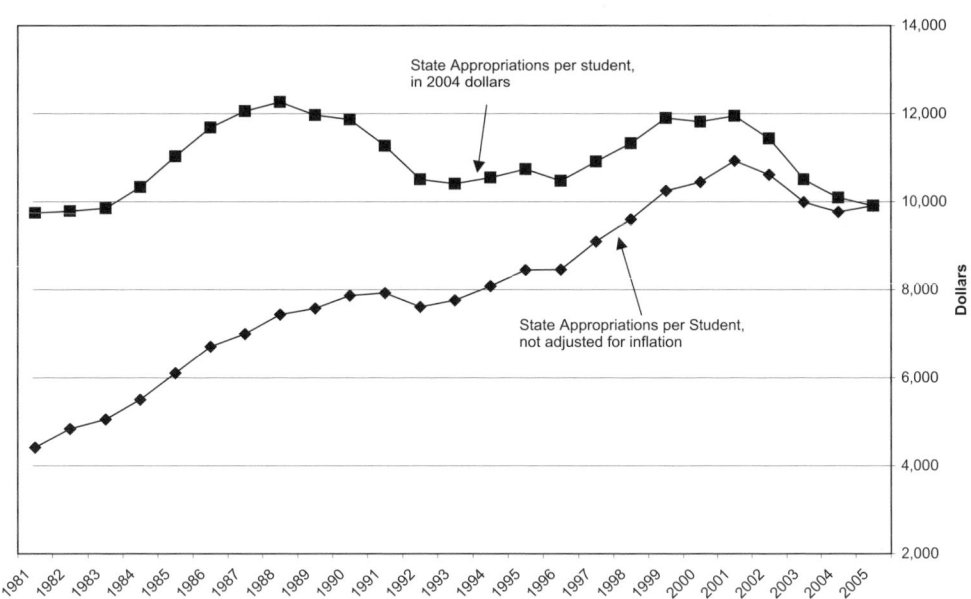

ECU State Appropriations

East Carolina University receives an appropriation of state funding through the UNC system, as do all other system schools. As illustrated in figure 5.4, ECU funding, as a proportion of system funding, has varied from a low of 8.5 percent in FY 2002 to a high of almost 11 percent in 1992. The FY 2004 proportion of about 9.5 percent is slightly below the long-term average of 9.7 percent.

ECU received $171 million in state appropriations in FY 2004, compared to FY 1981 appropriations of $44 million. Adjusted for inflation, appropriations started at a base of $94.8 million. Figure 5.5 illustrates the growth in state appropriations flowing to ECU.

In terms of inflation-adjusted dollars, figure 5.5 clearly shows that appropriations have increased only modestly since FY 1987, when they were $151.6 million. Over that same period, the student population grew from 14,459 to 21,756, an increase of 50 percent.

As a result, while per-student state appropriations have increased slightly, they have not kept pace with inflation. Figure 5.6 illustrates that inflation-adjusted state appropriations per student have fallen from a FY 1988 high of $10,780 to their current level of $7,860. Further, as was the case with inflation-adjusted per-student appropriations at the system level,

FIGURE 5.4   ECU Appropriations as a Percentage of UNC System Appropriations

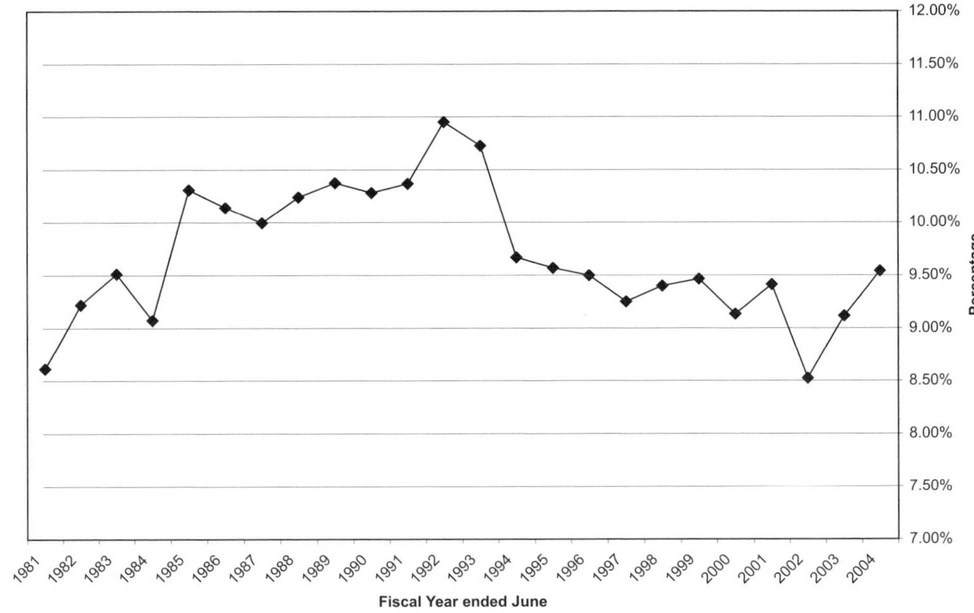

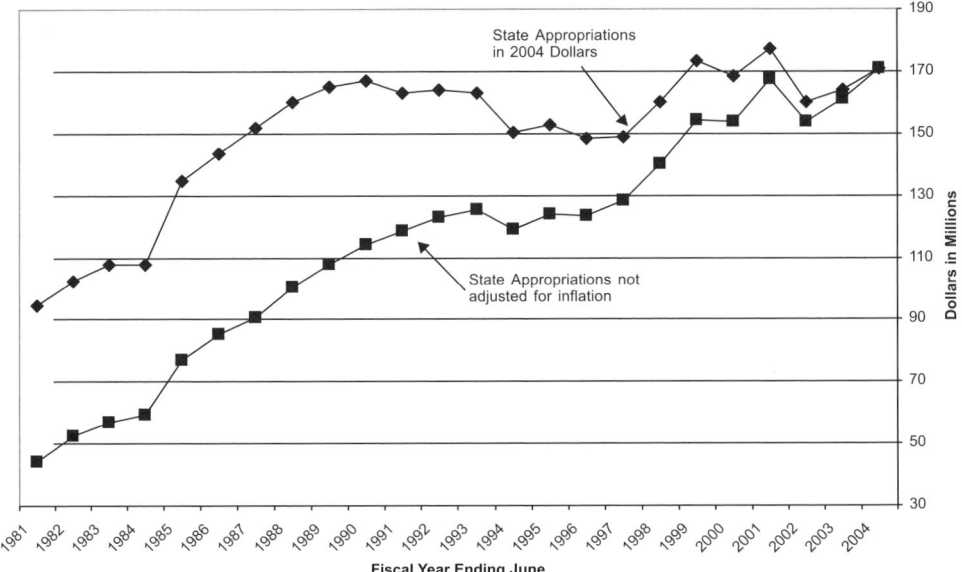

FIGURE 5.5   State Appropriations to ECU

FIGURE 5.6 Per-Student State Appropriations and Inflation-Adjusted State Appropriations to ECU

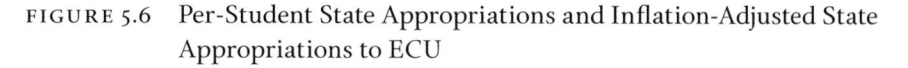

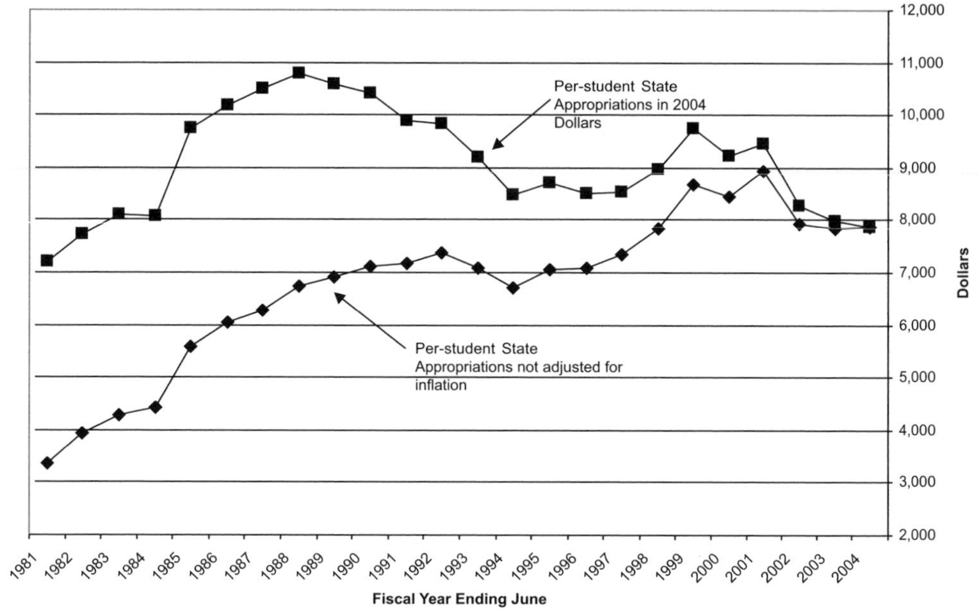

ECU's appropriations in FY 2004 were not materially different than they were in FY 1981 and were virtually identical to FY 1982.

On the surface, it may seem reasonable that, on an inflation-adjusted basis, appropriations are almost the same as they were twenty-five years ago. However, ECU is fundamentally different today. In FY 1981, there were ninety-seven degree programs, including five Ph.D.s, and now there are over two hundred degree programs and fifteen Ph.D.s. In FY 1981, ECU did not have an engineering program, had only a handful of personal computers, and had not yet thought of using robotics in the operating room. Then, ECU operated 76 buildings; now the number is 230. Without question, ECU is much more complex, academically and operationally, than it was in 1981, but state appropriations have not kept pace. The money must come from somewhere. Thus, we now turn to tuition and fees.

TUITION AND FEES

Public higher education is sold to the user (or his or her family) at a price far less than its cost. In other words, the amount paid by in-state students for tuition and fees does not approach the cost of that education.

In general, tuition revenue goes into the general operating fund to pay for academic-related costs such as salaries and benefits, business operations, utilities, maintenance, and the like, while the fee component is earmarked for specified student-related activities and expenses such as student health services, student recreation, intercollegiate athletics, the student newspaper, operation of the Mendenhall Student Center, and similar activities and programs.

Since FY 1981, annual in-state tuition and fees have increased from $578 ($1,234 in 2004 dollars) to $3,131 in FY 2004, an increase of 441 percent on an unadjusted basis, or 154 percent when taking inflation into account. The compounded annual growth rate in inflation-adjusted tuition and fees is 4.1 percent per year. Tuition and fee revenue over the FY 1981 to FY 2004 period is illustrated in figure 5.7.

The primary educational mission of the university is, for the most part, funded by tuition and fees and state appropriations. As noted, inflation-adjusted state appropriations have been falling for almost twenty years, particularly in the last six years (see figure 5.6). We also see that inflation-adjusted tuition and fees have increased, most significantly over the last five years (as shown in figure 5.7). These are not isolated, unrelated events. Let us now examine these two revenue streams in combination.

STATE APPROPRIATIONS AND TUITION AND FEES IN COMBINATION

For the last twenty years, the combination of tuition and fees and state appropriations has provided revenue of between $10,000 and $12,000 per student on an inflation-adjusted basis (figure 5.8).

Figure 5.8 is constructed by combining the per-student state appropriations information from figure 5.6 with the per-student tuition and fees information from figure 5.7. It clearly shows that the proportion of the total "education-related" revenue paid by tuition and fees has increased while the total revenue per student has not appreciably changed. For example, in FY 2002, per-student appropriations were $8,258 and per-student tuition and fees were $2,676, for a total of $10,934. In FY 2004, the total of the two categories was $10,991 (an increase of only $57), yet tuition and fees increased by $455 to $3,131, while state appropriations fell by $398 to $7,860. Also note that because the two components start at different levels, the percentage increase in tuition and fees (17 percent) is a far greater change than the percentage decrease in state appropriations (5 percent).

Another way to look at the changing relationship between tuition and fees and state appropriations is to examine them as proportions. If we com-

FIGURE 5.7 Annual In-State Tuition and Fees for an In-State Student

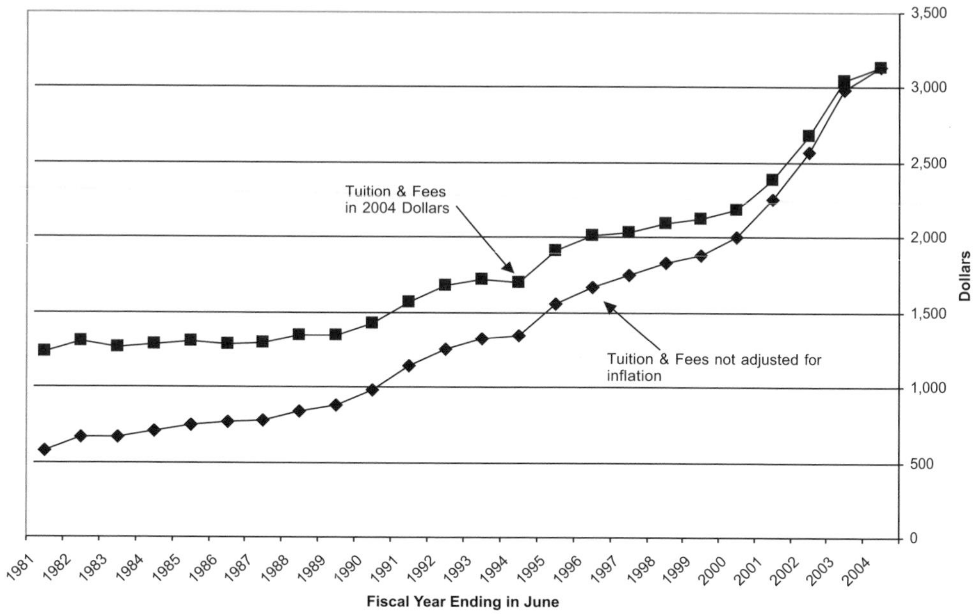

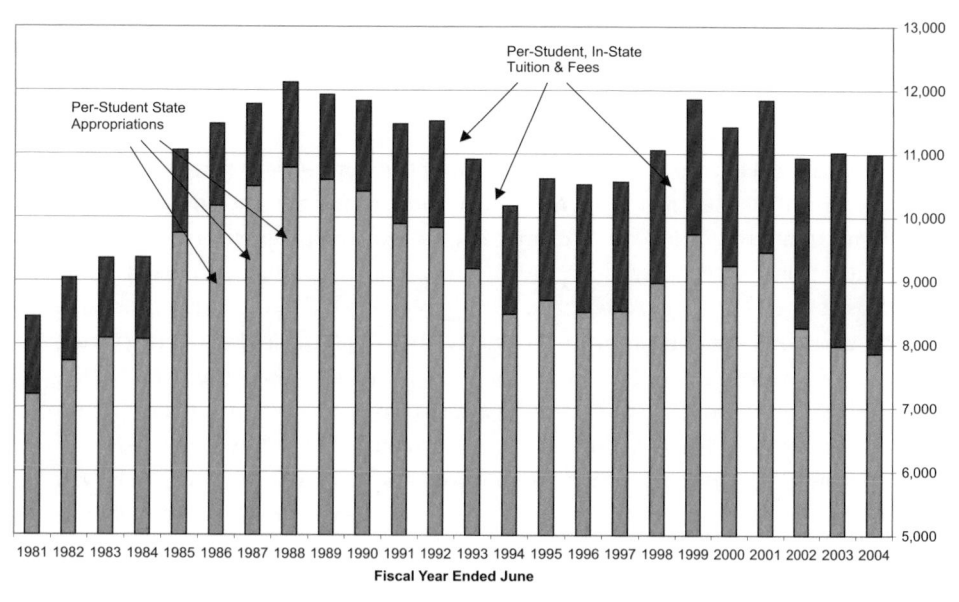

Tuition & Fees in 2004 Dollars

Tuition & Fees not adjusted for inflation

Fiscal Year Ending in June

Dollars

FIGURE 5.8   Inflation Adjusted Per-Student Appropriations and In-State
Tuition and Fees

Per-Student, In-State Tuition & Fees

Per-Student State Appropriations

Fiscal Year Ended June

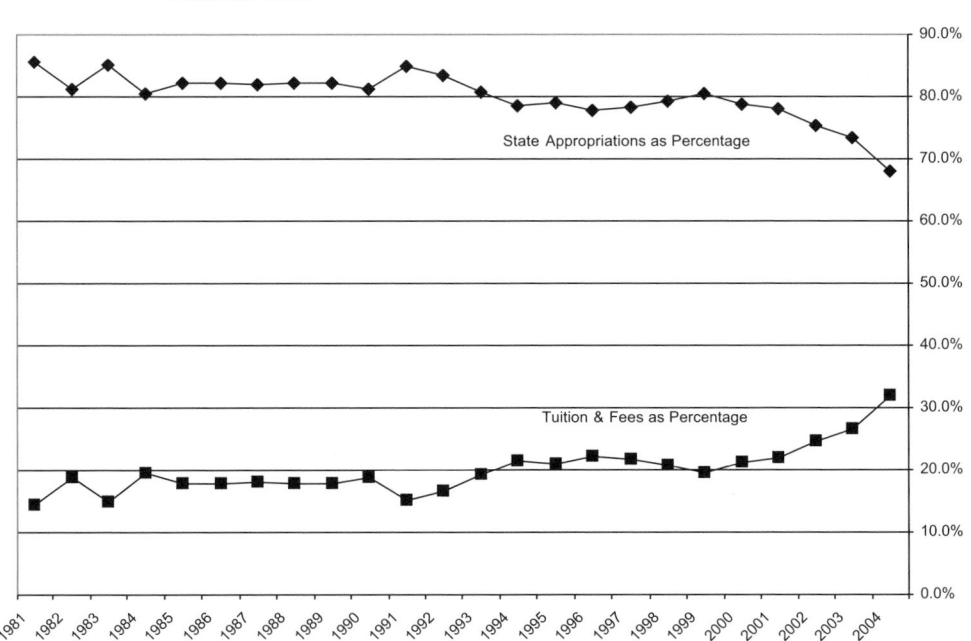

bine per-student state appropriations and tuition and fees, the appropriations component is about 80 percent of the total, with tuition and fees making up the remaining 20 percent. That was the case until about FY 2001.
From that point forward, the tuition and fees proportion has increased as
the appropriations proportion decreased until, in FY 2004, the proportions
were 68 percent/32 percent. Figure 5.9 provides data relative to these combined revenue streams from FY 1981 to 2004.

Of greater concern to higher education in North Carolina (and other
states) is that the downward trend in per-student state appropriations is
unlikely to reverse. Fundamentally, there are significant upward pressures
on state spending coming from such areas a Medicaid, public safety, and
unfunded federal mandates. For example, in 1981, Medicaid was about
4.5 percent of state budgets on a nationwide basis. The percentage is now
approaching 8 percent, with all indicators pointing to continual increases.
That reality is accompanied by a reluctance to increase state revenues
(taxes). In such an environment, something needs to give. Lately, it has been
education.

Grants and contracts provide an additional revenue stream that can support the research mission (primarily) or teaching mission (occasionally) of a university. Grants are generally provided to one or more researchers to explore a specific problem or issue, the outcome of which may not be known with certainty. Alternatively, individuals or the university may contract with an external governmental agency, corporation, or foundation to perform a defined task or tasks and provide the external group with a specified report or other deliverable end product.

Revenue provided by grants and contracts generally goes to the researcher to pay for equipment, graduate assistants, summer support, and other costs associated with performing the tasks outlined in the grant or contract. Some grants, generally from federal agencies, are accompanied by an additional payment for overhead. This additional payment is used to support the research infrastructure of the university.

Figure 5.10 gives the amount of revenue from grants and contracts in total and adjusted for inflation. It is important to note that the jump in revenue for FY 2002 is primarily, but not solely, because the accounting rules for grant reporting changed in that year. It is not feasible to reconcile between the two reporting systems.

FIGURE 5.10   Revenue from Grants and Contracts

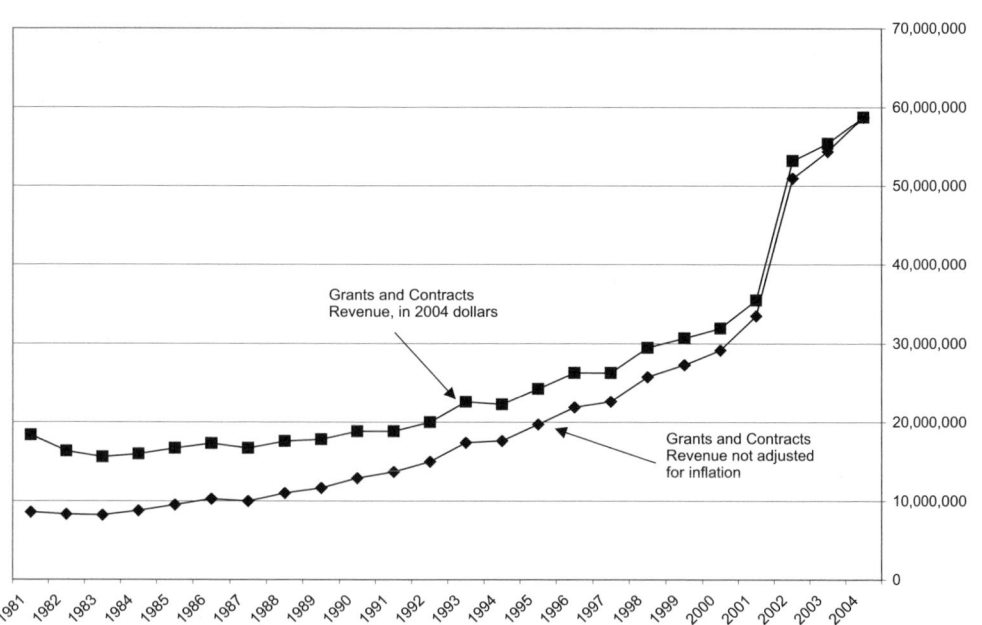

The university is placing an increased emphasis on grants and contracts funding. In part, this is because of the increased research activities engaged in by the faculty. It is also in response to the reduced level of state appropriations support and a realization that further reductions are likely to occur in the future.

COMBINED REVENUE FROM PRIMARY SOURCES

When we combine the three primary revenue streams—tuition and fees, state appropriations, and grants and contracts—we get a more complete picture of the funding relationships within the university.

Figure 5.11 tracks the proportions of the three major revenue sources over time. For many years, state appropriations accounted for around 75 percent of the total, but they have dropped to about 55 percent in FY 2004. The difference has been made up by tuition and fees that have risen from 12 percent to 26 percent and by additional grants and contracts that now account for 19 percent of the total. The information provided in figure 5.11 reinforces the trends noted when we examined the three revenue sources individually.

FIGURE 5.11   All Primary Funding Sources as a Percentage

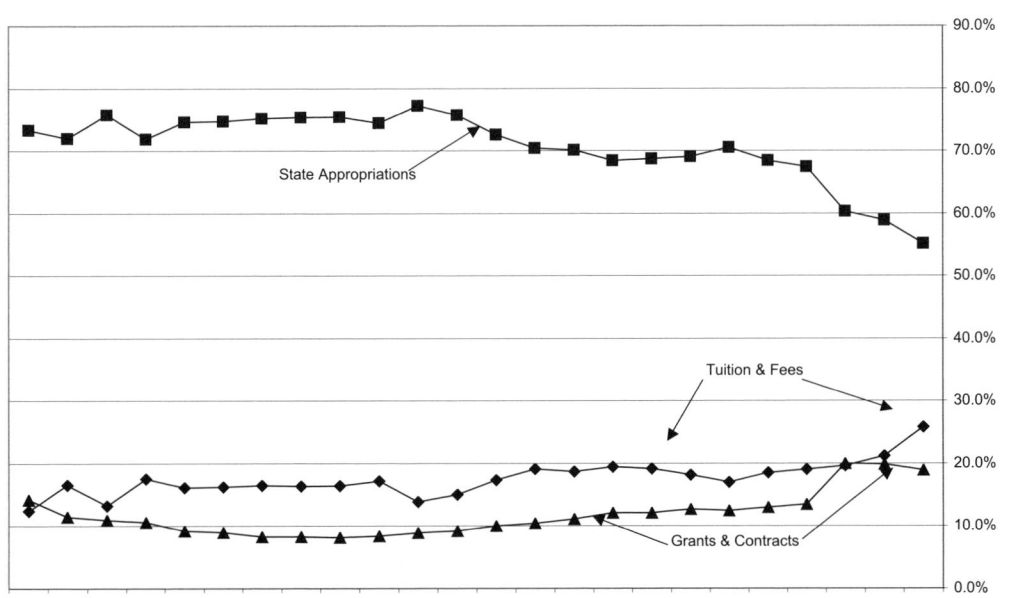

Another revenue source for a university is contributions from alumni and friends. This revenue stream provides funding for student scholarships, endowed chairs for faculty, operating money for departments and colleges, and general support for faculty and students. In many ways, private money (as this revenue stream is called) makes the difference between good and great. Throughout higher education and at ECU, it is increasingly difficult to provide a quality education, engage in meaningful research, and make a positive difference in the lives of students and those we serve without the availability of incremental dollars from contributors.

Contributions are administered by the ECU Foundation.[2] The ECU Foundation provides fund-raising assistance, allocates contributions to the proper account or purpose, invests foundation assets for long-term growth and stability, oversees disbursement of funds, and accounts for its activities to stakeholders.

Over the last twenty-five years, assets held by the ECU Foundation have grown substantially. As shown in figure 5.12, foundation assets were $3.6 million at the end of June 1981 and have steadily increased to almost $121 million at the end of FY 2005. The vast majority of foundation assets are invested in a diversified portfolio of stocks and bonds, CDs, and short-term

FIGURE 5.12   ECU Foundation Assets at Current Value

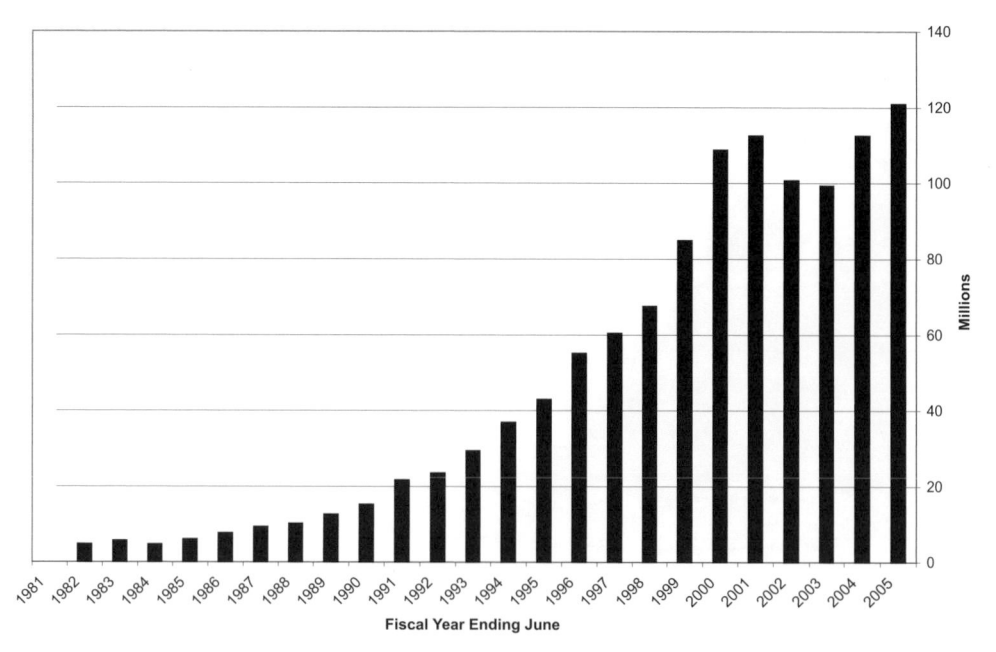

Fiscal Year Ending June

FIGURE 5.13   Annual Gifts to ECU (Excluding Deferred Gifts)

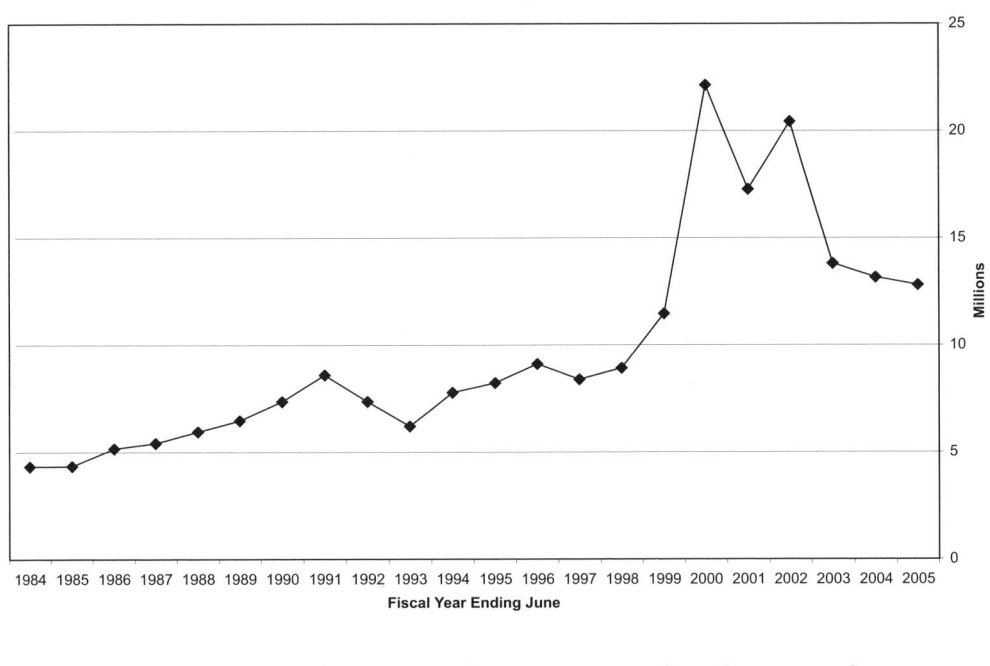

cash investments. The foundations do own some nonliquid assets such as land. The downturn in foundation assets in FY 2002 and FY 2003 is a direct result of the substantial downturn in the equity markets during that time.

The dollar amount of annual giving is provided in figure 5.13.[3] The general trend in annual giving has been a slow but steady increase from $4.3 million in FY 1984 to $12.8 million in FY 2005. The modest level of overall annual giving means that a gift of $5 million or more can have a noticeable effect on the total, as evidenced in FY 2000 and FY 2002.

REGIONAL AND NATIONAL DATA AND TRENDS

The economic challenges facing North Carolina are not unique to the state. Regionally and nationally, funding for higher education is dropping both on an inflation-adjusted basis and as a proportion of state budgets. While there is never enough money to do everything we would like, given the economic and political climate in the United States, North Carolina colleges and universities are better off than higher education institutions in most other states.[4]

Table 5.5 shows the percentage change in state funding to higher education over each of the last three fiscal years for North Carolina, states in our region, and nationally.

TABLE 5.5   Annual Percentage Change in Higher Education Funding:
North Carolina and States in the Region

	Percentage Change FY 2004– FY 2005	Percentage Change FY 2003– FY 2004	Percentage Change FY 2002– FY 2003	Cumulative Percentage Change
All States	3.8%	(2.1%)	0.0%	1.6%
North Carolina	6.2%	(0.1%)	0.3%	6.4%
Virginia	10.6%	(5.7%)	(5.3%)	(1.2%)
South Carolina	1.9%	(10.0%)	(3.0%)	(11.0%)
Tennessee	0.0%	(5.5%)	7.7%	1.8%
Kentucky	1.3%	4.4%	2.9%	8.8%
West Virginia	(3.9%)	(5.7%)	.4%	(9.0%)
Georgia	1.4%	0.2%	1.6%	3.2%
Maryland	2.1%	(6.3%)	1.5%	(2.9%)
Annual inflation	3.3%	1.9%	2.4%	7.8%

Note: The cumulative change column (right-hand column) is not simply the sum of the annual change columns because of the compounding effect of the annual changes. Numbers in parentheses indicate negative cumulative change.

Table 5.5 illustrates some key points.

Nationally, the cumulative change in state appropriations over the last three fiscal years is only 1.6 percent—far below the inflation rate over that time. Half the states have a positive cumulative change, while the other half are negative. Only North Carolina has fared better than the national average in each of the last three fiscal years. Over the last three fiscal years, only Kentucky has received cumulative increases in excess of the inflation rate. North Carolina comes close but is still 1.4 percent behind on an inflation-adjusted basis.

Table 5.5 examines only the change in total dollars to higher education. It does not take into account increases in the student population. As we noted earlier in this chapter (see table 5.3, for example), per-student appropriations have been falling in North Carolina even while total spending has increased. For states such as West Virginia, South Carolina, Maryland, or Virginia, in particular, the combination of rising student enrollment and decreases in the level of state funding has had a severe adverse effect on educational quality, student learning, and campus morale.

Another instructive comparison is to examine state funding per capita or per $1,000 in personal income. Table 5.6 provides relevant data.

TABLE 5.6   Appropriations for Higher Education per Capita and per
$1,000 of Personal Income: North Carolina and Selected
States in the Region

Fiscal Year 2005	Appropriations per $1,000 personal income		Appropriations per capita	
	Dollars	National Rank	Dollars	National Rank
All States	$6.59		$214.96	
North Carolina	$10.55	5	$307.74	6
Virginia	$5.68	38	$199.60	33
South Carolina	$5.90	35	$158.99	45
Tennessee	$6.23	29	$184.49	36
Kentucky	$9.93	10	$270.05	10
West Virginia	$7.27	20	$186.96	35
Georgia	$7.12	24	$215.58	27
Maryland	$5.36	41	$209.47	30

Table 5.6 shows that, nationwide, states provided appropriations to
higher education of $6.59 for each $1,000 of personal income of the residents of the state. Alternatively, states funded higher education at a rate of
$214.96 for each person living in the state.

It is clear that North Carolina provides state appropriations per unit of
income or per capita materially better than both the national average and
the states in our region. The high national ranking of North Carolina is not
a recent occurrence—North Carolina has been in the national top ten for
over twenty years.

The national trend of state appropriations per unit of income or per capita has been downward, similar to what we have seen in North Carolina.
Table 5.7 shows the trend of state appropriations per $1,000 of personal in-
come over the last fifteen years.

Note that, almost without exception, each period is lower than the one
before. It is also interesting to observe that, in FY 1990, appropriations
were relatively close from state to state. However, in FY 2005, the disparity
is significant.

The increase in tuition and fees at ECU is also not just a localized phe-
nomenon. Nationwide, tuition and fees have been rising, in large part to
compensate for the per-student decreases in state appropriations. Table 5.8
illustrates the change in inflation-adjusted tuition and fees over the last ten
years.

TABLE 5.7   State Appropriations to Higher Education per
$1,000 of Personal Income

	FY 1990	FY 1995	FY 2000	FY 2005
All States	$9.74	$8.02	$7.64	$6.59
North Carolina	$15.71	$13.28	$12.17	$10.55
Virginia	$10.42	$6.99	$7.35	$5.68
South Carolina	$13.66	$10.36	$9.31	$5.90
Tennessee	$10.71	$9.21	$7.25	$6.23
Kentucky	$11.51	$10.24	$10.34	$9.93
West Virginia	$11.42	$10.34	$10.19	$7.27
Georgia	$9.14	$8.43	$7.54	$7.12
Maryland	$9.14	$6.64	$6.37	$5.36

TABLE 5.8   Average Tuition and Fees, Inflation Adjusted
to 2004 Dollars: Four-Year Public Colleges and
Universities

	FY 1994	FY 2004	Change	Percentage change
Nationwide	$2,535	$4,694	$2,159	85%
South	$2,183	$3,758	$1,575	72%
ECU	$1,704	$3,131	$1,427	84%

Average tuition and fees in the South are less than the nationwide figures, and ECU is lower than the average in the South. Over the last ten years, ECU's tuition and fees increase (in dollars) is smaller than the average school in the South or the nation. On a percentage basis, the ECU increase is roughly at the national average and is slightly more than schools in the South (although ECU's dollar change is smaller, the percentage increase is higher because of the lower base).

CONCLUSION

In this chapter, we have examined both how East Carolina University is financed and the statewide and nationwide trends in university revenue streams. East Carolina University is a large and complex higher education institution. It has gone far beyond simply educating students, and its financing is far beyond simply tuition and fees.

The statewide and national trends in university financing—lower state appropriations, more tuition and fees, greater emphasis on grants and contracts and private fund-raising—are unlikely to reverse in future years. As ECU enters its second century, it will become increasingly important for the university to aggressively make the case for state appropriations and to seek and expand additional revenue sources to enable the institution to continue to serve the students, alumni, and citizens of the region and state.

NOTES

1. ECU is a component part of the state of North Carolina. As such, its accounting does not follow a calendar year but instead follows a fiscal year that runs from July 1 of one year until June 30 of the next. Thus, the 2003–4 fiscal year runs from July 1, 2003, to June 30, 2004. A fiscal year can be identified with reference to the ending year. For example, the 2003–4 fiscal year is called "fiscal 2004" or "FY 2004."
2. A number of different entities raise private funds for ECU. These include the ECU Foundation (the primary academic entity), the Alumni Foundation, the ECU Endowment Fund, the Real Estate Foundation, the Medical Foundation, and the Educational Foundation of ECU (the Pirate Club). For our purposes, we will refer to all these groups collectively as the "ECU Foundation."
3. Figure 5.13 excludes deferred gifts, such as the value of a bequest in a will or a gift that will be made in a future year. The amount of deferred gifts has historically been well under $1 million per year, except for FY 2000 and FY 2002, when ECU realized deferred gifts of $6.7 million and $12.5 million, respectively.
4. This section uses national data that include all spending beyond K–12. Thus, the data in this section include spending for state-supported community colleges as well as four-year colleges and universities.

REFERENCES

Center for the Study of Education Policy at Illinois State University. "Grapevine: An Annual Compilation of Data on State Tax Appropriations for the General Operation of Higher Education," www.coe.ilstu.edu/grapevine

ECU Foundation. Papers. East Carolina University.

ECU Vice Chancellor for Administration & Finance. *Annual Report*, 1980–2004, Greenville, NC: East Carolina University.

U.S. Bureau of Labor Statistics. *Consumer Price Index*, Washington, D.C.

UNC General Administration. Papers. University of North Carolina General Administration.

## CHAPTER SIX

Student Life

BRETT HURSEY

BY DEFINITION, students shape the core identity of any institution of higher education. Many of the changes at East Carolina University over the past generation have been directly reflected in the university's robust, diverse, and dynamic undergraduate and graduate population. Without doubt, the explosive growth in enrollment during the last twenty-three years has had a significant, permanent impact on the profile and character of the typical ECU student, but many other factors have played a part in gradually shaping today's student body—over 20,000 strong. Pride can be taken in the fact that East Carolina University not only has greatly increased its population, but also has significantly augmented the ethnic and cultural diversity of that population as well. Readers will undoubtedly notice a bittersweet "side-effect" of the university's growth—especially prevalent in the post-Vietnam era—a certain loss of innocence that sprang from a time when colleges were often perceived as a type of sanctuary, shielding students from the harsher realities of life. However, observers of the institution will also note that, despite its impressive numerical expansion, ECU's student body has maintained many of its best "small college" attributes—especially its long-standing active interest in student government and community relations, as well as the robust social activity that has traditionally been a widely acclaimed facet of East Carolina University's student life.

THE AWESOME EIGHTIES

1980

Ronald Reagan is elected, defeating Jimmy Carter. 3-M introduces Post-It Notes. CNN begins broadcasting as the world's first all-news network. Bill Gates licenses MS-DOS to IBM. Pink Floyd releases The Wall.

The decade at East Carolina University began with a bang as the long-anticipated "Liquor by the Drink" referendum easily passed in Greenville. Turnout was approximately 45 percent with 61.5 percent of voters supporting the new initiative. However, local merchants selling products potentially used as drug paraphernalia were in danger of being put out of business by the Federal Anti-paraphernalia Act proposed in the state's General Assembly. The far-reaching law made it a crime to own any equipment that could be used to plant, store, contain, conceal, inject, ingest, inhale, or otherwise introduce a controlled substance into the human body.

Meanwhile, entrance requirements were slowly rising at ECU, according to Ron Brown, assistant director of admissions. Chancellor Thomas Brewer supported the goal of raising the university's admission standards, saying he looked forward to a time when the average freshman SAT score would be "up from 950 to 970." Facility improvements at ECU included renovation of the Student Health Center and a proposal to add a new dining facility to the Mendenhall Student Center—especially noteworthy given criticism by a task force formed to examine the university's food services. Students were also faced with a significant shortage of on-campus housing and an increase in dormitory fees—up from the per semester cost of $295.

Internal problems within the staff of WZMB, the university's student-operated FM radio station, prompted the resignation of one of its advisers. The turnover at the station was further compounded when a new general manager, Sam Barwick, was named to the post. The university's fraternal organizations also faced challenges when Kappa Delta encountered resistance from local residents as it attempted to relocate closer to the campus on Fifth Street. Simultaneously, Tau Kappa Epsilon found itself in a mild conflict with its neighbor, the Catholic Newman Community Campus Ministry, over the verbal harassment of some of the ministry's visitors.

Students expressed disappointment when the plan for a concert featuring Pat Benatar fell through as a result of scheduling conflicts at Minges Coliseum. However, interest was rekindled when it was announced that Cheap Trick would be appearing at the arena. Additionally, many students enjoyed the comic performance of Jimmie Walker (who starred as "J.J." in the popular sitcom *Good Times*) in Hendrix Auditorium. Finally, the announcement of Dr. Mary Jo Bratton's forthcoming history of East Carolina University was greeted with great excitement and anticipation.

1981

The first space shuttle (Columbia) is launched. Pope John Paul is shot. Prince Charles marries Diana Spencer. MTV is born. Ronald Reagan is shot by John Hinkley. Rick James releases the hit "Super Freak."

The School of Medicine announced that its first class of physicians completed residency training, with most of the newly certified doctors stating their intention to practice medicine in North Carolina. Rick Atkinson, who majored in English and graduated from East Carolina University in 1974, won the Pulitzer Prize in Journalism for a series of stories written for the *Kansas City Times*. ECU graduate Lynn Marie Williford won the Miss North Carolina Pageant and received $3,000 in scholarship funds as well as $11,000 in additional prizes.

Students addressed minority-related issues on campus by holding a "Souls on the Mall" rally. Many students spoke on the unique challenges and obstacles facing African Americans at the university. Students living off-campus also faced a challenge when a new Greenville zoning law appeared to ban more than four unrelated people from sharing a house. However, housing-related turmoil was kept to a minimum when it turned out most residents were protected by the ordinance's grandfather clause. Senator Jesse Helms received a mixed, if vocal, reception during his visit to the university to speak about his support of the tobacco industry and his efforts to cut social programs. In other politically related events, a large group of ECU students joined the North Carolina Peace Network's vigil to protest the proliferation of nuclear arms.

A number of wheelchair thefts plagued disabled students living in the residence halls. However, the university took a step toward significantly deterring crime when it installed a Blue Light security system across campus. In stranger happenings, contestants in the Chi Omega–Elbo Room Fourth Annual Goldfish Eating contest managed to set a new record by downing forty-five fish in one sitting.

Eric Henderson's swearing in as SGA president created some controversy. Some students pointed to irregularities in the circumstances surrounding his election. However, the Review Board found the violations insufficient to disqualify Henderson's election. An "All-American" rating was bestowed on *The Buccaneer*, ECU's annual yearbook, by the American Collegiate Press. Many students were excited to learn that the university's housing office decided to convert Belk and Jarvis Halls into coed dormitories. However, residents of Greene Hall experienced a scare when a fire broke out in the residence hall after a cigarette lighter ignited a pom-pom —fortunately no one was hurt and property damage was minimal. Alpha Epsilon Delta won two awards at the premedical/predental honor society's national convention, and the Tau chapter of Phi Sigma Pi won its sixteenth consecutive Joseph Torchia Award. The year's on-campus festivities included concerts by Blackfoot and Def Leppard.

John Belushi dies in drug-related circumstances. The Vietnam Memorial is erected in Washington, D.C. The first artificial heart is transplanted. Ozzie Osbourne bites the head off a bat during a live performance. Michael Jackson creates a sensation with his album Thriller.

Freshmen across North Carolina received a shock when the North Carolina legislature raised the legal drinking age to nineteen. Several officials at East Carolina University spoke against the law, and students reacted with surprise and disgust after the measure passed almost unanimously in both legislative houses. Many business owners in Greenville added their voices to the general protest, including the owner of the Attic and other members of the Greenville Nightclub Association. The mood in and around the university did not improve after Greenville's City Council passed a noise ordinance that levied fines from $5 to $50 for disturbances louder than 70 decibels. Ironically, the growing sound of discontent at the university might have violated the noise ordinance as many students complained about a host of issues including overcrowded conditions in campus gymnasiums, Selective Service draft registration, placement of new buildings in the university's few remaining wooded areas, and lack of wheelchair accessibility at the popular Darryl's restaurant. Happily, Darryl's quickly installed ramps for its disabled patrons. A number of complaints were lodged against the university's wheelchair-accessible van, charging the vehicle was often undependable.

On a brighter note, the East Carolina Alumni Association and ECU Foundation set a record for fund-raising, and the registrar announced an increase in the enrollment of foreign students at the university. The *Rebel* magazine was awarded first place and a "medalist" ranking in the fifty-ninth Columbia University Scholastic Press Association contest, and the FCC granted WZMB an official license to broadcast through 1988. On campus, Dr. Elmer Myer, vice chancellor for student life, reported that use of the university's meal plan service had significantly increased, further helping to solidify plans to add a new kitchen wing to the Mendenhall Student Center. In other good news, Governor Jim Hunt visited Greenville to dedicate ECU's $26 million Brody Medical Sciences Building.

Tragedy struck the city and university when a huge predawn explosion rocked the Village Green apartment complex. One ECU student was killed, and twelve were injured (one critically) after liquid propane used to fuel dryers in a basement laundry room exploded. A special fund financed by public and private money was established by the university to help students replace personal items destroyed in the blast. Further misfortune visited the student body when a mysterious rash of fires suddenly struck

Tau Kappa Epsilon, Lamba Chi Alpha, and Kappa Sigma. All three houses suffered extensive damage from fire and smoke. No one perished or was seriously injured. Omega Psi Phi fraternity expressed relief when eight of its members were acquitted of assault charges stemming from an initiation ceremony, and students in general were gratified after a notorious campus rapist was sentenced to thirty-five years in prison. Finally, a homecoming concert by .38 Special was generally considered a resounding success.

1983

Forty people die when the American embassy in Beirut is bombed. The United States invades Grenada. Compact discs are first released. Scientists discover HIV. The blockbuster Flashdance *opens in theatres.*

After the elevation of the legal drinking age to nineteen, many ECU students were nearly apoplectic upon learning the U.S. Senate passed legislation intended to restrict legalized drinking to people twenty-one and older. Many merchants in and around Greenville predicted the new law would bring about particularly hard times for the bars, nightclubs, restaurants, and other local businesses with significant student clientele. In the same year it celebrated its second anniversary, WZMB announced the appointment of Greg Watkins as general manager after Jim Ensor's resignation of the position. Faculty pay raises were delayed by confusion over the manner in which student evaluations were to be used to assess teaching effectiveness with many professors expressing dissatisfaction with the survey's format and objectivity. A further irritation (or relief) to some faculty and students was the university's newly imposed ban on smoking in classrooms.

Off campus, many students donated food, clothing, and time to help victims of a series of tornadoes that swept through Pitt County. On campus, the College Republicans squared off against the Greenville Peace Committee over the U.S. invasion of Panama. *Rebel* magazine won the Columbia Scholastic Press Association's First-Place Medalist Award for the second straight year, and an ECU coed made news (after taking a summer course at N.C. State) by appearing nude in *Playboy*'s "Girls of the Atlantic Coast Conference" edition.

Confusion canceled the year's SGA elections after twenty candidates were controversially disqualified from the race. Controversy also arose over the creation and location of a university-sanctioned "quiet dorm." Some students opposed this proposal based upon the assertion that rules governing such a dorm were inherently "vague and subject to abuse." In other dorm-related happenings, a group of female students in Jones Residence Hall petitioned against a rule requiring male students to be escorted when visiting the second and third floors of the hall. Student affiliation with Greek societies continued to increase at the university even as the organizations themselves instituted a ban on drinking during the fraternity and sorority recruiting period. The dry rush experiment proved short-lived as the Greeks announced they would allow their members and guests of legal age to drink during the following year's recruitment events.

1984

Geraldine Ferraro becomes the first female vice presidential candidate. Reagan defeats Mondale. The Cosby Show *airs. The first black Miss America, Vanessa Williams, resigns after a scandal over nude photos.* Ghostbusters *debuts on screen.*

Enrollment at ECU officially reached 13,827, making plans for the university's new online registration system even more welcome to both students and faculty. C. Ralph Kinsey, chairman of the Board of Trustees, announced the establishment of a new scholarship program aimed at attracting gifted scholars from across the state and nation. However, times were hard for ECU's mascot, Pee Dee the Pirate. A survey of student opinion indicated a strong desire to get rid of the university's "cute" version of the symbolic buccaneer as well as to change his nickname. Things also "heated up" in McGinnis Auditorium after a prop malfunction caused a minor fire to break out during a performance of *Ozma of Oz: A Take of Time.* Unlike Pee Dee, all in the audience managed to escape unscathed.

Fire struck downtown Greenville as well when the landmark Attic nightclub was destroyed in a late-night blaze. However, the club reopened quickly in a new location to rejoin other nightspots including the Elbo Room, Rafters, Pantana Bob's, Papa Katz, Grogs, New Deli, and the Treehouse. Renovation was underway on campus as Cotten Hall got a major face-lift after sixty years of student occupancy. However, refurbishment of Fleming Hall ran into delays after asbestos and other potential biohazards were discovered. Safety around campus improved as the Pirate Walk escort service was reinstituted, and many residents were more than happy to use a new campus laundry service started and managed by two student entrepreneurs.

Although minority enrollment at the university was reported to be stable, lack of student involvement prompted Chrystal Fray, general manager of the *Ebony Herald,* to resign. After being appointed as the *Herald*'s new manager, Ruben Ingram announced his intention to change the name and general format of the paper. Meanwhile, the *East Carolinian* also experienced changes in its editorial staff when Hunter Fisher resigned as general manager and was replaced by Tom Norton. The *Rebel* made another strong showing by winning the prestigious Associated Collegiate Press Award.

SGA elections were once again invalidated—this time over campaign literature that was improperly posted too close to polls. David Brown was eventually named president in a landslide election later in the year. A lively debate broke out over use of student government funds to support Greek organizations, and, in further action, the SGA passed a resolution chastising the federal government for pressuring states to adopt bills raising the minimum drinking age to twenty-one.

In other Greek-related news, Phi Kappa Tau fraternity was recognized as the Roland Maxwell Outstanding Chapter Award winner. Concern over falling grade point averages prompted the Panhellenic Council to consider limiting the social activities of the university's sororities. On a tragic note, Greek and non-Greek students alike expressed shock and grief when Erskine Evans, a sprinter on the ECU track team, died from injuries sustained in a traffic accident.

1985

Nintendo introduces its home entertainment system. "New Coke" is launched and is an immediate flop. Mikhail Gorbachev is elected and becomes the last president of the USSR. "We Are the World" is released.

Numerous interesting details about ECU appeared in the *East Carolinian*, including enrollment growth from 11,341 in 1974 to 13,826 in 1984 (11,395 from North Carolina and 2,110 from Pitt County). Strikingly, the number of black students on campus had increased from 452 to 1,515 over the same period. However, students and enrollment were briefly overshadowed when 2,000 mothers and fathers attended the university's first Parents' Weekend. On a more painful note, many students got an unwanted shot in the arm after the legislature required college attendees in North Carolina to be properly immunized.

North Carolina Attorney General Laci H. Thornburg gave a well-received lecture on the importance of professional honesty and fair dealing. Honesty on campus was found suspect after an informal survey revealed that five out of ten ECU students admitted to cheating at one time in their college careers.

The Media Board approved WZMB's request for a power increase, but controversy arose when the station's change of frequency from 91.3 was announced. Many students were left wondering about mysterious melodies wafting across campus after the university's "carillon" (or mechanical musical box) was removed from storage and installed on top of Mendenhall.

Music was also on the minds of the Senior Class Council when it proposed a new bell tower be designed by students and installed on campus.

Expressions, ECU's minority-affairs publication, received a First Class rating and two Marks of Distinction from the Associated Collegiate Press, and a university committee was formed to devise ways of further improving the journal. Readers were surprised when the Media Board abruptly announced its decision to place the publication in a state of moratorium owing to organizational and financial problems. Happily, the journal's difficulties were addressed, and *Expressions* reappeared under a new publication schedule and format. The *Rebel* won the Pacemaker Award again, and *The Buccaneer* scored a success when it was awarded first place from the Associated College Press for its use of photography. In other good news, the university's ROTC cadets won the Governor's Trophy for their performance in advanced camp at Fort Bragg.

The SGA had a busy year, recommending changes in the fall break schedule and planning a crackdown on students with overdue emergency or medical loans. Additionally, the governing body decided to change its election rules, moving from a plurality to a majority system that required runoff elections. Plans to enlarge Mendenhall were well under way as the university announced a 30,000-square-foot expansion of the student center. Students and faculty in the nearby Jenkins Art Center experienced a scare after an early morning fire caused minor damage to the building. Lively discussion broke out on campus over which students would be given priority to live in the newly air conditioned wing of Scott Dormitory, and some residents in Fleming Hall voiced concerns over the plans to change the dorm to a male/female facility.

News that the rock band Heart was scheduled to play at Minges Coliseum created excitement on and off campus, as did the appearance of Alex Haley, author of *Roots,* who delivered a well-received lecture to a capacity crowd in the Hendrix Theatre.

1986

The Challenger *space shuttle explodes during liftoff. The Iran-Contra scandal breaks. A catastrophic nuclear meltdown occurs at Chernobyl. Martin Luther King Day becomes an official U.S. holiday. Singers Peter Gabriel and Robert Palmer each record hits—"Sledgehammer" and "Addicted to Love."*

Finding on-campus housing was becoming more of an issue as enrollment at the university grew to a record 14,464. C. D. Spangler, president of the University of North Carolina system, visited the campus and spoke on a variety of subjects. His primary concern centered on the ongoing search for a new chancellor to replace John Howell, who had held the position since

1982. A group of civic-minded students founded the East Carolina Friends —an organization dedicated to placing ECU students with young children throughout the Greenville area.

Many at the university expressed shock and disbelief after twenty-one ECU students were arrested for manufacturing and distributing counterfeit driver's licenses. It was generally believed that the fake IDs were produced with the intent to allow underaged students to purchase alcohol. Many of the Greek societies found themselves faced with the challenge of enforcing the newly established drinking age during recruitment activities, prompting fraternal organizations to reinstitute a highly unpopular dry rush policy. On the bright side, a new sorority—Zeta Tau Alpha—was established, and the university gave official recognition to Alpha Mu Phi, the army fraternal order. *The Buccaneer* claimed the prestigious Printing Industry Association Award, and the university's Forensic Society won multiple prizes in competition against schools such as Clemson, UNC-Charlotte, and William and Mary.

The SGA remained active, proposing a plan to rent microwave ovens to students and formally recognizing Martin Luther King Day by conducting special activities across the campus. Unfortunately, racial tensions rose dramatically during a rally organized to protest the outcome of the student body presidential race. After lengthy deliberation, the Review Board announced there was not enough evidence of voting irregularities to warrant another election.

Life on campus improved after a new food service began operation in the university dining halls, and many residents expressed excitement over plans to install cable television in the dormitories. Jarvis Hall held a party honoring its namesake and former governor Thomas Jarvis, and the Office of Housing Operations officially confirmed that Fletcher Hall would become a coed residence hall. Many students found studying a bit harder after Joyner Library suffered extensive water damage after a particularly strong rainstorm, and the ECU Faculty Facilities Committee met to discuss ways of funding the bell tower proposed by the previous year's senior class. Finally, the university's Sign Language Club gave a well-received performance of "Fantasy" in Hendrix Auditorium, and John Fogerty literally rocked the house during a rollicking concert in Minges Coliseum.

1987

The stock market loses 508 points (22.6 percent of its total value) on Black Monday. Baby Jessica is rescued after falling down a well. The Jim Bakker and Jessica Hahn scandal breaks. Les Misérables *wins Best Musical and eight other Tony awards. U2 releases "With or Without You."*

Conflict and controversy remained a consistent theme throughout the year as officials at North Carolina State University canceled its rematch with the Pirates in response to a riot following ECU's 32–14 football victory over the Wolfpack. Chancellor Richard Eakin denounced the destruction of property and violence at Carter-Finley Stadium as "inappropriate" and "unacceptable," declaring that ECU's image had been tarnished by the "behavior of a few." Mayhem also rattled Greenville when students and police clashed during a Biltmore Street block party. After many fines, arrests, and charges of police brutality, the city and ECU officials met to devise plans for preventing future recreationally based conflicts around the university. Further dampening student morale, news came that falsified work petitions had led to the cancellation of a popular financial aid program. On a brighter note, ECU graduate and Pulitzer Prize–winning author Rick Atkinson spoke on campus about his experiences at the university, and Tipper Gore and Richard Gephardt also made appearances on and around campus as the national presidential race accelerated.

Many improperly billed students were pleased when their $25 lab fees were promptly refunded. Chancellor Eakin's decision to cancel plans for turning the green space at the bottom of College Hill into a parking lot was highly popular with many campus residents. However, *The Buccaneer* encountered stormy weather amid complaints about the production schedule and general quality of the university's yearbook. Controversy also arose after the SGA passed a bill broadening the authority of the Honor Board to impose penalties on students—apart from judgments rendered in a court of law. Some opponents of the bill expressed fear that ECU attendees would be fined twice for the same violation.

Students across campus expressed shock and dismay after members of the Kappa Alpha Psi fraternity were accused of assaulting a resident of Garrett Dorm. The president of the Eta Psi chapter stated categorically that his organization did not condone violence and that a single individual, not the fraternity itself, was involved in the incident. The university weathered additional bad publicity after members of the ECU basketball team were arrested in connection with a series of thefts that occurred in Scott Hall and three residents of Umstead Hall were charged with counterfeiting North Carolina driver's licenses. Sadly, some off-campus residents also suffered serious misfortune when their homes were destroyed in a fire at Langston Park Apartments.

Social life continued to thrive around the university, with an estimated twenty thousand people attending the downtown's traditional Halloween celebration. The popular Susie's Treehouse announced plans to open franchises in other college towns, and WZMB celebrated its sixth anniversary at the Attic. Students also enjoyed local concerts by a variety of popular artists including The Fixx, Anita Baker, the Ramones, and Jimmy Buffett.

1988

George H. W. Bush defeats Michael Dukakis. The Soviet Union withdraws its military from Afghanistan. Televangelist Jimmy Swaggart admits to sexual "sinning." Sales of music on compact disc top vinyl for the first time. The Beach Boys record their comeback hit "Kokomo."

Although enrollment at the university reached an all-time high of 15,500, concern was expressed over a drop in the number of minority students attending ECU. Ethnic unease on campus was further heightened after the NAACP raised concerns about the university's treatment of an African American student allegedly involved with an assault on a Garrett Hall resident. Further controversy was sparked by an art project that included a black figure hanging by a rope from a tree. Creators of the sculpture asserted their intention had been to convey an "antiracist" message, and university officials acted quickly to dismantle the controversial portions of the project. In contrast, poet and author Maya Angelou appeared in Hendrix Auditorium and delivered an extremely well received lecture. Joyner Library announced that students would soon be able to use their identification cards to check out books. The university unveiled a new officially sanctioned logo. In off-campus news, ECU student Jackie Pageant represented North Carolina in the Miss USA Pageant, and many students and local Greenville residents mourned the closing of the Crow's Nest restaurant—a well-loved institution of "near campus" dining for twenty years.

Sadly, Greenville's traditional downtown Halloween celebration was canceled for an indefinite period following a full-scale riot that left over fifty people arrested and an undetermined number of revelers injured. Later in the year, misfortune struck on Cotanche Street when an early morning fire forced residents to leap from their apartment building's windows. Fortunately no one was killed or seriously injured in the blaze, although the structure suffered approximately $40,000 in damages.

The SGA debated a proposal directed to the UNC Board of Governors that mandated condom machines be placed in residence halls located on UNC system campuses. The machines were subsequently installed in selected dormitories. A faulty component caused WZMB to suspend broadcasting, forcing the university's radio station to request emergency funding to resolve the problem. Funding was also a concern of the on-campus dining service, prompting the university to consider instituting a mandatory meal plan for dorm residents. Students living in Belk Hall had to contend with over a hundred brown bats that invaded one of the dormitory's suites, and Clement Hall residents received a scare after a fire gutted a social room located on the sixth floor. Many in the Greek community were pleased when Phi Kappa Phi completed construction of the first house at ECU specifically intended for use by a fraternity and Theta Chi reestablished its charter at the university after a seventeen-year dormancy. Finally, many students and local residents enjoyed well-attended musical performances by Wynton Marsalis and UB40.

1989

The Berlin Wall falls. The Exxon Valdez spills oil in Alaska. Chinese students stage political protests in Tiananmen Square. The Unites States invades Panama and captures Manuel Noreiga. Radio stations air Aerosmith's "Love in an Elevator" and the B-52s' "Love Shack."

Once again, civil unrest sparked around the university when over one hundred students were arrested after a Halloween party turned into a riot at the Tar River apartment complex. However, charges were subsequently dropped against eighty of the defendants arrested in the incident. Student passions were also aroused when Greenville's City Council passed an ordinance further toughening noise restrictions within the city limits. Over 1,500 ECU students marched on City Hall and presented a petition to City Manager Greg Knowles calling for its repeal. A series of sexual assaults created tension on campus, prompting Greenville and ECU police to tighten security across the university. On-campus crime also made headlines when one former student and eight ECU attendees were arrested for the illegal sale and distribution of controlled substances. In contrast, many students were delighted when ECU finally declared July 4 an officially recognized holiday.

Expressions' spring and fall editions received first-place awards from the American Scholastic Press Association and Associated Collegiate Press, and the *Rebel* magazine won the prestigious All American Award from the National Scholastic Press Association and the Associated Collegiate Press. WZMB announced plans to expand its studio by constructing a new 1,000-square-foot facility in Mendenhall. Unfortunately, controversy continued to dog the SGA election process, resulting in protests of voting procedures, revotes, disqualifications, and runoff elections. After an arduous (and often confusing) electoral process, Allen Thomas was finally recognized as president of the Student Government Association.

Many campus residents were pleased to learn of a five-year, $3.5 million plan to renovate campus dormitories. Students also reacted with enthusiasm to an updated phone service in the dorms as well as the announcement that university dining services would continue to expand into new facilities. In the Greek community, Zeta Tau Alpha sorority signed a contract to buy Sigma Tau Gamma's fraternity house, and, after only a year and a half at ECU, Sigma Tau Epsilon announced that it would not return to the university the following year.

Social life around the campus continued to buzz as the Attic celebrated its eighteenth year of operation but later issued the surprising news that its owners were putting the famous nightclub up for sale. Another "clubbing" institution, the New Deli, commemorated its eighth anniversary, but the popular Susie's Treehouse saddened many devoted Greenville nightlifers when it closed its doors. Another ECU landmark was finally retired when the famous "Volkswagen on a pole" was dismantled after Evans Street Auto Service was purchased by the government and shut down. Perhaps in a fitting musical farewell to so many well-loved local landmarks, George Thorogood appeared in Minges Coliseum and delivered a veritable knock-out punch of classic rock and roll.

THE NEW AGE NINETIES

1990

Margaret Thatcher resigns as prime minister of Great Britain. Iraq invades Kuwait. Nelson Mandela is freed. The Hubble *telescope is launched into orbit. Dancer/singer M.C. Hammer releases "Can't Touch This."*

Students, staff, and faculty were unnerved when a gunman armed with a hunting rifle held police at bay at the Whichard Building. Fortunately, after a fifty-five-minute standoff, the distraught former postal employee surrendered to police without firing a shot. Local opposition to Greenville's noise ordinance continued to increase, prompting the city to consider reinstating noise permits to residents willing to pay a small fee. ECU attendees and employees expressed anger and frustration when the university announced another increase in the cost of on-campus parking and, adding insult to injury, parking fines were also increased twofold. Even students attempting to avoid the university's parking gauntlet experienced misfortune as the number of bicycle thefts on campus skyrocketed. ECU police scored a significant victory by identifying and shutting down a significant on-campus drug ring.

After the previous year's Halloween riot, university representatives, students, and city officials met to discuss alternative means of holding the traditional October celebration. Eventually, community leaders decided to hold a Halloween party at the Pitt County Fairgrounds—rather than in its usual downtown venue. On campus, political activism was alive and well as over 150 students met at the Mall to support U.S. troops sent to the Persian Gulf. Many graduate students found themselves in need of support when the university placed a twenty-hour cap on the number of hours graduate assistants could work per week.

Expressions continued to add to its list of accomplishments by winning a national Pacemaker Award. Prospects were not as rosy for the university's yearbook. The Media Board announced it was suspending *The Buccaneer*'s production from 1991–92. Students were charged a new $50 fee to update and improve ECU's high-tech facilities, and WZMB was happy to complete its move from Joyner Library to a new location in Mendenhall. In other campus-related developments, many students felt safer after the installation of the university's improved campus lighting system.

ECU's student government continued to create a stir. Controversy arose over the summer appointment (rather than election) of the SGA's vice president. Further questions followed the dismissal of the SGA's treasurer and the subsequent revelation that Office of the Dean of Students had inadvertently released the former officer's GPA. Despite these problems, the student government managed to remain active, passing legislation that included an antismoking ordinance that established many new smoke-free areas across campus.

Members of Theta Chi were elated to finally find a location for their new house on Eleventh Street, and the Kappa Alpha fraternity house was extensively renovated and repaired. On campus, security was further tightened after the dormitories began a practice of locking their doors after 8:00 p.m. Residents of White Hall were warned to be on the lookout for two scam artists hanging around the dorm, posing as donation collectors. Social life remained active as many on- and off-campus residents flocked to the Attic to enjoy performances by The Black Crowes and The Rembrandts.

1991

Iraq is invaded by U.N. forces. Magic Johnson tests positive for HIV. The navy "Tailhook" scandal breaks. Serial killer Jeffrey Dahmer is arrested. The Rodney King beating is aired. Prince Charles and Princess Diana separate. The Silence of the Lambs *opens in theatres.*

The university reacted with surprise and horror after an ECU student was found dead at the southern base of Ficklen Stadium. Circumstances surrounding the tragedy remained a mystery, but the unfortunate young man apparently died from injuries sustained after a fall of approximately a hundred feet (from the facility's press box). Violence erupted off campus when an attempted robbery at Georgetown Apartments left an ECU student critically wounded from multiple gunshots.

Despite these unhappy circumstances, the university reported a healthy increase in its nontraditional enrollment (students at least twenty-five years old, not holding a bachelor's degree). However, one of East Carolina's more traditional students created a stir when he filed to run for a seat on Greenville's city council. Sophomore Patrick Pitzer declared he wanted "to see a move to mutual cooperation between the two [city and students] rather than the policy of containment that the city has exercised on students in the past." Also active in the community were members of Alpha Phi Alpha and the Minority Arts Committee as they held a well-attended march to celebrate Martin Luther King Jr. Day. After a two-year hiatus, *The Buccaneer* made a return in a surprising new form—that of a "video" yearbook. WZMB was banned from affiliation with businesses serving alcohol—effectively ending the station's promotion of popular events often occurring in local nightclubs. ECU got a much-needed face-lift after the student government passed a project to clean up the campus. Courtney Jones's election reawoke the older East Carolina tradition of women SGA presidents held in abeyance since 1946.

Greek society members were unpleasantly surprised when a rash of break-ins and robberies occurred at the Sigma Phi Epsilon and Alpha Sigma Phi houses over spring break. Misfortune also struck Kappa Alpha Psi after a dance sponsored by the fraternity ended in a shooting. Fortunately, no one was seriously injured in the incident, and there were no arrests. On campus, controversy sparked in the dormitories after the popular Dungeons and Dragons game was banned in the residence halls. The restriction was quickly lifted after several highly vocal protests by residents and members of the university's Science Fiction and Fantasy Organization. A minor stir was created over the announcement that condom-dispensing machines were soon to be installed in all dormitories. Many people at the university were greatly troubled when an African American display in Jarvis Hall was destroyed by vandals who set fire to a bulletin board depicting minority awareness. Finally, a number of foreign-study students found themselves looking for a new place to live after the university's International House closed its doors to residents to make room for new administrative offices.

1992

Bill Clinton is elected president. Hurricane Andrew devastates Florida. Johnny Carson leaves The Tonight Show. *Dr. Mae C. Jemison becomes the first black female astronaut. Clint Eastwood directs and stars in* Unforgiven, *and the Spin Doctors record "Little Miss Can't Be Wrong."*

Sonic Plaza and Joyner Library, 2005

Bicyclist on the Mall in the fog

CHANCELLORS OF
EAST CAROLINA UNIVERSITY

Thomas Brewer, 1978–81

John Howell, 1982–88

Richard Eakin, 1988–2001

William Muse, 2001–3

William Shelton,
Interim 2003–4

Stephen Ballard, 2004–

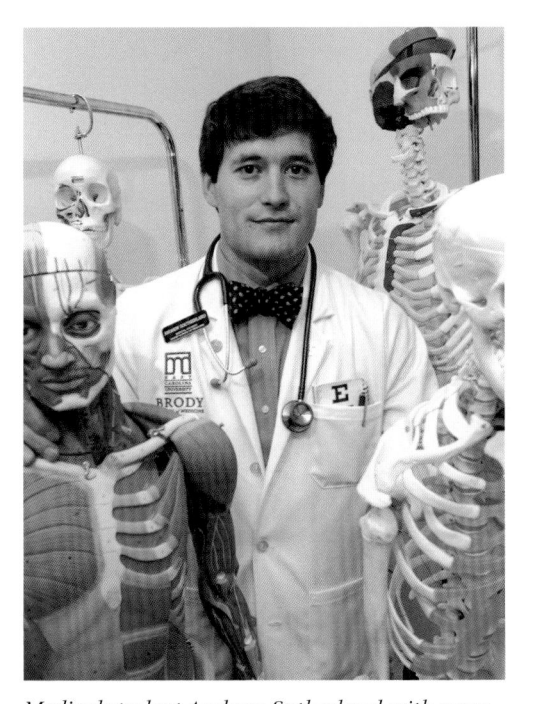

Air Corps Reserve Officers Training Corps at East Carolina

Randy Yiu goes to the Book Review Index to locate references for research

Medical student Andrew Sutherland with some special instructors

Moussa Badiane, basketball player

below: *A member of the biology department, Anthony Overton, pursues his disciplinary interests in ichthyology*

Maritime studies director William Still Jr. with Gordon Watts

Justin Vaughn and Sarah Dickens in Joyner Library

below: *Snow on main campus*

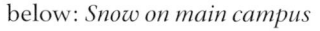

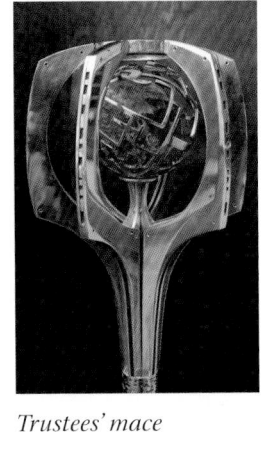

Trustees' mace

Ken White, lighting director, Messick Theatre   *Timekeeper*

above: *Director Daniel Barra and associates in the concert choir*

left: *Art student Ben Isenburg in the studio*

Cole Jones served his first term as Student Government Association president from 2005–7. He was elected to a second term in 2006.

Conversation in the East Carolina spring

Rivers Building

Art student Leah Foushee at work

*Coach Skip Holtz
and Pirates*

West End Dining Hall, 2005

Darryl's recreation

Art professor Gil Leebrick

Biology lecture hall

right: *Professor Patch Clark (middle) with theatre students*

below: *Course registration in the mid-eighties*

Bare bones of the Allied Health Complex on west campus

Enrollment at the university hit an all-time high of 17,400, causing a significant shortage of on-campus housing at the beginning of the school year. Susan Stewart, a North Carolina Teaching Fellow, received the Martin Luther King Student Leadership Award, and the Minority Cultural Center announced it would further expand its services. Local politics heated up as many pro-life and pro-choice ECU students met outside the Pitt County Courthouse to participate in demonstration marking the anniversary of *Roe v. Wade*. The national presidential election also made a local impact, as Marilyn Quayle made a campaign appearance in Greenville and Al Gore held a political rally at Minges Coliseum.

Students in need of quick, convenient cash were delighted when an automatic teller machine was installed on central campus. Some were hesitant to take advantage of the ATM after ECU crime statistics indicated a 500 percent increase in robberies on campus. *Expressions* continued to add to its list of accomplishments, receiving three awards at the North Carolina Inter-Collegiate Association Convention, and work began in earnest toward the production of the university's video yearbook.

Student government formally expressed its opposition to a proposed tuition increase and passed a resolution that denounced racial discrimination against ECU students by downtown Greenville businesses. Mild controversy appeared when WZMB was accused of defying the Media Board's advice by sponsoring an event at the downtown club O'Rockefeller's. The SGA subsequently passed a resolution supporting the station's right to broadcast from local nightclubs.

Members of the Lambda Chi Alpha fraternity and Alpha Delta Phi sorority held a charity car wash to support the victims of Hurricane Andrew, and the pledge class of Gamma Gamma Sigma, a service sorority, held a "Jailhouse Rock" event that raised money for two needy families in the Greenville area. In other Greek news, Delta Chi received a national charter, and Kappa Delta Rho was established as the university's newest fraternity.

Students flocked to live performances of Hootie and the Blowfish at the Attic and Ray Charles at Minges Coliseum. Many current and former Pirates were shocked and dismayed when the university limited tailgating activities before ECU football games.

1993

The Branch Davidian tragedy occurs in Waco, Texas. The World Trade Center is damaged by a bomb placed in its parking garage. Lorena Bobbitt's trial begins. Michael Jordan retires for the first time. The final episode of Cheers *airs.*

Many members of the university community were pleased when, despite increases in tuition, *U.S. News and World Report* rated ECU as one of the South's ten best buys in higher education. Renovations to the campus bookstore went smoothly, and the university broke ground for a future 150,000-square-foot recreation center. Significantly less enthusiasm greeted news of another increase in ECU's parking fees. Students were unnerved after an armed robbery occurred on campus, and, off campus, two women were abducted from the parking lot of the popular Chico's restaurant. Greenville police managed to apprehend four youths responsible for vandalizing cars around the campus.

SGA elections were again fraught with controversy. After a delay and a runoff election, Ian Eastman and Sheila Boswell were elected president and vice president. The student government kept busy by holding a tricycle marathon for the American Red Cross and proposing a Campus Safety Act designed to curb violence and crime at the university. Unfortunately, violence became an issue in the Greek community after a fight and gunshot at an Alpha Phi Alpha fraternity party led to several arrests, and, in an earlier incident, ECU's Interfraternity Council handed down several disciplinary rulings to the Pi Kappa Alpha fraternity for its actions during a fight at the ECU-Syracuse game in Ficklen Stadium.

Renovations of Slay and Umstead halls proceeded according to schedule. White Hall was selected as the next dormitory to turn coed. All incoming freshmen were now required to purchase meal plans upon signing a university housing contract. Other notable events occurred when resident advisers expressed concern about changes in their compensation packages, and Clement and Jarvis halls were both damaged by fires stemming from faulty wiring. Mendenhall didn't escape the year unscathed: heavy rains caused a flood in the Student Union's basement. In a bizarre off-campus incident, a runaway Pepsi delivery truck slammed into the City Market grocery before bursting into flames.

Downtown Greenville continued to deliver quality entertainment as Hootie and the Blowfish and the Dave Matthews Band both performed to packed audiences in the Attic, as did comedian Tommy Chong (half of the famous Cheech and Chong comedy team).

1994

Major League Baseball players strike. The "Chunnel" opens, linking Britain and France by rail. Astronomers observe a comet colliding with Jupiter. Susan Smith admits to drowning her two sons. Forrest Gump *packs theatres across the country.*

In a surprising development, the university announced that enrollment shrank by over two hundred students. Minority enrollment at ECU continued to expand thanks, in part, to the school's active recruitment programs. Many expressed satisfaction and relief after Greenville's Halloween festivities occurred without incident. A group of ECU students camping at Hammock's Beach State Park managed to save a beached whale. But satisfaction was in short supply when long lines at the bookstore and cafeteria led many students to express frustration with the Pirate Points purchasing system.

A sudden rash of accidents raised tensions. Students were struck by vehicles around campus, and, tragically, Detlev Bunger, a student and son of an ECU faculty member, was killed in one such incident. Compounding the shock and grief at the university was the fatal shooting at Darryl's restaurant of Dr. David Gobeski, a professor in the industrial technology department. The assailant was subsequently sentenced to serve thirty years for the murder.

A break-in at the SGA office created a minor stir after complaints were lodged that orientation students had received mailings from a local nightclub using copies of university-generated address labels. Another delay in class elections prompted recriminations and charges of voting irregularities. The controversy was finally put to rest after Bill Gheen was elected senior class president. And in an unusual demonstration of electoral support, Ian Eastman became ECU's first SGA president to be reelected to his post.

The Beta Chapter of Pi Kappa Phi received a Red Rose Club Award for doubling its philanthropic donations over the span of one year. All was not rosy in the Greek community when seven members of the Alpha Phi Alpha fraternity were suspended from the university for taking part in hazing activities alleged to have injured a pledge.

After three years, renovations to Slay Residence Hall neared completion. Joyner Library suffered a setback when its first floor flooded after a drainage pipe collapsed. Residents of Ringgold Towers received a scare when a cooking fire caused an evacuation of the high-rise apartment building. Fortunately there were no injuries and only minimal damage to property.

Entertainment on campus featured raucous performances at Wright Auditorium by comedians Gallagher and Carrot Top.

1995

One hundred and sixty-eight people are killed when the Federal Building in Oklahoma City is bombed. A major outbreak of the Ebola virus occurs in Zaire. Hootie and the Blowfish record "Only Wanna Be With You."

Students were less than thrilled after ECU raised tuition and fees again and the Board of Governors endorsed a recommendation to add an additional nine days to the UNC system's academic calendar. Considerably more enthusiasm was expressed over the work of a graduate student research team and its archeological study of a sunken Confederate gunboat in Chicod Creek near Grimesland.

Unfortunately, the student body found itself in a year fraught with unusually sorrowful circumstances. After ECU's victory over Syracuse, Greenville police sprayed pepper gas and mace into an unruly downtown crowd, creating pandemonium throughout the downtown area. Although city and university officials met after the incident to discuss ways of preventing future confrontations, relations between the student community and police remained tense. Misfortune continued to mount when a student was robbed at gunpoint near the campus. Construction major Terris Lee Jones was stabbed to death in Kinston, and Catalina Maria Villorente (a member of the Gamma Sigma Sigma sorority) was killed in an automobile accident. Many at the university were also deeply moved by the untimely death of the ECU basketball team's student manager, Jim Calhoun.

Student government was experiencing rocky times after election violations were uncovered. After a series of meetings, investigations, and the voluntary resignation by the SGA vice president, the controversy was finally put to rest without the call for a new election.

Expressions continued to make a good impression outside the university, winning "Best Student Magazine Published More Than Once a Year" honors from the Society of Professional Journalists. WZMB gained recognition for modifying and expanding its format to appeal to a greater range of listeners. Great debate swirled around the possibility of the return of a printed ECU yearbook. Although strong support was shown in the student population for the yearbook's return, the Media Board ultimately voted not to support the project, citing budget constraints.

Many at the university expressed pleasure at the construction of a new, centrally located cupola—long considered an unofficial symbol of the university. More disappointing was the news that construction on the library and recreation center was under a delay. Students were also disheartened by the decision not to allow fast food chains to operate on campus—despite the practice at Chapel Hill and N.C. State University. Residents on College Hill had to contend with a Dumpster fire outside Belk Hall that managed to spread to the fire truck trying to extinguish it. Although no one was seriously injured, a female resident needed treatment at the hospital. Further alarm was created in the on-campus living community when a resident in Garrett was attacked by four masked assailants, and a resident adviser in Fleming Hall was charged with possession of a weapon and a controlled substance.

Happily, on-campus entertainment continued to make a strong impression with a visit by renowned poet Joy Harjo as well as a performance by popular comedian Chris Rock. Off campus, many students packed the Attic to see .38 Special's high-energy brand of rock.

1996

The Unabomber, Ted Kaczynski, is arrested. One person is killed in the Olympic Park bombing. The English Patient *wins Best Picture Oscar, and Sheryl Crow releases her hit "If It Makes You Happy."*

East Carolina officially switched to the One Card system, distributing the all-purpose ID to incoming freshmen at orientation. While most students found the transition to the One Card easily dealt with, Greenville's weather proved a tougher challenge. Hurricane Fran made itself a destructive nuisance on and around campus, felling trees and knocking out local power. Many students were left without transportation when their vehicles were trapped in a flooded university parking lot. Additional heavy hearts were felt after alumnus and former football player Kevin Banks collapsed and died during an ECU basketball game. Levi Strauss announced a special contract with the university, providing eligible students with scholarships and dining allowances.

The *Rebel* magazine once again drew rave reviews after winning a national Pacemaker Award from the Associated Collegiate Press. *Expressions* followed suit, capturing a Gold Medal from Columbia Scholastic Press Association. Unfortunately, all was not so idyllic at WZMB after a raucous on-air altercation between two rap groups.

On campus, students applauded the culinary improvements made by dining services, and many flocked to the grand opening of the university's new 150,000-square-foot Student Recreation Center. Residents of Jarvis Hall were pleased to learn their building, the oldest dorm on campus, was being scheduled for remodeling. The university announced a plan to study the feasibility of installing card locks on all the dorms' entrances as a means to increase the security of on-campus residents. Not surprisingly, security measures at the university were highlighted even more after two Belk residents were stabbed in their dormitory. Students in Aycock Hall also received a scare after a visitor was bitten by a brown recluse spider, sparking a brief dormwide case of arachnophobia.

Celebrities and entertainers continued to make appearances on campus, including senatorial candidate Harvey Gantt. Actor James Earl Jones lectured to an enthusiastic audience in Hendrix Auditorium, and Carrot Top returned to ECU for a comedic repeat performance. The local music scene continued to buzz with rapper Busta Rhymes appearing at Minges Coliseum and Chapel Hill's Squirrel Nut Zippers playing at the Attic.

England returns control of Hong Kong to China. Dolly the sheep is cloned in Scotland. The Mars Pathfinder lands on target. Comet Hale-Bopp puts on a cosmic light show easily observed without the aid of a telescope. Titanic breaks box office records.

Enrollment at ECU increased to a record 17,851, and the average GPA of incoming freshmen reached an all-time high of 3.25. Further steps increased master's-level enrollment when the university implemented initiatives to improve salaries of underpaid graduate students. Many students were disappointed to learn that plans for a parking deck had once again been scuttled. Physics student Steve McLawhorn helped raise campus morale when he decided to run for a seat on Greenville's city council. Crime around campus continued to be a concern after a student and a nonstudent were arrested for hacking into the university's computer system. In an embarrassing off-campus incident, three ECU students were charged with assaulting a N.C. State student in the old substation parking lot. General relief was expressed after the notorious "backpack bandit" was apprehended in Minges Coliseum.

The university raised a few eyebrows when it sued Skully's music store over their highly popular skull-and-crossbones logo, claiming that the grinning cadaver clad in purple and gold infringed upon ECU's trademark registration. Happily, the store and university agreed to compromise on the use of the logo after Skully's promised to clearly display their name and location on their famous piratical symbol. Perhaps not by coincidence, ECU announced an updating of its own official logo that displayed a "tougher, bolder" version of the school's Pirate mascot.

WZMB continued to tinker with its format, adding more specialty shows in an attempt to attract more listeners. A minor scandal occurred after two *East Carolinian* newsstands were removed from Fleming Hall's front porch. Work orders showed that the associate director of housing for facility management and the hall coordinator had requested that the stands be sent to the dump. The SGA dealt with another bit of political turbulence when Vice President Sean McManus resigned after controversy arose over his eligibility to hold office.

On-campus residents were heartened to learn that ECU dining halls were ranked number one among North Carolina's public universities. Residents of Aycock Hall were less than pleased when a student's malfunctioning extension cord sparked a third-floor fire. Further alarm was created at the university after an assailant wearing a ski mask and wielding a knife assaulted and robbed residents of Belk Hall, and a student in Cotten Hall reported being sexually assaulted in her first-floor room.

Greek organizations continued to contribute to the local community, with Phi Kappa Psi making a sizable donation to the Greenville Community Shelter. Unfortunately, off-campus racial tensions ran high after a local nightclub was accused of enforcing a discriminatory admission policy. All lovers of poetry found equal treatment at the Percolator coffeehouse during its popular poetry slams. Poetry was also featured at the university when North Carolina's Poet Laureate Fred Chappell gave ECU's eighty-ninth commencement address.

1998

Newt Gingrich resigns as Speaker of the House. Mark McGwire and Sammy Sosa both break Roger Maris's home run record. Peace is declared in Northern Ireland. Three men associated with the Ku Klux Klan kill James Byrd Jr. by dragging him behind their vehicle. Shania Twain records "You're Still the One."

Programs designed to improve academic performance at ECU were obviously having a positive effect. The average GPA at the university rose to 2.7, and considerably fewer students were placed on academic probation. The campus was fortunate to suffer only minor damage from Hurricane Bonnie. The exploding population of stray cats inhabiting ECU's grounds created more than a few headaches for the university's maintenance personnel. The Child Development Lab was the recipient of a visit by Second Lady Tipper Gore, and the ECU Pirate Bridge Club was officially established. Many students took an opportunity to see more of the world, participating in university-sponsored trips to Russia and Belize. Travel around campus became a bit easier when the parking and traffic department further updated its transit system. ECU's police department was the only university law enforcement agency to receive a Governor's Award of Excellence. Unfortunately, that highly decorated police force was kept busy, arresting two students for possession of weapons and over a hundred pounds of marijuana. Other unusual criminal activity included the kidnapping and robbing of a student who was held, and later released unharmed, at the local Motel 6. The counterfeiting of residence parking permits by an enterprising, if misguided, freshman also resulted in arrest.

The Greek community celebrated news that Phi Beta Sigma, ECU's historically black service fraternity, was named North Carolina's Collegiate Chapter of the Year, and the university's Panhellenic Council announced, over the objections of some of its members, that the organization would sponsor only alcohol-free fraternity and sorority events. Members of Delta Sigma Phi experienced a difficult holiday season after their fraternity house was vandalized and robbed on Thanksgiving Day.

On campus, dismay also greeted news of the impending demolishment of the Flanagan Amphitheatre (long a favorite spot for sunbathing) to make room for a newly planned west campus dining hall. A minor fire in Clement Hall left no one hurt, but the discovery of asbestos in Belk and Fletcher Halls prompted many residents to question the environmental safety of their dorms. Crime continued to cause concern on campus after police chased and arrested a man caught burglarizing Fletcher Hall. Residents in Aycock were startled when a student fired a handgun in a parking lot near the dorm. Even more reacted with anger at a reported rape in Garrett Hall.

Festival '98, featuring Christian-oriented music and entertainment, attracted a crowd of over 25,000 to Dowdy-Ficklen Stadium. In downtown Greenville, a man was arrested for stabbing three bouncers at the popular Pantana Bob's nightclub.

1999

Bill Clinton is impeached by the House of Represenatives; the Senate acquits him of perjury and obstruction of justice. Two students go on a shooting rampage at Columbine High. Hurricane Floyd wreaks havoc in North Carolina. The Y2K *computer scare runs rampant. Film audiences flock to see* American Beauty.

A further 1.2 percent tuition increase by the UNC Board of Governors did not stop ECU from setting yet another enrollment record of over 18,000, which included the largest freshman class in school history. Additional good news came in the form of an *U.S. News and World Report* article that ranked ECU as the seventh "Top Southern Public University." However, shock and a sense of loss were visited on the university and its community when Hurricane Floyd struck the area, inflicting enormous ecological and economic damage on eastern North Carolina. On top of the tragic loss of life and property, many students faced the additional hardship of homelessness after this Flood of the Century.

Mild surprise greeted news that the university's dean of students position was being dissolved under an administrative reorganization plan. Some students reacted with disappointment after learning that ECU would no longer print graduates' majors on their diplomas. Construction projects created a hive of activity across the campus, and the university announced its intention to expand significantly many of its facilities over the upcoming decade.

Renovations to Jarvis Hall neared completion. A plan to reserve the newly remodeled hall for "university leaders" produced a call for a more democratic means of selecting the dorm's residents. Mendenhall's venerable Outer Limits bowling alley also underwent renovations, replacing its traditional wooden lanes with more durable synthetic material and installing a new automatic scoring system.

Criminal activity continued to dog the campus, including a late-night attack outside Joyner Library by multiple assailants that injured a student and his friend. Further tragedy occurred off campus when junior management major Reggie Ned Harris was shot and killed on Jarvis Street. Additional charges of racial discrimination were directed at many of Greenville's most popular downtown restaurants and bars, and, in a show of support for the university's minority population, the SGA passed a resolution to support actions against discriminatory business owners. The mood on campus was considerably more harmonious after a visit from George Clinton and the P. Funk All-Stars rocked Minges Coliseum.

BREAKING IN THE NEW MILLENNIUM

2000

The "I Love You" virus infects computers worldwide. Elian Gonzales returns to Cuba with his father. The Supreme Court orders a halt to vote recounts in Florida, effectively awarding the presidency to George W. Bush. Gladiator debuts in theatres.

News that tuition and fees were on the rise again did little to bolster students' spirits. However, despite the increase in educational expenses, minority enrollment at the university continued to increase, growing from approximately 50 African American students in 1966 to 2,343 in 1999. Not surprising during an election year, ECU was visited by a number of local and national political figures, including Congressman Walter Jones Jr., Senator John Edwards, and President George W. Bush. Students in the archeology department made news when they excavated two graves in Kinston, attempting to confirm the resting place of North Carolina's first governor. In accordance with Latin Heritage Month, university officials met with students to plan the establishment of a new Latino organization.

Sophomore Monica Palumbo represented North Carolina in the fiftieth annual Miss USA competition, winning "Miss Congeniality" honors in the pageant, and sophomore Cara Cousins and junior Jessica Mauch captured attention of a different kind after posing in *Playboy* magazine's "Girls of Conference USA" edition. ECU students remained politically active, forming a coalition to end alleged police brutality in Greenville—an issue highlighted even more after the city adopted an aggressive "zero tolerance" policy toward residential problems such as parking, pets, litter, and noise. The university police department admitted, and later apologized for, employing racial-profiling techniques during patrols.

Great sadness greeted the news that art major Caleb Dowd had suddenly died of heart complications. Nontraditional graduate student Joyce J. Stevenson's murder in her Grifton home elicited shock. The university community was further disheartened to learn that a former SGA president had been charged with felony and misdemeanor theft. Despite the negative publicity, the SGA remained active, endorsing a popular off-campus meal plan in partnership with local restaurants. Food-related issues were again in the news as students celebrated word that Chick-fil-A cuisine would soon be available at the Croatan.

The Greek community was alarmed when a machete-wielding student crashed a Tau Kappa Epsilon party. No one was injured in the incident, and the suspect was swiftly apprehended and arrested. Life in downtown Greenville continued to provide excitement (both good and bad) as 173 individuals were arrested for underage drinking during a single weekend, and further mayhem was created when two separate shootings occurred outside the popular Sports Pad nightclub. Happily, events on campus were much more low-key as gold medalist Mitch Gaylord gave a well-attended lecture on his experiences as an Olympic gymnast and comedian Lavell Crawford cracked up crowds in Wright Auditorium.

2001

Oklahoma City bomber Timothy McVeigh is executed. Enron Corporation files for bankruptcy. The World Trade Center and Pentagon are attacked by terrorists flying hijacked jetliners. A Beautiful Mind *wins the Best Picture Oscar.*

East Carolina joined the nation in mourning the devastating terrorist attacks in New York and Washington on September 11. Many student-led ceremonies in remembrance of the victims were held on campus, including an SGA-sponsored candlelight vigil outside Joyner Library. Even as the university community mourned the nation's loss, student life continued to diversify and expand—including the establishment of ECU's first Italian Club. The shortage of adequate parking around the campus remained a major problem but was partially offset by the welcomed arrival of four new transit buses. Controversy arose over the higher prices charged in campus convenience stores compared to local Greenville businesses. The variety of new food available through the university's dining services proved a big hit with both students and faculty. Three students suffered minor injuries when they were struck by cars on Tenth Street in three separate incidents.

WZMB continued to attract attention with its annual canned food drive to combat hunger as well as its popular "Talk of the Campus" show, which invited students to call in and voice their opinions and concerns. Junior class president Mike Reilly drew support for a plan to expand Joyner Library's operation to twenty-four hours a day, seven days a week, and the SGA began to seriously discuss implementing online voting in forthcoming elections. In further legislative developments, many students were particularly pleased when the student government proposed that a twenty-four-hour weekend visitation policy be implemented in all university residence halls.

Greek organizations remained active, with Phi Sigma Pi holding a teddy bear drive to raise money to combat child abuse. Alpha Phi Omega collected books to send to needy children in the Philippines. The Greek community was also greatly cheered when senior Jashun Gaddy, a member of Alpha Phi Alpha, awoke from a monthlong coma after suffering an aneurism. On-campus residents were excited to learn of plans to replace their door keys with electronic One Card readers, and the population on Campus Hill enjoyed the Great Race, ECU's first annual soapbox derby. A resident fell out of a fourth floor Jones Hall window, suffering serious but not fatal injuries.

Entertainment on campus included performances by folklorist Orville Hicks and Grammy-winning violinist Mark O'Connor as well as a visit by the award-winning *Reading Rainbow* televised children's show. Unfortunately, events in downtown Greenville were less idyllic when a brawl involving students and ECU baseball players erupted outside Pantana Bob's. Nevertheless, many in the university community braved the rowdy off-campus atmosphere to enjoy performances by Lake Trout at the Attic and guitarist Keller Williams at Peasants.

2002

The "DC Sniper" shooting spree creates panic in Washington. After making controversial remarks related to segregation, Trent Lott steps down as Republican leader. American Taliban soldier John Walker Lindh is captured in Afghanistan. The O Brother, Where Art Thou? *soundtrack wins Grammy's Best Album of the Year.*

Enrollment at ECU set a new record at 20,624 with a freshman class of approximately 3,470. The increase in student population did nothing to alleviate the university's parking shortage, and the problem was compounded when students expressed worry over safety and cost issues relating to the renovation of the school's freshman parking lot. Further controversy arose when falsified ordering and payment records were discovered in ECU's housing and dining services, and many at the university were surprised when a former vice chancellor of student experiences and director of housing pleaded guilty to embezzlement charges. Slightly less surprising was *Playboy* magazine's ranking of ECU as the nineteenth top party school in America, and the institution received additional national exposure after one of its students and an alumnus appeared on the popular game show *The Price Is Right*. In keeping with the ever-evolving image of the university, ECU adopted yet another official logo—an even fiercer version of the traditional skull-and-bones mascot.

Over twenty-five students found themselves homeless after a fire swept through the Tar River Estates apartment complex in a blaze that destroyed many rental units but produced no deaths or injuries. Owen Francis Carr and Caroline Virginia Allen were not as fortunate, perishing in an early morning fire in their apartment on Brownlea Drive. Further tragedy struck the student body when Crystal Roberts, Dana Wood, and Jessica Szymanski were killed in traffic-related accidents.

WZMB continued to overhaul its musical format in an attempt to appeal to the university's rapidly growing population, and the SGA followed suit by proposing a number of initiatives designed to spark interest and participation in student government.

The Greek community continued its active role with Alpha Xi Delta hosting an all-Greek cookout, Delta Sigma Phi raising funds to support the local Boys and Girls Club, and Phi Beta Sigma sponsoring a community fundraiser to help the homeless. Sigma Lambda Chi made news by inducting eighteen new members, and ECU's chapter of Phi Sigma Pi earned recognition after winning the Joseph Torchia Outstanding Chapter Award. Unfortunately, the Delta Chi fraternity found itself the recipient of unwanted attention after receiving disciplinary action for violations of the university's hazing policy.

Many on-campus eaters were delighted when a self-serve Java City station opened in the Croatan Food Store, and the university continued to update and renovate its facilities with construction projects in the Mendenhall Student Center and Dowdy Student Store. Campus entertainment included a lecture by Chief Richard Picciotto, the highest-ranking firefighter to escape from the World Trade Center, as well as a visit by MTV's Campus Invasion tour, featuring a concert by hip-hop artists Fabolous and Talib Kweli in Minges Coliseum. Finally, an era in downtown Greenville truly came to an end after the Blue Front Theatre, formally the famous Attic nightclub, closed for business.

The United States and Great Britain invade Iraq. The space shuttle Columbia *explodes, killing seven astronauts.* The Lord of the Rings: The Return
of the King *wins the Best Picture Oscar.*

The sudden resignation of Chancellor William Muse caught many at the
university by surprise. William Shelton stepped in as interim chancellor
until Steve Ballard was tapped to permanently fill the position. Further administrative turmoil ensued as a series of student and faculty protests preceded William Swart's resignation as provost. Despite these challenges, the
Office of Institutional Planning announced a record enrollment of 21,797
students, further solidifying East Carolina's status as the third-largest
school in the UNC system.

Hurricane Isabel largely spared the campus but knocked down trees and
power lines around Greenville. Students remained active on campus and in
the community, organizing a candlelight vigil for world peace on the steps
of Joyner Library and participating in a Red Cross blood drive at Mendenhall. However, students responded with much less enthusiasm to news that
departmental graduation ceremonies were being canceled. The ECU community was distressed by Maiisha Moore's death in a car accident.

Hannah Winslow became the first East Carolina undergraduate to publish a book when her collection of poetry titled *Once upon a Time, I Was Me:
Reflections on Living as a Teenager* was accepted by Canadian Press. Other
notable literary events included Patrick Minges's on-campus signing of his
book, *Black Indian Slave Narratives,* and the announcement that former creative writing student Dan Neil had won a Pulitzer Prize for his work at the
L.A. Times.

After summer repairs were completed, WZMB returned to the air. The
SGA endorsed a new $56 fee increase but rejected a proposed tuition hike of
$300. However, despite vocal student protest, the cost of tuition was even-
tually increased by $225. SGA elections were again disputed, prompting
the Judicial Board to intervene and rule in favor of upholding the contest's
original results.

Members of Gamma Sigma Sigma hosted the thirteenth annual Pick-
a-Pirate date auction to benefit the Family Support Network of Eastern
North Carolina, and nearly 150 ECU students wore white T-shirts while
they marched in protest of alleged discrimination against minority groups
by downtown nightclubs. Both Greek and non-Greek students mourned
the untimely death of Phi Kappa Tau member Nicholas A. Dragicevich.

On-campus residents were briefly evacuated after an electrical malfunction set a mattress on fire in Aycock Hall, and further alarm occurred upon
the discovery of a handgun in a Tyler Hall bathroom. After two incidents

of sexual assault in the dorms were reported, the Office of Campus Living moved swiftly to install automated cameras and additional lighting in and around ECU's residence halls.

Many notable speakers visited the university, including Arun Gandhi (grandson of Mohandas Gandhi) who gave a lecture on nonviolence, and Robert Dhan, a retired major who spoke about his firsthand experiences in three wars. Fans of popular television were excited by an on-campus appearance by *The People's Court* judge Marilyn Milian as well as a "diversity show" performed by five cast members from MTV's *The Real World*. But perhaps the knockout punch of the year was provided by East Carolina alumnus Vince McMahon when he brought his World Wrestling Entertainment show to Williams Arena.

The music scene on and around campus turned up the volume with a sellout downtown performance by the Chairmen of the Board. Hendrix Theatre screened a midnight showing of *The Rocky Horror Picture Show*, Mendenhall hosted a performance by local group Justincase, and Minges Coliseum staged a concert featuring six country music bands.

FINAL THOUGHTS

For over twenty years, student life at East Carolina University has evolved to reflect changes in the university as well as American culture. While a certain loss of innocence may have accompanied the explosive growth of the school, observers of the institution can take comfort in the fact that East Carolina's students—ambitious, spirited, and adaptable—have successfully kept their footing during both natural and manmade crises, emerging optimistic and well-equipped to face the challenges posed by an ever-changing world.

REFERENCE

ECU Media Board. *East Carolinian*,1982–2004, Greenville, NC: East Carolina University.

## CHAPTER SEVEN

Faculty Organization

BOB MORRISON

THE EAST CAROLINA University Faculty Senate was established and had its first meeting in 1965. A decade later President Leo Jenkins said, "The result has been a constructive relationship between faculty and administration which has, in only a few years, resulted in the most representative and responsible Faculty Senate in the entire university system." Don Sexauer, a faculty member in the School of Art, was instrumental in founding the Faculty Senate, and he was chair of the faculty from 1995 until 1998. In an article in *Pieces of Eight* in 1998, he wrote, "Shared governance in an academic setting is a fragile balancing act that takes place between the administration of the university and its faculty. It is the attempt by the administration and the faculty to solve problems and implement policies in a manner that benefits the constituencies of the university." This chapter details the attempt by the administration and the faculty to solve problems and implement policies in a manner that would benefit the constituencies of the university.

The East Carolina University Code (ECU Code), appendix L of the *Faculty Manual*, outlines the joint effort in the government of ECU. It provides for faculty participation in the governance of the university at the departmental, school, and college level, specifying procedures for appointment of administrative officials, for developing and altering departmental, school, and college codes of operation, and for the evaluation of unit programs and administrators. The code grew out of a code of operations for schools and departments proposed in 1972 by the Faculty Affairs Committee (FAC). That proposed code would have applied uniformly, having the same code for all academic units. The Administrative Academic Council opposed several features of the proposed code. The FAC presented a revised version of the ECU Code that the Faculty Senate adopted on November 14, 1972.

The code outlined processes for appointment of administrative officials, the development of codes for individual units (departments and schools), and the evaluation of unit administrators. A process was outlined for the faculty of each unit, department, or school to democratically develop their individual unit codes. These codes were then submitted to an ad hoc screening committee for review and submission to the senate for approval before going to the chancellor. Changes in unit codes went through the faculty governance committee. In 1986, the ad hoc screening committee became a senate standing committee, the unit code screening committee. This committee screened new unit codes and took over the responsibility for reviewing changes in established unit codes.

In the late 1970s, the Faculty Governance Committee undertook a major rewriting of the ECU Code, presenting its revision to the senate in October 1981. While the 1972 version of the code provided for similar processes for appointing academic administrative officials, including the vice chancellor for academic affairs, deans, and department chairs, this proposed version of the code had different levels of faculty participation for the selection and appointment of administrators, with the greatest faculty participation in the appointment of department chairs. In May 1983, the Board of Trustees rejected that revised code and amended the evaluation process in the old code in appendix L of the *Faculty Manual*. The resulting policy for the appointment of unit administrators required a nominating committee that had three-fifths of its members elected by the faculty of the unit and the remainder appointed by the next senior administrator. The nominating committee was to determine that candidates were acceptable by a majority of the tenured faculty of the unit—department, school, or college.

A key element of the code was the evaluation of a unit's programs and administrators by the faculty. Every four years the faculty voted by secret ballot on the effectiveness of its administrative officers. In the 1970s through the early 1990s a negative vote of three-fifths of the voting faculty was considered a de facto recommendation for removing the administrator. Administrators subject to this review and vote were the deans of the professional schools and the department chairs in the College of Arts and Sciences. The dean of the college was not formally evaluated by the faculty. In the early 1990s, this process was changed to require a negative vote by a majority of the voting faculty for a recommendation to remove a unit administrator. The code also stated that the decision to terminate an administrator's position would be made by the chancellor. This evaluation process by the faculty has provided a useful check on administrative performance, and over time several administrative officers were removed from their positions after receiving negative faculty votes.

The ECU Code was amended in 1993 to provide more detail on unit code development and changes in unit administrator evaluation. This new version of the code also included a change in the definition of a voting faculty member for purposes of appointment of administrators, code development, and unit evaluation. In 1996, the code was again amended to provide more detail on unit administrator evaluation.

In the late 1990s, concern was expressed by some senior administrators and Board of Trustees about what they considered to be veto power by the tenured faculty in the selection of deans and unit administrators. No corresponding changes to the code occurred. Several minor amendments were made to the code during 1998–2003. Through the Faculty Senate, the Faculty Governance Committee developed and implemented guidelines for organizing into code units so that groups of faculty, or departments, would have some guidelines on developing and changing unit structures.

The organization of colleges, schools, and departments required frequent adjustments, with new departments being formed or moved from one school to another as the university met changing societal needs and tried to develop a more efficient structure. In 1980, ECU had nine schools and one college. In the early 1980s, the economics department moved from the School of Business to the College of Arts and Sciences, where it joined anthropology and sociology. The drama and speech department was renamed theatre arts. In the mid-1980s, the Schools of Allied Health Sciences and Nursing moved from the Academic Affairs Division to the Health Sciences Division, which also included the School of Medicine. The Department of Sociology, Anthropology, and Economics divided into two units, a new sociology and anthropology department and the economics department, both remaining in the College of Arts and Sciences. A new communication department was formed in the College of Arts and Sciences.

In the early 1990s, the science education department moved from the College of Arts and Sciences to the School of Education. Home economics was renamed the School of Human Environmental Sciences. The aerospace department moved from the college to the School of Industry and Technology. Planning moved from the college to industry and technology. The health, physical education, and recreational safety department in the college became a new school, Health and Human Performance. Sociology and anthropology became two separate departments.

In 1993, a revised ECU Code stated that these kinds of reorganizations should be reviewed by the Educational Policies and Planning Committee (EPPC) for their recommendation and approval. During the 1998–99 academic year, the School of Social Work was renamed the School of Social Work and Criminal Justice Studies. During the 1999–2000 academic year, the communication department and the computer science division in the mathematics department in the college joined to form the School of Computer Science and Communication with the two departments—communication and broadcasting and computer science. The environmental health department was transferred from the School of Allied Health to the School of Industry and Technology in July 1999. It was also renamed the environmental health sciences safety and technology department.

In the fall semester of 2001, interim vice chancellor for academic affairs Bob Thompson proposed to move teacher education programs from the Departments of English, History, and Mathematics in the College of Arts and Sciences to the School of Education. The faculty associated with these programs would be transferred as well. The deans of education and the college had worked collaboratively with the vice chancellor to develop the proposal. Following the process outlined in the ECU Code, the proposal to move these teacher education programs was submitted to the faculty in the affected departments of the college and to the faculty in education. Then the proposal was sent to the EPPC and the Faculty Senate for their recommendations. The faculty in each of these departments voted against moving the programs, but the department chairs and the dean did not concur with that vote. The education faculty voted in favor of relocating these three programs, and their dean concurred.

During February and March 2002, the EPPC, chaired by George Bailey, collected written responses and heard oral responses from faculty and administrators of the affected units. On April 8, 2002, the EPPC met and voted to recommend that these three teacher education programs remain in the College of Arts and Sciences, and this recommendation was presented to the senate on April 23, 2002. After considerable discussion, the senate voted forty-seven to eight to accept the committee recommendation to keep the teacher education programs in the college. Chancellor William V. Muse overruled the senate recommendation, and in the summer of 2002 the teacher education programs and associated faculty moved.

In July 2002, the faculty of the environmental health sciences, safety, and technology department elected to move the environmental health sciences and safety program to the health education and promotion department in the School of Health and Human Performance. After approval by the faculty in these units, the EPPC voted to recommend that this program be reassigned again. The chancellor agreed.

In 2000, ECU had twelve schools and one college. Members of the Board of Trustees questioned whether this number was too large and whether some should be combined. In the 2002–3 academic year, the academic units underwent substantial reorganization. Part of the argument for the reorganization was that the new structure would be more efficient and less costly. The School of Social Work and Criminal Justice Studies and the School of Human Environmental Sciences merged to form the College of Human Ecology. The music and art schools, the communication and broadcasting department in the computer science and communication school, and the theatre and dance department in arts and sciences combined to form the College of Fine Arts and Communication. The communication and the theatre and dance departments both became schools in this new college. Computer science joined with the School of Industry and Technology to form a new College of Technology and Computer Science.

Several other schools became colleges: The College of Health and Human Performance, the College of Business, and the College of Education. In each of these cases the proposal to reorganize was approved by the faculty. The recommendations went through EPPC and the Faculty Senate before going to the chancellor and the Board of Trustees for final approval. The schools in the Division of Health Sciences remained intact during this reorganization. In the Academic Affairs Division, seven colleges reported to the provost/vice chancellor for academic affairs, a change from nine schools and one college before the reorganization.

The faculty plays a key role in appointment, promotion, and tenure decisions. Before 1975 personnel decisions relied heavily on the department chairs with informal processes for faculty participation in appointment, reappointment, and conferral of permanent tenure. The 1973–75 version of the *Faculty Manual* was reorganized with "Personnel Policy and Procedure for the Faculty" in appendix C and "Provisions Regarding Tenure and Academic Due Process" in appendix D. Appendix D had one page devoted to academic tenure and three and a half pages devoted to suspension and discharge and the hearing process on appeal. The department chairs and deans still held primary responsibility for promotion and salary determination and consulted with the faculty when they deemed appropriate. The statement in appendix C regarding promotion and salary increases read: "Recommendations for promotion and salary increases shall be initiated by the chairman of the department after such consultation with his staff as necessary to promote departmental concord and effectiveness."

Appointments without tenure were probationary. The department chair made the decision whether to retain a nontenured faculty member after such consultation with members of the faculty and the dean of the college or school as he or she deemed appropriate. The statement in appendix D on academic tenure defined the next step: "After the expiration of a probationary period, . . . full-time faculty members have tenure, and their services will be terminated only for adequate cause."

In 1976, appendix D was substantially revised, and departmental personnel committees made recommendations on promotion and tenure. These recommendations were then sent through the chain of command with concurring or nonconcurring recommendations by administrators along the chain. Recommendations of the unit personnel committee to both a unit administrator and his or her immediate supervisor were advisory in nature. There was specific reference to hiring faculty members without the benefit of the probationary track. A six-year limit was included to avoid creating "a liquid pool of faculty who would never be under tenure." In April 1978, appendix C was substantially revised and included grievance procedures as well as sections on selection and appointment of new faculty, professional advancement, and salary. In 1982, appendix C was revised again, and informal faculty grievance procedures for grievances involving sex discrimination and other equal employment opportunity complaints were put in appendix J of the *Faculty Manual*.

In late spring 1988, Chancellor Richard Eakin expressed concern for the consistency of review of personnel policies and appointed an ad hoc committee to consider revisions to appendix D. The ad hoc committee offered some major changes, which included the role of the permanently tenured faculty members in tenure decisions. They proposed that decisions made by personnel committees that did not approve promotion or tenure would not go forward. But the Faculty Governance Committee revised the ad hoc committee's recommendations, keeping a two-track system that had been adopted in the 1970s. On one track were the faculty committee recommendations on appointment, promotion, and tenure, and on the other track were the administrative recommendations. Appendix D stated that in personnel matters the unit administrator is an administrator rather than a faculty member and consequently does not have a faculty vote in personnel matters. It was thought that the unit administrator had a separate vote by concurring or not concurring with the personnel committee's recommendation. The unit personnel, tenure, and promotion committees' recommendations were to be forwarded to the next higher administrator along with the recommendation of the unit administrator.

The new appendix D was to include "material procedural irregularity" as one of the reasons a probationary-term faculty member had for appealing a nonreappointment or nonconferral of permanent tenure. This was taken from a similar statement in the University of North Carolina at Chapel Hill faculty manual and was included to ensure that administrators and faculty committees followed promotion and tenure processes. Minor revisions were made to appendix D from 1995 to 2004 that included revisions to voting procedures and to appellate processes.

The role that fixed-term non-tenure-track faculty members play in their contributions to the welfare of the university and to the education of students has changed significantly during the thirty-year period 1975–2005. A fixed-term non-tenure-track faculty member labors under a contract of fixed length, usually for one semester or one year. Although fixed-term faculty members could have their contracts renewed at the end of the contract term, there was no assurance that a contract would be renewed. Appointment to fixed-term positions was defined in section 604c of the Code of the Board of Governors of the University of North Carolina (UNC Code) and in part states, "All appointments of visiting faculty, adjunct faculty, or other special categories of faculty such as lecturers, artists-in-residence, or writers-in-residence shall be for only a specified term of service." Fixed-term faculty members did not have permanent tenure, nor were they eligible for permanent tenure. At ECU, temporary faculty members had titles such as lecturer, visiting professor, clinical professor, and research professor.

Before the 1980s, fixed-term non-tenure-track faculty members were primarily used to direct special programs, provide special skills, or serve as temporary replacements while a search was conducted for a permanent faculty member. At the beginning of the 1980s, there was a perceived need to have about 10 percent of the ECU faculty on fixed terms, non–tenure track, to provide flexibility in case of enrollment fluctuation.

The 1980s saw a steady rise in the percentage of the faculty on fixed-term appointments. It became a matter not of flexibility but of economics, as lower salaries were paid to faculty members who were not on the tenure track. They also had heavier teaching loads. While flexibility was the initial justification for increasing the number of faculty members without permanent tenure, economics became the overriding factor as the numbers increased. On a full-time-equivalent basis, ECU had about 18 percent of its faculty in non-tenure-track appointments by 1990. By 2000, 30 percent of the faculty was not on tenure track, and in the autumn of 2003 that number had increased to 35 percent (34 percent when the School of Medicine is excluded). In 2003, two academic units had more than 50 percent of their faculty on fixed-term appointments, while five other academic units had between 40 percent and 50 percent of the faculty on fixed-term appointments.

At the beginning of the 1980s, the Faculty Senate constitution defined general faculty: "The General Faculty shall consist of all regular members of the teaching or research staff who hold the rank of full-time instructor or above, all staff personnel who hold ranks equivalent to those of the teaching staff, and general administrative officers of East Carolina University and their assistants in policy making positions."

Lecturers and visiting faculty were not included as part of the general faculty. The constitution was amended in March 1984 with approval by

Chancellor John Howell in April 1984 to revise the definition of general faculty: "The General Faculty shall consist of all full-time members of the teaching, research, or administrative staff who hold an academic title, including those on special faculty appointment (cf. The UNC Code, section 604c)."

Fixed-term faculty members had limited opportunity to participate in shared governance, and that participation was primarily limited to the unit level. They did not vote for representatives for the Faculty Senate, nor did they serve on the senate or its committees.

Issues of freedom, economic security, faculty welfare, and the right to participate in the shared governance of the university are prevalent throughout the history of using fixed-term faculty in continuing positions. The American Association of University Professors (AAUP) addresses some of the issues in their policy documents. They support a normal maximum probationary period of seven years. About tenure, the AAUP policy states: "Tenure is a means to certain ends; specifically: (1) freedom of teaching and research and of extramural activities, and (2) a sufficient degree of economic security to make the profession attractive to men and women of ability. Freedom and economic security, hence, tenure, are indispensable to the success of an institution in fulfilling its obligations to its students and to society."

In line with this policy, ECU had a six-year cap on temporary appointments that would not permit a faculty member's employment beyond six years without being permanently tenured. The 1985 *Faculty Manual* describes the status of reemployment of fixed-term faculty during the 1980s: "It shall be the practice of East Carolina University not to re-employ faculty with fixed term appointments for extensive periods of time beyond their initial date of employment. Re-employment of a faculty member with a fixed term appointment beyond six years in a state-funded position in order to avoid the awarding of tenure is a misuse of this category of employment. Persons who are employed primarily as athletic coaches are excluded from this provision."

At its November 16, 1982, meeting, the Faculty Senate asked the Faculty Affairs Committee (FAC) to study the possibility of removing the six-year cap on hiring fixed-term faculty members. Within the university community, there was growing concern about losing well-qualified fixed-term faculty members. In January 1983, the faculty of the philosophy department passed a resolution asking the FAC to consider policies that would allow no more than 10 percent fixed-term faculty members in any unit, and to allow hiring fixed-term faculty members beyond the sixth year. In March 1983, the faculty of biology passed a resolution requesting that the six-year cap be removed immediately to avoid the loss of highly qualified individuals.

The FAC held open hearings in the fall and winter of 1983–84. Arguments in favor of removing the six-year cap said that fixed-term faculty members are an asset and in a position to make better contributions than someone hired new to replace them; fixed-term faculty members prefer the possibility of indefinite employment as opposed to only six years' work; multiple-year appointments would allow some job security; fixed-term faculty are needed in case of possible cutbacks in case of enrollment drops. Arguments against removing the cap said that indefinitely appointing workers again and again destroys the concept of tenure and threatens the concept of academic freedom, while reductions owing to financial exigency are addressed in the university code. The FAC recommended to the senate that the six-year cap not be removed.

At the February 21, 1984, meeting of the senate, the FAC submitted a resolution to keep the six-year cap in place. The resolution was amended to include: "In schools with clinical disciplines, non-tenured faculty in such positions may be reappointed by the appropriate vice chancellor and dean for continuing terms of one to five years." The senate took no formal action on the resolution and deferred it until the next meeting.

At the March 27, 1984, meeting the resolution was again considered. Vice Chancellor Angelo Volpe stated that about 12 percent of the faculty was in fixed-term positions, but the goal was to reduce that to 10 percent. Additional amendments were proposed, and concern was expressed about the effect on clinical positions in the medical school. The senate decided to establish a special task force to address the six-term cap issue.

At the April 17, 1984, meeting of the Faculty Senate, FAC chair Ione Ryan of the counseling center read a statement to the senate expressing concern about the lack of confidence the senate had in its committees when the senate proposes formation of a special task force to address an issue that was within the charge of a senate committee and for which the senate committee had made a report. The senate voted to rescind the formation of the task force and sent the report on the six-year cap back to the FAC. In its report to the senate at the March 26, 1985, meeting of the senate, the committee recommended that the senate not remove the six-year cap and that the administration review the fixed-term appointments and where appropriate convert them to tenurable, probationary appointments. At its April 23, 1985, meeting, the Faculty Senate voted forty to nine to accept the report, which read:

> All persons appointed to full-time wholly state-supported teaching positions at East Carolina University should either be tenured at the time of initial appointment or recipients of tenure upon the successful completion of an appropriate probationary period—save only those who

are visitors, temporary replacements, or for whose disciplines the institution expects in good faith to have only a short-term need. "Short term" should mean usually two or three years, but under no circumstances should exceed six years. Further, that the administration review all present fixed-term positions and, where appropriate, convert these positions to tenurable, probationary positions.

Chancellor Howell stated that the administration does and would continue to review, and where appropriate convert fixed-term appointments to tenurable, probationary appointments.

The six-year restriction was removed in 1993. March 29, 1994, the Faculty Senate approved a change in the wording: "Re-employment of faculty members for fixed-terms in state-funded positions as special faculty appointments when these faculty members are qualified and apply for vacancies in existing tenure-track positions is a misuse of this category of employment and is prohibited." This paragraph in appendix D of the *Faculty Manual* was subsequently replaced with a statement that made no reference to misuse of the category of employment.

The rights of fixed-term faculty to participate in shared governance was a sensitive issue, because those privileges have to be balanced with the diminished academic freedom associated with lack of permanent tenure. At the March 16, 1982, meeting of the Faculty Senate, the issue of voting rights of fixed-term faculty was addressed. On the eligibility of faculty to participate in electing representatives and to serve on the Faculty Senate, senate bylaws read, "All faculty members are eligible to vote for or serve in the faculty senate who have the rank of instructor or above and who are under yearly contracts with the university as full-time faculty members." This statement had been in the senate bylaws since the 1960s. In a 1982 interpretation, the faculty chair interpreted the wording in the bylaws to preclude fixed-term faculty from voting. After discussion by some senate members who opposed this interpretation, the senate sent the issue of the voting status of fixed-term faculty members to the Faculty Governance Committee. On December 7, 1982, after two readings, the senate voted to change the wording to read: "All full-time faculty members of East Carolina University are eligible to vote for representatives to the Faculty Senate. All full-time faculty members of East Carolina University holding permanent tenure or tenure-track positions are eligible to serve in the Faculty Senate."

An amendment that would allow fixed-term faculty to serve on the senate failed. This change in the bylaws then went to the general faculty on August 22, 1983. At that meeting of the general faculty the amendment was again offered to change the wording of the second sentence to "All full-time faculty members of East Carolina University in at least their second year of appointment to the unit which they will represent are eligible for election to the Faculty Senate."

The general faculty voted in favor of the amendment, and fixed-term faculty members were given the right to serve on the Faculty Senate and to vote for representatives for the senate.

Fixed-term faculty members did not have voting rights on policies in the ECU Code, which includes the appointment of administrative officials, development of unit codes, unit program evaluation, and unit administrator evaluation. Before the 1980s, the *Faculty Manual* appendix L had a definition of *voting faculty member* that included the wording, "A voting faculty person is defined for the purpose of this code as an individual with an academic title and not less than half a normal teaching or research program as practiced in his or her unit."

On February 21, 1984, the Faculty Senate voted to change the definition to "a full-time individual with an academic title or on special faculty appointment (cf. The UNC Code, 604c)." This provision gave fixed-term faculty the right to vote on ECU code issues and was approved by Chancellor John Howell and by the Board of Trustees on July 1, 1984. It was implemented in the 1985 *Faculty Manual*. In 1993, a new appendix L was approved that restricted voting faculty members with the wording:

> A voting faculty member is someone who is appointed to a full-time faculty position; who is a permanently tenured or probationary term faculty person; who has been employed in any faculty position for at least 12 consecutive months at East Carolina University; who has regular academic faculty rank (ECU Faculty Manual, Appendix D, Tenure and Promotion Policies and Procedures of ECU); and who must, except as noted below for faculty on leaves of absence, be carrying at East Carolina University, at the time of the voting, not less than half the normal teaching/ research program as practiced in the unit of appointment.

This changing voting eligibility illustrates the differing points of view on the importance of academic freedom as well as faculty members' long-term commitments to the university when making shared-governance decisions.

By the 1999–2000 academic year, nearly one-third of the faculty were in non-tenure-track positions. The faculty officers discussed the need to understand the role the increasing number of fixed-term faculty members was playing in the academic mission of the university. In his annual report on the employment category for faculty at the December 7, 1999, meeting of the Faculty Senate, Chancellor Eakin spoke of "the 'distressing' characteristic on the decline of tenure track faculty members since 1991, and the increase in non-tenure track positions. Compared to other UNC institutions, ECU has lower percentage of faculty not on tenure track, but a task force will be empanelled to discover reasons for the gradual increase in non-tenure track faculty" (Faculty Senate minutes, December 7, 1999).

In the late 1990s, the academic freedom and tenure committee and the faculty welfare and benefits committee of the UNC faculty assembly were also discussing the increasing numbers of non-tenure-track faculty in the UNC system and the concerns for academic freedom, job security, and benefits of non-tenure-track faculty. In February 2001, Gretchen Bataille, senior vice president for academic affairs, appointed a committee on non-tenure-track faculty to examine the employment of non-tenure-track faculty in the University of North Carolina system. The task force presented the report to the UNC Board of Governors, which on March 6, 2002, approved the recommendation that the staff of the Office of the President be charged to work with the campuses to implement the recommendations of the report of the committee on non-tenure-track faculty.

In January 2003 the ECU Faculty Welfare Committee and the provost jointly appointed a task force on fixed-term faculty that would report to both the provost and the Faculty Welfare Committee with monthly written progress reports and a final written report by the end of spring semester 2003. The final report in July 2003 addressed some of the UNC recommendations but left others open.

In February 2004, the Faculty Welfare Committee, in a resolution to the senate, asked the faculty chair and the chancellor to appoint a committee to further study the major recommendations approved by the UNC Board of Governors and to provide answers by September 2004. The process was delayed by changing administrations, and, in the fall of 2004, a fixed-term faculty committee was appointed to address the UNC recommendations.

Faculty members who have permanent tenure enjoy the guarantee of protection against arbitrary and unjust application of disciplinary penalties including discharge. Appendix D of the *Faculty Manual* states, "During the period of such guarantees, the faculty member may be discharged or suspended from employment or diminished in rank only for reasons of incompetence, neglect of duty, or misconduct of such a nature as to indicate that the individual is unfit to continue as a member of the faculty."

In the 1990s, there was a national trend to implement formal reviews of the performance of tenured faculty members. In July 1996, UNC president C. D. Spangler Jr. discussed posttenure review of tenured faculty members with the UNC Board of Governors. In August, he sent a memorandum to the chancellors requesting that they appoint a representative to an ad hoc committee to study post-tenure review and to develop a list describing the principal features of a posttenure review process.

In September 1996, the East Carolina Faculty Governance Committee began drafting a list of principles for post-tenure review that was sent to the Faculty Senate in October 1996. The cornerstone for the review would be annual written evaluations. Development plans were to be used to improve deficiencies of faculty who received a series of negative annual reviews. The Faculty Senate and the chancellor approved the principles. The UNC ad hoc committee subsequently developed a set of principles for the UNC system.

In April 1998, the Faculty Senate passed a post-tenure review process scheduled every five years. Each year in which tenured faculty members were to be reviewed, the unit tenure committees would elect at least a three-member cumulative review committee from the unit's tenured faculty, with one alternate. A faculty member would be rated by the cumulative review committee on a scale of "exemplary," "satisfactory," or "deficient." The Faculty Senate also passed a resolution, somewhat tongue-in-cheek, for the UNC Board of Governors to initiate a review every five years of the board and the UNC general administration to be undertaken by the tenured faculty in the UNC system. Both the post-tenure review process and the request to the UNC Board of Governors were approved by the chancellor on April 15. In November 1998, the Faculty Senate approved a clarifying amendment to the post-tenure review process, and the "Policy for the Cumulative Review of Permanently Tenured Faculty" was included in the *Faculty Manual* as appendix B.

In the period 1998–2003, over 4,000 faculty members completed post-tenure review in the UNC system, and 128 (3 percent) were found deficient. At ECU, 578 faculty were reviewed, and less than 1 percent of the faculty were found deficient.

Faculty members are evaluated annually on their contributions to teaching, research and creative activity, and service. In their monthly discussions during the 1999–2000 academic year, the faculty officers, chancellor, and vice chancellors discussed the role of faculty in shared governance and other service activities. The relatively low reward accorded to those faculty members who played a large role in the shared governance of the university was a key topic. Vice Chancellor Richard Ringeisen and faculty chair Brenda Killingsworth from the School of Business jointly appointed a task force on faculty roles and rewards. This group examined the changing role of faculty in an evolving university that was becoming more research-oriented and at the same time growing in student population. They recommended that rather than using the standard teaching, research, and service model for faculty workload, that there should be flexibility in faculty assignments. They agreed that faculty assignments should align with departmental needs and areas in which individual faculty members excel. Under this model some faculty members would be more involved in teaching and others more involved in research.

At the same time, ECU was in the initial phases of an accreditation study by the Southern Association of Colleges and Schools (SACS). The ECU SACS Education and Research Committee had drafted a "community of scholars" concept that included faculty assignment flexibility. They recommended that faculty who did not conduct research or creative activity programs be rewarded for their heavier teaching assignments. The community of scholars concept was incorporated into the faculty roles and rewards task force report. In November 2001, Charles Glassick, coauthor of *Scholarship Assessed,* was invited to campus to conduct a workshop on expanding the definition of scholarship and on evaluating that scholarship.

In the fall semester of 2002, the commission on scholarship was formed. The commission examined documents and processes from other universities. They reported to the Faculty Senate in the fall of 2003 recommending the definition of scholarship to include the scholarship of teaching, the scholarship of engagement (application), the scholarship of discovery (traditional research), and the scholarship of integration. The report recommended making any necessary changes in the *Faculty Manual* to incorporate the changes in the definition of scholarship. The report was forwarded to the faculty governance committee for their consideration.

University grievance appellate processes have been established to aid faculty members and administrators in resolving their grievances. These range from appeals because of nonreappointment and nonconferral of permanent tenure to salary and workload disputes. The UNC Code lists several categories of faculty grievances. In the UNC Code, the Board of Governors had stated, "When framing our system of governance, the Board of Governors invested heavily in the idea that persons of intelligence and goodwill ought to be able to work out many of their differences through relatively informal University-sponsored procedures." Sections 603, 604, 605, and 607 of the UNC Code listed the various types of faculty grievances.

In the early 1980s, the Faculty Senate appellate committees were the Faculty Affairs Committee for faculty grievances that included matters directly related to a faculty member's employment status and institutional relationships under section 607 of the UNC Code, the Hearing Committee for nonreappointment or not granting tenure under section 604 of the UNC Code, the Due Process Committee for termination due to serious sanction under section 603 of the UNC code, and the reconsideration committee to review appeals of dismissal due to financial exigency under section 605 of the UNC Code.

In the 1982–83 academic year, an ad hoc committee on faculty grievance procedures recommended making changes to these committees by combining some of the appellate processes. Richard Robinson, assistant to the UNC president for legal affairs, advised that committee processes should reflect the sections of the UNC Code. The Faculty Affairs Committee continued to hear faculty grievances in addition to its broader charge on governance issues. Most grievances during this time were related to salary or promotion. Tenure and reappointment appeals continued to be handled by the Hearing Committee.

In 1992, the Senate Grievance Board was formed to hear complaints of sexual or racial harassment or discrimination or conflicts of interest. In 1994, the Faculty Grievance Committee was formed to hear the grievances under section 607 of the UNC Code.

In the 1990s, the university attorneys became involved in the grievance process by advising administrator respondents and upper-level administrators. Faculty members frequently were retaining private attorneys at considerable personal expense. Some faculty members had the perception that grievance processes were becoming more adversarial. The chancellor's responses to grievance committee reports during this time included references to legal handbooks for out-of-context definitions of terms in the *Faculty Manual*. Grievance processes were not working on the ECU campus, and apparently there were problems on other UNC campuses as well.

The Office of the President formed a grievance task force to make recommendations to solve some of these problems. This report was submitted to the UNC Board of Governors in November 2002. UNC system 607 grievance processes were revised in 2003 and 2004, with mediation to play a primary role in the resolution process. In 2003–4, the ECU Faculty Grievance Committee rewrote, and the trustees approved, major sections of appendix Y of the *Faculty Manual* that addressed the 607 grievances. In this revised process, attorneys were to be excluded from the process at its early stages. Both grievants and respondents would have access to university counselors who had experience as leaders in shared governance. Outside mediators would be used in the early stages of the process in an attempt to resolve conflicts. These changes provided the framework for people of intelligence and goodwill to work out their differences.

The relationship between intercollegiate athletics and the academic mission of a university is complex and often controversial, and at the national level there have been many reported scandals and abuses related to universities' athletics programs. Often the entertainment aspects of intercollegiate athletics overshadow a university's academic mission. There have been a number of national attempts to reform intercollegiate athletics, including those of the Knight Commission on Athletics cochaired by

William Friday, former president of the University of North Carolina. The Knight Commission produced its *Report I* in 1991–93, *Report II* in 1999, and *Report III* in 2004.

Many of the reform efforts attempted to include an increasing role by the faculty in the governance of athletics. In a speech in October 2003, Myles Brand, president of the National Collegiate Athletic Association (NCAA), stated that he wanted to integrate intercollegiate athletics into the academic mission of the university and that faculty members are especially important in that effort. The AAUP has developed a set of principles and recommended practices on the role of faculty in the reform of intercollegiate athletics. These include among others the election of faculty members to a University Athletics Committee and the election of the committee chair by the Faculty Senate.

At its April meeting in 1985, the senate endorsed the statement on intercollegiate athletics made by university chief executive officers at meetings held in Miami, Florida, in March 1985. It in part stated that freshmen should be ineligible to participate in those varsity sports that create substantial threats to successful academic adjustment such as football and basketball. It recommended that there be no weakening of the requirements governing initial eligibility of student athletes in Division I-A schools. Consideration must be given to shortening the length of playing seasons and reducing the number of contests to provide student athletes with a more appropriate balance between academic and athletic activities. These issues were being studied by both the NCAA and the UNC Board of Governors.

In a report to the UNC Board of Governors in October 1985, a Special Committee on Intercollegiate Athletics recommended that faculty leaders have a more informed involvement and participation in the internal governance of intercollegiate athletics. The issues studied in that report also included freshman eligibility, admissions with exceptions, the number of contests, season lengths, drugs, and gambling. The UNC Board of Governors asked the chancellors to conduct a study on the length of seasons, number of contests, and recruitment practices and to submit reports to UNC President C. D. Spangler Jr. by October 1, 1986.

In the fall of 1989, Spangler presented a lengthy report to the Board of Governors that outlined academic abuses in the basketball program at North Carolina State University, later detailed in the book *Personal Fouls*, by Peter Golenbeck. The Board of Governors added some additional statements to its policies on athletics, including that the chancellors and boards of trustees shall insure that there is an effective faculty committee on athletics that reports annually to the Faculty Senate, or other appropriate office of faculty governance, on the operations of the athletic programs. In his report to the faculty assembly, Spangler stated: "The task to the faculty is to insist that athletic programs function within the academic standards of the University. I want to urge you to take that responsibility."

The UNC policy on intercollegiate athletics includes the statement adopted in 1989: "The chancellors and the Board of Trustees shall insure that there is an effective faculty committee on athletics that reports annually to the faculty senate, or other appropriate office of faculty governance, on the operations of the athletic programs."

In a resolution on October 10, 1989, ECU's Faculty Senate charged the "committee on committees to join with the Chancellor to encourage faculty participation in pursuing President Spangler's request that athletic programs function within the academic standards of the University." In November 1989, Chancellor Richard Eakin and the Faculty Senate impaneled a group consisting of the Committee on Committees and four members of the UAC to study the UAC structure and charge.

The group met in the fall and spring semesters of 1989–90 to fashion a new charge. The UAC charge in the 1980s read that it should "advise the Chancellor about general issues pertaining to intercollegiate athletics at East Carolina University, including but not restricted to conference matters, budget, compliance with legal regulations, fund raising and public relations." Part of the impaneled group's consideration was the statement put forward by the Faculty Assembly Governance Committee that the Athletics Committee should have a majority of its membership elected by the faculty, that the chair be elected by the committee, that the committee report at least annually to the faculty, and that the committee should have oversight responsibility for the maintenance of sound academic standards in relation to its student athletes.

At the April meeting of the UAC, several members expressed concern about the new UAC charge being proposed by the Committee on Committees. The UAC members thought the committee chair should be the faculty athletic representative (FAR) to the National Collegiate Athletic Association, and there was some question about the involvement of the Faculty Senate in UAC structure.

The Committee on Committees presented its recommended changes to the UAC at the April 1990 meeting of the senate. It adopted changes that revised the membership to include eight faculty members, five elected by the senate and three appointed by the chancellor. The chair of the committee was to be elected by the committee from among the faculty members. The committee would report at least once a year to the senate and other times as necessary.

The UAC would have an Academic Review Committee that would consist of the faculty members of the committee. They would be responsible to review the academic quality of the athletic programs and would make its recommendations and reports to the senate and the chancellor. The senate adopted changes to the UAC as Resolution 90-35.

At the September meeting of the UAC, Chancellor Eakin reported that he was adopting some of the senate's recommendations, but he chose to keep the FAR as the committee chair. He also adjusted the quorum to five faculty members, without the senate's stipulation that the quorum be from the elected members, and he made some adjustments to committee functions. In July 1992, he formally adopted Resolution 90-35 with the exception of the election of the chairperson, and the Academic Review Committee was renamed the Academic Integrity Committee. The committee chair would continue to be the FAR appointed by the chancellor. The revised charge of the committee read: "The Committee is concerned with issues pertaining to intercollegiate athletics at East Carolina University. Primary functions of the Committee are oversight responsibility in the area of academic integrity, compliance with NCAA rules and regulations, and the development of student athletes. General issues such as budget, conference matters, fund-raising, and public relations are inclusive in the charge, but not restricted to those cited. The Academic Integrity Subcommittee, composed of the faculty members of the committee, will report on the academic quality of the athletic program."

The Academic Integrity Committee would regularly review the academic records of student athletes to give oversight of student athletes' academic performance. The membership of the UAC included five faculty members elected by the senate; three faculty members appointed by the chancellor; the FAR, who served as chair; and the chair of the faculty. In 2002, the chair, or a representative, of the Faculty Senate Academic Standards Committee was added as an ex officio member. There were eight additional ex officio members. The UAC had its membership revised through the Committee on Committees in 2004 to include the provost/vice chancellor for academic affairs or his or her representative.

In the fall of 2004, the ECU senate joined the Coalition on Intercollegiate Athletics (COIA). The COIA is a national organization of faculty senates and councils that is proposing reform in the governance of athletics in Division I-A schools. In 2005, the UAC became a Faculty Senate committee.

GRADUATION RATES

The progress toward graduation of each student is important. In May 1991, Vice Chancellor Marlene Springer and Faculty Chair James Joyce of physics jointly appointed an Ad Hoc Committee on Academic Regulations. The ad hoc committee made a number of recommendations, which included revising the retention standards of all students. The old retention standards had no required grade point averages (GPA) for 1–7 completed hours of work; for 8–31 completed hours, a 1.35 cumulative GPA was required. For 32–63 completed hours, a 1.6 cumulative GPA was required; for 64–95 completed hours, a 1.8 cumulative GPA was required; and for more than 96 hours completed, a 1.9 cumulative GPA was required. A GPA of 2.0 was required for graduation. The committee brought its recommendations to the Faculty Senate in the fall semester of 1992, endorsed by the credits committee and EPPC. The senate passed the recommendations, after some revision. The new standards required a 1.75 cumulative GPA for completed hours 0–31 and a 2.0 cumulative GPA after 32 completed hours. Requiring a 2.0 cumulative GPA earlier in a student's academic career was consistent with national trends and was thought to result in higher graduation rates, as students would have more rigorous targets earlier in their academic studies. These new standards would be among the highest in the state.

At the April 1994 meeting of the Faculty Senate, Chancellor Richard Eakin reported some concerns the Board of Trustees had about the new standards. The board had concerns about losing an additional 150–250 students per year and about special student populations such as minorities and student athletes. Chancellor Eakin decided to proceed in the fall with the emphasis on the quality in the recommendations without implementing the penalties. He appointed an oversight committee including three members recommended by the faculty chair. The oversight committee would monitor student performance and develop intervention strategies for students who fell below the standards. In a report to the December 1997 meeting of the Faculty Senate, Chancellor Eakin announced that the Ad Hoc Committee on Academic Standards had concluded that the university should not implement the new standards but continue with intervention strategies. He asked for the senate's endorsement of a plan to have the enrollment services council, augmented with a representative from the Credits Committee, develop new standards to be presented to the senate. The recommendations of the enrollment services council would be forwarded to the appropriate senate committees.

The report on new academic standards was presented at the April 1998 meeting of the Faculty Senate. The standards required a 1.6 cumulative GPA for hours 0–29, a 1.8 cumulative GPA for hours 30–59, and a 2.0 cumulative GPA for more than 60 hours. The proposal included intervention strategies for students who dropped below the standards. The ensuing discussion centered mainly around requirements for student athletes. There was concern that student athletes would be at risk because NCAA rules didn't permit freshmen to take more than 25 percent of the normal semester load during the summer. Concerns were raised about the new retention standards being higher than those at the University of North Carolina at Chapel Hill and North Carolina State University. The report was sent back to committee for further review. The committee received response papers from the athletic program, to which the credits committee sent detailed explanations and the rationale for the new standards. The committee met with representatives of over twenty-five groups, including many campus offices. At the December 1998 meeting of the Faculty Senate, the credits committee presented slightly revised standards that included a requirement of a GPA of 1.9 for hours 60–74 and 2.0 for more than 75 hours. These standards had broad-based support within the campus community. The new standards were adopted by the Faculty Senate and approved by the chancellor.

CHANCELLOR SELECTION

Faculty involvement in chancellor selection processes is a recurring issue whenever a chancellor vacancy occurs. The first sentence in appendix 1, section 1.D on chancellor selection in the UNC Code reads, "In the event of a vacancy in the chancellorship, the board of trustees shall establish a search committee composed of representatives of the board of trustees, the faculty, the student body and the alumni."

The level of faculty involvement at East Carolina University varied from one chancellor search to another.

After Chancellor Thomas Brewer resigned in 1981, the Board of Trustees chair Ashley B. Futrell sent a memo to the ECU faculty stating that he was asking the Faculty Senate to nominate three faculty members to serve on the Chancellor Selection Committee and that he would appoint one at-large faculty member. Futrell believed that faculty representation and input in the selection process were vital to the success of the process. The senate met in special session on October 6, 1981, to elect the three members to the Chancellor Selection Committee. The faculty had sent thirty-four names to the senate as candidates for nomination to the committee. The senate elected the three nominees from the list of candidates in five ballots. The final search committee of twelve members included five faculty members, among them the three elected by the senate.

At its October 20, 1981, regular meeting, the senate passed a resolution requesting that the evaluation criteria used by the Chancellor Selection Committee be widely circulated in journals and newspapers. Senate members expressed concern that the advertisement for the position did not speak to the evaluation criteria and that the criteria to be used by the committee were to remain the personal privilege of the committee.

On November 3, 1981, the Faculty Senate held a special called meeting to meet with trustee chair Futrell to discuss the chancellor selection process. In answer to a number of questions, Futrell outlined the important attributes a candidate must have. He stated that learning would be put ahead of winning in athletics, and that strong, shared governance was a positive aspect of the university. In a resolution adopted in January 1982, the senate requested that procedures similar to those used in 1978 be employed in the current search to insure faculty involvement in the interview process. (In 1978, four candidates had been brought to campus and had met with faculty senators, student leaders, and other university leaders. Those who had participated in the interview process in 1978 had completed evaluation forms and returned them to the search committee.)

The faculty members of the Chancellor Selection Committee reported regularly to the senate. Four candidates were brought to campus to meet with faculty, administrative, staff, student, and community leaders. The candidates met separately with the senate. Faculty, staff, and students were provided with rating scales. After the interview process, the search committee made its recommendation, and President William Friday recommended John M. Howell Jr. to the UNC Board of Governors for appointment as chancellor. Chancellor Howell had been interim chancellor since the resignation of Chancellor Brewer.

In the fall of 1985, Chancellor Howell announced he would retire from the chancellorship by June 1987. This provided ample time to begin a search for a new chancellor. Board chair C. Ralph Kinsey Jr., in discussions with faculty chair Ken Wilson of sociology, requested recommendations from the senate on the criteria for selecting a new chancellor, and recommendations on the interview process. The senate elected three ad hoc committees, the Ad Hoc Committee on Criteria for Chancellor Selection, the Ad Hoc Committee on Development of Search Procedures, and the Ad Hoc Committee on Development of Campus Interview Procedures. These committees reported to the senate, and their reports were forwarded to the Chancellor Search Committee. Kinsey asked the senate to elect three members to the search committee. He asked for one from the medical school, at least one from the College of Arts and Sciences, and at least one minority or female faculty member. The three elected by the senate were all from the College of Arts and Sciences, so chair Kinsey selected two of the three and appointed another member from the school of medicine to make up the three faculty representatives on the search committee. In November 1986, two candidates were brought to the campus for open interviews with faculty, staff, students, and community leaders. Richard Eakin was selected as the new chancellor.

In the spring of 2000, Chancellor Eakin announced his resignation.

Board chair Phillip R. Dixon appointed a search committee that included four faculty members. All chancellor candidate interviews were closed, with no open on-campus interviews for the finalists. In spite of repeated requests by the faculty representatives on the committee, the interview process remained closed. Finalists visited the campus and met with top administrators, but no open interviews with faculty, staff, students, and community leaders occurred. Some finalists were concerned about the reaction the faculty would have at not being allowed to meet with chancellor candidates when they came to campus. In spite of this closed process, the news media were able to obtain the names of finalists, which were reported in local newspapers. William V. Muse, president of Auburn University, was selected chancellor beginning in August 2001.

Chancellor Muse stepped down in September 2003. Board of Trustees chair James Talton appointed a thirteen-member search committee that included four faculty members. While the on-campus interviews were not open to all faculty, staff, and students, they were conducted with an expanded committee that included selected faculty and administrative leaders. Once again the media obtained names of the finalists, and they were published in local newspapers. Steven Ballard was appointed chancellor in June 2004.

GRANTS AND AWARDS

To foster and support research at ECU, a system of offering university-sponsored grants for innovative research was begun in 1978. The University Research Committee was established to review research grant proposals and make recommendations on awarding grants. During the 1978–79 academic year, the committee received 115 grant proposals that asked for a total amount of $162,000. The committee recommended funding fifty-six proposals for a total amount of $46,000. The next year the committee received ninety-four proposals and recommended funding seventy proposals, for a total of $55,000. The total amount awarded for 1981–82 was $54,000, and by 1994–95 the total amount awarded was $81,000. The amount took a significant jump in the late 1990s to about $250,000 per year.

In the 1982–83 academic year, the Teaching Grants Committee was established and began to review proposals to develop innovative teaching methods. Three summer stipends were awarded the first year. In the 1983–84 academic year, the committee recommended funding ten proposals out of fourteen applications, for a total amount of $5,800. During the 1988–89 academic year, the awards were still relatively low, with six grants receiving a total of $5,300 for project expenses, and five summer stipends recommended by the committee. The next year saw a dramatic increase in funding of teaching grants to a total of $50,719, and the following two years teaching grant funding increased to about $60,000. Unlike the stable source of funding for research grants, the source of funding for teaching grants was not stable from year to year, and the later funding amounts fluctuated between about $50,000 and $100,000 depending on available funds.

Although considerably more funds have been awarded in research grants, most of the recognition of excellence awards have been for teaching. The ECU Alumni Association has a long history of providing teaching awards to faculty members. In 1980, the cash amount of the award was $500. That was changed to $1,000 in 1990. Two awards per year were made until 1994, when the university began awarding three $1,000 Alumni Association awards for outstanding teaching. In 2002–3, the association discontinued funding for two of the awards, and the chancellor's office funded the remaining two, which became university awards for outstanding teaching.

In 1994, the UNC Board of Governors began teaching excellence awards for faculty members on the sixteen UNC campuses. The board's awards for excellence in teaching were limited to one faculty member on each of the sixteen campuses and included a $7,500 cash award. ECU faculty members who have received recognition are Margaret Capen, business; Patricia Campbell, education; Rhonda Fleming, music; Richard Marks, medicine; Edward "Mel" Markowski, human environmental sciences; Karl L. Wuensch, psychology; Louise Toppin, music; Betty Peel, education; Iona Poston, nursing; Michael J. Spurr, mathematics; and J. Frank James, medicine.

In addition to the award for excellence in teaching, the board also awards a distinguished professor teaching award. Since 1994–95, these have been presented annually to six faculty members at each of the sixteen campuses.

In 2000, the academic affairs vice chancellor began recognizing faculty members who effectively integrate research/creative activity in classroom teaching. There have been between nine and thirteen scholar/teacher awards given to faculty members annually since the 1999–2000 academic year. In 1997, the Division of Continuing Education established the Max Ray Joyner award for "faculty service for continuing education." In 2001, the senate awards committee developed procedures and began selecting award winners.

In 1994–95, the Research Creative Activity Policy Committee of the senate was formed. It was charged with reviewing and developing policies for research and creativity and making recommendations to the senate as well as developing guidelines for new five-year and lifetime awards for research and creative activity. The first awards were given in the 1995–96 academic year. Initially two awards were given annually and came with a significant cash prize. Recipients were also considered for the title of distinguished research professor. Beginning in 2002–3, up to four awards were given.

Each year the UNC Board of Governors names a recipient of the O. Max Gardner Award. This award is made to a faculty member in the UNC system who has made the greatest contribution to the welfare of the human race. Since 1980, the East Carolina University recipients have been Stanley R. Riggs in geology in 1983, Edgar Loessin in theatre in 1986, William E. Laupus in medicine in 1989, Walter J. Pories in medicine in 2001, and W. Randolph Chitwood in medicine in 2004.

At its March 2005 meeting, the Faculty Senate celebrated its fortieth anniversary. Faculty chairs since 1980 were Thomas H. Johnson, 1979–82, health and human performance; Caroline L. Ayers, 1982–83, chemistry; James Le-Roy Smith, 1983–85, philosophy; Kenneth R. Wilson, 1985–87, sociology; John Conner Atkeson, 1987–89, history; James M. Joyce, 1989–91, physics; John C. Moskop, 1991–93, medicine; Patricia J. Anderson, 1993–95, education; Donald R. Sexauer, 1995–98, fine arts and communication; Brenda L. Killingsworth, 1998–2000, business; Robert C. Morrison, 2000–3, chemistry; Frederick D. Niswander, 2003–4, business; and Catherine Rigsby, 2004–5, geology.

AS PRESIDENT Leo Jenkins said in the mid-1970s, the constructive relationship between faculty and administration has resulted in the most representative and responsible Faculty Senate in the entire university system. The above examples illustrate that the administration and the faculty work together to solve problems and implement policies in a manner that benefits the constituencies of the university. They often succeed in the fragile balancing act that occurs between the administration of the university and its faculty. This has required good leadership by both the faculty and the administration. ECU has benefited from the long-term leadership of faculty members such as Don Sexauer and Henry Ferrell, who were there in the mid-1960s when shared governance was formalized in the creation of the senate. The future of ECU depends on the active participation in shared governance by the younger faculty, who will become the leaders of tomorrow.

NOTE

The author wishes to acknowledge the notes provided by John Conner Atkeson. Thanks to Lori Lee for invaluable assistance in locating information in Faculty Senate documents and for comments on the manuscript for this chapter.

## CHAPTER EIGHT

Administration

JIM SMITH AND MARY ANN ROSE

FROM 1975 to the present, East Carolina University experienced a remarkable period of memorable leadership. Just as Robert Wright had combined locality and experience from afar in his own successful career, the senior administration during this period included local skill and experience as well as talented people traveling to the institution from other places. Here is a summary sketch of some of the more significant moments in this blending. Five different chancellors have led the university during this period.

JOHN MCDADE HOWELL

John McDade Howell became chancellor in 1982. A native Alabaman, he is also a longtime member of the ECU community, and he was a stabilizing presence as he assumed the chancellorship. He was sixty years old, a respected faculty member and administrator, and five years away from retirement. He had a short time to accomplish a great deal, and he did just that.

John Howell was the youngest in a family of nine children. The eldest child was a boy and the next seven were girls. His mother died when he was only twelve, so he was raised primarily by his father.

Howell grew up on a farm in rural Alabama. While he respected the rural values that his family instilled in him at an early age, he recognized that growing cotton was not something that he wanted to do for his entire life. Most of his sisters were teachers, and he made up his mind early on that he didn't want to assume that role. Yet later he was to become a teacher and to regard teaching as his most enjoyable work. He left the farm at eighteen to join the Air Force.

In the Air Force, Howell served as a master sergeant in a service unit responsible for aircraft maintenance. He was stationed primarily in England and France and notes that he saw very little combat in that assignment, unless he went into London on leave, where there was bombing. He served from 1942 through 1945.

Returning from the war, Howell used the GI Bill to obtain his education. His original ambition was to go into journalism, and he entered the University of Alabama, majoring in journalism with a minor in political science. Spending only two and a half years to complete the bachelor's degree, he went on immediately for the master's degree. Howell notes that his father was always interested in politics and there were many dinner table conversations around that subject. Realizing that he was finding political science more interesting than journalism, he studied it for his master's degree. After finishing that degree in one year, he moved on to Duke University for his doctorate.

While he was in dissertation, his doctoral adviser took a Fulbright and was gone for a year. John Howell took a teaching position for that year at Randolph-Macon Woman's College and there met his lifelong partner, Gladys David, an instructor in sociology and anthropology. They were married in August 1952. Howell returned to Duke to complete the doctorate, and the new Mrs. Howell completed her contract at Randolph-Macon, commuting on the weekends to be with her husband.

Howell's next job took the young couple to Memphis State University. While on faculty there, he received a telephone call from President Messick at East Carolina University. Howell had never heard of the university in eastern North Carolina, but Messick was offering him a job! He asked for a day to think it over and used that time to call his professor at Duke. He found that President Messick had called seeking a recommendation and learned of young Dr. Howell. Although Howell had never heard of East Carolina, he had an acquaintance at Memphis who was originally from Tarboro, North Carolina. She was enthusiastic about ECU. That was enough for him, and the couple made their way to Greenville. The year was 1957.

Howell began as an associate professor in what was then the Department of Social Studies, encompassing the fields of history and government. In 1963, President Messick asked him if he would consider chairing the department. He quipped that he would much rather chair a department of political science than one that included history, so the department was divided, with Howell chairing political science and Dr. Herbert R. Pascal chairing the new Department of History. This step marked the beginning of Howell's administrative career, a career that would move him from the position of department chair all the way up to that of chancellor.

Three years later, in 1966, Howell became dean of the College of Arts

Dr. Howell speaks at the 1983 Commencement.

and Sciences, a position he held for three years. In 1969, he was named dean of the graduate school, a position that he again held for three years. Next he became provost, a position later renamed vice chancellor for academic affairs. He served as the vice chancellor for academic affairs for six years, leaving administration to return to the classroom. After remaining out of the administrative role for two and a half years, he returned to administration as interim chancellor.

While Howell was moving up the administrative ladder, his wife Gladys returned to teaching. With their children now of school age, she was free to join the sociology department where she was a popular teacher. She continued to serve on faculty until her husband became chancellor. Then, leaving the position of faculty member, she became first lady of the university.

When Leo Jenkins retired, his successor, Thomas Bowman Brewer, assumed the role of chancellor in 1978. Dr. Brewer came to ECU from Texas Christian University and served for a relatively brief time. He left his position at the end of the fall semester 1981, and the president of the University of North Carolina, William Friday, asked Howell to serve as the interim chancellor. He did so for about six months, in 1982 becoming the permanent chancellor.

The Department of Athletics

The first challenge that confronted the new chancellor was a problem in the Department of Athletics. Contributions to the Pirate Club had decreased, and there was a resulting $500,000 deficit in the budget of the athletics department. The director of athletics, Dr. O. Kenneth Karr Jr., was fairly new to his position, having arrived in 1980, and he and the new chancellor set out to solve the problem. Howell appointed a committee to help raise the needed money, and the group was successful.

There was also a problem with the admission requirements in athletics. It was a fairly universal practice, according to Howell, for departments of athletics to recruit students who would be good athletes but held no promise of being good students. A strong movement was developing in the universities in the southeastern United States. Howell attended a meeting in Miami of the chief executive officers of many of those institutions to pass a resolution calling upon the NCAA to mandate higher admission standards. When it became clear that the NCAA would indeed set new admission standards, Howell and the Admissions Committee at ECU abolished the old admission practice.

Howell noted later that he knew most of the faculty and they knew him, so it was no secret that he was not much of a sportsman. Nevertheless, he brought about a great deal of change in that department and later referred to that work as some of the most satisfying of his time as chancellor.

Expanding Development

During his brief tenure as chancellor, Brewer had moved to expand the development effort. He hired a development officer, Mr. Donald L. Lemish, and had that position established at a vice chancellor level. When Dr. Brewer left the university, Mr. Lemish left the university as well. Howell conducted a search for a new individual to head the effort, and James Lanier was brought to campus.

There were two facets within the broad area of development that Howell and Lanier focused on in particular. They recognized the importance of having named professorships and also wanted to establish academic scholarships for talented students that would allow the university to compete more effectively for the brightest and best students.

When W. Riley Roberson III, of Washington, North Carolina, chair of the Trustee Committee on Development, brought to the Board of Trustees the concept of the University Scholars Award, he announced that he and his sister, Robin Potts, would endow the first scholarship in honor of their parents, Bill and Frances Roberson. Two more trustees, Chairman C. Ralph Kinsey Jr. and John F. Minges, announced that they, too, would fund scholarships. With that auspicious beginning, the establishment of additional scholarships grew rapidly.

The idea of named professorships was to allow the university to bring in highly talented and successful professors who could then teach and also assist the junior faculty. ECU needed $500,000 to establish a named professorship, a portion to be provided by the General Administration from a fund appropriated by the General Assembly. The first named chair was funded by the Dillard Teer family in honor of their son, Robert, a graduate of ECU's School of Business.

Accomplishments During the Howell Years

Howell always said that president Leo Jenkins was a master at relating to people in the region, and he followed in his footsteps by reaching out to the various constituencies in the region. The chancellor's home became the center of gracious entertaining, with Gladys Howell supervising dinners, receptions, and other events geared to welcoming and getting to know the people of the region. Howell had come through the ranks of the faculty, and he had great respect for them. Earlier in his career he had been supportive of the movement to establish a Faculty Senate, and during his tenure he worked actively with the Faculty Senate to strengthen the concept of faculty governance at ECU.

During Howell's tenure as chancellor, the university marked its seventy-fifth birthday. Dr. Caroline Ayers, a respected faculty member and chair of the chemistry department, headed the planning, and the result was a week of activities and festivities.

During the tenure of Leo Jenkins, and then in the few years of Dr. Brewer's tenure, the university experienced many changes. Dr. Howell was felt by many to be the calm, soothing influence that allowed these changes to solidify and begin to have an effect. His experience as an administrator and his thorough knowledge of the university allowed him to bring a feeling of calm and order to the campus that allowed for the next major changes to take place under the tenure of Chancellor Richard R. Eakin.

Howell's keen sense of humor permeated his work. He particularly enjoyed telling the story of the John M. and Gladys D. Howell Science Complex. Max Ray Joyner, chair of the Naming Committee of the Board of Trustees, told him that the trustees had made the decision about the name. Howell commented that he was glad that the building's name included Gladys, since he felt that she had done so much to assist the university. According to Howell, Joyner replied: "John, you didn't need to worry. When we decided to name a building for Gladys, we were going to work your name in somehow."

In his installation remarks on February 4, 1983, John Howell had stated that he thought that higher education had two futures to consider: the immediate years of declining enrollments through the 1980s, to be followed by expanding enrollments in the 1990s. We must, he said, not let coping with the former prevent us from preparing for the latter. He was successful in that endeavor, as he laid the groundwork for financial stability, academic program development, and athletics success with his senior associates Cliff Moore in business affairs, Robert Maier and Angelo Volpe in academic affairs, and Ken Karr and Dave Hart in athletics.

Moreover, he foresaw four primary hazards: a crisis of confidence within society about the value of traditional higher education; a lack of a single-minded front in higher education in the state of North Carolina, including relations with the community colleges; the looming potential hegemony of procedure over substance in the educational world; and the danger to the sense of community that only trust and mutual respect can preserve.

His actions guided East Carolina University well through those hazards and thereby continued to prepare the ground for continued excellence of service to the region, the state, and beyond.

RICHARD RONALD EAKIN

Richard Ronald Eakin became ECU's chancellor in 1987. A veteran of twenty-three years in faculty and administrative roles at Bowling Green State University in Ohio, he undertook the role with enthusiasm and led East Carolina University to new heights for fourteen years. He became the institution's third longest officeholding leader, exceeded only by Robert Wright and Leo Jenkins and surpassing national averages by nearly a decade.

Dick Eakin grew up in New Castle, Pennsylvania, and attended Geneva College in Beaver Falls, Pennsylvania, as an undergraduate. Long encouraged by his parents in things academic and always remembering that Miss Ryan, his fifth-grade teacher, made it seem that mathematics was the most important thing in the world, Dick was the first of his family to attend college. He went to college wanting to become a high school math teacher and a basketball coach. He studied mathematics and physics and graduated, crediting the passion of his professors, with the goal of teaching mathematics at the university level.

As important as that was, in his senior year something equally momentous occurred. He met a Geneva College undergraduate named Jo. The next year they were married, and they moved across the country to begin their life together.

Dick became a National Defense Educational Administration Fellow at Washington State University, completed his doctorate in mathematics, and became a faculty member at Bowling Green State University in Ohio. There he eventually worked in the graduate school administration with Charles Leone, whom Dick considered to be one of his greatest mentors. As Jo Eakin completed her degree in clothing and textiles, Dick's administrative talents eventually gave him responsibility for student life, then for planning and budgeting. Finally he became Bowling Green's financial vice president. From that position he was recruited to East Carolina University.

Several significant themes became central to Eakin's work as ECU's chancellor, the most immediately visible of which was communications. Richard Edwards was hired as the chancellor's executive assistant and brought to campus. Mr. Edwards's experience in communications began to improve this aspect of the university. The news bureau and the office of university publications were realigned to report to the new executive assistant. There followed an extensive process of choosing the university logo and designing letterhead and other printed materials to give the university a more modern and consistent look. The present logo with three arches was chosen at the time and has endured. Much more was to come.

University Planning and Regional Accreditation

One of the tasks facing the chancellor was grappling with the new accreditation criteria adopted in the mid-1980s by the university's regional accrediting body, the Southern Association of Colleges and Schools. Chancellor Howell had begun planning for consideration of these new criteria by inviting officials to campus to discuss the changes.

The primary emphasis would now be on "institutional effectiveness," as defined by setting goals, developing criteria whereby goal attainment could be measured, applying those criteria, and then using the results of that evaluation to improve processes. Applied institutionally, this paradigm was designed to improve all functions from teaching to facilities development. Obviously, a planning process that was comprehensive and cyclical would be required. Earlier planning efforts at East Carolina lacked these evaluational linkages and cycles.

Eakin's background in planning led him to hire Sue Hodges as a planning officer, and the office of institutional research became the office of planning and institutional research. James LeRoy Smith and Emily S. Boyce, two long-standing faculty members, were asked to direct the 1990–92 regional accreditation self-study. The self-study was successful in large part because of the implemented planning process. Before the study ended, Ms. Hodges took a position at the University of Louisville, and Robert J. Thompson, faculty member and chair of the Department of Political Science, assumed the role of director of planning and institutional research. The 1990–92 self-study led to ECU being invited, along with four other universities, to the annual regional accreditation meeting to give a presentation on how to do a successful self-study. In 1993, as Dick Edwards returned to Ohio, James

LeRoy Smith became executive assistant to the chancellor. Dr. Thompson would later serve as interim vice chancellor of academic affairs for fifteen months, beginning in April 2001.

Faculty Governance: Fourteen More Years of a Growing Legacy

As did his predecessor John Howell, Dick Eakin had an abiding respect for the faculty and faculty roles in university life. A mathematics faculty member himself for the first five years of his postdoctoral career, he honored the long tradition of shared governance at East Carolina and sought faculty opinion and advice regularly. He worked with faculty leadership that included faculty chairs Conner Atkeson (history), James Joyce (physics), John Moskop (medical humanities), Patricia Anderson (education), Don Sexauer (art), and Robert Morrison (chemistry). Dr. Eakin successfully completed his fourteen-year tenure without a single instance of major disagreement or friction with the faculty. This was a truly notable aspect of his career as chancellor and a continuing contribution to the growing legacy of shared governance at the university.

THE LOOK OF A CAMPUS:
RENOVATION AND LANDSCAPE

The 1980s, 1990s, and early 2000s were periods of feast or famine for East Carolina University when it came to repair and renovation funding. Dick and Jo Eakin had a great interest in improving the appearance of the university while preserving its traditional beauty. Eakin hired Richard Brown from SUNY-Binghamton as vice chancellor for business affairs, and one of his first responsibilities was to tackle the problem of repair and renovation.

The 1980s had seen little funding for major repairs, and by the end of that decade, roofs leaked, plastic sheeting covered books in parts of the main library, and mechanical systems were failing. Not only had funding been scarce in the past, but a modern approach to maintenance management was missing.

Dr. Eakin and Mr. Brown, working with newly hired Associate Vice Chancellor for Facilities George Harrell, who joined the university from Florida, instituted a program of preventive maintenance. The funding situation improved dramatically as the campus benefited from one of the best periods of repair and renovation funding in its history. Good funding and a quality maintenance approach resulted in a significant improvement in the reliability of the building systems and the aesthetics of the campus.

Changes were visible all over the campus. Gone from the core of the

Impromptu groundbreaking for Joyner addition.
Left to right: Richard Eakin, Richard Brown, Charles Coble,
Keith Dyer with Marlene Springer with shovel, Jim Smith
and James Hallock behind them, Bob Thompson, Patricia Anderson,
Ernie Uhr, and Jim Lanier with shovel.

main academic campus were the trailers and the "old green barn," themselves old and particularly ugly landmarks. New and attractive plantings were abundant. All of this allowed Dick Eakin's abiding desire for an attractive, well-functioning campus significant fulfillment.

Joyner Library Renovation: The 1993 Bond Issue

The success of the 1993 UNC statewide bond issue referendum allowed ECU to undertake a $28 million renovation of Joyner Library, one of Chancellor Eakin's most important and dear objectives. The regional accreditation visit of 1992 had resulted in the university receiving more than half of the twelve peer review "recommendations" for deficiencies in the library. The bond passage changed all of that and allowed East Carolina to bring the Joyner Library forward as a showcase for the UNC system, rather than languishing any longer among the rearguard of the university libraries. This accomplishment was one of the most satisfying of his tenure for Chancellor Eakin.

"Eakin's Folly" Was Not: Science and Technology Come of Age

Dr. Eakin and other members of the senior administration could recite the tour script of the Flanagan Building by heart. The building was a WPA project in the 1930s. The facilities were as close to being unsafe as an institution dared to trod and still be responsible. The cramped spaces constituted a curricular bottleneck for hundreds of students who needed chemistry credits to advance in their major fields. The chemistry faculty carried forward in their work with almost heroic fortitude in facilities long ago outlived.

Planning dollars were acquired by a sympathetic UNC General Administration and a helpful North Carolina General Assembly. Construction funding was promised in the next legislative session. Knowing that such funding is never guaranteed but knowing even more how deep was the need for this new science and technology building at East Carolina University, Chancellor Eakin gave the word to begin the process of site preparation. He knew that if the funding were held up for any reason, it would delay the project by many months. He remarked that this project would either provide what has long been needed at East Carolina, or, "if we fail in acquiring the funding, the hole in the ground will be referred to as 'Eakin's Folly.'"

Indeed, funding came, and the project took three years to complete. The new facility housed four large auditorium-style classrooms and state-of-the-art laboratories. There was also "flex" laboratory space designed to accommodate future opportunities.

The Science and Technology Building was dedicated on October 12, 2003. At the dedication, Dick Eakin was recognized for his hard work in advancing yet another project essentially important in the university's evolution. He received a standing ovation by all gathered at the celebration, including the applause of UNC president Molly Corbett Broad.

The Student Recreation Center: State of the Art for the Students

Dick Eakin knew there was an absence of legitimate student recreation opportunities on campus. The old Christenbury Gymnasium was in poor condition, and there was no other facility available. The chancellor was well aware of the benefit a good recreation facility would bring to the students. Vice Chancellor for Student Life Alfred Matthews put it succinctly: "If students rest well, eat well, and have stimulating recreational and leisure experiences, they will function well in the academic setting." In addition, Eakin knew that the students were willing to be assessed a portion of their student fees to finance the construction.

The result was an $18 million facility with 150,000 gross square feet, 6

Richard Eakin with basketball players.

basketball courts, a natatorium with a lap pool, and numerous multipurpose areas.

The facility quickly became a favorite on campus, with a great deal of use by students and faculty and staff members. It also quickly became evident that the facility was a strong draw for potential students and their parents visiting campus.

Doctoral II Status

The attainment of doctoral status is among the crowning achievements of the Eakin era. Some background is needed to understand this momentous event.

One of the administrative changes that Chancellor Eakin oversaw was the creation of a new division at East Carolina University, the Division of Research and Graduate Studies. He brought Dr. Thomas Feldbush to campus as the university's first vice chancellor for research and dean of the graduate school. As the university developed more doctoral programs, the advance of research efforts and the manner in which research fit into those programs demanded a new effort at organization and planning. In developing this new division, East Carolina joined with most Doctoral I and Doctoral II institutions in managing research and graduate study.

Universities are ranked by the complexity of their mission under a system known as the Carnegie classification system. Under the system, a number of objective criteria determine whether a university is deemed "Comprehensive," "Doctoral Granting II," or "Doctoral Granting I," the highest classification. A university's classification determines its funding level within the University of North Carolina, with doctoral institutions funded at a higher level because of higher costs incurred in producing higher degrees.

In order to move into the doctoral granting classification, ECU was required to show that it was producing a certain number of doctoral degrees in a required number of areas. ECU was recognized as having achieved Doctoral II designation by the UNC Board of Governors in April 1998. The University of North Carolina at Greensboro was the only other Doctoral II institution in the University of North Carolina, with UNC–Chapel Hill and North Carolina State University in the next higher category of Doctoral I.

With the designation, the ECU administration anticipated funding at a level equal to that of UNC–Greensboro. President of the University of North Carolina Molly Broad indicated that UNCG was a mature Doctoral II institution, while ECU had just attained Doctoral II status.

East Carolina University's funding was adjusted to the midpoint between comprehensive universities and that of the University of North Carolina at Greensboro. Fringe benefits and other support costs were adjusted based on the funding formula, and tuition rates were also raised to the midpoint. In total, ECU would receive more than $8 million in new funds, including thirty new faculty positions. Given the state's fiscal problems, it took more than four years for this new funding to be phased in, but it went a long way to make ECU more competitive with similar universities around the country. The new ranking and additional funding greatly improved the university's status and effectiveness in serving the state and the region and was the result of effective planning.

Conference USA: Another Giant Step for ECU Athletics

During the 1990s, many athletic conferences were changing membership, and others were being formed. Athletics Director Dave Hart left ECU for Florida State, and Mike Hamrick became ECU's athletics director. Dick Eakin and his athletics directors followed the changing scenes intently.

In 1997, in the midst of these changes, East Carolina University accepted a football membership in Conference USA. This was the first step in building the relationships that would ultimately result in ECU becoming a comprehensive all-sport member of Conference USA in 2001.

Eakin served on the Conference USA Board of Directors and was also named to the Executive Committee of the board in 1997. These relationships helped him position East Carolina University to be included in the conference. Many institutions across the nation sought to be invited; however, as the decisions were being made, Eakin made it clear to the conference leadership and to the other university presidents in the conference that ECU was prepared to make the commitment necessary for the total East Carolina University athletics program to compete on a national level. The move to Conference USA was beneficial, not only to the athletics program but also to the institution as a whole, given the high national profile provided by the conference.

Two Successful Campaigns: Shared Visions
and the Campaign for ECU Scholarships

East Carolina University embarked upon Shared Visions, its first major comprehensive campaign, on July 1, 1990. The goal was to raise $50 million, which would be used for a variety of needs across the campus. The cochairs of Shared Visions were Robert Ward and Henry Williamson. Not only was this the first major comprehensive campaign, but also it was the first time that all three foundations on campus (the ECU Foundation, the ECU Educational Foundation [Pirate Club], and the Medical Foundation) had worked together to raise funds.

Dick Eakin was tireless in his efforts to visit friends of the university and to put forth the university's cause. Vice Chancellor for Advancement Jim Lanier and his staff helped coordinate the campaign. The university was successful. On December 31, 1995, at a major celebratory gala, the university announced that a total of $55.5 million had been raised. Shared Visions was a resounding success.

One of Richard R. Eakin's major contributions to the university was the East Carolina Scholars Program. John Howell had begun a program to establish scholarships at ECU for the best and brightest students. During Chancellor Howell's administration, funds were raised to endow nearly twenty-five merit scholarships that funded $3,000 annual awards. At the time, these were the largest academic awards on campus. Eakin wanted to dramatically expand this scholarship program.

Work on this program began during the Shared Visions Campaign. Although not a major part of the campaign, slightly over $3 million was raised for merit scholarships. This reinforced Eakin's commitment to significantly increase the number and level of merit scholarships. He wanted ECU to be more competitive in recruiting the state's brightest and best young leaders.

A separate East Carolina Scholars Campaign was launched July 1, 1998, and concluded at the end of 2000. One of the primary goals was to create or significantly expand one hundred scholarship endowments. During the campaign, Eakin made many visits to potential donors, speaking eloquently and convincingly that high-level scholarships were needed to recruit the brightest students to ECU. His zeal prompted Sam Wornom, a member of the campaign Steering Committee, to comment that the topic of merit scholarships was Dick Eakin's "hot button."

The East Carolina Scholars Campaign was extremely successful. The original goal was to raise $12 million, and it was later raised to $15 million. Total gifts and pledges totaled more than $15.4 million. The focus of the campaign was to endow named scholarships to provide awards between $5,000 and $10,000 annually that could be used to recruit outstanding freshmen.

The merit scholars who came as a result of the scholarship program had an impact on the campus and were very active in leadership positions. Eakin followed their on-campus careers in a very personal way. Each year as the students were ready to graduate, he and his wife would invite the scholars to dinner in his home, giving him another opportunity to learn about them and wish them well.

Information Technology at ECU

The dawning of the 1990s proved to be a most challenging time for ECU's information technology infrastructure. It had been difficult to make adequate investment in this area, and the campus was at a strategic disadvantage during a time when information technology was exploding everywhere else. An old broadband network suffered from numerous outages and failures, not to mention its high cost of maintenance and limited expandability. Both academic and administrative computing ran, for the most part, under outdated operating systems on Sperry mainframe computers.

The telephone system was ancient, and the switch could not handle the additional lines needed for a growing campus. The residence halls did not have cable TV or computer access. Student computing was at a minimal level—but no worse than the computing facilities available to faculty and staff. Realistically, ECU stood at least ten years behind its peers in most areas of IT.

Recognizing these issues but knowing that financial resources were constrained, a bold initiative was needed. Chancellor Eakin put forth a bold proposal to the UNC General Administration requesting that it finance the purchase of a state-of-the-art fiber–optic network and telephone switch with a bond issue. It would be repaid over a ten-year period from a combination of state appropriations, residence hall charges, student fees, and other sources of funds.

Fiber was laid throughout the campus, and every building was rewired to handle both voice and data. At the same time as this was being done in the residence halls, an agreement was reached with the local cable TV company to place cable into each dorm room and provide service. This twelve-month project placed ECU at the very forefront of universities in terms of network availability and made it the envy of other UNC institutions.

In combination with the network upgrade, IBM mainframes were acquired on the secondary market, and a process was implemented to buy packaged systems or to convert existing administrative software to a DB2 database format. Since the software, hardware, and network were integrally related in many ways, the simultaneous implementation of all components of this multifaceted initiative was required to achieve success and keep the campus operations flowing. That goal was achieved.

Building upon the foundation of the new campus IT infrastructure, resources were dedicated to improving faculty, student, and administrative computer equipment. Microsoft Exchange was installed as the campus-wide e-mail system, with great acceptance by the user community. A new student educational technology fee was implemented to provide funds to establish hands-on, discipline-specific student computing labs throughout the campus. Faculty members were provided new desktop or laptop computers with a three-year replacement cycle. Likewise, administrative departments received funding to replace their desktop computers.

Even though funding proved to be challenging over the remainder of the decade, the commitment to retaining leadership in this area remained. A new position, that of chief information officer (CIO), and the recruitment of an outstanding information technology leader, Dr. Jeffrey Huskamp, were significant steps. Dr. Huskamp and his staff propelled ECU into the future with supercomputing, visualization, wireless networks, and many grants and contracts. ECU entered the new millennium with demonstrated leadership in the field of information technology.

A Brush with Disaster: Hurricane Floyd

The most difficult event of the Eakin administration was Hurricane Floyd and the ensuing flood of eastern North Carolina. It was the greatest physical challenge that the university had ever faced, and it had the potential to cause irreparable harm.

The beginning of the problem can be traced to Hurricane Dennis, a hurricane that made landfall in early September 1999. Dennis dropped approximately 6 inches of rain on the east. Moreover, as it moved northward out over the ocean, it reversed course and returned as Tropical Storm Dennis to add even more rain. The ground was saturated.

The crisis began insidiously on Wednesday, September 15, 1999. Radar had been tracking another hurricane, Hurricane Floyd, as it moved up the east coast, and the prediction was that it would make landfall near Wilmington, North Carolina. ECU employees were dismissed at midafternoon that day to prepare their homes. The hurricane made landfall late that night and dropped an additional 15 inches of rain on the already saturated soil.

Wind damage in the east was not extensive, and by Thursday afternoon, September 16, the sun was back out. Greenville residents were cleaning up downed limbs and generally concluding that they had dodged the bullet. Electricity was still out, but, in general, things looked good. They had no idea what lay ahead.

By Friday the water began to rise. Rivers, creeks, and tributaries began inching over their banks. Eakin began to receive reports that the flooding would be extensive, as there was simply no place for the water to go. Tenth Street was quickly flooded, and students were wading—and swimming— in several feet of water.

There were approximately six thousand students living in the residence halls on campus, and Eakin and the vice chancellor for administration, Richard Brown, faced the decision of whether to send these students home. Authorities warned that the roads were impassable, but Eakin and Brown drove from Greenville to Wilson with no problem. They concluded that it was preferable to dismiss the students than to try to provide for them on campus in case the flooding became more severe. The chancellor asked the students to leave campus and return to their homes, and they did so immediately.

This left only about one hundred students in the residence halls, and, as the crisis deepened, they were transported to residence halls at North Carolina State University to remain until school resumed.

The ECU Pirates were scheduled to play a football game on Saturday against the Gamecocks of the University of South Carolina. That same Friday the student athletes were taken to South Carolina on buses. They were victorious over the Gamecocks, but by Saturday evening it was impossible for them to return to Greenville, which was now inundated with floodwaters. They remained at USC and practiced for the upcoming game the following Saturday.

As the water continued to rise, students and employees who lived around the university were flooded out of their homes. There were many accounts of residents awakening as water flowed into their homes, leaving them little time to gather their belongings and escape. Water rose as much as 6 to 8 inches in an hour. Clothes, books, computers, and work were all lost. By Saturday, it was estimated that between 1,600 and 1,800 students were displaced, either temporarily or permanently, from their homes. One student, freshman Aaron Child, drowned in a swollen creek near campus.

Eakin met each morning with a group of administrators to deal with the crisis. By the beginning of the week the Tar River had risen so much that it had submerged the gauge that read the water level at the Greenville Utilities Commission! Approximately 60 percent of Pitt County was now under water, and the damage to businesses, livestock, and crops was extensive.

Although the electricity had been restored, university officials were notified by the city officials that if the water rose even 1 inch further, the city water would be lost. Arrangements were made by university officials to transport "water buffaloes," gigantic trucks filled with water, from the western part of the state to the campus. Portable lavatories were set up throughout campus. The loss of the city water supply did not happen, however. The Tar River crested 24 feet above the flood stage.

Eakin established the Hurricane Floyd Relief Resource Center to provide a one-stop shop for students and employees seeking counseling or assistance in dealing with FEMA, the Red Cross, or other financial concerns. Students who had literally lost everything were given donations of $100 in cash to help ease them over this crisis. The crisis center, managed by Dr. Kris Smith, remained open to students and employees until everyone who needed assistance had been served.

The dining facility was the only one open in the city, and word went out that anyone who needed to do so could have a meal there. Rescue workers, police, National Guardsmen, and university employees found hot food available at no cost.

There was considerable damage to the campus itself, and estimates of those costs exceeded $7 million. There were many accounts of university employees working long hours of overtime to repair the campus, knowing that their own homes had also been lost.

Relief poured in. The ECU Family Relief Fund was established to accept donations, and these exceeded $316,000. IBM donated one hundred ThinkPads to help ECU students who lost their computers. The campus bookstore replaced destroyed books for free, with the request that they be returned when they were no longer needed. Tons of clothing, bedding, and equipment were donated by other campuses in the UNC system and by other colleges and universities across the country.

Classes resumed after a nine-day shutdown. Eakin and his administrative team were fearful that the university was so damaged that the students would not be able to return, but return they did.

Although recovery from the flood required years, there was one bright light that marked the end of the acute phase. It was the "big game." Nobody who was there that day will ever forget it.

The ECU Pirates were scheduled to play the Miami Hurricanes on Saturday, September 25, but the extensive flooding in Greenville made it impossible to play there. Accordingly, the game was moved to Carter-Finley Stadium in Raleigh, home of ECU's rival, the North Carolina State University Wolfpack. The Pirates went directly from South Carolina to Raleigh.

ECU fans packed the stadium, but the first half was grim. Miami was the ninth-ranked team in the country, and at the half the score was 20-3 with Miami in the lead. The ECU band had come to Raleigh, but many of the students in the band had lost their uniforms in the flood, so they were clad in jeans and T shirts. Instruments were borrowed, and the effort was valiant. But the overall effect was depressing for the Greenville crowd that had already been through so much.

Nobody knows for certain what went on in the locker room during the halftime, but when the Pirates came back on the field, they were invincible. It was one of the greatest comebacks in the history of college football. As the fans screamed virtually nonstop, the Pirates came from behind to beat the Hurricanes by a score of 27–23.

Following the game, posters began appearing on doors, in the residence halls, and all over campus, bearing the slogan "ECU Beats Hurricanes— Miami and Floyd."

Commencement, December 9, 2000

In his last graduation ceremony as the chancellor of East Carolina University, Dick Eakin offered inspiration and advice to the 2,400 graduates. Members of the chancellor's staff unanimously requested that he deliver the commencement address. Richard Ronald Eakin offered his personal insights on things that he had learned during his thirty-six-year career in higher education. These insights serve to summarize the good humor, comprehensive intelligence, and unsurpassed integrity of the ninth leader of East Carolina University:

- Intelligence is a valuable commodity whose value is only fully realized through old-fashioned hard work.
- There is no substitute in a marriage for the liberal use of two words: "yes, dear."
- When faced with the choice between honesty and expediency, be honest.
- There is no more liberating experience than a top-down ride in a convertible.
- The first job out of college should be selected with care, but with the knowledge that it is not likely to determine the destiny of a career.
- The stock market is not for the faint of heart.
- Friends are a blessing, but it is family that sustains us.
- Dimples are good on babies and bad on ballots.

- Tastes in food become more and more sophisticated, but ice cream remains as soothing and delicious as it was the day you had your tonsils out.
- Most people have good hearts and consciously or innately practice the Golden Rule.
- The more experience you have, the greater your realization of the limits of your knowledge.
- Faith is the underpinning of any truly successful venture.
- Whether we wish for it or not, each of us will have a real and lasting effect on the lives of others, even those in generations to come.
- The admonition to say or write nothing that you wouldn't want quoted on the front page of the *New York Times* has great merit.
- A sense of humor is important, but the capacity to laugh at oneself is essential.
- Peace is better than war, honor surpasses deceit, and love overcomes hate.

Many other initiatives than the ones noted here continued successfully under Dick Eakin's chancellorship, preeminently among them the continuing success of the School of Medicine under the leadership of Vice Chancellor and Dean of the Medical School James A. Hallock. Under Dr. Hallock's leadership, the East Carolina University School of Medicine continued to achieve high rankings in rural and family medicine and to graduate classes of physicians dedicated to serving the medical needs of the region and the state.

In his installation address on April 15, 1988, Richard R. Eakin reminded everyone of the mission of service given by the institution's founders and pledged his steadfast devotion to that mission. Moreover, he spoke eloquently of an ever-brightening light on the eastern Carolina horizon, a rising beacon for those who believe that education, inquiry, and service are the best hope for our shared destiny. Indeed, in their fourteen-year tenure as Chancellor and First Lady, Dick and Jo Eakin were devoted keepers of the light.

Since his retirement as chancellor in July 2001, Dr. Eakin continues to contribute to East Carolina University and its students as professor in the College of Education's Department of Educational Leadership.

WILLIAM VAN MUSE

Bill and Marlene Muse visited East Carolina University on a midwinter Sunday late in the search process for Dick Eakin's successor. They met members of the senior administration, visited the School of Medicine, and had lunch with key supporters. As president of Auburn University, as past president of the University of Akron, and as a successful university administrator who began his administrative career as the first dean of the School of Business at Appalachian State University and who had held high-level positions at several major universities, Chancellor Muse enjoyed a national reputation as an educator with an unsurpassed work ethic and a passion for moving institutions forward.

Chancellor and Mrs. Muse responded favorably to what they saw at East Carolina that day, and Bill Muse quickly became the first choice of the search committee and was named the next chancellor of ECU in February 2001. Muse began his duties at the university on August 1, 2001.

He immediately undertook a yearlong review of the various colleges and schools at the university by making lengthy visits with deans and faculties. He also undertook what came to be called his "Hometown Tours," in which he gained familiarity with eastern North Carolina. In town-gown meetings, Muse brought his experience and reputation in campus-city relations, having been instrumental in a renewed relation between the Ohio city of Akron and the University of Akron when he was president there.

As Richard Ringeisen departed the Office of the Vice Chancellor of Academic Affairs, Chancellor Eakin appointed Robert J. Thompson as interim vice chancellor for academic affairs. When James A. Hallock left ECU as vice chancellor for health sciences and dean of the medical school, Phyllis Horns, dean of the university's School of Nursing, became the interim vice chancellor for health sciences, and Dr. Peter Kragel became interim dean of the School of Medicine.

As Muse began the 2001–2 academic year, important searches were under way for a provost and vice chancellor for academic affairs, a vice chancellor for health sciences, and a dean for the Brody School of Medicine.

As the year progressed, Dr. Michael J. Lewis arrived from West Virginia as ECU's new vice chancellor for health sciences. On July 1, 2002, Dr. Muse appointed Dr. William Swart from Old Dominion University as provost and vice chancellor for academic affairs. Eventually, Dr. Lewis oversaw a search that resulted in Dr. Cynda Johnson joining the university as dean of the Brody School of Medicine. Also, Dr. Muse brought Ruth Ann Cook to ECU from the University of North Carolina at Greensboro to serve as his administrative assistant. She had served as his assistant at Appalachian State University when he was dean there. During the 2002–3 academic year, Dr. Swart oversaw several new initiatives, including reorganization of many of the schools in academic affairs into colleges. Additionally, athletics conference affiliation became a central focus of attention, with the Big East and the ACC giving consideration to new memberships.

Muse underwent successful heart surgery early in 2003. As the spring and summer of 2003 went by, Muse focused on several issues, including athletics matters and questions related to audits of time and effort reporting in a federal grant in the School of Medicine. Athletics Director Mike Hamrick left for the University of Nevada at Las Vegas, and Associate Athletics Director Nick Floyd was named interim director of athletics. Also, after a national search, Muse appointed William Shelton as vice chancellor for university advancement. Shelton had served as development officer at Kent State and was for eleven years president of Eastern Michigan University.

After discussion with UNC President Molly Broad on September 8 and 9 and with the ECU Board of Trustees on September 11, 2003, Muse submitted his resignation to President Broad on September 12, 2003.

In his installation address, on March 8, 2002, Muse had underscored the centrality at East Carolina of four basic thrusts or areas of emphasis: teacher education, human health, the fine and performing arts, and economic development. He saw these areas as resting appropriately on the foundation of excellent programs in the humanities. Indeed, he reconfigured the division of Research and Graduate Studies to include economic development and outreach.

William Muse also listed ten conditions that should be attained and maintained in order for the university to reach the even higher level of performance and service that were his motivation in accepting the responsibility of the chancellorship:

- a highly effective undergraduate educational program
- a growing graduate doctoral program where faculty are ready and need exists
- a research program that serves the region and can attract external support
- a heightened emphasis on engagement with the region
- the development of a community of scholars that emphasizes strengths
- an enhanced student life program where diversity is fostered
- a dominant athletics program that reflects positively in all ways
- a dedicated team of administrators and support
- a commitment to diversity and equal opportunity throughout the university
- a greater international presence for students and faculty.

Such contributions and vision serve to advance both the potential and the achievement of East Carolina University and will remain as part of the dialogue among university constituents going forward.

When President Molly Corbett Broad visited East Carolina University on September 15, 2003, to discuss the appointment of an interim chancellor, she met with the vice chancellors, the deans, and the faculty leadership. She was concerned to discover whether the leadership of the university could or would support an internal candidate. If that were not the case, she would seek an appointee elsewhere. She discovered a thorough support for William Everett Shelton, a veteran administrator who had served as development vice president for Kent State and as president at Eastern Michigan University. Shelton had worked with Bill Muse in Ohio and had kept in touch over the years. Muse's confidence in Shelton was evidently well placed, as he had won the support of so many in the short weeks between July 1 and September 15.

President Broad discovered that substantial support in her daylong visit, and later that week she prevailed upon Shelton, and he agreed to serve as interim chancellor. President Broad indicated that although she normally required that interim chancellors not be candidates for the permanent position, she would not make that stipulation in this appointment. After discussions with the president about goals and directions at East Carolina University and within the University of North Carolina, Bill Shelton took office.

Shelton asked Richard Brown, veteran vice chancellor for administration and finance, to return from retirement to assist in guiding the university. Provost William Swart was reassigned to a faculty position in the College of Business, where he held tenure. Longtime philosophy faculty member and senior administrator James LeRoy Smith was asked to serve as interim vice chancellor for academic affairs. As the fall progressed, Vice Chancellor for Research and Economic Outreach Tom Feldbush decided to resign and join the faculty in biology, the department in which he held tenure. John Lehman, senior administrator for research in the Brody School of Medicine, assumed the interim vice chancellor for research role, and well-known chemistry professor Paul Gemperline became interim associate vice chancellor for research, so that both the east and west campuses would be represented in the office of research. Veteran administrator and institutional research and planning officer Robert J. Thompson assumed the additional responsibility for overseeing the economic outreach activities.

Over the next eight weeks, Bill Shelton, Richard Brown, and other members of the senior administration worked to develop a list of critical issues for East Carolina University. To better understand the challenges at hand, vice chancellors, deans, and unit heads were asked to identify challenges and concerns. What developed out of this broad-based effort was a list of priorities that would be important to address in this period of transition. Ten areas were singled out for special attention.

1. *Maintaining momentum.* It was clear that ECU must continue to push forward with positive initiatives that supported the four areas of emphasis for the campus (teacher education, human health, cultural enrichment, and economic development). Some sixteen major examples were singled out, including implementation of a general engineering program, development of a new 124-acre recreation site, downtown redevelopment efforts, and the cardiovascular center.

2. *Leadership.* Both interim and future permanent leaders must not only demonstrate vision, enthusiasm, and energy, but they must also exhibit daily a high level of integrity and a love for this university. Competence and experience are not enough. These leaders must understand ECU's history, the support of the region, and be committed to an honest, open, and consultative ethics of leadership.

3. *Mission.* Basic questions of direction for ECU must be answered in the next phase of the planning process. Questions of enrollment growth, quality of delivery, level of research productivity, sufficiency of facilities, and adequacy of resources must be carefully examined.

4. *Research.* Investments in labs, start-up packages, infrastructure, additional graduate student support, tuition waivers, and goals for grant and contract support must be set and achieved.

5. *Budget adequacy.* Adequacy of operating budgets and support staff must be addressed. Also, a clear, open, and equitable method for resource distribution must be developed. Private support must be increased.

6. *Personnel compensation.* Recruitment has been affected by the relative absence of raises and the high cost of health insurance. In lieu of compensation adjustments, other avenues of faculty and staff assistance must be pursued.

7. *Facilities.* An updated and enrollment-driven facilities plan is needed to ascertain the extent and timing of space needs.

8. *Diversity.* There continues to be a need for a clear and well-focused diversity initiative that is comprehensive in nature, improves communication, and unites the campus community.

9. *Athletics.* Budgetary considerations must be analyzed and communicated, compliance issues must be continually monitored and supported, and competitiveness of our teams must be emphasized.

10. *Student issues.* Academic advising must continue to be improved, the importance of unit graduation ceremonies must be reviewed, and student access while maintaining and improving quality must be pursued.

As the search for a permanent chancellor proceeded over the winter and into the spring of 2003–4, the initiatives listed above were advanced and developed. Bill Shelton developed many valuable relations with external constituencies, including alumni, financial supporters, friends of the university, and members of the legislature. Indeed, many of those supporters urged Shelton to apply for the permanent chancellor position.

As the search neared the final stages, Bill Shelton agreed to apply and was one of four finalists. As the search committee rendered its list of finalists and conveyed it to the Board of Trustees, the campus realized that East Carolina University had four candidates, at least two of whom had impressed many of the university's constituencies as being excellent candidates. President Molly Broad would have a challenging decision to make.

STEVEN C. BALLARD

On April 19, 2004, Steven C. Ballard was appointed as chancellor of East Carolina University. An administrator with experience in public policy, research administration, and academic management as provost, Chancellor-Elect Ballard found the challenge at ECU to be an attractive one. Plus, ECU's baseball team had been knocking on the door at Omaha for several years, a door that Steve Ballard and his teammates at the University of Arizona had opened some years earlier, before Ballard's time in professional baseball.

Apparently chosen for his experience and skill in the combined areas of public policy, research, and academic management, Ballard inherited a search for an athletics director as a major focus before he could even begin to evaluate the deeper structure of the university's academic, research, and public service programs.

Long before he took office officially on May 31, 2004, he had invested hundreds of hours in discussions with trustees, campus officials, university supporters, and national colleagues in working through the list of finalists that the search committee had ready for his consideration. In the end, there was triumph: nationally known basketball coach and athletics administrator Terry Holland joined East Carolina University as director of athletics. Nick Floyd, associate athletics director, who had been the successful interim director for many months, stayed on as Coach Holland's associate director, a condition on which Mr. Holland was insistent.

This was only the beginning of the work of forming a senior administrative team. With interim officers in three of six vice chancellorships, there was much searching to be done. That number became four of six as Bill Shelton decided at mid–academic year to return to the faculty in the College of Education beginning in the summer of 2005. Only Vice Chancellor for Health Sciences Mike Lewis, and Vice Chancellor for Student Life Garrie Moore were permanent division-level officers. As a next step, Dr. Ballard named Interim Internal Auditor Stacie Tronto to the permanent position.

As the 2004–5 academic year progressed, University Attorney Ben Irons left office to return postretirement to serve in the advising center in the fall of 2005. Kitty Wetherington became interim university attorney. Also, Interim Vice Chancellor for Administration and Finance Chuck Hawkins assumed an associate finance role, and College of Business dean Rick Niswander served as interim vice chancellor for administration and finance until Kevin Seitz, longtime finance officer at SUNY-Buffalo, joined ECU in February as vice chancellor for administration and finance.

In April 2005, after serving as interim vice chancellor for academic affairs for eighteen months, longtime ECU faculty member and administrator James LeRoy Smith was named as provost and vice chancellor for academic affairs. In June, Ballard appointed John Durham, director of public affairs since 1993, as interim assistant to the chancellor for communications, and, in July, Mr. Durham was elected by the ECU Board of Trustees as assistant secretary to the board, a position held by Dr. Smith since 1993.

Interim Vice Chancellor for Research John Lehman continued until mid-spring, when College of Health and Human Performance dean Glen Gilbert became interim vice chancellor for research until Deirdre Mageean, associate vice president for research at the University of Maine, joined ECU in July as vice chancellor for research.

In June 2005, College of Education dean Marilyn Sheerer assumed the additional role of interim vice chancellor for university advancement. President of the ECU Foundation Jim Lanier announced his retirement. Lanier had served many years in the role of vice chancellor for institutional advancement, including the period of ECU's first major capital campaign, Shared Visions, during the 1990s.

Also, in the summer of 2005, Robert J. Thompson, after fifteen years in senior administration, including fifteen months as interim vice chancellor for academic affairs, resigned and rejoined the political science faculty, the department in which he held tenure and had earlier served as chair. Vice provost Henry Peel was appointed as interim university planner. Finally, in July 2005, Dr. Sallye McKee, a veteran administrator from the University of Minnesota, joined ECU as assistant to the chancellor for diversity.

Throughout 2005, the primary focus of the senior administration has been the development of an interdivisional, transparent budget process, further involvement of the deans in the administrative work of the university through their service on the chancellor's cabinet, continued emphasis on strategic planning, and further restructuring of university advancement.

On March 31, 2005, as the keystone event of Founders' Week, Steve Ballard was officially installed as the tenth chancellor of East Carolina University. In his installation speech, Ballard illuminated the foundation of East Carolina University: nearly a century of academic endeavor based on service, spirit, leadership, and character. ECU is part of a public university system that is the envy of the higher education community, and opportunities abound.

Quoting Yogi Berra that you can see a lot just by watching, Ballard described his first six months of watching and listening to the community. He found three things: ECU has always focused on social responsibility, ECU is a national-quality university with a state focus, and ECU has a special affection and eye toward eastern North Carolina. ECU must continue to be relevant, responsive, and respectful.

In imagining ECU in 2015, ECU's tenth chancellor proposed these six characteristics:

- the leadership university: undergraduates will nurture those skills here
- athletics and academics: these will be mutually reinforcing activities
- service and engagement: public service redefined and made essential
- access and diversity: we must live the values of inclusiveness
- economic partner and catalyst: partnerships and collaboration everywhere
- a center for medical innovation and health technology.

These are characteristics that resonate with East Carolina's history.

As this brief review of Chancellor Ballard's first fifteen months concludes, he has just addressed the faculty at the start of the 2005–6 academic year. The work to chart ECU's course for the 2005–10 five-year period is beginning to jell: the official strategic plan at the university level will be completed during the fall semester. Thereafter, the six divisions and the colleges and schools within two of those divisions will complete their plans for 2005–10. There is discussion of some alteration of the planning structure that has been in place since 1988, to allow for unit variation and creative difference. A collaborative process is requested at all levels.

In his August 22, 2005, address, Chancellor Ballard asserted five strategic challenges: achieving growth with quality; fostering faculty success; clarifying our status for ourselves, for North Carolina, and for the region; fostering student access and engagement; and defining our goals for research productivity. He also envisioned five strategic opportunities: students should come first at ECU, we should provide educators for the twenty-first century, we should lead the region culturally and artistically, we should transform the economy of the region, and we should lead in medical innovation and technology transfer. These are good and great things. They are in the natural evolutionary reach of this university and the natural twenty-first-century outcome of its history.

With the promise of collaborative leadership on the parts of the faculties and the administration, the next five years should be interesting ones for East Carolina University.

REFERENCES

Bratton, Mary Jo Jackson. *East Carolina University: The Formative Years.* Greenville, NC: East Carolina University Alumni Association; 1986.
Howell, Gladys, personal interview with authors, August 5, 2003.
Howell, John, personal interview with authors, August 5, 2003.
Howell, John. Interview by James Bearden, video recording, no date, East Carolina University Archives.

## CHAPTER NINE

The Brody School of Medicine

WALTER J. PORIES

MEDICAL SCHOOLS are misnamed. They are much more than a school for medical students; they are truly health care universities that offer a broad range of educational programs, support multiple research trys, and, most important, provide health care, especially to the disadvantaged and those with challenging diseases.

Our school is a major educational resource that accomplishes far more than the education of seventy medical students each year. It contributes to the professional preparation of nurses, undergraduates, allied health professionals, residents, fellows, and physicians who seek continuing education. Our faculties extend far beyond our walls. We teach in the grade and high schools, the community colleges, and our regional hospitals. ECU professors also provide leadership at state, national, and international meetings.

Our school is a major research institute. For medical schools, research is more than a pursuit of academic contributions and the attainment of tenure; it is a matter of survival. The Brody School of Medicine is well known for its worldwide leadership in research in immunology, cardiac function, and insulin action, leadership that translates into the flow of ideas and the recruitment of fine faculty, as well as outside funding.

The biggest responsibility, however, is the mission of service. The Brody School of Medicine provides primary, secondary, and tertiary care throughout twenty-nine counties in eastern North Carolina, one of the most underserved regions in the United States. Nine of those counties qualify as the poorest counties in the country. We are not only confronted with far higher rates of diabetes, cancer, and hypertension than are seen in the rest of the country, we also deal with a population that is older and poorer. We don't

Brody-PCMH Medical Center

have to fight for market share; instead we wonder how we can continue to operate at a loss caring for the many uninsured.

It is difficult to describe the history of such a complex organization in one chapter. The choices are few for the historian: a superficial overview of trends over a quarter of a century or a phone book of names, dates, and titles. Neither provides the flavor of our school—an institution founded against great opposition; a remarkable mix of academia and private interests; a forced marriage of a state university with a county, now not-for-profit hospital; a center that is now the largest employer and the economic engine of eastern North Carolina.

I chose a more personal approach that allows the listing of the important dates and events in the life of our school enriched by the reminiscences of selected leaders. If I can't offer a full meal, let me at least offer an interesting appetizer that could lead someone to write the full story.

Brody School of Medicine Timeline

1957   School of Nursing founded.

1964   Advisory Budget Committee of the General Assembly considers funding a medical school.

1966   Consultants recommend allied health sciences curricula instead of medical school.

1968   Ed Monroe appointed dean of allied health and social professions.

1969   Leo Jenkins and Ed Monroe ask for $2,460,000 for two-year medical school.

Health Science library established.

1970   Wallace R. Wooles joined the School of Medicine faculty as director of medical science and professor and chair of pharmacology.

1971   General Assembly appropriates $1.8 million for one-year medical program at ECU.

1972   First class of students in one-year medical program admitted to ECU.

1974   General Assembly of North Carolina appropriated the funds to establish a four-year medical school at East Carolina University.

Wallace Wooles resigns; William Cromartie appointed interim director.

Second-year program added to ECU School of Medicine.

1975   N.C. General Assembly authorizes four-year medical school at ECU.

Pitt County Memorial Hospital–ECU affiliation approved.

William Laupus appointed dean.

1976   Land purchased for medical school.

1977   Charter class of students begins studies in ECU's four-year medical program.

1978   Thirty-two students are enrolled in the freshman class.

Jenkins retires after thirty-one years of service to the university, eighteen as either president or chancellor.

Thomas Brewer becomes chancellor.

1979   Ground broken for $26 million, 451,000-square-foot Brody Medical Sciences Building.

1981   School of Medicine construction completed; building has 451,000 square feet over 9 floors.

First class of ECU medical students graduates.

School of Medicine yearbook first published by medical students.

Thomas Brewer resigns, John Howell becomes interim chancellor.

Region's only kidney transplant program is created.

1982   John M. Howell installed as chancellor.

New quarters for the Health Sciences Library.

Brody Medical Sciences Building dedicated and opened.

1983   The Brody Scholars Program established, which annually provides merit awards for students who demonstrate outstanding academic performance and leadership skills.

First doctoral degree awarded.

1984   Radiation Therapy Center, a $5.2 million structure of 24,000 feet, opens.

1985   Leo W. Jenkins Cancer Center, $7.4 million, 39,000 square-foot facility is opened (expanded in 1992 and named in memory of the former chancellor).

1986   Wallace Wooles becomes the first to hold the office of vice chancellor for health sciences.

Magnetic resonance imaging facility added.

1988   Richard R. Eakin named chancellor.

Biotechnology Building built for $2.2 million.

1989   James Hallock succeeds William Laupus as dean of the school and vice chancellor for health affairs.

1996   Addition to the ECU School of Medicine's Life Sciences Building costing $15 million.

School renamed the Brody School of Medicine at East Carolina University in recognition of the largest gift in the history of the university.

2000   Brody School of Medicine at East Carolina University performs three-dimensional ultrasound.

2001   Ann Jobe succeeds James Hallock in the position of interim vice chancellor after Peter Kragel takes the position of interim dean of the school of medicine.

BSOM ranked seventeenth in the United States for primary care.

William V. Muse named chancellor.

2002   Michael Lewis hired as vice chancellor for health sciences.

First distinguished professorship endowed at Brody School of Medicine.

2003   Cynda Johnson named dean of Brody School of Medicine.
        William Shelton takes the position of interim chancellor.

2004   Steven Ballard named chancellor of the university.

Pitt County Memorial Hospital Timeline

1951   Pitt County Memorial Hospital (PCMH) opens a $1.4 million,
        120-bed facility, honoring those killed in World Wars I and II.

1961   PCMH adds 85 beds, increasing capacity to 205.

1970 $9 million bond issue passes to build replacement hospital.
        Remaining funds will come from the state and East Carolina
        University.

1974   Ground broken for $15.9 million, 370-bed facility.

1975   PCMH and ECU sign affiliation agreement making PCMH the
        school's primary teaching hospital.

1977   New PCMH opens.

1978   First medical residents arrive at PCMH.

1979   Ground broken for $5.5 million, 166-bed west tower.

1981   Former Pitt General Hospital building demolished. West tower
        opens.

1983   Ground broken for new PCMH emergency department.

1984   Open-heart surgery begins at PCMH.

1985   EastCare begins air transport service.

1986   First Children's Miracle Network telethon held, raising $67,000.

1987   EastCare helicopter crashes, killing three crew members and
        one patient.

        Malcolm Huffman becomes PCMH's first heart-transplant
        recipient.

1994   Heart center opens.

1995   New Children's Hospital wing opens.

1997   Roanoke-Chowan Hospital in Ahoskie and Bertie Memorial
        Hospital in Windsor leased.

1998   Heritage Hospital in Tarboro purchased from Columbia/HCA
        for $80 million.

        PCMH and Chesapeake (Va.) Health get state approval to build
        $20 million, nineteen-bed hospital in Dare County.

        PCMH becomes a private, not-for-profit hospital.

1999   University Health Systems of Eastern Carolina becomes a legal
        entity and PCMH's parent company.

2000   Second EastCare helicopter added.

ViQuest Center opens.

Ground broken for new emergency department and neonatal intensive care unit.

2001   PCMH celebrates its fiftieth birthday.

PCMH aerial view.

To the passenger landing today at the Greenville airport, the medical center complex, with its gleaming collection of buildings, appears as if it had always been there. It is hard to imagine the voices screaming that it was not needed, that it would be a "white elephant." A full story of the struggle is well recounted by Wayne Williams in The Beginnings of the School of Medicine at East Carolina University, 1964–1977. *Dr. Edwin W. Monroe, who deserves most of the credit for the victory, and Dr. Christopher J. Mansfield, our resident historian and epidemiologist, offer a brief synopsis of the struggle far better than I can. —WJP*

Edwin W. Monroe, M.D.

Vice Chancellor, Health Affairs, January 1968–
February 1990

When East Carolina College in 1964 broached the subject of developing a medical school, few people took it seriously. After all, the only state-supported medical school in Chapel Hill had expanded to four years from its long-standing two-year status just twelve years earlier, and its leaders were proclaiming that it and the private medical schools in Durham and Winston-Salem would educate all the physicians needed across the state. Unfortunately, the expansion did little to correct the long-standing shortages in medical, nursing, and allied health manpower, especially in the east.

To address this need, Chancellor Leo Jenkins determined that a second state school should be founded at East Carolina University. As news of this decision circulated, a groundswell of support and opposition arose with the metropolitan areas and the three existing medical schools, Bowman Gray, Duke, and UNC, adamantly against the proposition and the more rural areas of the east and west heavily in favor of it. Even so, in June 1965, the General Assembly authorized the development of a two-year school with the stipulation, added by the opponents, that if accreditation were not achieved by January 1, 1967, the N.C. Board of Higher Education would study whether or not to continue the effort and unspent state funds would revert to the board. The bill's supporters were not aware of the impossibility of meeting the deadline imposed by this amendment, since none of them had any experience in medical school accreditation. Thus, the stage was set for the ensuing ten-year struggle to establish the school—a fight that pitted the urban Piedmont against the more rural east and west;

forces loyal to the University of North Carolina (then a three-campus system) against the regional colleges such as East Carolina and Western Carolina; and, surprisingly, moderate Republicans against their more traditional conservative party members.

During the 1967 legislative session, East Carolina supporters were successful in obtaining approval for university status. To insure the bill's passage, regional university designation included Western Carolina, Appalachian State, and NC A&T in Greensboro. Included in this bill was a little-noticed section that authorized East Carolina to continue planning a two-year school of medicine. Two years later, this mostly overlooked item assumed great importance as once again planning funds ($375,000) were appropriated, directly to ECU this time, without any action required of the Board of Higher Education for expenditure. To head this effort, Jenkins recruited Edwin W. Monroe, M.D., a local internist, who immediately surveyed similar concepts elsewhere in the country and requested that the new unit be called the School of Allied Health Professions. The trustees approved this change and named Monroe as dean and director of health affairs, to start his duties in January 1968.

During the 1960s, physicians in Greenville led the effort to improve the county hospital and to support the proposed new health programs in East Carolina. The original 110-bed typical Hill-Burton funded facility was expanded with 100 more beds, larger surgical and X-ray facilities, and additional emergency rooms, which continued to be staffed around the clock seven days a week by the active medical staff without compensation. Local physicians also steadfastly worked with community leaders of Greenville, Pitt County, and East Carolina to have the state choose Greenville as the location of an alcoholic rehabilitation center for the eastern region. Since Dr. Monroe was becoming known as the medical spokesman for health matters in the east, he was often asked to represent the region on study commissions or boards dealing with new state and federal health initiatives such as the Regional Medical Program (RMP), established by President Lyndon B. Johnson, to improve the care of patients with heart, stroke, and hypertension problems. As a board member of the N.C. RMP, Monroe had ready access to its director and his staff, who had just completed a comprehensive study of health manpower and facilities in the state. With permission of the director, Monroe used this study as background documentation for a booklet produced early in 1969 and distributed widely to legislators and other interested state officials and medical leaders. This graphic depiction of severe medical manpower shortages in the east was an eye-opener for many and contributed to East Carolina's success in the 1969 legislature.

Simultaneously, Pitt County authorities decided to obtain voter approval of a $9 million bond issue to build a new county-owned hospital rather than expanding the existing facility. With urging by university officials and local physicians, the county commissioners turned down overtures by for-profit hospital corporations to own and operate the much-needed new one. The county voters' decision to pursue at least a three-hundred-bed hospital brought a sigh of relief from medical school supporters, who saw a corporate for-profit institution as a threat to their goals. Also, when coupled with the earlier state decisions, Greenville and ECU were seen more and more as a developing medical center.

In the spring of 1970, Monroe recruited an experienced medical educator to join the East Carolina family. Wallace R. Wooles, Ph.D., associate professor of pharmacology at the Medical College of Virginia in Richmond, agreed to head what was anticipated to be a two-year school of medicine. Within four years, the General Assembly approved the funding for a four-year school; in 1977, the school enrolled its first students.

Monroe served as the vice chancellor for health affairs, an office that included the responsibility for the new medical library as well as the Schools of Medicine, Nursing, and Allied Health, until 1986. In twenty-two years, he managed to turn a soybean field into a major medical center providing care to 1.2 million patients, a resource to meet the crushing need for physicians in the east, and, finally, an open door for the entry of minority students into the health care professions.

Christopher J. Mansfield, Ph.D.

1983–Present
Professor, Department of Family Medicine
Director, Center for Health Services Research and
    Development

In the spring of 1964, Dr. Ernest Furgurson, a general practitioner from Plymouth, N.C., was returning home on a Sunday from a medical conference at Duke. He spoke at the conference on how great the need for medical care was in the eastern region of the state and how much trouble he was having recruiting a doctor to join his practice. He stopped in Greenville to tell Dr. Leo Jenkins, president of East Carolina College (ECC), about the need for doctors in eastern North Carolina and to recommend ECC do something about it. Dr. Jenkins wasn't home, but Mrs. Jenkins received him. She told him she wasn't informed enough to talk about it but asked him to please call Dr. Jenkins the next day. When he did call to tell Dr. Jenkins that ECC should start a medical school, Dr. Jenkins said that ECC wasn't in the medical business, to which Dr. Furgurson replied: "Well, you have a motto, which is 'to serve.' Why don't you live up to the motto? Who are you serving if you just sit in this cesspool?"

The above vignette is from Wayne Williams's extensive history of the School of Medicine. What follows is mostly a summary of his work, re-cast to describe how a university, practicing physicians, and community leaders across a large, poor, and underserved region realized a vision to "grow their own" doctors in spite of concerted opposition from an elitist academic establishment and a self-interested profession.

Leo Jenkins accepted Dr. Furgurson's challenge. He asked Dr. Ed Monroe, a local practicing physician, and Professor Robert Williams to evaluate the need that Dr. Furgurson claimed. They confirmed the need, and Dr. Monroe was recruited to lead the planning for a medical school. Dr. Jenkins was a frequent speaker at civic events throughout the region, and he found considerable support for the idea of starting a medical school at ECC.

The North Carolina Board of Higher Education immediately rejected the idea when ECC proposed in 1965 to create a two-year medical school that would send students to the School of Medicine at the University of North Carolina at Chapel Hill for the remainder of their medical education. The idea was strongly opposed by the School of Medicine at Chapel Hill and the private medical schools at Duke and Wake Forest (Bowman Gray). The reaction echoed the way the two private medical schools fought expansion of the two-year public medical school at Chapel Hill when it sought to become a four-year school and build a teaching hospital in 1947.

Jenkins carried the idea to the North Carolina General Assembly, which authorized and appropriated funds in 1965 to plan a two-year medical school at ECC, if accreditation could be obtained. East Carolina was discouraged from seeking accreditation by the Liaison Committee on Medical Education (LCME), however. A panel of consultants recommended that it expand its allied health programs instead. In 1967, ECC requested independent status as East Carolina University. The legislature rejected the proposal and made it one of the constituent universities of the consolidated University of North Carolina system. It also authorized creation of a Health Sciences Institute, which became the School of Allied Health and Social Professions.

Eventually, people recognized the need for more physicians in the state. North Carolina ranked forty-third of the fifty states in the ratio of physicians to population and forty-sixth in the number of medical students per state resident. Mortality statistics described it to be one of the least healthy regions in the nation. In 1969, a Committee on Physician Shortage in Rural

North Carolina, appointed by the Legislative Research Commission, acknowledged the need for better access to medical care. Its solution was to recommend expansion of the UNC School of Medicine from seventy-five to two hundred graduates a year and to provide a subsidy to Duke and Bowman Gray to train North Carolina residents.

Popular support for a medical school at ECU continued, however. In 1970, the North Carolina General Assembly appropriated funds to develop a two-year medical school at ECU. It would train sixteen to twenty future doctors in the basic sciences. They would be recruited from the eastern region and go to one of the three other medical schools to finish their training. Deans at the other schools resisted, claiming they had never agreed to accept the students from ECU. A draft report of a new evaluation of the accreditation potential of ECU by a LCME review team was encouraging. It spoke highly of ECU's ability to achieve accreditation and stated that it was clear that the number of medical students trained in the state should be increased. In the final report, however, the page stating that ECU had reasonable assurance of accreditation was omitted. Circumstances suggest that leaders of one or more of the other medical schools may have influenced the final report.

Persistence resulted in passage of a bill to fund a one-year school with twenty students, who would be guaranteed admission at Chapel Hill. Chapel Hill then claimed its own accreditation was at stake, as the LCME said that ECU could be accredited only as part of Chapel Hill. East Carolina accepted compromise and started the one-year program. It admitted its first class of twenty in 1972, but ECU did not give up the fight to become a two-year school. As a two-year school, it could apply for federal funding. The consensus at the national level was that there was a serious shortage of the primary care physicians that ECU intended to train. By the end of the next decade, the number of medical schools in the nation increased from 75 to 120, with virtually all emphasizing primary care.

Leaders in the medical schools in North Carolina were heavily invested in training specialists. They argued that if there was a crisis in access to primary care in North Carolina, it could best be addressed by training physician assistants and nurse practitioners. They also claimed that the problem was not a lack of medical students but rather the lack of capacity for residency training. The federal demonstration program of Area Health Education Centers (AHEC) was a preferred alternative for established leaders of medical education in North Carolina. In the AHEC model, graduate medical education was decentralized, so that residency training for family medicine and other specialties would occur in community hospitals and continuing education of health professionals would be regionalized, with educational expertise supplied by academic health science schools.

Confronted with legislated direction to develop a second medical school, the newly created UNC Board of Governors and its president, William Friday, were quite concerned that ECU was politicizing the higher education process. The UNC board's autonomy in educational policy was challenged. The Board of Governors appointed a five-man committee, headed by Robert Jordan, to advise it on health manpower needs and the feasibility of establishing a second state medical school. In December 1972, the Jordan Committee recommended that the need for more doctors could be met by:

- the state of North Carolina paying Duke and Bowman Gray Schools of Medicine to train North Carolina students ($5,000 for each North Carolina student in 1975, $6,000 each in 1977)
- paying Meharry Medical College $65,000 a year to provide space for twenty North Carolina medical students (which would be $3,250 per year for minority medical students)
- renovating MacNider Hall and constructing a new laboratory/office building at UNC-CH
- increasing the medical school class size at UNC-CH to 160
- establishing a standing Committee on the Health Sciences to advise President Friday
- creating a position for a senior-level staff officer knowledgeable in health sciences for the UNC General Administration
- continuing to enroll twenty "degree candidates" in the one-year program at ECU
- commissioning "a team of national consultants to evaluate the need for an additional degree-granting school of medicine . . . and . . . examine all possible institutional alternatives . . . for the provision of additional doctors in all regions of the state.

In May 1973, the House of Delegates of the North Carolina Medical Society took a similar but more protectionist position. It adopted the Glasson Report, which called for abolishment of the ECU School of Medicine, expansion of class size at Chapel Hill, subsidy to Duke and Bowman Gray, and funding of AHECs.

Popular concern about a crisis in physician supply nevertheless continued. Responding to other evidence and sentiment, the 1973 legislature appointed two groups to study the problem. One was the Medical Manpower Study Commission, the other was the Joint Committees on Health of the General Assembly. Each found there to be a substantial undersupply of primary care physicians in the state.

The UNC Board of Governors, following recommendation of one committee, appointed another one to study the problem further. It commissioned a panel of outside experts in medical education to evaluate the alleged crisis of medical manpower and recommend whether another medical school would be a wise investment. This panel, known as the Bennett Committee (for its chairman, Dr. Ivan Bennett Jr., M.D., dean of the School of Medicine at New York University), seemed to proponents of the ECU medical school to be stacked against ECU. It reported that there was no health crisis in North Carolina, despite the fact that the state ranked forty-third in population-to-physician ratio. It stated that increasing the number of physicians would aggravate the access situation because physicians would raise fees to increase income. The committee recommended that three hundred new residency slots be created through AHEC, even though there was an 11 percent vacancy rate in existing ones. There were not enough North Carolina medical school graduates to fill existing residencies. Foreign medical graduates filled a high proportion of them, and the entire nation was experiencing a shortage of primary care physicians.

The UNC Board of Governors accepted the Bennett Report immediately and did not consider or try to resolve the conflicting evidence in reports of the Medical Manpower Study Commission or the Joint Committees on Health of the legislature. It didn't abolish the ECU school as recommended by the Medical Society but placed control of the one-year program under the dean at Chapel Hill.

The North Carolina legislature that year took quite different action. Considering the report of its Medical Manpower Study Commission, the 1974 General Assembly appropriated funds to further develop the school, added a second year emphasizing family medicine, and encouraged recruitment of minorities. After years of trying to prevent it, the Board of Governors finally accepted the challenge of developing a second medical school at ECU. In November 1974, President Friday proposed to the Board of Governors that the ECU School of Medicine become a full, four-year medical school. The 1975 General Assembly appropriated funds to make it a reality. Once they had accepted it, President Friday and the Board of Governors were committed to making it a school the state could be proud of. East Carolina enthusiastically accepted the challenge to train primary care physicians for North Carolina, improve opportunity for minorities to enter the medical profession, and improve the health of citizens in the region.

Wally Wooles, Ph.D.

Dean of the Medical School, 1970–1974

Watching the steady and confident development of the School of Medicine from its humble beginning in an office (a desk with three legs, a chair with two, a half-used roll of toilet paper tilting precariously on the desk, and no telephone) in an office in the Biology Complex has been my good fortune since July 1, 1970, when I arrived as dean of the medical school. I soon learned that the school was neither authorized nor funded, but I guess I was too dumb or too numb to worry then about the many trials and tribulations that were to come. Since that time a lot has happened, more is happening, and still more is yet to come. The school has succeeded beyond the wildest hopes of those who dreamed the initial dreams and those who made the dreams become reality.

But it wasn't easy. The development of the school in its early years was slow and tentative, mainly because anything we did or even planned to do instantly met with opposition from the entrenched academic medical centers and organized medicine throughout the state. Both were united in their vigorous opposition to a new School of Medicine in the state, particularly one at East Carolina University. There also was resentment toward us on campus, not for what we were doing but for our constant need of space, due mainly to a lack of space set aside for the school. As a result, whatever space we needed had to be taken from someone. And that someone always turned out to be the Department of Biology. The poor Department of Biology had just moved into the new Biology Complex after many years of sharing space in the inadequate Flanagan Building with the Department of Chemistry. They had no time to enjoy their new space when there we were with space needs they, and others on campus, couldn't or wouldn't understand. Each new faculty person added required displacing someone. It was especially hard when we needed space for a library, laboratories for the academic disciplines that required them, and places to store and embalm cadavers. We created problems for many, but we did what was necessary to survive and grow. Thankfully, Ragsdale Hall on Fifth Street become available in 1973, and we were able to accommodate everything in Ragsdale except the Departments of Anatomy and Biochemistry and the library.

These and other problems convinced me that the school needed to be located off campus. For example, we once received a cadaver we badly needed for gross anatomy. The cadaver arrived unannounced in the late morning at the peak of campus activity at the loading dock of the biology building.

The cadaver was a tall, large man, and we were unable to get his carrying case into the small elevator. It was necessary to remove the cadaver and stand him up in the elevator to get to the fourth floor. Unfortunately, this elevator serviced the entire biology tower. On our way to the cadaver storage area on the fourth floor, we were lucky that it stopped only on the third floor. But before we could get the doors closed, two chatting and totally unaware young coeds entered. When they looked up, one fainted into the arms of the other (fortunately), and the other was screaming. We felt bad that we had to leave them there, but we thought we would only cause more confusion and disruption by staying. By the time we returned to check on the two students, they were gone. Long gone, we were told. We never heard from the two unfortunate and scared young women, but we did hear from the elderly: the president, the provost, assorted deans, and an irate chairman of the Department of Biology.

I could understand the frustration we caused many while on campus, but what was hard to understand was the determined opposition of the established in-state schools of medicine. In my naïveté, I just assumed they would be willing to help a sister institution get started. To get some perspective into these attitudes, I met with the then–dean of medicine at the Medical College of Georgia. I had met him while he was a professor of medicine at the University of North Carolina involved in developing a new curriculum for their medical school and I was doing the same at the Medical College of Virginia. For the better part of an afternoon in Augusta, Georgia (no, we did not play Augusta National), we had a wide-ranging discussion in which I told him what we were about and he gave me his opinion of the attitudes of the in-state schools. They seemed to boil down to (1) the lack of an adequate university infrastructure upon which to build a medical school; (2) the lack of any doctoral programs and the unlikelihood any would be established; (3) the lack of sufficient financial resources to support yet another medical school would lead to increased competition for very limited funds, thus weakening existing programs. All were reasonable points, but, as history has proven, they were irrelevant, and we have done quite well without points one and two. Of course, we've done much better since they were added. Similarly, our existence does not seem to have hurt the excellence of any of the other in-state schools. By the way, that dean of the Medical College of Georgia became the dean of medicine at the University of North Carolina shortly after my visit.

In retrospect, we were really lucky. The fate of the School of Medicine was not to be decided by an entrenched academic medical community or by organized medicine. It was also not decided on the front pages or the editorial pages of practically every major newspaper in the state, each of which vehemently opposed the school. Rather, it was to be decided by the people in eastern North Carolina and throughout the state who were dissatisfied with inadequate health care and felt it was time to do something positive.

We all know how it turned out. We won. They lost. And the medical school continued its inexorable march to excellence. But as happy as we were to have won, it was not without some bittersweet memories. For example, shortly after we successfully won authorization and funding for the school, I attended a performance at the ECU Summer Theatre, which was then the most important summer event in eastern North Carolina. It was the pride and joy of our region. Its audience came from throughout the state, and it was not unusual to see the governor, legislators, and other influential people in attendance. Productions took place in July, four different weekly plays, usually musicals, mainly with local talent, with the leads played by recognizable Broadway names. All performances were in McGinnis Auditorium, which then was not the magnificent facility we know today. The acoustics were poor, the stage small and inadequate. Worst of all, the roof leaked, and it was quite common to see water dripping onto the stage during a heavy rain. Naturally, this always seemed to occur during the show-stopping song-and-dance numbers, such as Gypsy Rose Lee, in *Gypsy*, practicing her bumps and grinds to "If You Gotta Bump It, Bump It with a Trumpet."

The night I was there, it didn't rain. The performance began on time, and the lights dimmed, then darkened. There, spotlighted at the side of the stage, was Edgar Loessin, the genius who developed and was responsible for the phenomenal success of the Summer Theatre and who was also the chairman of the drama department. He wanted to explain to the audience why the promised renovations of McGinnis had not occurred. He quickly explained that it was not his fault that badly needed renovations could not be made and, as he pointed out, all available state funds for new projects that year were withdrawn and used to fund the medical school. I thought for a split second that it sure was nice of Mr. Loessin to explain that. But as soon as a loud chorus of nos and boos began, I really didn't. The rising curtain stopped the boos, and the play was great. However, the intermission seemed to be interminably long and somewhat lonely. It was a strange and disconcerting feeling to be booed at home after we had won an impossible victory. Clearly, we had gored the wrong ox that night.

However, there was a happy ending. Within two years the medical-school short-circuited renovation of McGinnis was under way, and we all have enjoyed the new McGinnis since. And the medical school has not yet stopped building and growing and adding new programs to meet the needs of the people of eastern North Carolina and throughout the state. With continued good luck, hard work, visionary leaders and, most important, with the help and goodwill of the people we serve, the school will only get better.

William Edward Laupus

Dean of the Medical School, 1975–1988
Vice Chancellor, East Carolina University, 1982
Vice Chancellor for Health Sciences, 1987–1989

I interviewed Bill Laupus on a sunny afternoon in Cypress Glen, a retirement facility where he was in skilled care. We recalled our first meeting when I came down for my interviews, and, after some conversation while he was cutting mushrooms for a salad in an eternally slow cadence, he offered me the chairmanship of surgery. I was so taken with his methodic dissection of the mushrooms that I was not prepared for such a rapid decision. I blurted out that I would take it, we shook hands, and the next morning I was back on the six-seater airplane out of the Kinston airport. When I came home, my wife, Mary Ann, was not happy with the news. "What will be your rank? Will you get tenure? What kind of salary did he offer? Where will we live? How could you accept a job without talking with me?" I had none of the answers. I only knew that this could be the most exciting school in the United States and I wanted to be a part of it. Within twenty-four hours, we were both on a plane back to Greenville. It did not take long for Bill and Evelyn Laupus, with some help from Terry Lawler, professor of nursing at ECU and my wife's former classmate, to convince her as well.

Bill's quiet, steady leadership was remarkable. Somehow, with little apparent direction, buildings appeared, faculty took their places, students learned, research flowered, and patients received better care than they had believed possible. At meetings, he would rarely speak but sit there, a big mountain of a man who sometimes even seemed to be dozing but who could repeat every sentence if called upon. It was not surprising that he held some of the highest posts in the land including the chairmanship of the Board of Medical Specialties and many presidencies of pediatric societies.

During his tenure, he gave me instructions only once, on my first day as chair. "Walter, recruit only the best. We are not Harvard; we cannot afford mediocrity."

Evelyn Laupus was such an important partner in the founding of the school that I thought it only appropriate to ask her to contribute as well. —WJP

Mrs. Evelyn Laupus, R.N.

Life in Greenville has always been different from most places Bill and I have lived since we were married. As the medical school and hospital grew, so did the east campus. The town changed and traffic began to be a challenge. We bought a home overlooking the golf course of Greenville Country Club. A lovely little cottage came with the house, and we used it for some candidates who were interested in joining the medical school. That was always the fun part—I loved meeting new people from different parts of the country and especially those who thought Greenville, and eastern North Carolina, was a bit of heaven. One of the most important things I did in the early years was to start a club for the new wives. It enabled them to have new friends and to feel a part of the school. We named it the "Pill Guild." Another reason for the club was to support the medical students as much as possible. During exam time, we set up a long table and filled it with sandwiches, cookies, cakes, and fruit. The students were most appreciative. Recently I have restarted the club, now named the "Old Pill Guild." We have about twenty members and meet once a month for lunch. We talk about old times, new times, children, grandkids, and life in general.

I often think of the early years and pioneers who joined the school—all outstanding—and they brought in others with the same work ethic who help to make the school a success.

James A. Hallock, M.D.

Dean of the Medical School and Vice Chancellor for
    Health Sciences, 1988–2001

When I arrived at East Carolina University in September 1988, I was told that one of the strengths and key issues was that there were no worries about the budget. Almost immediately, the state announced a shortfall in funds that was followed by a freeze in travel funds. After that introduction, I was constantly alert to budget issues for our institution.

Shortly after my arrival at ECU, one of the trustees challenged me to achieve positive national recognition for the School of Medicine. I told him that one didn't just go out and get recognition but that one earned that on merit. Nonetheless, I took this as a challenge and thought that if I could become involved nationally with a few key organizations that the school might be seen in a different light. I then became involved with the Association of American Medical Colleges (AAMC) and Council of Deans (COD); I chaired a committee for the National Board of Medical Examiners (NBME) and served the Liaison Committee for Medical Education (LCME) as a site visitor. While in these interactions, I became chair of the COD, a member of the NBME executive governing committee, and a member of the LCME board. The challenge and resulting activities had a marked dual beneficial effect, first, on the school, which I believe benefited from its name being associated with national organizations and by its dean being in key leadership positions nationally. Second, I benefited personally with each of the activities, which allowed me to have input and to grow as I assumed the new responsibilities. While I expended a great deal of time and energy, I am convinced that the school and I benefited tremendously from my activities.

It was clear to me when I was recruited that a distinguishing factor of the East Carolina medical school was its unique mission of service to the region, access for minority and disadvantaged students, and production of primary care physicians. I attempted to relate any undertakings to that mission. We had an early flurry of activity regarding the creation of a diabetes center, cancer center, and heart center, all of which met the three missions. Primary care physicians needed to be well schooled in matters regarding diabetes, cancer, and heart disease.

The various centers moved at different rates, but the diabetes center progressed more quickly, due in major part to the activities of Dr. Jose Caro and Dr. Walter Pories, both of whom pushed me to move these issues along. The heart center was the next most rapid to move forward, with my recruitment back to East Carolina of Dr. Randy Chitwood, who was the focal point for the creation of the heart center. Unfortunately, the cancer center never took the shape and pace that the other two did, but I believe it was an important step for the School of Medicine.

A recurring theme during my tenure was curriculum revision. We were able to make the transition to methods of small-group and problem-based learning while retaining the strengths in the curriculum. One issue that emerged from this was the need to pursue clinical skills assessment. The four medical schools in North Carolina were part of a Macy grant to look at the study of clinical skills assessment and standardized patients. This study led to the creation of a twenty-center clinical skills facility, which represented a national leadership role for East Carolina.

The creation of a telemedicine center and an institute for telemedicine for the entire university was driven, in large part, by David Balch. Our telemedicine program emerged as one of the national leaders in the application of technology for distribution of telemedicine into rural settings. The other center that emerged during my tenure was the AgriMedicine Center, which followed a series of negotiations between East Carolina and North Carolina State University.

While all these programmatic issues were being accomplished, several other themes were threaded throughout my tenure at East Carolina. First, we had two very successful LCME accreditation visits, which resulted in full accreditation for the institution. Second, I made a conscious decision to replace the departmental chairs at an even, balanced pace so that the institution would never suffer a sudden loss of leadership. The third theme of my tenure was my ongoing efforts to garner national recognition for the school in the areas of primary care and rural medicine.

Obviously the interactions with Pitt County Memorial Hospital were areas of positive growth for the school. This relationship allowed for interaction between the clinical facilities and the clinical programs at East Carolina. And as I neared the end of my tenure, I realized significant progress had been made in the application of an electronic medical record throughout the clinical care system and the hospital.

The Brody family's unparalleled largesse allowed us to accomplish many good things. The interactions I had with the university administration were central to my success over thirteen years. I had the benefit of Richard Eakin's leadership through the entire time of my deanship, and I am very grateful to him.

Michael Lewis, M.D.

Vice Chancellor for Health Sciences, 2002–Present

Michael Lewis is one of the most effective but humble men I've ever known. Note that he does not take credit for what happened during his short tenure so far: a new major Cardiovascular Institute, construction of the Learning Village for a new School of Nursing, a new School of Allied Health, and a new Library of Medicine, and the naming of ECU as one of the six national NIH Bariatric Surgery Centers. In that same time, he facilitated cooperation between the university and the hospital, recruited a new dean, and launched a major assault on dealing with the school's deficit, a problem not caused by a lack of production by the faculty but rather by the inability of our citizens to pay for the care they desperately need. —WJP

The Brody School of Medicine is a young school that, in a relatively short period, has achieved national and international recognition. The school has made great strides in meeting its mission of providing an opportunity for disadvantaged students and underrepresented minorities, improving the health status of the people of eastern North Carolina, and motivating medical students to pursue careers in primary care medicine.

This is a time of transition for the Brody School of Medicine. The school presently faces significant challenges as it strives to continue to provide excellent medical education and outstanding medical care to those with the most serious illnesses and to those who are medically underinsured or indigent.

The future is bright. The school will continue to honor its commitment to its three founding missions but, with the support of university leadership, faculty, and the citizens of the region, will also grow and expand upon these missions, with a new focus on research and building specialty centers and programs. This growth will enhance the school's ability to meet its mission, further provide opportunities for national and international recognition, provide fiscal stability, and enable the Brody School of Medicine to continue to serve the region and the state in an exemplary fashion.

Peter Kragel, M.D.

Interim Dean, January 2001–October 2003

As is the case with most interim administrations, some programs that we built and implemented, and even some programs that had very positive results, must make way for new leadership and new vision. This was a particularly difficult time to provide interim leadership, due to the number of vacancies in other leadership positions and continual state budget cuts coupled with increasing overhead and decreasing professional reimbursements. Quite rapidly, it became apparent that the School of Medicine would be rocked by cuts, audit findings, and instability of leadership both internally at the chair level and externally at the vice chancellor and chancellor levels.

Even so, we accomplished much during these interim years:

- started a master educator program
- started a schoolwide quality committee, leading (among other things) to changes in handling of U.S. Medical Licensure Examination (USMLE) results, course directors actually taking the USMLE I exam, and a summer program offered to prepare for USMLE, leading to highest pass rate and scores on USMLE in the history of the school
- took several steps to enable research by providing salary match for extramural salary support, the opportunity to include researchers in incentive plan, and restructuring researcher salary so that extramural support could result in increased compensation
- started schoolwide diversity program
- reengineered clinical compensation to include a productivity component
- recruited our first endowed professorship (Jefferson Pilot), tasked with keeping our focus and success with primary care mission at a time when market forces would make students pursue more specialized training

- started to better market the school through *Mission Magazine* (and sending *Mission Magazine* to other deans) and advertising (the "Two Incredible Decades" campaign)
- met with the *U.S. News and World Report* editor in charge of medical school rankings, causing changes in ranking methodology, resulting in higher ranking for ECU

These are some highlights. One other event worth mentioning was the presentation of Senator Ed Warren with a white coat in recognition of all he had done for the School of Medicine. I am very pleased that we were able to do this before Ed passed away, since he was our constant active supporter and strong advocate.

Cynda Johnson, M.D., M.B.A.

Dean, Brody School of Medicine, 2003–Present

As only the fourth dean at the Brody School of Medicine, I came to the school at a time when the institution was ready to enter adulthood. Nearly thirty years old, the school had established itself as a strong, community-based, mission-based school. It was, in fact, the special mission of the school, encompassing but extending beyond the traditional medical school missions of education, research, and clinical care, that caught my attention. On my first visit to campus, I was hooked by the energy and friendliness of all members of the Brody School family.

The school is all I'd hoped for and more. Brody medical students are a special group, selected on many factors in addition to the traditional criteria of grade point average and test scores. These are students selected for their professionalism and sense of mission. I was drawn to a school with a mission that includes opportunities for disadvantaged and minority students. While busy with medical school, these students continuously live out the Brody mission and their own mission to serve the community. There is a give and take between caring faculty who give of their time for one-on-one attention and appreciative students, eager to learn.

Practice location of our graduates is a testament to its success, with 50 percent of graduates in primary care specialties, 50 percent in North Carolina and 27 percent in eastern North Carolina. The most remarkable statistic for practice location relates to those students who matriculate at Brody for medical school and residency training: 76 percent of those students remain in North Carolina to practice. Few schools can demonstrate similar success in training physicians for their region.

As I assessed the clinical care here at Brody, I realized that most of the facilities were bursting at the seams as well as functionally dated. The Family Medicine Clinic, for example, housed 66,000 patient visits per year in a facility designed for half that many. An unexpected opportunity in February 2004 resulted in a rapidly planned but well-conceived strategic analysis of our space needs in the next five years. I saw inadequate facilities to be one of many issues that resulted in the startling, sad statistic that only 11 percent of ECU employees sought their medical care with ECU physicians. Tripling that number quickly became a target I knew we'd need to meet within the first couple years of my tenure.

I have also focused on expanding two incompletely tapped resources: research and philanthropy dollars. Preceding me by nearly a year at ECU, Dr. John Lehman was hired as associate vice chancellor for research. He quickly began to repair the research infrastructure of the school. Upon my arrival, we began to strategize on the most effective methods to jump-start the inflow of grant dollars to the institution, focusing also on dollars allocated toward salary offset and distribution of facility and administration dollars. I committed to hiring chairs who could bring grant dollars and/or who had a track record of building research in their previous units. On my arrival in November 2003, total NIH dollars awarded to Brody totaled $3.7 million, placing it 116th out of 126 allopathic schools of medicine.

Indeed, Brody was transitioning to adulthood at the time of my arrival. Along with many other faculty members and staff, I saw many opportunities for success across the institution. An air of hope surrounded me, and I knew I had made the correct decision to join the Brody team.

A CHANCELLOR

Chancellor Eakin's influence on the school and campus were enormous. With unfailing courtesy, good humor, and integrity, he transformed the campus, inspired athletics, and elevated academics to the level of a true university.
—WJP

Richard Eakin, Ph.D.

Chancellor, East Carolina University, 1987–2001

As part of my introduction to East Carolina University, innumerable people made it quite clear to me that the medical school did not have an easy beginning. Those who successfully founded the medical school had to overcome strong opposition from many quarters, including the objections of then–UNC president William Friday. But in my tenure as chancellor, I came to admire and respect Mr. Friday. It was during interviews with him on his television program *North Carolina People* that I recognized that he had come to a full appreciation of the importance of the School of Medicine to eastern North Carolina and to the state. He asked questions that revealed his understanding of the school's emergence as an important factor in the health of the region. He was complimentary in reviewing the school's progress and praised its contributions. Mr. Friday, ever the professional and gentleman, celebrated the worth of the school he had opposed. It was a heartwarming experience.

To understand how far we have come, it's worth remembering that in the late 1980s and early 1990s I would occasionally receive a telephone call from the dean of the School of Medicine alerting me to the fact that a significant surgical procedure was under way. Most often, the procedure involved an organ transplant. After a time I realized that the calls no longer were being made, simply because the surgical specialties were so well developed that transplantation had become a regular, expected part of medical practice in the School of Medicine.

But perhaps most significant in charting the success of the School of Medicine is the coveted O. Max Gardner Award, given each year by the University of North Carolina Board of Governors to a member of the faculty of the North Carolina system who "has made the greatest contributions to the welfare of the human race." Two members of the school of medicine, Dr. William E. Laupus and Dr. Walter J. Pories, received the O. Max Gardner Award during my tenure as chancellor. A third recipient, Dr. Randolph W. Chitwood Jr., received the award in 2004. Their receipt of this award is powerful evidence of not only the importance of their contributions to the field of medicine overall but also of the quality of the School of Medicine today.

THE CHAIRS

The chairs compose the management team of a school. These are the individuals who set the tone, provide the leadership, deal with crises, and battle the budgets. All should be allowed to speak, but a single chapter won't allow so many voices. Accordingly, a few will speak for the group. —WJP

Seymour Bakerman

Chairman of Pathology, 1976–1989

"A mighty oak under which all may find shelter." This was the apt description of Seymour Bakerman by one of his faculty members celebrating his life following his untimely death in 1989. "Sy" Bakerman was one of the founding chairs of the School of Medicine brought to this campus in 1976 by Dr. William Laupus from the Medical College of Virginia.

Sy was a native New Yorker and a combat veteran of World War II, like many of his generation. He did graduate work in physical chemistry and was awarded a Ph.D. in this subject. Medicine then called. He took great pride in being an early participant in Western Reserve's innovative medical curriculum. Residency in pathology with an emphasis in clinical chemistry allowed him to combine his expertise in chemistry and instrumentation with his clinical practice. He held faculty appointments at the University of Kansas Medical Center and the Medical College of Virginia before employment here. He gave an internationally known board review course in clinical chemistry biannually while at the Medical College of Virginia and continued to do so while here in Greenville. From this grew Bakerman's *ABCs of Interpretive Laboratory Data,* a book still being updated and published in much of its original form.

His door was always open. In fact, I think he enjoyed being disturbed. The front door entered into an outer office, followed by an inner office occupied by the executive secretary of the department. However, all students, staff and faculty knew there was a side door, always open, which led directly to the boss. Only the uninitiated or administrators went through the front door.

Sy Bakerman was well loved by students. His midterm hot dog and chili party (kosher, of course, and personally imported from Richmond, Virginia) and end of year party were looked forward to by every class. In the early years of the school, he was a consistent winner of the Golden Caduceus Award, an award given by the graduating class to the one faculty member felt by the class to be the most outstanding basic science instructor. Following Dr. Bakerman's death, this award's name was changed by the students to the Bakerman Award in his honor. Bakerman's concern for students was legendary and exemplified by an incident in which he arranged and funded hepatitis B vaccine immunizations for the whole second-year class when the university refused to do so.

Staff and faculty could always depend on Dr. Bakerman for support and encouragement. His concept of chair and departmental administration was to support the individual. Many times he told me: "The institution will always be here. It is the little guy, the individual who you need to look out for and support."

The staff and faculty of the department planted an oak tree in Dr. Bakerman's remembrance. It may be found on Moye Boulevard at the entrance to the Brody Building and is known as the "Bakerman tree" by the faculty and staff who knew him.

Robert Brame, M.D.

Professor and Chair, Obstetrics and Gynecology, 1977–1984
Chief of Staff, 1987

Discussion of the beginning of the School of Medicine at East Carolina University must include Ragsdale Hall. The dean's office was there in 1977, as were the offices of most of the clinical chairmen. At the outset, there were few clinical faculty in that building; in fact, there were few clinical full-time faculty. The internal medicine chair was filled when the OB/GYN chairman arrived, and the chairman of pediatrics was present although he had not yet been named chairman. The chairman of surgery came later that summer, so that the groundwork had been laid for the development of the clinical departments. The members of the faculty remained in that building, where life midcampus was a bit more serene than hospitals usually are, until the Medical School Annex, along with the new hospital, opened across town in 1978. Nurse-midwife Josie Hookway was really the first faculty member of the Department of OB/GYN when the chairman arrived, and she made important contributions to the success of the department. There developed a camaraderie among clinical and preclinical faculty not commonly seen in medical schools, possibly enhanced by the campus proximity of one group to the other.

When the medical school building was completed, we all noted how the hospital had the appearance of a square Taj Mahal because of the bright white finish, punctuated by windows that appeared from the outside to be black. The Brody Building, eastern North Carolina's tallest, was not finished until later, where for the first time there developed clinics, essential to clinical training, operating under the complete control and direction of the Medical School Annex. The early challenges in the department included recruiting faculty members and resident physicians. One of the more difficult tasks in starting any postgraduate program was the struggle to achieve tentative approval of a residency training program, and, in 1979, the first four residents were admitted. That program became the home of superior postgraduate education. Medical student education required an equal amount of planning with the development of a core curriculum utilizing both full-time faculty and private physicians. The growth of the department could not have been accomplished without the solid support of the private practice community in Greenville as well as several surrounding communities. The support of the dean and his staff was also critical, as was financial support made possible by the people of North Carolina through the legislature. Integration of other support services, previously geared only to a private practice community, such as pathology, radiology, and anesthesiology, occurred as painlessly as one could have hoped, given the newness of the institution.

Educational programs in a specialty cannot be developed in isolation, and cross-pollination among all the programs was essential to success. An organization of clinical chairs was initiated after the clinical departments opened, and while this group had many disputatious meetings, comity prevailed, and the goals of the school were greatly enhanced by the deliberations of this group.

William A. Burke, M.D.

Chief of Dermatology,
1997–Present

Ralph Whatley, M.D.

Chair of Internal Medicine,
2000–Present

In November 1967, shortly after East Carolina College was granted university status by the University of North Carolina system, a Greenville, N.C. internist, Dr. Edwin Monroe, was approached by the university chancellor, Dr. Leo Jenkins, to ask him to assist with the development of a new medical school at East Carolina University. Several months later, Dr. Monroe was appointed as the dean of the new School of Allied Health and Social Professions, and also as the director of health affairs. It was largely through the efforts of Jenkins and Monroe that the groundwork was laid for the establishment of the East Carolina University School of Medicine, and Monroe recruited Dr. Wallace Wooles, a pharmacologist, as director of medical sciences in 1970.

The first faculty clinician who was attracted to the proposed School of Medicine and was hired by Dr. Wooles in 1970 was Dr. William Waugh, an internist who was put in charge of clinical internal medicine. As one of the founding faculty of the East Carolina University School of Medicine, he played a major role in assisting with the planning and development of the new one-year school, which opened its doors to its first class of twenty students in the fall of 1972. Dr. Waugh served on several committees and panels that eventually led to the formation of a new four-year medical school at East Carolina University.

Dr. William Laupus was hired in 1975 as the new dean of the now four-year ECU School of Medicine, and in August 1976, he hired Dr. Eugene Furth, an endocrinologist from Albany Medical College, as the new chairman of the Department of Internal Medicine. Dr. Furth immediately began the task of developing his new department, and the first two faculty hired by him were Dr. Spencer Raab, the founder of the section of hematology-oncology, and his wife Dr. Mary Raab, who also practiced hematology-oncology. Dr. Jack Chamberlain was hired soon thereafter into the section. Other early/founding section heads in the new department hired between 1976 and 1980 were Dr. Allen Bowyer (cardiology), Dr. Alan Halperin (general medicine), Dr. Yash Kataria (pulmonary), Dr. Bruce Campbell (infectious diseases), Dr. Thomas O'Brien, Jr. (gastroenterology), Dr. Richard Merrill (nephrology), and Dr. Billy Jones (dermatology). Sections of rheumatology and allergy/immunology were added over the next few years and were founded by Dr. Edward Treadwell and Dr. James Metzger in 1982 and 1984 respectively.

Many of the private practice physicians in Greenville and the surrounding communities gave of themselves in the teaching of medical students and residents at the new school. Among others, early private practice internal medicine clinical faculty included Dr. Eric Fearrington, Dr. Al Ferguson, Dr. Frank Fleming, Dr. William Fore, Dr. J. Gregg Hardy, Dr. John Hendrix, Dr. P. Wayne Kendrick, Dr. C. Michael Ramsdell, Dr. Cecil Rand, Dr. John Rose, Dr. Cameron Smith, Dr. Sumiko Ts'Kamura, Dr. Donald Tucker, and Dr. Lynwood Williams.

The early years of the Department of Internal Medicine were housed primarily on the third floor of the Teaching Annex of Pitt County Memorial Hospital with a few offices (as well as clinics) in the A-wing section of the "old hospital" (now the Pitt County Office Building). Internal medicine classroom teaching for residents and medical students took place in room TA-347 in the Teaching Annex, and "Morning Report" took place in a small conference room off the main departmental office in room TA-308.

The first internal medicine resident physician was Dr. Jesse Aronowitz, who began his three-year internal medicine residency at Pitt County Memorial Hospital in July 1977 and graduated in 1980. Other early residents beginning in 1978 in internal medicine included Dr. Jan Creech, Dr. George Hughes, Dr. Janice Strom, Dr. Nick Patrone, and two doing only a preliminary year, Dr. Ed Kitces and Dr. Steve Mamerow. The third group of residents beginning in 1979 (and rounding out a full three years of residents) included Dr. Lynn Anderson, Dr. Edwin Robinson, Dr. Lynn Davis, Dr. Mike Messino, and Dr. Richard Young. Dr. Glenn Gafford was also in this group but was called to military service and later completed his residency in the department in 1986.

The first four-year medical school class of twenty-eight students began their first year of medical school basic sciences curriculum in August 1977 in a classroom in the south end of the biology building on the main ECU campus. Formal teaching by the Department of Internal Medicine faculty began during the pathophysiology and physical diagnosis courses in the 1978–79 school year. As mentioned earlier, these courses were taught in room TA-347 in the teaching annex of the new Pitt County Memorial Hospital. Grand Rounds for the Department of Internal Medicine has always been held in the main auditorium at Pitt County Memorial Hospital.

Early memories of the Department of Internal Medicine include Gene Furth's "prayer bench" (which was bought from state surplus by Gene), which represented the "almighty power" of the departmental chair. His abacus (also bought from surplus) was also present in his office purportedly to simplify and explain to faculty even very complex budgetary issues. "The Gospel According to Eugene" was regularly posted by Dr. George Hughes to impart a bit of biblical humor into his early written accounts of the department. Finally, Dr. Furth gave all graduating senior internal medicine residents an old wooden "tobacco stick" embossed with their name to remind them of their "roots" back in eastern North Carolina.

The Brody Building opened in the fall of 1982, allowing movement of internal medicine outpatient clinics to the first floor outpatient clinics area on the "back side" of Brody, a location that still houses many of the ECU clinics today. The Internal Medicine Clinic was initially in module C, where some medicine clinics are still located.

The teaching of the medical students for the former pathophysiology (now introduction to clinical medicine) course was moved to the second-floor medical student classrooms in Brody. Subspecialty conferences (for students/residents) were held in room TA-347 in the hospital teaching annex, and other lectures to medical students were also done in room TA-391.

During 1986–87, Dr. Furth took a sabbatical year from East Carolina University to do the Hartford Geriatrics Fellowship at the Johns Hopkins University School of Medicine in Baltimore. Dr. Yash Kataria led as interim/acting chairman during his absence. Dr. Furth resumed command on his return in 1987, covering geriatrics as well as endocrinology.

During the latter years in the 1980s, the department was very active in basic sciences and clinical research with thriving grant-supported research being done in endocrinology, allergy/immunology, hematology/oncology, and pulmonary medicine. Most of the laboratory bench research was done in laboratories on the second and third floors of the Brody Building.

Dermatology was the first internal medicine outpatient clinic to be moved outside of the Brody Building in 1988. It was placed in a modular unit next to the parking area for the School of Medicine Outpatient Center. Many other internal medicine clinics followed with a dislocation from the Brody Building as the department as well as the medical center thrived in numbers of patients seen.

Dr. Furth retired as the chair of the internal medicine department in 1992. Following a search, the dean of the School of Medicine (since 1988), Dr. James Hallock then hired Dr. Robert Wortmann as the new chairman of internal medicine in 1993.

During Dr. Wortmann's tenure as chair (from 1993 to 1999), the department struggled with issues of financial constraints and fiscal budget issues, and there was a high turnover of personnel. The school was beginning to face real budgetary deficits due to changes occurring on a national level in both the clinical as well as research arenas, and Dr. Wortmann worked to try to address these difficult problems.

In 1999, Dr. Ralph Whatley was appointed interim chairman of internal medicine. After a careful search for a new chair, Dr. Whatley was given permanent chairman status for the department in early 2001. The Department of Internal Medicine is undergoing change and is continuing to improve under Dr. Whatley's vision and direction. It is currently composed of ten divisions: (1) cardiology; (2) dermatology; (3) endocrinology; (4) gastroenterology; (5) general internal medicine; (6) hematology-oncology; (7) infectious diseases; (8) nephrology; (9) pulmonary/critical care medicine; and (10) rheumatology. The department currently has twenty-three fellows in fellowships in cardiology, interventional cardiology, gastroenterology, infectious diseases, pulmonary/critical care medicine, nephrology, and hematology-oncology. A fellowship in diabetes is in the application stages. The department also has a new residency program in its Division of Dermatology.

Research is also beginning to be revamped with a strong program being developed under Dr. Wayne Cascio's divisional leadership in cardiology. This division will play a major role in the recently funded building for the ECU Cardiovascular Center. Active research is also under way in endocrinology (as the main driver for the School of Medicine's Diabetes Center) and in renal medicine. Major research drives in the Division of Hematology-Oncology as well as research into photodynamic therapy in pulmonary/critical care medicine are being studied within the Department of Internal Medicine as part of the ECU Cancer Center.

The department currently has a full-time faculty of seventy-five physicians and three Ph.D. research scientists. It currently matches for twelve categorical and six preliminary match slots per year for internal medicine residency positions. The department is also active in the training of twenty-three medicine-pediatrics resident trainees and six medicine-psychiatry trainees as well as some in other residencies as well. In addition to clinics in the Brody Building, internal medicine clinics are also located in Medical Pavilion Medical Offices and Executive Park Medical Offices. New clinical space in a contiguous "medical mall" is currently being contemplated as the medical school campus expands to adjoining lands further to the west of the Brody Building. Other funded buildings already planned on this medical campus to be used by the department include a Cardiovascular Research Center, a new medical library, and a new cafeteria.

The future for the Department of Internal Medicine within the Brody School of Medicine is bright. The department is actively involved in all aspects of an academic environment including clinical, educational, research, and service activities and is emphasizing these attributes to its resident trainees. It is important to emphasize that the future of internal medicine rests with our current trainees (students, residents, and fellows). Without proper direction, training, and foresight by these individuals, the future of the field of medicine itself is uncertain.

James Jones, M.D.

Chair of Family Medicine, 1976–1994

In 1973, as president of the North Carolina Academy of Family Physicians, I commissioned a study of the medical manpower in the state. That study revealed some alarming data: medical school graduates from the state's three medical schools, in keeping with the pervasive academic thinking of most U.S. medical schools, were influenced to specialize in increasingly narrow specialties. Very few young physicians were entering primary care, and virtually none were choosing careers in family medicine. Compounding the problem, 50 percent of the general practice doctors east of Raleigh were fifty or older. This meant that the state would face a major shortage of doctors for the most underserved areas within ten to fifteen years.

As I listened to Dr. Ed Monroe and other leaders from ECU, I became convinced that a new school committed to training family doctors had the best probability of making an impact on the pending medical manpower crisis. I joined the political battle in support of the new school at ECU. The N.C. Academy of Family Physicians publicly endorsed the school despite opposition from the N.C. Medical Society and the other three medical schools.

As the debate evolved, it became clear that if the state funded a new school it would have a clearly different mission: (1) to increase the number of primary care physicians, especially family physicians; (2) to develop tertiary medical services for the eastern region of the state; and (3) to provide opportunities for underrepresented minority and disadvantaged students.

I was recruited to develop a family practice residency program at Pitt Hospital as part of the AHEC program before the final approval of the School of Medicine. Within less than a decade, the department was nationally recognized as one of the ten best programs in the United States. More than 58 percent of the graduates have remained in North Carolina, and many practice in rural and underserved areas.

At the insistence of Dr. Walter Pories, the clinical chairs met as a group frequently, assuring good communication and team decision-making. The importance of the close interpersonal relationships that developed cannot be overstated. I recall the first time I met Walter Pories. Dean Laupus asked me to interview him as a candidate for the chairman of the Department of Surgery. At that time the Family Practice Center was housed in trailers behind the old hospital in the middle of a soybean field. As we walked through the field, Walter started picking the soybeans. "What are these?" Walter asked. "Soybeans. Now tell me your vision of this new department," I said, trying to return the conversation to the serious task. "Can you eat them?" Walter persisted. "I suppose. Usually they are processed first," I said. Whereupon Walter threw the shelled soybeans in his mouth and ate them.

Later, Dr. Laupus inquired about my opinion of this candidate for surgery chair. "Superb background, but a weird fellow," I said, "How so?" he asked. "Well," I said, "he ate soybeans out of the field." "That may be because he is a nationally renowned scholar in trace element research," the dean said. After that, Walter and I spent a lot of time together, walking through the woods, learning computers, having quiet breakfasts with him and Mary Ann. I could tell similar stories about each of the other chairs. It was the cohesiveness, mutual respect, and friendships that forged a unique school with an environment where students felt comfortable approaching anyone from the chairs down.

Family medicine was given responsibility for a very large amount of curriculum time in all four years of medical school. This included one of the first required family medicine clerkships in U.S. medical schools. I shall always be grateful for the support of the practicing family doctors all across the state in opening their offices and homes to these students. They did so without pay or regard for the intrusion of our evaluation instruments or requirement for preceptor training. Allowing students to experience the rewards and frustrations of primary care from the first year of medical school helped many students decide for and against similar careers.

At the undergraduate level, the Department of Family Medicine has been recognized as a national leader. We were one of the first departments to introduce simulated patients for teaching students as well as one of the first departments to introduce standard clinical exams for evaluation of clerkship experience.

Many of our residency grads have gone on to distinguished careers such as president of the N.C. Academy of Family Physicians, director of residency programs, Family Doctor of the Year for North Carolina, and many other local and national honors. I am honored and blessed to have been a part of so noble an effort.

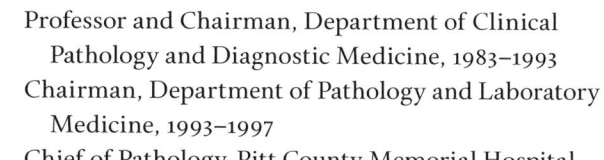

H. Thomas Norris, M.D., F.A.C.P., F.A.S.C.P., F.C.A.P.

Professor and Chairman, Department of Clinical
    Pathology and Diagnostic Medicine, 1983–1993
Chairman, Department of Pathology and Laboratory
    Medicine, 1993–1997
Chief of Pathology, Pitt County Memorial Hospital,
    1983–1997

I was recruited by Bill Laupus in the early 1980s when a solid base in diagnostic pathology was needed. The medical center was moving from one exclusively focused on only patient care to a center that would be able to support both medical student training and residency training in a wide variety of specialties. The hospital had a very meager pathology laboratory housed in about 5,000 square feet of space, and while the hospital was only 250 beds, this amount of space was very inadequate.

My recruitment took six visits to Greenville. In preparation for my last visit, it was suggested that I formulate a list of what was needed. When one formulates such a list, the first pages are the essentials, then come the less essential but nice particulars, and then the things that really would make your job very, very easy. My list was over six pages long, and if the first pages were not granted, there was no way the Norrises were coming to Greenville. I was prepared to argue for the middle pages, and the last pages were things I was willing to give in on.

I arrived in Kinston, and I was met by Bill Laupus late one Friday night. Bill asked me for the list as he dropped me off at the old Holiday Inn. No discussions.

As I shaved the next morning, I put the finishing touches on my defense of the want list.

We had the usual breakfast, with no mention of the list. As he prepared to let me off for my next meeting, he said, "Oh, by the way, I have already discussed the want list with Jack Richardson, and between the hospital and the School of Medicine, we can meet all of your wishes." It was time to shift gears and get to work.

The chance to build an outstanding Department of Pathology in a developing academic medical center does not happen often. It was a very exciting time. As it turned out, the job was a lot of work but also a lot of fun.

As I arrived for my first day at the medical center, April 1, 1983, the hospital was already adding an additional 4,000 square feet of laboratory space. However, at least 40,000 square feet of laboratory space were needed in the hospital. The hospital had a very primitive computer system, run out of the east campus of ECU. There was no laboratory computer system at all.

The first Thanksgiving I spent in Greenville was very memorable. It gained the name of Black Thursday in the hospital. The rudimentary computer system in the hospital crashed Thanksgiving morning, and those responsible for the system maintenance were located on the main campus of ECU. They were all away for the holiday. No one was there to fix the problem. Fortunately, manual systems and lots of extra work by a dedicated staff got us though the weekend.

On the next Monday morning, it was Dave McRae's and my task to inform Cliff Moore, one of the ECU top administrators, about the problem. Cliff Moore had a regularly scheduled Monday meeting with the hospital about future development of computer services and had assembled a group of computer people but was unaware of the problem. He called the meeting to order, but before he started the agenda, Dave and I informed him that there was a problem that could impede further development of computer services between ECU and PCMH. We told Mr. Moore of the problem. He said he would look into it and abruptly adjourned the meeting. The entire event was one of the great stimulators for the hospital to develop its own freestanding computer system.

Sunquest won the bid at PCMH for the pathology laboratory system. Sunquest was the best on the market and was very innovative in its system. They were willing to develop in collaboration with the hospital computer system and interface so that pathology laboratory values could be published on the hospital computer system and could follow patients wherever they went in the hospital. In 1986, PCMH was the only hospital with such a system, which is now standard for all computer systems.

At the same time that computerization was going on, the Hospital Board agreed to a laboratory expansion to 40,000 net square feet of space. This provided the hospital with a state-of-the-art diagnostic pathology laboratory.

All of these accomplishments could not be obtained without the very hard work of a vast number of pathologists, Ph.D.s, technologists, technicians, and support staff. I am truly appreciative of all of the help and support that the department has received.

Joseph G. Cory, Ph.D.

Chair of Biochemistry and Molecular Biology,
   1990–Present

The biochemistry program at East Carolina University started under the direction of a dedicated man, Dr. Sam Pennington. Then in 1976, Dr. William E. Laupus, dean of the School of Medicine, formally recognized biochemistry as a department by hiring Wilhelm R. Frisell, Ph.D., as the chair. The department grew under his direction to a faculty of nine. Bill was an academician of the highest order. The word *gentleman* is overused, but Bill Frisell was a gentleman and, more important, a gentle man. He had a wonderful view of what the East Carolina University School of Medicine should and could be, and he made tremendous contributions to the school both as chair of biochemistry and as the first associate dean for research and graduate studies in the School of Medicine.

Bill Frisell's legacy lies in the faculty that he recruited and in the Ph.D. program that he developed. The biochemistry faculty has been exceptional in their commitment to teaching medical and graduate students; the biochemistry course taught to medical students is one of the courses rated most highly by the students. The biochemistry faculty received the highest teaching award presented by the University of North Carolina Board of Governors, and two received the highest teaching award presented by East Carolina University. So close is the relationship of the biochemistry faculty to the medical students in a mentoring capacity that four of our medical students who carried out research in the laboratories of the biochemistry faculty subsequently received the prestigious Howard Hughes Medical Student Research Fellowships to spend a year at the National Institutes of Health, competing against students from Harvard, Johns Hopkins, Stanford, and others. In competition with other medical schools, on five different occasions the department was awarded the Burroughs-Wellcome Visiting Professorship in Basic Medical Sciences.

Since the beginning, the biochemistry faculty have carried out high-level research activities. The faculty have been one of the most heavily grant-funded departments in the School of Medicine over the period of its existence. Because of their high level of research, faculty have been asked to serve on American Cancer Society and National Institutes of Health Study

Sections, on editorial boards of scientific journals, and as site visitors for the National Institutes of Health.

The department also has a strong commitment to the Greenville community and is actively involved with the Greenville Community Shelter, Habitat for Humanity, the Ulster Project, and the activities of faculty's respective churches and organizations.

Edward R. Newton, M.D.

Professor and Chair of Obstetrics and Gynecology, 1998–Present

I was struck by a comment one of my residents made a couple of weeks ago. We had just performed a cesarean section in a very large woman at twenty-eight weeks' gestation. Her pregnancy was complicated by chronic hypertension and insulin-resistant diabetes. The resident was awestruck that I could hold the 340-gram little girl in the palm of my hand. While very small and with "a long row to hoe," the baby's chances for healthy survival are good.

This case illustrates major improvements in adverse pregnancy outcomes in eastern North Carolina in the last thirty years. In 1974, the mother, who lives outside of Greenville, would have arrived for prenatal care at the public health clinic after twenty weeks of pregnancy. Her fetus would have died in utero. Before the advent of the Brody School Medicine, maternal and infant mortality rates were some of the worst in the country and were similar to death rates of many developing countries. From 1995 to 2002, perinatal mortality has dropped 7 percent (16.9 per 1,000 births to 15.7 per 1,000 births), and infant mortality has dropped 14 percent (11.8 per 1,000 live births to 10.2 per 1,000 live births) in eastern North Carolina. Since 1974, there has been a 70 percent drop in neonatal mortality among the highest risk group of neonates, from 576 per 1,000 births to 173 per 1,000 births in 2002.

On the downside, we are seeing massive increases in obesity, with the comorbidities of hypertension and diabetes. We deliver eight to ten women a month with a predelivery weight greater than 350 pounds. In one week in January 2004, I delivered 2 patients greater than 550 pounds, 1 greater than 450 pounds, and 3 who exceeded 350 pounds.

The success has been due to a long-term effort by the maternal fetal medicine specialists and their colleagues, the neonatologists, to develop a regional system for perinatal care. The Division of Maternal Fetal Medicine has the only fellowship-trained and certified MFM specialists east of Interstate 95 and north of Interstate 40 and provides outpatient and inpatient care for about one thousand high-risk patients in the Regional Perinatal Center and three hundred hospital-to-hospital maternal transports. The Regional Perinatal Center also provides state-of-the-art fetal diagnosis and therapy.

Their success would not be possible without the resources of the North Carolina Division of Maternal and Child Health, which has supported us with a yearly grant since 1979 for the salaries of key support individuals, nurses, nutrition specialists, social workers, and sonologists. More recently, the ECU Department of Obstetrics and Gynecology has supervised the development of the Access III Community Care Program for pregnant women. The changes in risk assessment and appropriate referral, case management, and early postpartum follow-up has enhanced the primary and secondary prevention of adverse pregnancy outcomes in a cost-efficient fashion. When compared to patients with traditional Medicaid coverage, patients in the Community Care Plan have better screening and referral for maternal risk factors, fewer patient days in the neonatal intensive care unit, and improved breast feeding rates. As the Access III Community Care rolls out to more counties in eastern North Carolina, we estimate that total mother-baby charges will be reduced by 15 to 20 percent if patients participate in Access III Community Care Plan.

Early in the development of Pitt County Memorial Hospital, a commitment was made to improving maternal-child health. The hospital management has allowed for space, equipment, support personnel, and service management to produce a state-of-the-art neonatal unit. The increasing number of maternal high-risk referrals has recently exceeded the bed capacity for the current neonatal intensive care unit of thirty-seven beds, but within the year, we will have a fifty-bed unit.

Our success has led to problems for the future. While survival is routine for the infant born after twenty-five weeks, there remain major morbidities from the maternal complications associated with high-risk birth and from being born early. As many as 30–40 percent of infants born at under twenty-nine weeks will have major long-term morbidity. The chronic care of these infants will need to be supported to allow these children to meet their maximum potential in a cost-efficient fashion.

Another challenge is the societal expectation that every child should be born without maternal or childhood morbidity. This has fueled an explosion of litigation and has driven up malpractice premiums and has driven obstetricians out of practice in eastern North Carolina. Most obstetricians in eastern North Carolina have had their premiums increase by more than 40 percent in the last year. Like the rest of the country, 5–10 percent of obstetricians per year in eastern North Carolina will stop obstetric care. For the rural areas of eastern North Carolina, access to quality prenatal care and delivery is a crisis today; for the large cities—Greenville, New Bern, Tarboro, Rocky Mount, Jacksonville, Goldsboro—there will be a crisis in the next two to four years. Our improvements in maternal-child health will be challenged if the malpractice crisis is not solved.

Before 1995, patients with infertility left eastern North Carolina to receive care at other universities and groups in the central part of the state. Now they are choosing care at the Brody School of Medicine. Like the MFM Division, the Reproductive Endocrine and Infertility (REI) Group has the only fellowship-trained and certified REI specialists in eastern North Carolina. The clinical pregnancy rates and "take-home baby" rates of IVF at Brody School of Medicine REI Division exceed the national rates.

Assisted reproductive technologies (ART) present a major clinical challenge: multiple gestation increases geometrically with ART, and multiple gestations have a high risk of preterm birth. The average gestational age at birth in triplets is thirty-two weeks; quadruplets deliver at twenty-eight weeks on average. This represents an enormous amount of clinical work, cost, and potential long-term childhood disability. Our future goal is to better understand, prevent, and manage these preterm births.

We now see fewer cases of advanced gynecologic cancer because more women in eastern Carolina have access to regular health care and are being referred to the Brody School of Medicine for the diagnosis and management of early disease. The increases in annual Pap smear screening and the access to our colposcopy clinic by the neighborhood health clinics have lead to the decreasing rate of advanced-stage carcinoma of the cervix.

Before the mid 1980s, patients with gynecologic cancer left families and friends to receive care at programs in the central part of the state. Now, they are close to home with access to state-of-the-art surgery, chemotherapy, and radiotherapy. While advanced-stage gynecologic cancers remain difficult to cure, disease-free survival has increased with most tumor types.

Since the inception of the Brody School of Medicine, senior gynecologists have provided support for women, especially the indigent, with a need for advanced benign gynecologic surgery. The day-to-day morbidity of pelvic floor prolapse, urinary incontinence, pelvic pain, sexually transmitted disease, and heavy, irregular vaginal bleeding was high before 1975. The ability for indigent women to get relief in our gynecology clinic has been sentinel.

One of the greatest improvements in the health care for women in eastern North Carolina has been effective family planning and contraception. In 1975, women in this region had four to six pregnancies; now in 2004, they have one to three. Our generalists have provided primary care service to women but, more important, have educated other primary care providers in eastern North Carolina. Their good care has been multiplied many fold by their education of medical students and residents.

I am most proud of our record in guiding our medical students toward a career in obstetrics and gynecology and training residents to be exceptional obstetricians and gynecologists for the people of North Carolina. About 10 percent of our medical school class chooses a career in this specialty year in and year out. While many stay at ECU, others are joining nationally recognized programs like Duke, the University of North Carolina at Chapel Hill, the University of Pittsburgh Magee Medical Center, and the University of Chicago. About one in five residents goes into a fellowship immediately after graduation; in the last two years, one resident each year has entered the uro-gynecology fellowship at the University of Pittsburgh-Magee Medical Center. Of the remainder, 80 percent have entered practice in North Carolina. I believe we train great practitioners.

Our successes would not have been possible without the support of the citizens of North Carolina, especially those of eastern North Carolina, the support of the medical school and Pitt County Memorial Hospital, and the commitment, knowledge and skills of my faculty.

Jon B. Tingelstad, M.D.

Chair of Pediatrics, 1977–2000

Dr. Jon Tinglestad's contributions to the community are legendary. He helped to integrate the Pitt County Schools as the chairman of the Board of Education and stimulated our economy as the chairman of the Chamber of Commerce. More than anyone else, he is responsible for the founding of the Children's Hospital, the McDonald Center, the telethon, and even the Med-Law Classic. Characteristically, he does not mention these great accomplishments. —WJP

As a prospective faculty member, I first met Bill Laupus early in 1967 when he was professor and chairman of the Department of Pediatrics at the Medical College of Virginia (MCV). Bill was highly respected in the medical communities—local, regional, and national—and served in many leadership roles. These various attributes became readily apparent to me as a potential faculty candidate. I was offered and accepted a position in Bill's department in July 1967. For approximately eight years at MCV, I was a beneficiary of his vision and leadership skills.

Having been on vacation during the spring of 1975, when I returned I was surprised and somewhat saddened to read in the *Richmond Times Dis-*

patch that Dr. Laupus was leaving to become the first dean of the new four-year medical school at East Carolina University. To quote the slogan on the pins worn by the University of Missouri football fans when the Pirates played in Columbia a number of years ago, my response was, "Where the hell is East Carolina?" I quickly and easily found Greenville on the map.

The following spring I accepted the position of vice chairman, Department of Pediatrics, and chief of pediatric cardiology at the East Carolina University School of Medicine, and later that year my family and I moved to Greenville.

The medical school faculty was small in number but was industrious and collegial. There were several new chairs and other members of the earlier one-year medical student program faculty. There were frequent planning meetings, and everyone worked hard. I spent several nights in the Laupus guest house and would often seek encouragement and reassurance from the dean's most wonderful and courageous spouse that this "enormous project was going to be a success." Evelyn was most reassuring, and I was always calm and collected by the time the dean arrived home for dinner.

Following a national search, I was named chairman of the Department of Pediatrics on October 1, 1977. What a thrill but a daunting task. Recruitment of faculty became my highest priority, because at that point in time, I *was* the Department of Pediatrics. My first job offer was to a neonatologist who rejected my invitation. What a disappointment! I often compare it to the feeling of rejection when you are turned down on your first attempt at dating a beautiful young lady. Needless to say, things improved rather rapidly, and over time we brought together a faculty of outstanding clinicians, teachers, and researchers. Over the past quarter century, the department has had a significant impact on the health of eastern North Carolina's infants, children, and adolescents.

However, in some areas progress did come slowly. Initially, facilities were rather Spartan. I examined my first pediatric cardiac referral patient on a cleared-off desktop in Ragsdale Hall on the university's east campus. One morning, one of our general pediatric attendings and our lone (or perhaps lonely) pediatric resident traveled to Grimesland to staff the new satellite clinic at the Health Department. Only one patient was scheduled and fortunately showed up. What a comprehensive evaluation that child must have received! The department's first research project was my performing blood pressure measurements in J. H. Rose High School students to detect unrecognized hypertension. This was done in collaboration with ECU School of Nursing students.

Over the past two and a half decades, the department has experienced phenomenal progress and growth and is now composed of a large number of excellent general pediatricians and pediatric subspecialists. They are expert clinicians, superb teachers, and productive researchers who are backed up by an extremely competent support staff.

The pediatric and medicine/pediatric resident training programs have graduated physicians who have contributed significantly to the improvement of pediatric health care across the state and nation and especially in eastern North Carolina.

In 1976, Pitt County Memorial Hospital had a capacity of less than two hundred beds, ten to twelve of which were designated for pediatric patients. The unit was closed briefly at times during the summer months because all of the patients had been discharged. There was no neonatal intensive care unit and no pediatric intensive care unit.

Again, what a difference a quarter of a century makes. In 1978, a thirty-three-bed neonatal intensive care unit was opened. In 1985, a new pediatric intensive care unit was constructed on 2 West. In 1986, the "hospital within a hospital" concept was adopted for the pediatric units, and they were designated as the Children's Hospital of Eastern North Carolina. That same year, the department began participating in the Children's Miracle Network Telethon, and over $65,000 was raised. In 2003, that figure exceeded $1 million! In 1987, the Ronald McDonald House was opened. A new twelve-bed pediatric intensive care unit was completed in 1995. The new fifty-bed neonatal intensive care unit opened in 2004. Work is progressing on a unit that will provide palliative care for terminally ill patients.

The exciting progress described above has been the result of the untiring efforts of the members of the Department of Pediatrics at East Carolina University's Brody School of Medicine, dedicated staff at the Children's Hospital, practicing pediatricians, the University Health Systems of East Carolina's leadership, county health departments, regional hospitals, and other health care providers. Challenges remain, but under the direction of Ronald Perkin, M.D., who became chairman of the department in 2000, we anticipate a future of unlimited potential for the health care of eastern North Carolina's infant, children, and adolescents.

Gene Furth, M.D., F.A.C.P.

Chair of Medicine, 1976–1992

Walter J. Pories, M.D., F.A.C.S.

Chair of Surgery, 1977–1996

Gene Furth, the first chairman of the Department of Medicine, is no longer with us, so my version will have to do for both of us. It's a fitting approach.

We were close and very much alike—both graduates of Wesleyan University in Connecticut; voluble, eccentric, blessed with outrageous senses of humor, and short. He kept a kneeling step in front of his desk, probably purloined from some church sale; I rarely wore a white coat.

Chairmen of medicine and surgery do not usually get along, much less cooperate. Our approach was just the opposite. We joined in the pursuit of ideas, in the care of patients, and especially in the pursuit of endocrine research, an area in which he was an undisputed master.

One of my favorite memories was the time we decided that departments of medicine and surgery were hopeless anachronisms. Medical schools and hospitals, we reasoned, would be far more effective if the departments were systems- or disease-oriented focusing on gastrointestinal, cardiovascular, neuromuscular, and metabolic issues and so on. These divisions would include internists, surgeons, and basic scientists in an environment that would facilitate care, encourage shared research, and sharply improve the opportunities for teaching. To dramatize our intent, we marched into Bill's office together with our resignations as chairs with a request to reorganize our programs and to get his permission to recruit the basic scientists to join us. He loved the idea, agreeing that it was long overdue. Unfortunately, the American Association of Medical Colleges (AAMC) did not agree and instead warned the dean that we would not receive accreditation if we pursued the plan. Disappointed, we fell back in line and managed our task in the traditional manner. It's still a good idea. In my surgical career, I worked far more closely with internists and basic scientists than I did with some of my own colleagues in the surgical specialties.

I also ended up caring for this magnificent leader, husband, father, scientist, and doctor during his last illness. It was a special privilege to see that his courage and his integrity never flagged. I miss him deeply. —WJP

Jack Allison, M.D.

Chair of Emergency Medicine, 1980–1995

The Department of Emergency Medicine was the brainchild of Dean William E. Laupus and was initiated in 1980 because of his vision of the need for emergency medicine, including upgrading the Emergency Medical Services (EMS) throughout eastern North Carolina. E. Jackson Allison Jr., M.D., M.P.H., served as the department's first professor and chairman, from 1980 through 1996.

The Department of Emergency Medicine was predated by the EMS project, which began in 1978 and trained the first paramedics east of Raleigh, which initially included the Outer Banks and later Eastern Pines; the latter became the very first all-volunteer paramedic program in the state of North Carolina. The EMS also spawned the first intermediate-level EMT programs in the state.

EastCare, the emergency helicopter system based at Pitt County Memorial Hospital, first lifted off in 1985 and is now recognized nationally as a stalwart leader in air medical services.

Over the years, the Department of Emergency Medicine has provided consultations to numerous countries establishing academic departments of emergency medicine: Costa Rica, Austria, Mexico, New Zealand, China, the Dominican Republic, and Israel.

Dean Laupus will always be remembered and revered for his vision, integrity and undying support for the Department of Emergency Medicine.

W. Randolph Chitwood Jr., M.D., F.A.C.S., F.R.C.S. (Eng.)

Senior Associate Vice Chancellor, Cardiovascular
  Disease, Health Sciences Division, 2003–Present
Chief, Division of Cardiothoracic and Vascular
  Surgery, 2003–Present
Chairman, Department of Surgery, 1996–1993

Dr. W. Randolph Chitwood fails to note his two greatest contributions: heading the first center in the United States to perform robotic cardiac surgery and his development of a methodology for salvaging mitral valves by intricate repairs. For these accomplishments and in recognition of his international reputation, he was awarded the O. Max Joyner Award, UNC's highest honor for a faculty member, in 2004. —WJP

When at Duke as the last-year superchief, I was called to Dr. Sabiston's office and asked if I would like to look at the chief cardiac surgeon's position at ECU. There was a chance to start a new university program from scratch. I had already told Jim Cox that I would come to Washington University in St. Louis for a junior faculty position. He understood my change in interest, as his son had gone to ECU.

The East Carolina University cardiac surgery program started on July 10, 1984. There were many obstacles and interesting obstructions, from people saying, "No one will stay in Greenville for heart surgery," to the head operating-room nurse saying, "It's just like a kidney transplant—you don't need any special equipment." Over 250 operations were done that year with this same team with a very low mortality. Many of our nurses like Rene Grainger in the OR are still with us.

The entire hospital was abuzz with excitement when we did those early cases. Before this, most people went to Raleigh for surgery, considered the standard, as were Duke and UNC. Larry King, R.N., and I traveled throughout the region to all physicians' offices and local medical societies and told them about our program. We were on the road with Mr. Cherry as our driver; the routine was to finish surgery, stabilize the patient, and then drive to an outlying hospital for a chicken dinner and a short talk with other doctors. We would take on any engagement larger than one doctor.

One night I was summoned to Washington, N.C., to repair a ruptured thoracoabdominal aneurysm that couldn't be moved to PCMH. The State Police took me to Beaufort County Hospital, sirens screaming at ninety miles per hour. Barr Coleman and I completed the operation early that morning, and my wife came and picked me up. We then had breakfast at the Waffle House. The patient lived nearly fifteen years longer. Another day during year two, a doctor in Rocky Mount had his finger in a stab wound to the right ventricle and didn't know what to do. Dr. Erle Austin went to Rocky Mount, where Dr. Clever still had his finger dutifully in the hole. Erle used Claude Beck's cross-stitch method, as the OR team didn't have a clue about the pledget. Erle improvised using the 1930s method that Dr. Sabiston had taught us.

Darnell Jones, M.D.

Chair of Obstetrics and Gynecology, 1984–1997

Dr. Robert G. Brame was both the first chair and the only faculty member of the Department of Obstetrics and Gynecology in July of 1977. Dr. Darnell Jones arrived as the second faculty member of the department in December of that year. Over the following three and a half years, additional faculty joined the department, and the training program filled to its full enrollment of twelve residents.

A regional prenatal center was quickly established to provide tertiary prenatal assessment and care for high-risk patients. The parallel development of a neonatal intensive care unit allowed for expert management of late pregnancy complications and preterm labor. A regional center for the evaluation and management of patients with abnormal Pap smears and pre-invasive and early invasive cervical cancer now provides care to patients who historically had no access to such care. The development of radiation oncology services and the expertise of existing faculty in the surgical management of advanced gynelogic cancer promoted the development of regional referral pathways for the care of patients for gynologic oncology care.

Dr. Darnell Jones was appointed as chair of the department in July 1984, and during the following fourteen years the department progressively created resources and programs to provide comprehensive care to women in Greenville and eastern North Carolina. Academic divisions of maternal-fetal medicine, gynecology oncology, and reproductive endocrinology infertility were established, as well as the first, and still only, in vitro program in the region. Advanced laparoscopic procedures began to be used in the surgical management of endocrine and infertility disorders. Dr. Hamid Hadi joined the faculty as chief of the Maternal-Fetal Medicine Division. As additional certified faculty joined the division, the fetal ultrasound program permitted comprehensive evaluation of the fetus and fostered the introduction of fetal interventional procedures, percutaneous umbilical blood sampling, chorion villous sampling, ultrasound guided amniocentesis, and intrauterine fetal transfusion. Parallel development of cytogenetic laboratories in the Department of Pediatrics enabled regional referral systems for fetal evaluation.

Dr. Larry Bandy established the Gynecologic Oncology Division in the mid-1980s. Dr. Diane Semer, an ECU medical student, subsequently joined the faculty. Most recently, Dr. Samuel Lentz has assumed the leadership of the division. The development of the Leo Jenkins Cancer Center has facilitated the development of regional cancer care.

Dr. Samuel Atkinson was recruited to be the director of General Obstetrics and Gynecology and subsequently assumed the role as residency program director. Dr. Narinder Sehgal and later Dr. Steven Green assumed responsibility for medical student education in OB-GYN, and the excellence of resident and student education is largely a result of the dedication of these three individuals.

Since its establishment, the department has developed regional clinical referral resources in all areas of OB-GYN, participated in training of our 1,600 medical students, and trained 60 residents. The residency program has expanded to five residents in each of the four years of training, and of its sixty graduates, twenty-five practice in North Carolina, seventeen of them in eastern North Carolina; ten subsequently completed subspecialty fellowships; and thirteen have become faculty members of academic OB/GYN departments.

THE BENEFACTORS

The School of Medicine is appropriately named after the Brody family, whose continuing generosity has made the impossible a reality for our young and often struggling rural medical center. David Brody, who served on the boards of the hospital and East Carolina University, is well suited to tell the story. —WJP

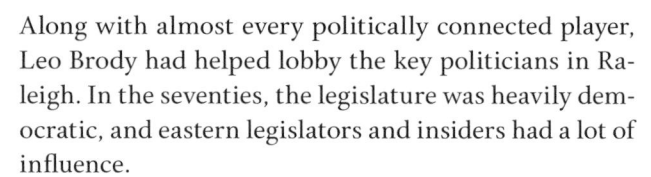

David S. Brody

Family Contributions in Excess of $22 million

Along with almost every politically connected player, Leo Brody had helped lobby the key politicians in Raleigh. In the seventies, the legislature was heavily democratic, and eastern legislators and insiders had a lot of influence.

However, as is often the case, timing plays a key role in the course of events. Soon after the school was announced and planning begun, my Uncle Sammy decided to sell his business, as was his habit. Whenever he had good luck financially, he would make a philanthropic gift.

Meanwhile, although Leo Jenkins and Leo Brody where good friends, Chancellor Jenkins had allied Morris Brody to help him convince Sammy and Leo Brody to make a major gift to help the medical school. I remember Morris bringing Leo Jenkins over to Kinston one day and the group going out to lunch. I was in my mid-twenties at the time and was not included. However, several weeks later Sammy called me into his office and told me about the gift and an announcement dinner being planned.

There was the original $1.2 million gift that funded the Brody Scholars program. The purpose to attract the best and brightest to a new school with merit-based scholarships. Since then the program has grown with additional gifts to an endowment of $8.6 million.

Neither Sammy, Leo, nor any of the Brody family attended ECU. Sammy had attended UNC, and as the lead benefactor had been considering a gift to either UNC or Duke. Although I am not positive, I believe it was the combination of Leo Jenkins and Morris Brody who turned the tide for ECU. Remembering the times, this was a huge leap of faith.

The announcement really went against Sammy's style: he wanted it to be anonymous or with as little fanfare as possible. However, Jenkins wanted the gift to set an example for others who had not attended ECU and to make a bold statement of local support. So a large new public dinner with much press and celebration was held to announce the gift. True to his form, Sammy had Leo Brody make the speech and invited all of his brothers to share in the credit.

In the mid-eighties, I became very involved with PCMH as a board member, and my cousin Hyman joined the board of the Brody Medical Foundation and then the ECU Medical Foundation. Over the next ten years, we each in our different areas assumed leadership roles.

In 1994, J. S. Brody died and in his will left a large gift to the Brody Brothers Foundation, which Hyman and I comanaged. It had been his charge to us to make large gifts that could make a difference. Hyman and I decided not to rush out but to take our time to find a project worthy of such a donation.

I was commuting between Kinston and Greenville at the time and would often use the drive to do my thinking. One day I came to Hyman and suggested the medical school gift. He was unsure at first and wanted to think about it. As it turned out, a few weeks later he was visiting a friend in Greensboro who had made the lead gift to the Children's Hospital there. His friend told him of how much good it had done and how gratified his family felt. So the idea started to gain traction. Again a few months later, Hyman was on the Shared Visions Campaign and was approached about a family gift to ECU. I was the chairman of PCMH and heavily involved in School of Medicine issues. Once again, the timing was fortuitous.

I had a number of concerns about how the money could be best spent. At a meeting in Dean Hallock's office, we outlined a gift that was to be used to provide "seed money" grants to researchers in their initial state of project development. The research was to focus on health issues of eastern North Carolina. It was a good decision. Our family is pleased that we were able to participate in the development of this great institution.

THE HOSPITAL: STAGES IN THE BUILDING OF A MEDICAL CENTER

A history of the Brody School of Medicine would be incomplete if it did not include the Pitt County Memorial Hospital, the teaching institution where students and residents learn under the supervision of practicing faculty members. Mr. Douglas Boyd provided an excellent overview of its history during the celebration of its fiftieth anniversary. —WJP

Citizens Vote for Better Health

In a special election on September 16, 1947, Pitt County voters approved $452,000 in bonds toward building a new facility to replace the aging and outdated fifty-two-bed Pitt General Hospital, started in 1924 by four local physicians. The state and federal governments picked up the rest of the tab, which grew from an estimated $900,000 in 1947 to $1.4 million by the time the hospital was complete.

Groundbreaking for the new hospital was held March 22, 1949, on nearly 20 acres of land on West Fifth Street donated by the J. S. Moye family. Crews soon got to work, and PCMH opened its doors February 8, 1951. The first patients were Mamie Dews of Winterville and her one-week-old son, Kenneth, transferred from Pitt General at 8:30 a.m. Lillie Wilson of Have-

PCMH during original building construction.

lock was the first outside patient admitted, and she gave birth to a daughter at 11:39 a.m.

PCMH received its first license from the state in May 1951 and its first accreditation from the Joint Commission on Accreditation of Hospitals on May 4, 1956.

By the 1960s, however, PCMH was already beginning to show its age. Space was cramped, patients waited on beds in the hallways to be admitted, and the design and construction of the facility made expansion impractical. Plus, a new medical school being established at East Carolina University that would need a modern teaching hospital looked like a real possibility. Thus, a new hospital was proposed. As they had twenty years earlier, community and medical leaders fanned out across the county to lobby for the new hospital. Their efforts paid off on November 3, 1970, when voters approved $9 million in bonds for a new hospital.

The current site of approximately 95 acres was selected, construction began, and on March 26, 1977, local leaders and Governor Jim Hunt cut the ribbon on the new $15.9 million, 370-bed PCMH. On that day, PCMH was 450,000 square feet and had approximately 200 nurses and a budget of $18 million. The emergency department consisted of sixteen beds, and the operating area had twelve surgical rooms.

Brody School of Medicine

How times change. After twenty-three years of almost constant construction and expansion, PCMH now has 731 beds and more than 1.1 million
square feet in the main facility, plus another 161,201 square feet at Venture
Tower, the Gaskins-Leslie Center, the SurgiCenter, and the ViQuest Center
and more office, clinical, and storage space in various other buildings and
warehouses. More than 1,100 nurses care for patients. The current fiscal
year has a budget of approximately $400 million. Surgeons have twenty-two
operating suites in which to work, and the planned Emergency Department
expansion will have sixty beds.

Kenneth Dews was chairman of the PCMH Board of Trustees during
the 1970 bond election and again in 1977 when the new hospital opened. He
recalled that after the original PCMH was expanded to 205 beds in 1961,
local and medical leaders thought that would be more than enough to satisfy the area's needs.

"We looked at it like, 'That'll pretty much take care of us,'" Dews recalled recently. "But as the university grew and the industrial base grew, we
knew we were going to have to do something." That something was issue $9
million in general obligation bonds for a new hospital, add to that money
from the state to build the Regional Rehabilitation Center plus money from
ECU for the teaching annex, and the total came to $15.9 million for a facil-
ity on approximately 95 acres of land. And that seemed to be enough at the
time.

"We had a consultant come down from the Medical College of Virginia before we got started, and he said, 'You get 100 acres, you won't ever need any more.' But he didn't see the growth that was about to happen here," Dews said.

Actually, that growth was far from a sure thing. Only a two-year medical school was approved so far, but not even that was a certainty. ECU began its School of Medicine by admitting students for just one year of study in 1972, then transferring them to UNC–Chapel Hill. Thus, Pitt County was putting a lot on the line when it built the new PCMH.

"It was a big risk for the County Commission," Dews said. "Nine million was a huge amount of money then."

The Medical School Arrives

The eventual approval and establishment of the medical school, however, helped push PCMH from primarily a community hospital with some regional referrals to primarily a referral center where patients could receive advanced care for nearly all types of illnesses and injuries. The medical school recruited top academic physicians, which in turn prompted private physician practices to seek out the best doctors they could find. Early on, ECU paid for advanced radiology suites at PCMH. The hospital has pitched in money, space, and other resources for important medical school programs, such as trauma services. The synergistic effect built a strong health care center in Greenville.

"The amazing thing is there were people of vision who were willing to fight for this and saw something strong and powerful coming out of the effort," said Dr. Tom Irons. In the 1970s, his parents were physicians in Greenville, and he was entering medical residency. The topic of the medical school and regional hospital were hot conversation topics, he said.

The medical school and PCMH's role as its teaching hospital didn't come without some reservation, however. Private physicians were concerned they would lose hospital beds to teaching purposes and that they may be required to perform some teaching duties without compensation. State officials were worried about funding a medical school when they didn't have control over its teaching hospital and were unsure of the need for another school. The leadership of Dr. William Laupus, dean of the medical school; Dr. Frank Longino, an influential private physician; and Jack Richardson, then president of PCMH; helped guide the formation of the relationship between ECU and PCMH.

"He was the right dean at the right time," PCMH chief executive officer Dave McRae said of Laupus. "He was able to create peace and move forward with the medical school in its most fragile days. He, Jack Richardson, and Dr. Frank Longino were the glue that held things together during the most fragile times."

Laupus recalled the period as a time of anxiety for private physicians, who were concerned they would be put out of business by the medical school, and a time when cooperation on all sides was vital to success. Blending those two wasn't always easy.

"Most of the private physicians were cooperative, but that didn't allay all their concerns," Laupus said recently in his trademark measured, soothing tone. Over time, he, Richardson, and others worked to make private physicians a partner in the success of the hospital and medical school. For many, Laupus said, relationships have turned out well, as has the agreement between PCMH and ECU.

"My forty years of experience in medical school and hospital relationships tell me that these types of relationships continue to be things that are bargained from time to time," Laupus said. "This is probably as good a relationship that exists in this state and in many places in the nation."

Dews agreed. "He not only was a first-class pediatrician," he said of Laupus, "but also a diplomat in getting things done in a quiet way."

Of Richardson, Dews said: "He was an easy-going fellow who never got excited or lost his temper. He was a gentleman and a Christian, and he worked at accommodating people."

Laupus added, "Jack and I worked together for a number of years, and we discussed everything and made sure we didn't have a lot of difference that would lead to major troubles."

McRae said the efforts of the men and women who patiently worked out the affiliation agreement between the institutions have paid off many times over with the current success of the hospital and medical school. "Neither would be at this level of accomplishment without the other," he said.

Today and Tomorrow: Building a Health System

While physical growth has been the hallmark of the past fifty years, Dave McRae sees the next half century bringing a solidification of the health system and measures to improve the health status of those in eastern North Carolina. In the late 1990s, PCMH joined with regional hospitals through lease and purchase arrangements to form University Health Systems of Eastern Carolina. In January 1999, the health system became a legal entity comprising PCMH, Heritage Hospital in Tarboro, Roanoke-Chowan Hospital in Ahoskie, Bertie Memorial Hospital in Windsor, Chowan Hospital in Edenton, and the Outer Banks Hospital under construction in Nags Head. Physician practices and an urgent care center in Dare County are also part of the system.

"In the health system, I'm convinced the next fifty years will bring more rapid and exciting change than we've seen in the past fifty years," McRae said. "That progress will allow us to make Pitt Memorial and its associated parts fulfill its mission of improving the health of the citizens of the region."

Irons, who also works as president of the health system subsidiary Health-East, believes the health system and medical school will continue to grow but added the two may evolve into something that looks very different from today.

"The two entities are bound to grow much more closely integrated in terms of meeting the health care needs of the region," Irons said. "There are a lot of things that could derail us, but I think we'll just get stronger."

He also predicted the partnerships the health system and medical school have with private physicians and public agencies will grow stronger in coming years.

The success of the medical center has brought economic success for much of Pitt County, too. According to a 1997 study by the Regional Development Institute at ECU, operational spending by the hospital, its payroll expenditures, and visitor spending exceed $246 million in additional goods and services circulating through the local economy. In addition, more than $80 million in additional earnings are fueled by hospital-related spending, and more than 4,000 workers in businesses other than the hospital directly benefit from hospital-generated revenues. According to the study, 21 percent of the Pitt County workforce is either employed by PCMH or has a job that is directly affected by the hospital.

"Pitt Memorial has brought good jobs to Pitt County and eastern North Carolina, and not only jobs but opportunity for advancement," McRae said. For example, nurses and respiratory therapists with associate degrees can start out earning $30,000 to $40,000 a year at PCMH. In addition, recent articles in *UHS People* have noted employees who have upgraded their skills through hospital career-advancement programs.

PCMH's current solid status is due in part to a painful but necessary effort to reorganize the hospital as a private not-for-profit institution. That change has been largely invisible to the public and to patients but has resulted in the hospital being able to invest some of its cash reserves in stocks and finance projects outside the county, such as the Outer Banks Hospital. The change, however, was complex and not easily explained, and it brought some public mistrust and cost the hospital some goodwill.

Dews was again in a position of leadership, this time County Commission chairman, and he helped shepherd the change through the county board.

"I believe it was the right thing to do and it will be the right thing for the future," Dews said. "When I give talks to groups today, I still get asked why I gave away the hospital. But I believe the facility now has the freedom to reach out and grow."

In the future, Dews sees medical technology and discovery continuing to create new cures and treatments for diseases and injuries, with a continued increase in life expectancy. How those cures and treatments will be paid for, however, is a different matter. He's certain the government will continue to tinker and perhaps even radically change how it reimburses hospitals under Medicare and Medicaid but is less sure about other factors.

"Will our health care system break itself?" Dews wondered. "Will care have to be rationed?"

Relations among private physicians, medical school physicians, and the hospital should continue to be good, according to Dr. Marcus Albernaz, PCMH chief of medical staff and a private physician.

"For an enterprise of this size and the numbers involved, there's surprisingly little town-gown conflict," Albernaz said. "Sure, there's competition and at times conflict, but that competition in ways can be good and the conflict secondary."

From the grassroots effort that built the original PCMH to the vision of leaders who saw the need for a modern hospital in the late 1960s and early 1970s to today's regional referral center recognized in academic, trade, and popular media as a health care leader, the PCMH family has a lot to feel good about, McRae said.

"Things are very different today, but you have to appreciate the small beginnings that brought you here," McRae said. "Those who are working today should be proud of those who preceded them, and they should be proud of the position they've allowed this hospital to take as we enter a new millennium."

REFERENCES

Bratton, Mary Jo Jackson. *East Carolina University: The Formative Years*. Greenville, NC: East Carolina University Alumni Association; 1986.

ECU Chancellor's Office. Leo Jenkins Papers. East Carolina University Archives.

Williams, Wayne C. *Beginning of the School of Medicine at East Carolina University, 1964–1977*. Greenville, NC: Brookliff, 1998.

## CHAPTER TEN

Athletics and Entertainment

ROGER BILES

UNIVERSITIES HAVE frequently provided entertainment as well as education to their many constituencies. Located in one of the principal cities of eastern North Carolina, ECU has been an entertainment capital for the region. Along with ECU students, university faculty and staff, townspeople, and others living in the vicinity have attended a wide variety of campus events. Because of its heralded performing arts programs such as theatre, music, and dance, the university has provided a regular schedule of presentations that have enriched on- and off-campus communities. Through a variety of agencies, most prominently the Department of Recreation Services, the university has proffered a host of intramural sports and recreational activities. As in hundreds of other college towns across the nation, intercollegiate athletics have played a leading role in attracting multitudes of visitors to the campus and in establishing a national identity for the university.

Intercollegiate competition by varsity teams has attracted more attention than any other activity sponsored by East Carolina University. Just as enthusiastic University of Michigan fans don their maize and blue clothing to cheer on their Wolverine teams and University of Tennessee fans wear orange from head to toe in support of their beloved Volunteers, Pirate loyalists resplendent in purple and gold lend their support to ECU teams in football, basketball, baseball, and a host of other sports. Moreover, as the University of Notre Dame's countless "subway alumni" cheer avidly for the Fighting Irish despite not having attended classes in South Bend, Indiana, great numbers of the Pirate faithful never matriculated at ECU. Eastern North Carolinians supported ECU athletics just as New Yorkers rooted for the Yankees or Chicagoans cheered for the Bears—and with equal or even more passion. Growing up in eastern North Carolina, a historically poor region of the state that took a backseat to the more affluent Piedmont, Pirate fans have seen themselves as underdogs in sports, just as in other areas of life. The football field or baseball diamond could be one place where the upstart university prevailed over its more heralded neighbors. Winning athletic teams at ECU thereby provided vicarious satisfaction and satisfied a longing for recognition among area residents.

Since 1980, during a time when both collegiate and professional sports have developed into multimillion-dollar entertainment businesses, the administrative leadership at ECU has consistently affirmed its commitment to competing at the highest levels sanctioned by the National Collegiate Athletic Association (NCAA). Ballooning athletic budgets; the construction, expansion, and improvement of athletic facilities; and the continuing search for membership in more prestigious conferences for ECU teams underscored the importance of intercollegiate athletics. Although some faculty have questioned this course of action, dismissing the educational value of such activities and criticizing the extraordinary sums of money spent on sports when other university needs remained unmet, ECU's chancellors, Boards of Trustees, and other community leaders have repeatedly confirmed their support of Pirate athletics.

Unequivocal support of ECU athletics from the highest administrative sources could be traced back to Chancellor Leo Jenkins, who identified the improvement of Pirate teams as one of his principal goals. The emphasis on spectator sports, Jenkins insisted, dovetailed with his belief in physical fitness for the entire population of eastern North Carolina. The chancellor presided over an unprecedented expansion of athletic facilities on campus and proudly played a leading role in the attraction of private funds to supplement state construction dollars. In the 1960s, when iconoclasts called for the subordination of intercollegiate athletics, Jenkins became nationally renowned as a spokesman for the alternative viewpoint. He traveled extensively to speak on behalf of big-time college sports and, closer to home, unabashedly cheered for the purple and gold at every opportunity.

Shortly after becoming chancellor in 1982, John Howell confronted a crisis in athletic funding that forced him to decide whether the university would maintain its extensive commitment to big-time college sports; he promptly assured Pirate boosters of his intention to follow in Leo Jenkins's footsteps. In February 1982, the NCAA reorganized its hierarchy of colleges and universities, ostensibly to enhance the competition among schools of comparable size and financial commitment. The organization reduced the number of schools included in Division I-A, generally the largest institutions with the most extensive investments in athletics, by about one-third and relegated some universities to Division I-AA. Howell gratefully announced that ECU had been selected as one of the ninety-two institutions still included in Division I-A but also warned the denizens of eastern North Carolina about the increasing monetary challenges of remaining in the elite ranks.

Continued participation in Division I-A, Howell explained, would require friends of the university to enhance their financial commitments. Acknowledging that the university's athletic budget already operated at a deficit, the chancellor noted that the situation would only worsen in the future. Because Division I-A schools had to schedule at least seven of their ten football games against other Division I-A teams, ECU could no longer play as many games against smaller schools in the region. Increased travel expenses would result from the necessity to play larger schools farther from Greenville. Exacerbating the problem for ECU, Division I-A schools within the state, such as the University of North Carolina at Chapel Hill, North Carolina State University, Duke University, and Wake Forest University, infrequently agreed to schedule the Pirates in football. The University of North Carolina at Chapel Hill canceled its contract with ECU in 1982, while Duke and North Carolina State played the Pirates intermittently thereafter. Undeterred by the imminent increase in operating costs, however, Howell resolved to raise the additional funds necessary to compete at the highest level. He said:

> We at the University are determined not only to stay in the top category, but to compete successfully there. We like to be in the top ranks in any of our programs and we will strive to stay there. It is not simply a matter of school pride, though we have such devotion to our institution. It is a matter of demonstrating to the state and the nation that this is a university of great use to the community it serves. A fine athletic program, like a fine drama, art, music, or business program, serves that purpose. I have supervised admissions of students long enough to know that an outstanding athletic program attracts outstanding students in all parts of the University.

By the summer of 1982, Howell was working with a number of longtime financial contributors led by Dr. Ray Minges to devise a five-year, $1 million fund-raising initiative to pay off existing debts and sustain the athletic program. As the chancellor explained to potential contributors, the million-dollar campaign would supplement the ongoing fund-raising efforts of the University Educational Foundation (more commonly known as the Pirate Club). In the future, the athletic department would expand facilities, implement more aggressive marketing techniques, and recruit more members for the Pirate Club to increase revenues. When a group of potential contributors sought a formal commitment from the ECU administration and the Board of Trustees that the university would take the necessary steps to retain Division I-A status, Howell urged compliance. On August 23, 1982, the trustees issued a resolution "reaffirming a total commitment to the goal of building and maintaining a strong and highly competitive NCAA Division 1A athletic program" and pledging to engage in "vigorous fund raising activities." Howell appealed to ECU faculty and staff to make financial contributions to the campaign as well, arguing that a solid record of giving by campus personnel would impress potential donors. The chancellor even persuaded Leo Jenkins, whose popularity in eastern North Carolina remained high after three years of retirement, to deliver a series of fundraising speeches at banquets throughout the region.

In 1987, Richard Eakin replaced Howell as chancellor and quickly followed his predecessors' lead in endorsing the growth of intercollegiate athletics. For Eakin, who earned a national reputation as an advocate of sport on campus, athletics provided an excellent venue for the development of a sense of community at the university. "It seems to me there is nothing quite like bringing together the university community and its supporters on a Saturday for a football game," the chancellor observed, "and hav[ing] thirty to sixty or a hundred thousand people joined together to enjoy the university and its offerings. It seems to me that's an important part of what we do." He suggested that athletics constituted the most visible part of the university, the only aspect of the institution that newspapers and other media discussed virtually every day. Sport provided a window on the university, he felt, offering the opportunity for free publicity that would otherwise be inaccessible. Eakin's national prominence among university leaders who endorsed athletics resulted in his selection as chairman of the College Football Association in 1993–94, an honor usually bestowed upon the presidents and chancellors of football powerhouses such as the University of Alabama, the University of Southern California, and the like.

Working closely with ECU's chancellors, the three athletic directors who served between 1980 and 2000 strove to elevate the Pirates to greater national prominence. After serving as athletic director for ten years at San Diego State University, Kenneth Karr filled the same position at ECU from 1980 to 1987. Assistant Athletic Director David Hart Jr. replaced Karr in 1987 and remained in the position until 1995, when he became athletic director at Florida State University. His successor, Mike Hamrick, had been athletic director at the University of Arkansas at Little Rock before coming to ECU in 1995. In 2003, he left to become the athletic director at the University of Nevada at Las Vegas; Terry Holland, the former basketball coach and athletic director at the University of Virginia, replaced Hamrick in 2004. Karr, Hart, and Hamrick benefited from the uniform support offered by the university leadership.

ECU's chancellors, working in conjunction with the trustees, under-wrote their support of athletics with expanding budget allocations in the two decades before 2000. In 1980, the university authorized expenditures from the athletic fund totaling $1,928,599, approximately $355,000 more than existing revenues; the Pirate Club's contribution of $85,500 offset part of the deficit. (The Pirate Club's assets totaled $570,191.) To counter the financial shortfall, Athletic Director Kenneth Karr announced the university would discontinue three sports (men's wrestling, women's field hockey, and women's gymnastics) while adding two less costly women's sports (cross-country and golf). Wrestling fans objected strenuously and obtained over nine thousand signatures on a petition urging the athletic department to reconsider, but Karr remained adamant. "In order to make the major sports go," he argued, "we must draw purse strings." In subsequent years, the university consistently elevated funding levels so that in the fiscal year ending on June 30, 2004, athletic fund expenditures surpassed $17.5 million. In twenty years, the university's allocation of dollars for athletics grew more than eightfold. Even more impressive, the Pirate Club reported a market value of $3.3 million in endowments in 2003–4. Clearly, the remarkable financial yields achieved by Pirate Club personnel vindicated the trustees' vow in 1980 to promulgate "vigorous fund raising activities."

Increasing revenue became vitally important in underwriting scholar-ships, equipment, coaches' and administrators' salaries, and rising trans-portation costs but even more so in the improvement and expansion of fa-cilities. To compete in Division I-A, coaches, athletic directors, and boosters contended, the university had to provide larger and newer venues for games and practices. Not only would gleaming structures attract the top-flight recruits necessary to compete at the highest levels, but larger stadiums and arenas allowed for more fans to pay admission to see the Pirates perform. The need to stage athletic contests in state-of-the-art venues, a necessity in the NCAA's Division I-A, justified considerable renovation and construc-tion costs.

Nowhere was the pressure greater to update facilities than in football, the principal moneymaker for the athletic program. James Skinner Ficklen Memorial Stadium, which had been dedicated on September 21, 1963, orig-inally contained permanent seating only on the south side. In 1968 the uni-versity added permanent seating to the north side, increasing the stadium's seating capacity to 20,000. Ten years later, following completion of many fund-raising efforts, the addition of permanent seats in all four corners of the stadium raised seating capacity to 35,000. In 1994, Ron Dowdy, a mem-ber of the Board of Trustees, contributed $1 million to the Pirate Club for the expansion of the stadium, which thereafter became known as Dowdy-Ficklen Stadium. Although some questioned whether additional seats were necessary, particularly when the Pirates seldom played in front of capacity crowds at home, athletic officials began discussing another expansion. To those who contended that existing attendance figures hardly indicated an urgent demand for more seating, Athletic Director Mike Hamrick answered that improved home schedules in which the Pirates played top-flight competition would increase the demand for tickets. "Build it and they will come" seemed to be the operative philosophy. Accordingly, construction crews completed an upper deck on the north side in 1998, and seating capacity of Dowdy-Ficklen Stadium rose to 40,000. Completion of club-level seating on that side the following year edged the seating capacity to 43,000.

Improvement of other athletic facilities continued. The Ward Sports Medicine/Physical Education Building, which opened in 1990, contained the offices of all coaches and athletic administrators. The sports medicine department's three-story, 82,000-square-foot structure also featured injury treatment and rehabilitation centers, as well as a 5,000-square-foot strength training facility, human performance laboratory, classrooms, and locker rooms for several sports. Complete renovation of Minges Coliseum, which contained Williams Arena for basketball as well as the swim team's pools, concluded in 1995. Looming over the west end zone of the football field and connected by a suspended corridor to Minges Coliseum, the Murphy Center opened in 2002. Constructed at a cost of $13 million, this multipurpose facility contained an extensive weight lifting and conditioning area that supplanted the Ward Building's antiquated equipment, banquet rooms, and study spaces for student athletes. Its walls glittered with plaques and other memorabilia. In 2000, under Hamrick's direction, the athletic department completed the design of a new baseball stadium that would be constructed on the site of the existing structure, Harrington Field. The $8 million field, which opened in the 2005 season, increased Harrington Field's seating capacity of 1,750 to an estimated 3,000 and contained such amenities as a new scoreboard, picnic areas, locker rooms, and an indoor batting tunnel.

The commitment to big-time sports also involved the university's ongoing efforts to affiliate with a larger and more prestigious conference. After a decade of persistent effort, ECU became a member of the Southern Conference in 1964. Twelve years later, believing that the conference had weakened substantially, the Pirates withdrew to become independent while pursuing affiliation with a stronger conference. In 1981, for all sports except football, ECU became a charter member of the Eastern College Athletic Conference (ECAC) South with the University of Richmond, the College of William and Mary, James Madison University, Old Dominion University, George Mason University, and the U.S. Naval Academy. Almost immediately, however, ECU initiated talks with the commissioner of the Metro-politan Collegiate Athletic Conference about the feasibility of joining the Metro Conference. Discussions with the Metro Conference continued from 1982 to 1985, even after ECU became a charter member of the Colonial Ath-letic Association (CAA) in January 1985. In 1990, ECU sought unsuccess-fully to become a charter member of the Big East Conference; in 1993, an-other attempt to join the Big East failed. In 1996, ECU joined Conference USA for football only while remaining a member of the CAA for all other sports.

On October 31, 1999, ECU accepted an invitation from Conference USA to join as an all-sports member. The following day, Chancellor Eakin in-formed Thomas Yeager, CAA commissioner, of ECU's intention to sever all connections with the CAA on June 30, 2001, so that it could compete in Conference USA during the 2001–2 academic year. Eakin pointed out that, at ECU's insistence, the CAA constitution explicitly provided that any member could leave the conference without financial penalty to become an all-sports member of a Division I-A conference. Separation from the CAA proved far from amicable, however, as some of the presidents of the con-ference's institutions demanded that ECU be expelled immediately. When Yeager spoke of imposing financial penalties and recommended that ECU not be allowed to compete in the CAA during its "lame duck" (2000–2001) academic year, Eakin responded forcefully and threatened litigation. In a December 1999 meeting of the CAA's Council of Presidents, ECU accepted a compromise that foreswore financial penalties but restricted the Pirates from competing in conference championships during its last year. ECU's passage from the CAA to Conference USA, while achieved with consider-able acrimony, represented an advance for the athletic program.

The quest for membership in the most prestigious conference contin-ued early in the twenty-first century. When the Atlantic Coast Conference (ACC) expanded by enticing members from the Big East Conference, the resulting reshuffling of conference memberships affected Conference USA and other associations as well. At an unsettled time when long-standing alignments unraveled, the most ambitious ECU alumni and boosters hoped to obtain membership in the ACC. The university resumed its efforts to join the Big East, employing as a consultant a former Big East official, ap-parently with as little success as before. The game of conference musical chairs, with revenue from football bowl games and lucrative television con-tracts at stake, symbolized the scramble for prestige and money common in the highest echelons of intercollegiate athletics.

The sustained commitment of ECU's leadership notwithstanding, did the university's teams compete effectively in the last decades of the twen-tieth century? Were the Pirates able to hold their own against much larger institutions that fortified their athletic programs with much more generous budgets? Did the Pirate Club and other benefactors raise sufficient funds in a historically poor region to supplement inadequate university appropriations? Echoing Leo Jenkins and John Howell, Richard Eakin answered these questions affirmatively. A paucity of resources constituted a significant hurdle and would doubtless continue to plague ECU, Eakin averred, but ECU had demonstrated the ability to compete consistently and excel occasionally.

After a somewhat lackluster beginning, the record of the football team during the last twenty years of the twentieth century seemed to corroborate Eakin's assessment. Under head coach Ed Emory, a former star player for the Pirates, the team achieved a mediocre record of 26–29–0 from 1980 to 1984. Following his dismissal in December 1984, Emory filed a lawsuit against the university that resulted in an out-of-court settlement. In the course of its in-house investigation of the football program, the university uncovered a series of NCAA violations involving Emory's misuse of athletic funds. Subsequent to its own investigation, the NCAA placed ECU on one-year probation in 1986 but applied no additional sanctions. ECU declined to appeal and vowed to supervise athletic expenditures more diligently. Emory's successor, Art Baker, compiled a disappointing 12–32–0 record during the 1985–88 seasons. Bill Lewis, who coached for the next three years, restored a sense of respectability to the embattled program and achieved considerable success with an overall record of 21–12–1. Most memorable for Pirate fans, ECU defeated intrastate rival North Carolina State University in the 1992 Peach Bowl in a thrilling comeback, 37–34. ECU finished that season ranked ninth nationally, its highest ranking ever, and several players such as quarterback Jeff Blake and linebacker Robert Jones, who was one of three finalists for college football's Butkus Award, enjoyed successful, long-lasting careers in the National Football League. Sadly for Pirate fans, however, Bill Lewis took advantage of the team's stellar performance to secure a more lucrative coaching assignment at Georgia Tech University.

ECU replaced Lewis with Steve Logan, a veteran coach who had served as an assistant for the Pirates for the preceding three years after earlier jobs at the University of Mississippi, Oklahoma State University, the University of Tulsa, and the University of Colorado. A quiet, intense leader widely respected as an innovative offensive tactician, Logan won more games during his eleven-year tenure at the school than any other ECU football coach had. From 1992 to 2002, his teams won sixty-nine games and lost fifty-eight while appearing in five bowl games. Under his leadership, the Pirates went 9–3 in the 1995 season and beat Stanford University in the Liberty Bowl; both the 1995 and 1999 squads finished in the top-twenty rankings.

He could also boast of running a scandal-free program with good graduation rates.

After the team won only four games in 2002—and just four of the last fifteen, including the 2001 season—speculation arose that Logan would be fired. The beleaguered coach affirmed his intention of retaining his post, saying that the school would have to write "an awful big check" to buy out the remaining years of his contract. The following day, however, Athletic Director Mike Hamrick announced that he and Logan had "reached a mutual agreement that he would resign." ECU agreed to pay the deposed coach's $200,000 annual salary for the next three years, less any income he managed to earn during that time. Logan's scrappy teams achieved a winning record during the 1990s and registered impressive wins over such football powers as the University of Miami, the University of Pittsburgh, Syracuse University, Virginia Tech University, and the University of South Carolina. If such success fell short of heightened expectations, Logan seemingly demonstrated the football team's ability to meet Eakin's goal of competing consistently and excelling occasionally.

The baseball team arguably met the same standard, consistently posting winning records and often qualifying for postseason tournament play. Under head coach Hal Baird (1980–84), the Pirates won 145 games, advanced to the NCAA regional tournament three times, and once finished in the top-twenty national rankings. Baird left ECU to become the head coach at Auburn University, where he coached successfully for many years. During head coach Gary Overton's years (1985–97), ECU won five conference championships and played in five NCAA regional tournaments. Overton's teams won 427 games, the most ever under one coach, but compiled lackluster records of 29–26, 22–24, and 29–27 during his last three years. From 1998 to 2002, under the leadership of Keith LeClair, the baseball team enjoyed its greatest success. Following a very successful coaching career at Western Carolina University, LeClair moved across the state to ECU and achieved an even better record. During his five years as head coach of the Pirates, LeClair recorded the second most wins in school history (212). His teams won three CAA championships and one Conference USA Tournament championship, appeared in four consecutive NCAA regional tournaments, and advanced to one NCAA superregional tournament. The 2001 squad finished the season ranked eleventh in the national polls. Tragically, the thirty-six-year-old LeClair resigned after the 2002 season because of failing health; he suffered from amyotrophic lateral sclerosis (Lou Gehrig's disease). Randy Mazey, an assistant coach at the University of Tennessee, replaced LeClair.

Pirate basketball teams enjoyed decidedly less success than the football and baseball squads. Playing in the shadow of ACC powerhouses Duke University, the University of North Carolina at Chapel Hill, North Carolina State University, and Wake Forest University, ECU struggled to recruit outstanding players and achieve winning records. A series of coaches paraded through Greenville, usually remaining a few years before disgruntled fans and impatient administrators sought the quick fix of a coaching change. Dave Odom, who coached from 1979 to 1982, enjoyed the most success and went on to a distinguished career at other universities, but Charlie Harrison (1982–87), Mike Steele (1987–91), Eddie Payne (1991–95), and Joe Dooley (1995–99) fared less well. In 1999, ECU hired Bill Herrion, an accomplished coach for many years at Drexel University, and ECU fans hoped that the legacy of mediocrity might end. Herrion faced an imposing challenge of winning at a school noted more for its football and baseball prowess, a task made even more difficult with the move from the CAA to Conference USA, where a number of universities repeatedly fielded outstanding teams. ECU replaced Herrion, whose teams achieved a 70–98 record in six years, with Ricky Stokes, an assistant coach at the University of South Carolina. Few ECU basketball players achieved great success in professional leagues, although Theodore "Blue" Edwards became the first Pirate to be selected in the first round of the National Basketball Association draft when chosen by the Utah Jazz in 1989.

The university's male athletes who competed in less-publicized sports (including soccer, track and field, cross-country, golf, swimming and diving, and tennis) compiled some noteworthy achievements during the era. In 1985, sprinter Lee McNeill beat Olympic gold medalist Carl Lewis in the semifinals of the 100-meter dash at the USA Outdoor Track and Field Championships and finished second in the finals. Three years later, he became a member of the U.S. Olympic Team's 400-meter relay team in Seoul, South Korea. In 1992, sprinter Brian Irvin earned his sixth All-America award at the NCAA championships, becoming the most decorated track and field athlete in ECU history. In 1994, the golf team won its seventh CAA championship in eight seasons. In 2002, seven Pirates earned All-America honors in track and field, a school record. Also that year, ECU sponsored its first NCAA postseason event when the men's cross-country team hosted the Southeast Regional Tournament at Overton's Lake Kristi.

ECU's women athletes uniformly attracted less attention than their male counterparts but played a larger role in the last two decades of the twentieth century than they had in the preceding years. Owing to its origins as a women's teacher's college, ECU had a long tradition of organized athletics for women. After World War II, however, men's athletics became much more important as the rising number of male veterans and recent high school graduates altered the demographics of the traditionally female campus —a transformation completed when the university accepted membership in the NCAA in 1961. Women's athletics, governed first by the Commission on Intercollegiate Athletics for Women (CIAW) and then by the Association for Intercollegiate Athletics for Women (AIAW), took a backseat to the burgeoning men's sports in the 1950s and 1960s. During those years, women received no athletic scholarships, played their games before tiny crowds in out-of-the-way venues, and received virtually no publicity in the print and electronic media.

A resurgence in women's athletics came after the passage of Title IX of the Omnibus Education Act of 1972, which mandated gender equity in higher education. Many athletic administrators failed to recognize the significance of the law at first, but in 1974 the U.S. Department of Health, Education, and Welfare (HEW) confirmed that the measure's prescriptions for universities included athletics. The following year, HEW issued its final guidelines for Title IX and provided a three-year grace period for implementation. To comply, universities would need to meet one of three conditions —assure that participation opportunities for men and women are "substantially proportionate" to their undergraduate enrollments; demonstrate that they had a history of and continuing practice of program expansion responsive to the developing interests and abilities of the underrepresented sex (usually women); or meet the interests and abilities of female students even when disproportionately fewer females than males participated in sports. No longer could universities brazenly consign women's athletics to the second-class status characterized by inadequate facilities, hand-me-down equipment, and minuscule budgets. When the AIAW dissolved in the mid-1980s and the NCAA became the governing body for women's as well as men's sports, the impact of Title IX became clear. To the degree that federal legislation required uniformity, the model of men's sports rather than women's sports prevailed. The ideals and practices promulgated by the AIAW—prohibitions on recruiting, treating athletes no differently from other college students, and placing high graduation rates before championships, for example—seemed anachronistic in an era when college sport became big business. Title IX turned out to be, in one wag's assessment, "the biggest thing to happen to sports since the invention of the whistle."

University athletic directors initially wailed that Title IX would destroy intercollegiate athletics in a misguided attempt to enforce gender equality. The cost of athletic scholarships, improved facilities, and other increased appropriations for so many women's teams would create financial chaos, they charged, and force universities to dismantle existing men's teams to maintain balanced budgets. But savvy administrators soon saw the possibility of reaching an accommodation with federal officials by meeting any one of the three conditions necessary for compliance. Significantly, universities need not always demonstrate "substantial proportionality." At

ECU, as at so many other institutions, Title IX led not to true equality between men's and women's sports but to a substantial enhancement of the latter. The Lady Pirates competing in volleyball, tennis, cross-country, basketball, softball, swimming and diving, track and field, golf, and tennis did so with more generous financial support than in the past. Although women's athletic budgets continued to lag far behind the outlays for men's teams, the increased opportunities for women showed in the increases in expenditures they enjoyed over time. In the year ending June 30, 1980, ECU spent $174,200 on women's athletic teams as compared with $2,270,000 in the fiscal year ending June 30, 2001.

From 1980 to 2000, Lady Pirate athletes and teams scored a number of notable successes. During her six years as head coach of women's basketball at ECU (1978–84), Cathy Andruzzi guided the Lady Pirates to three post-season appearances and an Associated Press top–twenty-five ranking while achieving a 105–66 record. In 1983, Mary Denkler received All-America honors in basketball, becoming the first ECU woman athlete to earn that distinction in any sport. Leora Jones starred for the basketball team during the 1980–81 and 1981–82 seasons before playing for the U.S. Olympic teams in the 1984 and 1988 summer games. Swimmer Meredith Bridgers became the first ECU woman athlete to qualify for the NCAA championships, doing so in 1990 and 1991. In 1994, Dava Rhodes finished eighth in the nation in the 10,000 meters and became ECU's first female All-America selection in track and field. That same year, softball player Michelle Ward set new NCAA season and career stolen-base records. From 1995 to 1997, the swimming team won three consecutive CAA championships. In 1998 the softball team appeared in its first NCAA regional tournament, and track and field standout Michelle Clayton earned All-America honors in the hammer throw event at the NCAA championship meet.

While a relatively few men and women participated in intercollegiate sports, the university continued its tradition of providing opportunities for athletic competition and recreation to the entire student body. Aware of eastern North Carolina's historical reputation as a poorly drained, unhealthy region plagued by malaria and other diseases, Leo Jenkins had repeatedly urged the development of programs on campus to improve the health of students. Beginning in 1975 under the direction of Wayne Edwards, the Department of Intramural Recreational Services offered students a large and growing number of physical activities. After Edwards left the university, Steve Cohen (1985–87) and Nancy Mize (1987–) directed the various intramural and recreational programs. Embracing the increasing emphasis upon health and fitness in American society in the late twentieth century, these directors expanded programs for students and added activities for faculty and staff as well. They sought to promote healthier lifestyles, provide alternative activities to the hedonistic practices common among many college students, educate their publics about wellness strategies, and foster lifelong commitments to physical activity that as alumni they could maintain. The Department of Recreational Services adopted the following mission statement: "To promote, organize, and administer structured, self-directed, educationally oriented and leadership development programs and services to enhance positive recreation and wellness lifestyles of the University community. Recreational services is committed to imparting a sense of responsible citizenship, providing relevant student leadership experiences, enhancing individual potential, and fostering a life-long commitment to learn skills associated with physical, social, emotional, and mental well-being."

As the university grew significantly, the paucity of facilities seriously limited the delivery of the kind of programs that recreation professionals judged necessary. Christenbury Gymnasium, the home of ECU's physical education department and athletic offices as well as the center of intramural and recreational activities, proved to be wholly inadequate to so many tasks by the 1980s. Shortly after assuming the directorship, Mize and Associate Director Pat Cox initiated a campaign to construct a new building that would be devoted entirely to intramural sports and recreation. Such facilities were appearing on university campuses across the country, and Mize accurately foresaw the time when they would be commonplace. Prospective students began including state-of-the-art recreational facilities on their checklists along with academic programs, job placement, and livable residence halls when considering what university to attend. Many students considered their own developmental opportunities more important than the triumphs and failures of the university's varsity teams.

Mize and her staff commenced a long, arduous task of marshaling support for the project. Having conducted studies and amassed statistics to demonstrate ECU's need for a new facility, they found influential allies in Chancellor Richard Eakin and Vice Chancellor for Student Life Alfred Matthews, both of whom enthusiastically supported the idea. In 1987, Student Government Association President Scott Thomas prepared a resolution indicating the student body's "overwhelming support" for construction of a new recreation center to be funded out of student fees. The SGA declined to hold a referendum on the issue, but all major student organizations on campus endorsed the proposal. In 1988, the ECU Board of Trustees approved the planning, financing, and construction of the self-liquidating capital improvement project; the University of North Carolina Board of Governors followed suit in 1990. Plans for the future expansion of athletic department facilities ruled out a site near Minges Coliseum, which intramural and recreation staff preferred, so that the final plans called for the building's location immediately west of Mendenhall Student Center. The ECU Board of Trustees ratified the Mendenhall site in 1991, with the groundbreaking ceremony for the construction conducted three years later. The dedication ceremony for the completed project came in 1997, a full decade after the SGA president had initiated action.

The Student Recreation Center (SRC), a sprawling 150,000-square-foot structure built at the cost of $18 million, housed 6 courts usable for basketball, volleyball, badminton, and other events; 1 squash and 6 racquetball courts; a suspended one-seventh-mile track; an indoor aquatics area with an 8-lane, 25-yard pool and a 4-lane, 19-yard pool; a 30-foot by 40-foot outdoor pool surrounded by a large deck and sunbathing area; a 10,000-square foot cardiovascular and weight training area; a 32-foot climbing wall; three 2,000-square-foot exercise studios; an outdoor adventure center; locker rooms; and administrative offices. Funded exclusively by student fees, the SRC automatically awarded memberships to currently enrolled students who had paid activity fees; distance education students, faculty, staff, and their spouses could purchase memberships. (Beginning in 1999, alumni could also buy memberships.) Students flocked to the facility from its opening, and rising enrollments pushed participation levels to capacity at certain times of the day. With continued enrollment increases projected for the first decade of the twenty-first century, the university announced that additional facilities for intramurals and club sports would be located at an off-campus site in northeastern Greenville.

From its offices in the SRC, the Department of Recreational Services administered a variety of programs to serve the needs of a disparate campus population. A generous menu of intramural sports allowed students the opportunity to compete individually or as a member of a team throughout the academic year. The Blount Sports Complex, completed in the fall of 1998 with an expanse of 18 acres located west of Charles Boulevard behind the Belk Building, included 10 flag football fields, 6 soccer fields, 5 softball diamonds, and a field house. In addition, ECU sponsored more than twenty-five club sports developed and organized by students with financial aid and supervision provided by Recreational Services. Requiring less commitment and skill than participation in varsity athletics, club sports allowed non-scholarship athletes to compete against other universities in sports ranging from rugby to martial arts to ultimate Frisbee.

The adventure program conducted excursions for such outdoor activities as backpacking, rock climbing, snow skiing, white-water rafting, and surfing. Trained leaders conducted these single- and multiday trips throughout North Carolina and in adjacent states. Spring break trips included kayaking and canoeing in Florida's Everglades and spelunking in West Virginia's New River Gorge. The New Adventures Program used ropes courses and climbing activities to build effective teams for groups of at least ten and no more than fourteen people. SRC staff customized trips for small groups involving such activities as horseback riding and hang gliding. Adventure Outfitters in the SRC also rented outdoor gear to individuals and groups for unsupervised trips.

The SRC offered a number of other programs for the campus community. The aquatics program offered swimming lessons, lifeguard training, and training and certification in community first aid and safety. The fitness program provided personal training as well as group classes for instruction in yoga, kickboxing, cycling, and several other exercise techniques. The innovative Adapted Recreation and Intramural Sports Enrichment (ARISE) program provided recreational opportunities for individuals with physical disabilities. As part of the ARISE effort, the Partners Assisting in Recreational Services (PAIRS) program matched a disabled person with someone possessing skills in a particular activity for one-on-one instruction. (The staffing of such an array of programs depended upon the hiring of a significant number of student workers, so that the SRC and its satellite operations stood second only to the Joyner Library in student workers employed.) In sum, the variegated programs dispensed by Recreational Services sustained a multitude of activities for students along with information about establishing lifelong health maintenance.

Although its primary constituency remained ECU students, faculty, and staff, the Department of Recreation Services designed some programs for area residents when local agencies lacked resources or expertise. During the academic year, facilities in the SRC became available at designated times for community use. In the summers, the SRC offered a series of weeklong adventure camps for children of varying ages—nature discovery camps for children up to the age of eight and kayaking, surfing, and climbing camps for those between the ages of nine and seventeen. An adult summer camp included hiking and climbing activities.

ECU also found it possible to combine education with leisure through the theatre department's sponsorship of dramatic and musical productions on campus. Students majoring in theatre would learn their craft while audiences from Greenville and the surrounding area benefited from the university's proximity. Furthermore, in keeping with progressive educational theory, the university had for decades identified the enhancement of artistic literacy as part of its mission in eastern North Carolina. For Chancellor Leo Jenkins, whose leadership proved vital in so many different areas of the university's development, a robust theatre arts program could contribute to the fulfillment of his vision of ECU as the region's cultural capital.

Moreover, he believed that a university could gain distinction through the cultivation of athletics and the fine arts. Such activities would bring visitors to campus, increase the university's visibility beyond eastern North Carolina, and attract additional extramural funding. In 1962, Jenkins hired Edgar Loessin, an experienced director and stage manager from New York with a bachelor of fine arts (B.F.A.) degree from Yale University, to chair the Department of Drama and Speech, which the university created the following year.

Loessin immediately established the East Carolina Playhouse as the principal vehicle for training B.F.A. students and staging first-rate theatrical productions for the university and the surrounding area. Following its initial production, Archibald Macleash's *JB*, the Playhouse settled into a routine of producing five performances per academic year (three plays, one musical, and one dance concert). Directed by faculty members in the Department of Theatre and Dance, the performances featured mostly students in performing roles supplemented by a few faculty and community members. Occasionally, a professional guest artist contributed to the performances, but limited academic year budgets kept students in the forefront of the productions.

In 1964, Loessin initiated the East Carolina Summer Theatre, one of the few professional theatres operating on any college campus. Unlike the Playhouse season, the summer theatre offered professional-quality performances replete with full production values. Troupes of professional actors, musicians, and crew members, augmented by a few students, came to Greenville for several weeks during the summer for the rehearsals and performances. With several different performances staged during the summer months, twenty-five to thirty thousand people attended each year. The university provided limited subsidies, while ticket sales provided most of the revenue to meet costs. In 2001, the university renamed the summer theatre the ECU/Loessin Summer Theatre in recognition of its founder's contributions.

In 1977, Loessin and Patricia Pertalion, a choreographer and wife of a Department of Theatre and Dance faculty member, initiated the Day of Dance as an annual event. The university brought to campus a number of professional dancers who held workshops for aspiring dancers of every age and ability in the community. The list of renowned dancers who participated included Jacques d'Amboise, Edward Villella, Peter Gennaro, Ira Bernstein, Jean-Pierre Bonnefoux, and Melissa Hayden. Profits from the Day of Dance paid for the appearances of other guest artists and helped defray the expenses incurred by students attending the American College Dance Festival.

Loessin and his cohorts staged theatrical productions in the McGinnis

Auditorium, which had been constructed in 1951 as an all-purpose facility for the university and which provided several challenges for directors, set designers, and other members of the production crew. Because it was not designed specifically for theatrical presentations, the auditorium lacked an orchestra pit, storage space in the wings, rooms for constructing and storing scenery, and "fly space" above the stage from which scenery backdrops could be lowered and raised. Sorely in need of repair by the 1970s, the McGinnis Auditorium became a fire hazard, with faulty electrical lighting and antiquated sound equipment that frequently overheated. In 1978, complete renovation of the stage house began, and, by 1982, adequate fly and wing space had been provided along with entirely new cushioned chairs in place of the wooden seats for the audience. A gala celebration on April 3, 1982, with an exclusive guest list of administrators, alumni, and influential patrons, commemorated the opening of the "New McGinnis."

The adjacent Messick Building, which housed the Studio Theatre, rehearsal and performance rooms, dance studios, and the offices of the Department of Theatre and Dance, had also fallen upon hard times by the end of the 1970s. Faculty and students complained about the lack of air conditioning, paint peeling from the walls, and falling ceiling tiles. In 1980, extensive renovations began in the Messick Building, and all personnel and facilities relocated to a vacated funeral home just west of campus on Evans Street. Faculty and students acclimated during that time to the unusual environment in which they found themselves. One professor established his office in the former embalming room, and stagehands used the coffin lift for storing scenery and props. Production designers built scenery in the hearse garage, and performances occurred in the former chapel. Productions during that time, such as *Sexual Perversity in Chicago,* occurred below a well-illuminated stained glass window of religious figures. A year and a half later, faculty and students eagerly returned to less-morbid surroundings in the refurbished Messick Building.

In 1990, Loessin retired, and ECU hired John Shearin as the new chair of the Department of Theatre and Dance. Shearin possessed impressive academic credentials—he graduated Phi Beta Kappa from the College of William and Mary and received a master of fine arts degree from Pennsylvania State University—as well as extensive experience as a professional stage, television, and movie actor and a professional stage director-producer. Shearin inherited very successful programs and largely continued along familiar paths but made one substantive change in the summer theatre offerings. Loessin had for the most part employed highly recognizable television actors, believing that they would attract larger audiences. Despite his extensive television acting experience (having appeared regularly in such series as *Hunter, Matlock,* and *The Young and the Restless*), Shearin decided to employ more stage performers in the summer theatre's leading roles. He believed that veteran stage actors would perform better and often at lower salaries, and the continued success of the summer theatre presentations proved him correct. Even so, rising production costs and reduced financial support from the university resulted in unbalanced budgets by the end of the 1990s. ECU had for years accepted a certain amount of red ink as the price of providing summer entertainment to the community, but a heightened emphasis on fiscal accountability in the midst of a statewide budget crisis forced the cancellation of the 2002 summer season. Productions resumed in 2003, but economic clouds still darkened the skies and made the future of the summer theatre program uncertain.

Financial problems notwithstanding, the ECU theater program maintained a stellar reputation based not only upon the consistently high quality of its theatrical productions but also upon the training of talented performers, technicians, and creative artists. Any list of successful theatre alumni begins with Sandra Bullock, who graduated in 1986 and became one of the leading Hollywood actresses of the 1990s. Following starring roles in such popular films as *Speed, Hope Floats, While You Were Sleeping, Murder by Number,* and *Divine Secrets of the Ya-Ya Sisterhood,* she received in 1997 the ECU Outstanding Alumni Award. Emily Procter, who majored in journalism and dance, parlayed a recurring role on the award-winning television series *The West Wing* into a starring role in another popular series, *C.S.I. Miami.* Kevin Williamson, who received a B.F.A. degree in 1987, served as the executive producer of the television series *Dawson's Creek,* wrote screenplays for such films as *The Faculty* and *Scream 2,* and directed the film *Killing Mrs. Tingle.* Robert Gardner danced for several years with the Joffrey Ballet before joining the Minnesota Ballet as ballet master in 1992; he later became the resident choreographer for the company.

Outstanding artistic performances also came to the ECU campus under the auspices of the Student Union, which had been created by a merger of the University Union and the Student Government Association in 1972. The Board of Trustees funded the Student Union from student activity fees and located the new organization in the Mendenhall Student Center, which was dedicated in 1974. The Student Union administered the Artists Series and the Theatre Arts Series, which were merged in 1987 into the Performing Arts Series. Renamed the S. Rudolph Alexander Performing Arts Series in 1995 after its founder at the time of his retirement, it presented internationally acclaimed vocalists, music ensembles, choral groups, instrumentalists, and theatrical and dance companies in Wright Auditorium. In large measure because of the generous contributions of the Friends of the S. Rudolph Alexander Performing Arts Series, ECU audiences thrilled to the performances of such renowned artists as Tony Bennett, Itzhak Perlman,

Harry Belafonte, Judy Collins, Yo Yo Ma, Marcel Marceau, Arthur Rubinstein, the Juilliard String Quartet, and the Bolshoi Symphony Orchestra. Beginning in 1963, the series brought internationally acclaimed acts from Russia, China, Israel, Africa, the United Kingdom, and Bulgaria as well as from the four corners of the United States. From 1984 to 1992, the university sponsored a chamber music series.

On a more modest scale, the Student Union underwrote a number of other programs catering to community and campus audiences. The Young Audiences Performing Arts Series debuted in 1990 and included musical plays, puppet shows, and magic shows for children on Saturday afternoons. In 1994, the series split into the Family Fare and Art Smart Series. A film series brought mainstream Hollywood productions and more obscure independent movies weekly to the Mendenhall Student Center. The Spectrum Committee booked guest lectures, novelty acts, and other special events to a variety of campus locations. The Popular Entertainment Committee presented concerts by an eclectic mix of folk, pop, jazz, and rhythm and blues performers. The Cultural Awareness Committee sponsored films, festivals, and other gatherings that promoted awareness of and appreciation for minority cultures. The Student Union also staged the annual Barefoot on the Mall celebration, an all-day spring festival featuring live music and other activities. The visual arts committee kept the Mendenhall Student Center Art Gallery filled with exhibits by ECU art students, guest artists, and traveling exhibits.

The Student Union also provided programs for eastern North Carolinians interested in travel. For an invitingly low fee, individuals and groups could take an annual excursion to New York City each Thanksgiving on a chartered bus, stay at a midtown Manhattan hotel, and explore the Big Apple for three days before returning to Greenville. The Travel-Adventure Film and Theme Dinner Series allowed community residents to satisfy their wanderlust without leaving the ECU campus. Participants viewed travel films concentrating on particular exotic locations in Mendenhall's Hendrix Theatre and then adjourn to Mendenhall's Great Room to consume gourmet dinners from the countries featured in the films.

Several of ECU's academic units sponsored performances, activities, and exhibitions for the enrichment of the local population. Beginning in 2000, ECU hosted the Walker Cup International Women's Wheelchair Basketball Tournament. Named in honor of Dr. L. T. Walker, the past president of the U.S. Olympic Committee and a member of the U.S. Olympic Hall of Fame, the tournament attracted teams from Canada, Japan, Mexico, and Australia as well as the United States. Sponsored by ECU's L. T. Walker International Human Performance Center and the Regional Rehabilitation Center of University Health Systems of Eastern Carolina, this event was the first international wheelchair basketball tournament for women in the United States. In addition to playing in the games, participants from the different nations conducted clinics and made presentations at area schools so that the able-bodied public could see the recreational opportunities available to people with severe disabilities.

ECU also offered programs in more traditional academic subjects. The East Carolina University Poetry Forum, under the aegis of the English Department, conducted informal workshops in the Mendenhall Student Center on the first and third Thursdays of the academic year and scheduled visits by such outstanding poets as James Dickey, Robert Creely, William Stafford, Lucille Clifton, Fred Chappell, Louis Simpson, Patricia Goedicke, and Carolyn Kizer. The department also collaborated with the North Carolina Arts Council, which received funding from the National Endowment for the Arts, to sponsor the Writers Reading Series of Eastern North Carolina. Designed to allow community readers and aspiring writers to hear and talk with some of the leading contemporary authors, the series featured such noted writers as Karenne Wood, Terry Davis, Ethelbert Miller, Theresa Williams, Bland Simpson, and Tim Gautreaux.

The School of Music presented an extensive concert program, which was open to the public, utilizing the talents of faculty, students, and visiting artists. In addition to regularly scheduled faculty and student recitals, the School of Music also offered a series of chamber music concerts, opera workshop productions, concerts by orchestral and choral groups, and a major choral-orchestral work performed by the school's combined units—including premier performances of compositions by faculty and student composers. In the 2000–2001 academic year, the School of Music launched the annual Four Seasons Chamber Music Festival of Eastern North Carolina. Under the direction of Ara Gregorian, the concerts, master classes, open rehearsals, and children's concerts featured performances by nationally and internationally acclaimed musicians and vocalists. The number and variety of performances provided music aficionados with a vast array of selections.

Campus audiences usually enjoyed several performances each year, often during family weekend, by the award-winning ECU Jazz Ensemble. Led by bassist Carroll Dashiell Jr., whom *Downbeat Magazine* recognized as jazz educator of the year, the group performed in the most prestigious venues, including Carnegie Hall; the Smithsonian Institution, in Washington, D.C.; the Montreaux, Switzerland, Jazz Festival; and the Birdland Jazz Club in New York City. The ensemble received the Jazz Fest USA 1997 Gold Award and hosted the annual ECU School of Music Spring Jazz Festival, at which such legendary musicians as Billy Taylor, Branford Marsalis, Russell Ferrante, Maynard Ferguson, and Peter Erskine performed. In addition, the

Contemporary Jazz Ensemble performed two concerts annually, each focusing on the work of one major composer.

In a variety of ways, the School of Art sought to bring art into people's everyday lives. The Wellington B. Gray Art Gallery in the Leo W. Jenkins Fine Arts Center, which has been operated by the School of Art, installed temporary exhibits of contemporary art. These shows included faculty and student work as well as national and international traveling exhibits. Having received more than five hundred pieces of African art, the Gray Gallery opened a new African Art Gallery in 1999 and created an interactive African art gallery on the World Wide Web, "Museum without Walls." School of Art majors exhibited their work in the Jenkins Fine Arts Center, the Mendenhall Student Center, the Baptist Student Center, the Greenville Museum of Art, and other locations throughout the community. In 1995, following the conclusion of the Tri-State Sculpture Conference at ECU, faculty created a sculpture park next to the Jenkins Center for the outdoor display of work by students and professional artists. Such student groups as Craftsmen East, Ceramics Guild, Printmakers Guild, Painting Guild, Designers Associates, Visual Arts Forum, the Student Chapter of the National Art Education Association and other student art organizations sponsored exhibitions, held programs, and sold their work at regular intervals. The East Carolina Art Society sponsored several public art auctions beginning in 1987 and continuing through the 1990s.

In a variety of formats and venues, East Carolina University has educated and entertained thousands of students outside of classrooms. Many of the programs offered by the university have enriched the lives of faculty, staff, and many off campus as well. Although often overshadowed by Pirate athletic teams, which the university administration continues to support generously, countless other programs have improved the quality of life of eastern North Carolinians. Great numbers of people living in Greenville and surrounding communities, many of whom never attended ECU, have benefited from living in or near the college town. Such service to the region is surely gratifying to the university's educators, who hold a vision of a vital university enriching the lives of eastern North Carolinians.

REFERENCE

ECU Athletics Office. Paper. East Carolina University Archives.

CHAPTER ELEVEN

Alumni and Friends

PAT BIZZARO AND JIM KIRKLAND

IN THE AUTUMN of 1980, few people expected East Carolina University to change and grow as rapidly as it did. Enrollment increased by almost ten thousand students over the next twenty-five years, with concomitant additions in the number of faculty, administrators, and staff. The university gained reclassification from a comprehensive university to a Research II institution offering doctoral degrees not only in medicine but also in various other fields. New facilities joined other renovated ones. And private donations increased exponentially. East Carolina moved from a state-funded to a state-supported institution.

Amid these changes, however, there existed one constant: the loyalty and commitment of ECU's alumni and friends. Some of them have supported the university financially with gifts large and small. Others have contributed their time and energy to the Alumni Association, the Pirate Club, the ECU Foundation, the Medical Foundation, and other organizations. Still others have served by example, as representatives and emissaries of ECU in their communities, schools, and workplaces. Many have been publicly honored, their accomplishments recognized in awards ceremonies, their names officially linked to the scholarships they have funded, the professorships they have endowed, the facilities their donations have helped to construct. Many more have worked behind the scenes, assisting in fundraising drives, working on bond referendums, lobbying legislators, and recruiting outstanding students.

Because these individuals number in the thousands and span many generations, there is no way to acknowledge them all. Fortunately, a rich store of information is available in Mary Jo Bratton's *East Carolina University: The*

Formative Years, 1907–1982; in the publications of the ECU Alumni Association, especially *The ECU Report* and its successor *East* magazine; in *Pieces of Eight;* in the Greenvillle *Daily Reflector;* and in other local, state, and national publications.

By August 1980, when the faculty gathered in Hendrix Theatre for the fall convocation, Thomas Brewer was beginning his third academic year as chancellor. A record 13,161 students had been admitted to the university. Membership in the Alumni Association had more than doubled during the previous decade. The Chancellor's Planning Commission, established shortly after Brewer assumed his duties, was poised to move forward with its efforts to establish a blueprint for the university's development during the coming decade. The chancellor himself seemed well positioned to confront what Mary Jo Bratton characterized in her history of ECU's formative years as "the emerging realities of the eighties, clearly a time of moderate growth, academic enhancement, fine tuning of existing programs, deliberate planning and initiation of modest change, and an expanded base of private funding."

Many of those expectations were indeed fulfilled during the 1980–81 year. The Alumni Honors Scholarship Program awarded full tuition and fees scholarships to forty students. The Chancellor's Society, established the preceding year, made significant gains in both membership and contributions. And a number of individuals lent their support to the university through memorial gifts, scholarships, and property. Esther Spencer Williams left a substantial portion of her estate (over $125,000) to ECU in memory of her daughter, ECU alumna Virginia Page Spencer. A. J. Fletcher's Educational and Opera Foundation provided a gift of $20,000 to support various projects in the School of Music. And E. Marvin Slaughter Jr. and Luther M. Taylor's generosity made possible the purchase of the Taylor-Slaughter Alumni Center.

Other alumni and friends contributed in different ways, serving on boards and committees, participating in local, state, or national politics, or enhancing the university's prominence and prestige through their personal accomplishments in business, education, and the performing arts. Among those featured in various issues of *The ECU Report* for 1980 were writer Nell Wise Wechter, well-known author of books about the Outer Banks; business executives James H. Maynard, and Samuel Wornom III; U.S. senators Robert Morgan and John East; Board of Trustees members Dr. Andrew Best; Mebane Burgwyn (children's book author); Troy Pate (president of First Federal Savings and Loan of Goldsboro and chair of the Board of Trustees for six years); James Dixon, owner of JMD Construction; Dr. Harvey Beech, partner in the law firm of Beech and Pollard; and

Emma L. Hooper, whose personal notes and records, accumulated during her thirty-four years as an English teacher, provided an invaluable resource for any history of ECU.

Even as the university publicly celebrated its successes, however, internal conflicts surfaced between Chancellor Brewer and the Board of Trustees as well as between the chancellor and the faculty over a number of different personnel and program issues—conflicts that eventually led to his resignation in September 1981. Though usually attributed to his failure to apprise the Board of Trustees of his candidacy for a position at another institution, Brewer's resignation, according to Bratton, resulted from the tensions and uncertainties marking the transition from one era to another.

Five years of calm followed, owing to the stabilizing influence of Dr. John Howell, who was named acting chancellor in January of 1982 and appointed chancellor in May of the same year. A respected scholar, teacher, and administrator, Howell was also an experienced fund-raiser and alumni leader with a clear understanding of the resources that would be needed to foster the institutional growth he envisioned.

Howell took office as the university was beginning a semester-long celebration of its seventy-fifth anniversary. The spring of 1982 was significant for other reasons as well. In January, the medical school began moving from the main campus to its first permanent home, the Brody Medical Sciences Building. And a few months later, the newly renovated Messick Theatre was dedicated in honor of another distinguished leader, John Messick.

John Howell, too, understood very well that ECU's progress was dependent on leaders like Messick and Jenkins and other alumni and friends with the same dedication and energy, and he took every opportunity to communicate that message to his constituents both within and outside the university. As he explained in the Chancellor's Corner section of the July 1982 edition of *The ECU Report*, the alumni are not only an invaluable source of financial support but also a bridge between the university and the public.

The pace of alumni giving had accelerated during the spring of 1982, and that trend continued through the summer and fall. Contributions to the ECU Foundation reached the $175,000 mark; the Z. Smith Reynolds Foundation awarded the Rural Education Institute a $25,000 grant; BB&T donated $250,000 to create a Center for Management Development in the School of Business; maritime history received federal grants to explore the wreck of the U.S.S. *Monitor;* the athletics fund-raising drive reached its midpoint goal of $500,000; Professor Emeritus Richard Todd, together with other emeriti, established a $7,500 scholarship for student emergency loans.

Many of these initiatives not only helped to expand the university's financial base but also heightened public awareness of its past accomplishments and potential for future success. Especially important from both a practical and a symbolic perspective was the dedication of the new Brody Medical Sciences Building in October 1982, an event that prompted featured speaker Governor James Hunt to affirm "how much can be accomplished when people of vision believe in a mission of mercy and work hard to make it a reality." James Bearden, former dean of the ECU Business School and director of the newly created BB&T Center for Management Development, sounded a similar theme in an interview published in *The ECU Report*, where he emphasized the center's role as a "vehicle to relate new knowledge, new information, and to give practicing professionals the opportunity to resort, reorient, and invigorate their performance in the managerial world."

That process of reorientation and reinvigoration became evident in almost every aspect of campus life in the months that followed. The ceremonies accompanying John Howell's installation as the university's eighth chief administrator in February of 1983 at the conclusion of the annual Phi Kappa Phi Symposium helped to focus upon the future and its requirements, as did the announcement several months later that ECU alumnus James Lanier had been appointed Vice Chancellor for Institutional Advancement, a position that the new chancellor believed to be crucial to the university's efforts to intensify its fund-raising activities and to continue strengthening ties with the alumni and the community.

Also significant was the substantial increase in financial contributions of alumni and friends during the 1982–83 academic year. Don Leggett, director of alumni relations, praised these individuals in the fall 1983 issue of *The ECU Report* for doing everything possible to help the university "reach and maintain the degree of national prominence that alumni and friends are seeking for their University."

The success of the Pirates' football team further enhanced ECU's public image in 1983, when it rose to national prominence with an 8–3 record and a near victory over national champion Miami in the Orange Bowl. As significant was the recovery of the anchor of the Union ironclad the U.S.S. *Monitor* by a team from the university's maritime history and underwater research program. The editors of the January 15, 1984, issue of *Pieces of Eight* cited this endeavor as evidence of ECU's "full-blown maturity in research and scholarship and the attainment of new stature and recognition." There were other signs of that maturity and attainment, a "pulsing eagerness to press forward toward new and higher goals."

Those words proved to be highly prophetic. Early in 1984, there was a concerted effort to establish a new University Scholars Awards program —a major, privately supported initiative designed to provide twenty or more full-expense and tuition scholarships to students with outstanding academic records. The Alumni Association presented its first University

Awards to two graduating seniors in recognition of their achievements in academics, service, and leadership. Longtime benefactors Richard and Clauda Todd created one of the largest scholarship endowments in ECU history with the aim of generating at least a million dollars a year. And the state legislature appropriated over $14 million for construction of a much-needed classroom building.

Donations increased even more dramatically during 1985, making it possible for the university to grant seven University Scholars Awards, fifteen Alumni Honors Scholarships, and a number of smaller awards and scholarships. Among the most generous contributors were C. D. Langston, senior vice president for First Citizens Bank of Greenville, who endowed four University Scholars Awards; alumnus Ronald Dowdy, a Florida business entrepreneur, who made a $100,000 challenge gift; and another alumnus, Sidney Mason, who established a $100,000 endowment fund, in honor of his mother Beulah Little Mason, for students with strong academic credentials and documented financial need.

The School of Business received another major donation in the spring of 1986, when a gift from the Dillard Teer Sr. family of Durham, together with a state grant, provided $500,000 to endow the Robert Dillard Teer Jr. Distinguished Professorship of Business. That gift was one of many that helped to launch the Business School's $2 million Golden Anniversary fund-raising campaign.

Just as important in its own way was the publication of Mary Jo Bratton's much-anticipated history of East Carolina. Published by the Alumni Association in April of 1987, the book not only offered the first systematic and comprehensive study of the university's formative years but also provided a rich source of primary materials that had previously been unavailable to the public. It also contributed to friends' and alumni's awareness of their university.

This same kind of symbiotic relationship between the university and its alumni took many other forms during the Howell era. Among the most distinguished of these alumni were Ruth Gwynn Shaw, the first female president of Central Piedmont Community College in Charlotte; Sandy Rowe, executive editor and vice president of the *Virginian-Pilot/Ledger Star;* and Rick Atkinson, award-winning journalist for the *Washington Post,* who received a Pulitzer Prize for national reporting in 1982.

By the time John Howell left office in the spring of 1987, a foundation existed for the next major phase of the university's development under the leadership of Richard Eakin. Appointed by the Board of Governors early in 1987, Chancellor Eakin took office in March, reaffirming from the outset his predecessor's commitment to seek reclassification of ECU as a doctoral degree–granting institution and to develop a blueprint for future growth.

There were a number of signs early in Eakin's administration that the university was entering a new period of growth and change. At the fall convocation of 1987, the new chancellor announced a $1 million gift from Clarence B. (Pop) Beasley and Lynn N. Kelso of New Bern. A few months later, in January 1988, the new $10.7 million general classroom building opened, while two other major building projects were completed. The university embarked on an unprecedented multimillion-dollar fund-raising campaign. Major gifts from ECU's own Student Stores, which contributed $75,000 of its profits for a scholarship endowment, and from a group of young alumni who made a $150,000 challenge gift to fund scholarships helped the university meet other pressing needs. By the end of the year, so much had been accomplished that the editors of *Pieces of Eight* aptly proclaimed 1988 "A Year of Change, Growth and Promise for ECU."

The same might have been said about 1989 as well. Enrollment for spring semester approached the 15,000 mark, the Kate B. Reynolds Health Care Trust awarded a $287,565 grant to the gerontology program, and the Thomas W. Rivers estate donated $1.3 million to support international programs.

Despite severe austerity measures imposed by the state legislature the following year, ECU moved forward with its long-range planning process. The state approved the university's plan to construct two major, self-funded building projects with student fees (a recreation center and a dining facility). Both private gifts and institutional grants helped to compensate for cuts in the institution's operating budget. The National Science Foundation awarded a $1.5 million grant to ECU and UNC-Wilmington for a joint project to improve science education in middle grades and high school.

In 1991, as in the previous year, everyone on campus continued what the editors of *Pieces of Eight* termed a "heroic struggle to cope with, manage, and control the damage from a second year of budget austerity and cutbacks in funding because of a state revenue shortfall." Once again, however, ECU's alumni and friends joined the struggle and helped the university avoid a potentially devastating financial blow. Lora Wilson King left a bequest to the School of Education to establish a distinguished professorship. Lawrence F. Brewster, emeritus professor of history, created a $400,000 endowment for the history department. The Whichard family established a distinguished professorship in the humanities. Many private and governmental institutions made substantial contributions as well, most notably BB&T, which established, in partnership with ECU, a $350,000 multiyear program designed to foster leadership and leadership study.

Rick Atkinson, a Pulitzer Prize winner, critically acclaimed author, successful journalist, and 1974 ECU graduate, returned to Greenville to address spring graduates. His speech continued the "We Believe!" slogan drawn from the victorious football Pirates. Atkinson cautioned the graduates, "You're going to be asked to believe in something larger than your-selves.'" Connie Ray, a 1977 graduate of the university, played the lead role in the weekly television show *The Torkelsons,* and like Atkinson she cred-ited ECU for teaching her the basic skills she needed to succeed. The ECU School of Medicine, apparently providing more than basics, was ranked first in the nation as a producer of family physicians.

Under the continuing strain of tight state funding, the university be-gan 1993 by launching its Shared Visions Campaign in an effort to raise $50 million. Chancellor Eakin observed that Shared Visions is the "most ambitious fund raising campaign undertaken by the university." He added, "'No university can become truly distinctive without private support. Public tax dollars have made East Carolina University a good university. Enough private dollars can make it a great university.'"

Funds from this campaign were earmarked to support academics, ath-letics, research, and medicine. The campaign aimed for $50 million by December 1995. Cochaired by Henry G. Williamson and Robert A. Ward, Shared Visions intended to unite the ECU Educational Foundation, the East Carolina University Foundation, and the Medical Foundation of East Carolina University.

The oldest of these three organizations, the Educational Foundation, was established in 1953 as the Pirate Club through the efforts of longtime ECU supporter Edwin Rawl, and it continues to serve as the primary fund-raiser for athletic scholarships, facilities, and other needs related to the university's intercollegiate sports programs. The East Carolina University Foundation was created shortly thereafter to generate funds to support ac-ademic scholarships and programs. And the Medical Foundation received its charter in the late 1960s as the organization responsible for securing re-sources to support teaching and research in the various disciplines com-prising the health sciences. Although each foundation is an autonomous organization with its own director and staff, their willingness to work with one another and with other organizations such as the Alumni Asso-ciation and the alumni relations office in support of the Shared Visions Campaign helped to make this fund-raising initiative the most successful in ECU history.

As the university considered expanding by acquiring new space in down-town Greenville, the Shared Visions Campaign spilled over in the form of major contributions by alumni and friends and the naming of buildings in their honor. Wachovia Corporation presented a $667,000 grant to the School of Education for an endowed chair, and Burroughs Wellcome estab-lished a $390,000 fellowship endowment in organic chemistry. The foot-ball stadium was renamed Dowdy-Ficklen Stadium after Ronald and Mary Ellen Dowdy, million-dollar donors to the Shared Visions Campaign. Ronald was elected to the Board of Trustees in the autumn of 1993. Walter Williams, founder and president of Trade Oil Company, likewise contributed $1 million as part of the Shared Visions Campaign to help finance an $11.4 million renovation and expansion of Minges Coliseum. Hereafter the arena would be named Williams Arena at Minges Coliseum.

Much construction began during 1994. Ground was broken for the new $17 million Student Recreation Center, a project funded by student fees. And work began also on two other major projects: a renovation and expansion of Joyner Library, a two-year project funded by money from a bond referendum passed the year before, and a $12.3 million expansion of the life science building.

The generosity of the university's friends also enhanced academics. East Carolina Bank established a $100,000 scholarship program for outstanding graduates of high schools in areas served by the bank. Grants from the General Assembly and the North Carolina Biotechnology Center provided support for the university's efforts to further implement the North Carolina Information Highway project and to improve biotechnology teaching and training.

The year ended on a high note when Chancellor Eakin noted in a news conference that Shared Visions had done better than anyone had anticipated, owing to the generosity of ECU's alumni and friends: "'Our total today for the campaign is $52.4 million. This is a magnificent achievement for East Carolina University and for all our students, faculty, staff, alumni and friends throughout the state and the nation." In the early 1990s, the generosity of alumni and friends hit a high mark.

In 1996, one year before its twentieth birthday, the School of Medicine—one of the university's greatest success stories—was the focus of a feature article in *The ECU Report* by Jeannine Manning Huston. Noting that *U.S. News & World Report* placed ECU's medical school fourteenth among the country's seventy-six medical schools that emphasize training in family medicine, Huston wrote: "Recognition like that comes in part from ECU's Generalist Physician Program, a comprehensive effort to increase the number of primary care physicians in eastern NC" and a clear reminder that ECU has been "true to its mission." While many people have helped the Medical School in this and other endeavors, none have done more than the Brody family, which continued its long history of support by presenting ECU with a gift of $1.5 million for a scholarship fund to honor longtime supporter J. S. "Sammy" Brody.

The same issue of *The ECU Report* listed the names of ten ECU alumni serving in the state legislature, reminding us of our past success as a place of learning and our future influence on the state: Rep. Henry Aldridge, Republican, a periodontist from Greenville, in his first term; Sen. J. Richard Conder, Democrat, a banker from Rockingham, in his fifth term; Rep. Mary McAllister, Democrat, ad agency director from Fayetteville, in her third term; Rep. John Nichols, Republican, a mortgage banker from New Bern, in his second term; Rep. Jean Preston, Republican, a retired educator from Emerald Isle, in her first term; Rep. David Redwine, Democrat, a businessperson from Ocean Isle Beach, in his seventh term; Rep. Carolyn Russell, Republican, a former personnel director and psychologist from Goldsboro, in her third term; Rep. Alex Warner, Democrat, a businessperson and educator from Hope Mills, in his fifth term; Sen. Ed Warren, Democrat, an investor from Greenville, in his third term; and Rep. Doug Yongue, Democrat, a retired educator and general contractor from Laurinburg, in his second term.

Continuing with what seemed to be a theme for the year—pride in the past accomplishments of ECU supporters—the university focused upon many other alumni and friends. Alumni J. Gary Danford and Macon Pierce were promoted to vice presidents of Wachovia Bank in Greenville. Honorary ECU alumnus William G. Blount and ECU alumni Hilton O. Chesson and John P. Hudson were named to the ECU Foundation. Henry G. Williamson and Thomas A. Bennett, ECU alumni and past members of the ECU Board of Trustees, were elected to the Board of Directors of the Medical Foundation of ECU. Additionally, Senator Marc Basnight was presented the Honorary Alumni Award, which recognizes individuals who did not attend ECU but who have demonstrated exceptional loyalty and support for the university. Honorary alumni awards for 1996 were also presented to Bill and Barbara Blount and Jack Whichard at the annual Leadership Awards Dinner in January.

Eight North Carolina educators, ECU alumni, were honored in 1996 with the James W. Batten Distinguished Educator Awards. This group included Charles Coble, former dean, ECU School of Education; and honorees Ann R. Weaver of Kenly, Nancy T. Harris of Farmville, Vivian Martin Covington of Farmville, Janie E. Manning of Bethel, and Judith H. Budacz of Greenville. Also included were Bradford L. Sneeden of New Bern, Phillip R. Dixon of Greenville, Robert N. Joyner of Greenville, and ECU Professor Emeritus James W. Batten, for whom the Distinguished Educator Awards and annual lecture were named.

ECU also found symbolic ways to express its appreciation to its many supporters, notably the construction of a replica of the Old Austin Cupola and a commemorative walkway to honor ECU alumni and their families. The cupola project also benefited the Shared Visions Campaign, generating approximately $250,000 in unrestricted gifts by alumni and friends who wished to have a name inscribed on a brick.

Yet another addition, the first phase of a $30 million expansion, was completed at Joyner Library. This addition, a three-story wing, doubled the size of the library. According to George Threewitts in his *ECU Report* column, "East Carolina Today," the renovation "also adds features such as state-of-the-art sections for book preservation and conservation and for linking the library with the resources of the information highway."

The university celebrated its ninetieth anniversary in 1997. Chancellor Eakin, in his tenth year as ECU's chief administrative officer, remarked during the March 8 Founder's Day celebration: "For its entire history, this institution has displayed a remarkable 'can-do' spirit. It has refused to acknowledge the so-called experts who said it couldn't be done."

It was not surprising, then, that during 1997 further developments on campus, supported by alumni and friends, pointed to a proud future as well an interesting and determined past. Among the most notable events of that year were the opening of ECU's Student Recreation Center, one of the largest and best-equipped recreation and fitness facilities in the region, and the dedication of the Rivers Building, named in honor of Thomas Wilson Rivers, who gave the university more than $1 million to fund student scholarships and a Distinguished Professorship of International Studies. The ECU Board of Trustees named the International Human Performance Center for Dr. LeRoy T. Walker, the former president of the U.S. Olympic Committee, who developed the idea for the center. Athletes may have their physiology and performance tested and evaluated at the center where athletes, coaches, and others may also be taught the latest scientific training methods and techniques for improving human performance.

While ECU was celebrating its ninetieth year, changes were taking place in administrative offices, including in the Office of the President. Foremost among those changes was the election on April 10 of Margaret "Molly" Broad as president of the sixteen-campus UNC system. Of more local import, however, three new members were appointed to the East Carolina University Board of Trustees by the University of North Carolina Board of Governors, each for four-year terms: Dan V. Kinlaw of Fayetteville; Willie Martin of Wilmington, Delaware; and Henry G. Williamson of Winston-Salem.

Although the makeup of the Board of Trustees is continually changing, its members have always been united by their commitment to the university and to the various constituencies that it serves. Consisting of twelve appointed members—eight chosen by the Board of Governors and four by the Governor—plus one ex officio member, the president of the Student Government Association, the board has historically drawn its members predominantly from the ranks of the alumni, many of whom have also served as chairs. Of the thirteen people who chaired the board during the past twenty-five years, for example, ten were ECU alumni: Troy W. Pate Jr. (1975–81), C. Ralph Kinsey (1982–87), Thomas A. Bennett (1987–88), Max Ray Joyner Sr. (1988–90), Samuel J. Wornom III (1990–91), D. Wayne Peterson (1991–93), Robert Ward (1995–97), H. E. Rayfield (1997–99), Phillip R. Dixon (1999–2000), and James R. Talton (2003–present).

All of these individuals also served with distinction as members of the board before assuming leadership responsibilities, as did the three non-alumni chairs, Ashley Futrell (1981–82), Craig Souza (1993–95), and Charles Franklin (2000–2003). In these efforts they have been ably assisted by many other alumni and friends who in various ways have helped to further the university's interests. Although an extended treatment of their contributions would far exceed the scope of this chapter, it is worth noting that many of their names—Minges, Dowdy, Ward, Whichard, and Williams, to mention but a few—appear not only on the rolls of the Board of Trustees but also in the university's list of major donors and on the campus buildings dedicated in their honor.

Trustees have also been among the many alumni and friends recognized for other contributions to the university and community, as evidenced by Craig Souza's selection as one of three recipients of the university's distinguished service awards in 1998, the same year that the Alumni Awards Committee presented Outstanding Alumni Awards to Sandra Bullock, Major General Walter T. Worthington, Sandra Mims Rowe, and Frances Eason.

In May of the same year, the university Board of Governors, on the recommendation of UNC President Molly Broad, voted to designate ECU a Doctoral II university, effective May 1, 1998. The spring 1998 issue of *The ECU Report* marked the occasion with a short feature proclaiming, "A Great Day for East Carolina," echoing the words and sentiments of H. E. "Gene" Rayfield Jr., chair of the ECU Board of Trustees. "It is a tremendous accomplishment for our faculty, staff and students,'" remarked Rayfield. "'I am proud of them and their achievements."

A sidebar to that story focused on "ECU's first doctoral recipient 15 years later." Dr. Tom Curry received his doctorate in anatomy in 1983. After graduating, he was a postdoctoral fellow and research associate at the University of Miami and then moved to the University of Kentucky where he became full professor, holding a joint appointment in the Departments of Obstetrics and Gynecology and Anatomy and Neurobiology.

New Ph.D. programs in Coastal Resource Management and Biomedical Physics were authorized on April 9 by the University of North Carolina Board of Governors, thereby making ECU the only doctoral institution in the UNC system besides UNC–Chapel Hill, UNC–Greensboro, and North Carolina State University. The academic world changed.

There were many reasons to celebrate on Founder's Day, as a result. Much of the pride of ECU could be found in Chancellor Eakin's decision to focus during his address on the early leaders of the university. Eakin said, "I was delighted to find clear evidence in the writings of the founders that after 10 years of classes, their resolve was, if anything stronger than ever."

Another source of pride was ECU's emergence as a leader in technology, which earned the university a top twenty-five ranking in 1998 among "most wired" campuses. What's more, for the second year in a row, ECU was noted as the only public university in North Carolina included in the listing. In keeping with this pride in maintaining an updated profile, Friends of Joyner Library had a new logo designed and set a goal to raise $1 million by 2000. Friends president Steve Smiley, the youngest child of the late Wendell Smiley, who served as ECU's chief librarian from 1943 to 1973, noted ECU's continual need "to play catch-up," reinforcing the theme the chancellor began during his Founder's Day address.

The Harvey family from Kinston, through the C. Felix Harvey Jr. Foundation, created a $500,000 endowment to improve the teaching of reading. As Margaret Blount Harvey, family member and member of the State Board of Education, explained in *The ECU Report*, "Our family has been very concerned about the lack of the variety of skills necessary among new teachers to teach basic reading to all students." In noting that ECU's School of Education has been a leader nationally in reforming teacher training, she said the family thought ECU was the right place for such an investment.

Other efforts to recognize contributions by alumni and friends to ECU that have made possible the development of campus landmarks, research projects, and scholarships included the Order of the Cupola. During 1998, charter members to this new benefactor recognition program were honored at a reception in the chancellor's home. Members of the order, according to Chancellor Eakin, have donated more than $40 million to the university; eleven of the gifts were for more than $1 million. To be recognized by the order, individuals, businesses, and foundations must make cumulative gifts of $100,000 or more.

In an important appointment in alumni affairs, J. Philip Horne, a 1983 graduate of ECU, was hired to succeed Don Leggett, who retired at the end of 1997, as associate vice chancellor for alumni relations.

In a much-contested move, ECU reached an all-inclusive soft drink contract with Pepsi Cola. The national trend of awarding an exclusive beverage contract brought certain benefits: $2 million was set aside for athletics department capital projects, while the remaining revenues were to be used to establish endowments for academic scholarships, grants-in-aid to student-athletes, and a faculty/student leadership fund. The university also continued to benefit from private donations, one of the most significant of which was a $100,000 endowment for the School of Art from Irwin Belk, who had received an honorary degree from ECU in 1997.

This trend continued into the new year, when the Brody family gave the School of Medicine the largest gift ever bestowed on the university, $8 million to support the school's regional service mission. During a press conference in December 1999 in the School of Medicine, the Board of Trustees decided to honor the Brody family by naming the medical school the Brody School of Medicine at East Carolina University.

ECU also obtained what was termed the "Millennium Campus." The old Voice of America Site C became the university's property when the federal government deeded the site to Greenville and Pitt County. City and county officials hoped the new site would enable ECU to expand medical services to treat and prevent agricultural-related injuries.

There was expansion, too, in the area of technology. The university was among twenty-nine campuses selected for the U.S. Department of Education's "Learning Anywhere, Anytime" partnership, receiving $4.6 million to support the School of Industry and Technology's Online Wireless Learning Internet Solutions project, and ECU also received a $341,000 grant from the National Science Foundation and a $4.6 million contract from the National Institutes of Health and the National Library of Medicine for Internet-related research initiatives.

Further enhancing the university's reputation and well-being were the accomplishments of its alumni and friends, many of whom were featured throughout the year in *The ECU Report*. Reggie Edgerton, a professor in the Department of Physiological Sciences at UCLA, returned to ECU to give a presentation in the area of spinal cord research. William Lindsey was awarded the *Miami Herald* Charles Whited Spirit of Excellence Award in recognition of extraordinary contributions he has made in South Florida. Sarah Matyiko, along with other members of the family-run Matyiko Bros. Expert House Movers business, moved the Hatteras Lighthouse 2,900 feet inland. Garrie Moore was made vice chancellor for student life. Annette Wysocki, Grover Whitehurst, Beth Grant, and Layton Getsinger were named outstanding alumni for 1999. And David J. Whichard II and David B. Stevens received the 1999 Honorary Alumni Award, given to individuals who, though they are not ECU graduates, have nonetheless shown uncommon support for the university.

No matter what else happened at ECU in 1999, it will always be remembered as the year of the flood. On September 15, as Hurricane Floyd bore down on the coast, Governor Hunt ordered ECU to close. By the next day, Floyd's aftermath produced what many called "the flood of the century," shutting down the campus until September 27, causing nearly $7 million in damage, and claiming the life of one student, Aaron Child. Led by ECU alumnus Glenn Woodard, director of FEMA for the southeast region, recovery efforts began immediately and brought everyone together in a remarkable demonstration of Pirate resilience.

The hard work of restoration continued in 2000, a year marked by new challenges and successes. On April 27, Chancellor Richard Eakin announced his plan to retire as chancellor in 2001. Also in the spring, the Joint Select Committee on Education Facilities was briefed by officials from ECU on pressing construction needs and then toured the aging and outmoded Flanagan Building. The fall 2000 issue of *The ECU Report* featured continued concerns over the upcoming bond referendum, which would determine whether the university would receive the funds needed to meet its critical facilities construction needs.

Of particular concern to ECU officials were the university's capital facilities needs. The highest priorities were a new science and technology building on the main campus and a nursing, allied health, and developmental evaluation clinic complex near the medical school, but funds were needed for other projects as well, especially for classroom renovations, for technology upgrades, and for expansion of the university computing center. Also required was the acquisition of additional property for construction of new facilities that would answer some space problems caused by increased student enrollment.

There was much encouraging financial news during 2000. The Campaign for East Carolina Scholars concluded a two-and-a-half year effort with the announcement that the campaign had generated more than $15 million. The largest gift to this campaign thus far came from Irwin and Carol Belk, a contribution that was expected to produce $3.78 million and lead to the creation of twenty endowed scholarships over three decades. There were other large donations as well. Alumna Gail McClelland created a $600,000 scholarship fund for students in the School of Music and the School of Medicine, and Bryan Latham gave $250,000 to the School of Education in honor of his parents, Walter and Daisy Carson Latham.

During this same period, ECU attracted grants from various foundations and companies. The Z. Smith Reynolds Foundation provided a $70,000 grant for the Coffee in the Kitchen program, designed to foster fuller discussion and deeper understanding of race relations in eastern North Carolina. The university became part of a consortium of schools receiving $1.03 million from the National Science Foundation to "develop a core of about 200 high school math and science teachers trained in the latest computer technologies." In addition, ECU received a $1.5 million federal grant to prepare teachers to work in the field of special education. The ECU Surgical Research Center was awarded a Doris Duke Innovation in Clinical Research Award in Cardiovascular Disease Research for $400,000. And officials from Blue Cross and Blue Shield of North Carolina announced a $100,000 contribution to the bond campaign, thus reaffirming the company's long-standing commitment to supporting higher education in North Carolina. Just a few weeks later, the state's voters did the same by approving the bond referendum, assuring that the university's most pressing facilities needs would be met.

Other alumni made significant contributions as well. Alumna Jan Greenwood, vice president of the executive search company A. T. Kearney, was hired to help the university select a replacement for retiring chancellor Dr. Richard Eakin. David Swink was featured on CBS's *60 Minutes II* in March for his work in preventing school violence. Wade Hobgood became chancellor of the North Carolina School of the Arts. Emily Mercer became the ninth woman in her family to earn a degree from ECU's School of Education, continuing the Mercer family's 190-year tradition of teaching.

The spring and summer of 2001 brought news of other contributions by ECU alumni and friends. Among the most noteworthy financial gifts was a multimillion-dollar donation from the estate of alumna Verona Joyner Langford—the largest amount ever for the main campus—to establish an endowment for Joyner Library. As librarian Carroll Varner, director of Joyner Library, observed in *The ECU Report,* this endowment "is a wonderful and significant contribution to ECU students and faculty." It would enable the library not only to expand its main collection but also to purchase first editions of important works and to support new areas of faculty research. Other benefactors recognized in the same issue were longtime friend and supporter Harold Bate, whose multimillion-dollar contributions prompted the university to name the new general classroom building in his honor.

Alumni and friends contributed to the university in other ways, too. Margaret Ward continued her long and distinguished service to ECU by accepting an appointment to serve on the Board of Trustees, as did Charles R. Franklin, who in the spring of 2000 was elected chair of the board for the 2001–2 academic year. In the entertainment field, ECU graduate Emily Procter completed another successful season on NBC's award-winning series *The West Wing,* and current student Monica Palumbo won the Miss Congeniality award at the Miss USA pageant. In sports, the Pirates baseball team gave the university increased national visibility by winning a school-record forty-seven games and the NCAA regional tournament. In the political sphere, campus and community supporters of George W. Bush brought the newly elected president to Minges Coliseum in April to deliver a major economic policy address. In the public service arena, ECU alumna Janice Faulkner—noted for her accomplishments as an educator, state political party executive, state commissioner, and secretary of state—returned to campus as a member of the Chancellor Search Committee. And in February that committee selected Dr. William Muse as successor to Dr. Richard Eakin, who retired in the spring of 2001 after fourteen years' service as chancellor.

Chancellor Eakin's retirement marked the end of one of the longest and most productive eras in ECU history—one that would be followed by a period of transition and change quite different than most imagined at the time. Even as Chancellor-Elect Muse was preparing to assume his duties, North Carolina legislators were calling for major spending cuts, and the new State Health Plan that went into effect July 1 included not only increased deductibles and copayments but also substantial increases in premiums for coverage of employees' families.

Despite the state budgetary problems that surfaced during the summer, the fall semester began on a positive note. Enrollment was up again following the previous year's unanticipated decline. Construction on the new science and technology building and a number of other facilities proceeded according to schedule. And the university welcomed its new leader, Chancellor William Muse, who at the fall convocation offered praise for the institution's past accomplishments and affirmed his commitment to its continuing success in academics, athletics, and all its other endeavors.

There were early indications, too, of continuing financial support from various sources and new accomplishments by ECU alumni and friends. The National Science Foundation donated two nuclear magnetic resonance spectrometers valued at approximately $500,000; IBM designated ECU as one of a number of state institutions to receive a share of a $6.353 million grant to support research and classroom instruction; and one of the country's most prestigious teaching awards was presented to ECU alumnus Ron Clark, who was named Disney National Teacher of the Year.

The sense of optimism and anticipation with which the semester began was soon shattered by the September 11 terrorist attacks on the World Trade Center and the Pentagon—a tragedy that brought people together in much the same way that Hurricane Floyd had done two years before. Blood drives at Mendenhall Student Center and Minges Coliseum drew more donors than the facilities and staff could accommodate; members of the Greenville community joined with ECU faculty, students, and staff in memorial services and candlelight vigils; the ECU Student Government Association and other groups organized fund-raising drives; various campus and community agencies began the long-term healing process by offering special programs, discussion forums, individual counseling, and other services; and faculty provided much-needed ongoing support to students both within and outside their classrooms.

Even during this time of unprecedented upheaval and uncertainty, there were many signs of recovery and renewal. Retired theatre department faculty member Edgar Loessin, who founded the ECU Playhouse and served as its director for twenty-eight years, was honored at the opening performance of the newly renamed ECU/Loessin Playhouse. Chancellor Muse began preparations for a "Hometown Tour" designed to give him an opportunity to strengthen ties between the university and people throughout the region. Hart, Inc., donated software valued at $500,000 to the UNC Teacher Education Technology Council, over $30,000 of which was allocated to ECU. The North Carolina Agromedicine Institute received a federal grant of $3 million for a regional center that would serve to promote the health and safety of workers in the agricultural, forestry, and fisheries industries. And the U.S. State Department's Bureau of Educational and Cultural Affairs provided a $250,000 grant to support an M.A. in public administration, developed jointly by ECU and Russia's Urals Academy of Public Administration.

There were a number of positive developments during the spring semester as well. The campus bookstore announced that it was contributing $375,000 to ECU scholarship funds. At about the same time, the Department of Materials Management and ECU Central Receiving and Stores announced a new partnership agreement with Staples. By the end of May, construction was completed on the Strength and Conditioning Center, and the last beam was erected on the Science and Technology Building.

Less encouraging was the news concerning the state's financial condition. A continuing decline in revenues prompted the legislature and the governor to propose substantial cuts in the budgets of all sixteen universities as well as reversions of allocated funds. In response, the chancellor announced two major initiatives, both designed to increase private giving. The first was to realign ECU Foundation president and vice chancellor for institutional advancement James Lanier's responsibilities, a move designed to strengthen the ECU Foundation and provide the impetus for major fund-raising efforts; the second was to create a new vice chancellorship and charge the person appointed to that position with responsibility for coordinating university related fund-raising and alumni affairs.

By the beginning of the 2002–3 academic year, the university seemed well positioned to meet the challenges ahead. University officials announced a record enrollment of 20,636 students and reaffirmed their commitment to increase enrollment to 27,000 students over the next eight years. And several construction projects financed through the 2000 bond referendum and various other sources neared completion.

There were other reasons for optimism as well. In late August, the special collections department of Joyner Library held a dedication ceremony honoring Bodo Nischan, the late history professor and Reformation scholar, and announced that with the support of the Bodo Nischan Manuscript Endowment the library had added a number of new volumes to its rare book collection. A few weeks later, the School of Social Work announced a $5.1 million gift from Charles and Hazel Freeze in honor of their daughter, the late Carolyn Freeze Baynes. The school was later renamed in her honor.

During the remainder of the fall semester, and throughout the spring, ECU continued both its fund-raising initiatives and its efforts to strengthen ties with varied constituencies throughout the state. The February issue of *Pieces of Eight* published an encouraging report on the status of the university's endowment fund, which according to the National Association of College and University Business Officers increased by 8 percent over the previous year, reaching a total of $55.3 million. Equally welcome was an announcement in the same issue that the UNC system had allocated $166,000 to the School of Education to further its efforts. And the following month, Dowdy Student Stores announced that it was contributing a record $400,000 of its profits for student scholarships.

While there was much to celebrate during the 2002–3 academic year, there were concerns as well, not only about the economy but also about the changes being proposed by the university's top administrators. The specific nature of those priorities became apparent at the beginning of the spring semester with the announcement of sweeping changes in administrative personnel and institutional organization. Accompanying these initiatives were a number of programmatic and organizational changes, including the implementation of a three-year-degree program, a proposal for a new School of Engineering, and an extensive reorganization of existing departments and schools into six colleges. New data indicating a further decline in state revenues coupled with rumored cuts in state appropriations prompted the chancellor to announce a number of new cost-cutting measures, including a hiring freeze, rigorous spending controls, elimination of all nonessential equipment and supplies purchases, cancellation of nonessential professional travel, and delayed reimbursements for essential travel.

Despite these economic pressures and the resignation of William Muse as chancellor shortly after the fall 2003 convocation, the university continued to move forward in its fund-raising initiatives, first under the leadership of Interim Chancellor William Shelton and then under the direction of Chancellor Steven Ballard.

During spring 2004 alone, the university received over $2.5 million in grants from the National Institutes of Health, NASA, the U.S. Department of Education, and other federal agencies to support scientific research and educational initiatives. Various corporations and other organizations made substantial contributions also, among them Wachovia, which awarded the School of Education $1.25 million—the largest corporate gift in the university's history—to support ECU's Partnership East initiative. Many private donors offered their support as well, most notably Irene Smith Howell, who gave $1 million to the College of Education's Assistive Technology Lab, and the William H. Clark family, whose earlier $1.5 million gift made possible the construction of the new state-of-the-art Clark-LeClair Stadium, named in honor of the donors and former ECU baseball coach Keith LeClair, which opened in March 2004.

ECU experienced similar success during the summer of 2004 and throughout the 2004–5 academic year. The National Institutes of Health awarded grants totaling more than $2 million to support research by faculty in chemistry and medicine, and other federal agencies provided support for various educational programs, notably the College of Education's Project Heart initiative. The state legislature continued its strong commitment to the ECU Medical School by appropriating $60 million for a new Cardiovascular Diseases Center. BB&T announced a $1 million gift to support leadership development initiatives through the BB&T Center. Dowdy Student Stores donated $365,000 for student scholarships. And an anonymous supporter donated $152,000 to endow the Rives Chair, named in honor of retired English professor Ralph Rives.

Although the state's budget picture still looks bleak, ECU seems well prepared to weather the latest crisis as it moves closer to its centennial year. The total amount of academic advancement funds rose to more than $60 million in 2004, an accomplishment that earned ECU Foundation president James Lanier a national award from the Council of Advancement and Support of Education. The university's other two foundations—the Medical School Foundation and the Education Foundation (ECU Pirate Club)—have also been extremely active under the leadership of their respective directors, Donna McLees and Dennis Young, as have the Alumni Association and its director Paul Clifford.

Especially encouraging is the Alumni Association's recently announced five-year strategic plan, which is designed to improve communications and strengthen ties with the university's alumni and to coordinate the association's alumni relations initiatives with the fund-raising efforts of the university's advancement foundations. While it is too early to tell what the specific outcomes of this plan will be, this much is clear: ECU's alumni, who now number more than 108,000, and countless other supporters within and outside the university family, await the opportunity to join with faculty, students, and administrators in making ECU's second hundred years as exciting and productive as the first.

REFERENCES

ECU Alumni Association. *The ECU Report*. East Carolina University Archives.

ECU News & Communications Services. *Pieces of Eight*. East Carolina University Archives.

ECU News & Communications Services. Press Releases. East Carolina University.

ACKNOWLEDGMENTS

We would like to thank the individuals who helped us at various stages of this project, especially University Archivist Suellyn Lathrop and the staff of Special Collections, who located and made available to us back issues of *The ECU Report*, *Pieces of Eight*, and other important resources; Information and Communications Specialist Nancy McGillicuddy, who culled the ECU News and Communications Services archives for press releases and other items that helped us fill in gaps in the historical record; undergraduate honors assistant Heather Willis, who helped in proofreading the manuscript, checking sources to verify the accuracy of quotations, and searching for new sources of information where details were lacking; Provost James Smith and his staff, who provided data about past members and chairs of the Board of Trustees; and Henry Ferrell, who offered invaluable editorial suggestions.

## CHAPTER TWELVE

Beyond the University

MULATU WUBNEH

THE 1980S USHERED in a new era of development that transformed the characteristics of East Carolina University and Greenville. Two factors— qualitative and quantitative—contributed to this transformation. The qualitative factors are related to the change precipitated by the development of new academic programs. With the addition of the medical school in 1975 and the introduction of new professional programs, ECU's reputation as an institution focusing only on education and the liberal arts changed. By the mid-1980s, the university, which had been largely known as a teacher training institution, was home to several professional programs including business, criminal justice, medicine, nursing, technology, and several science programs. The university aspired to become a comprehensive Doctoral II institution home to diverse academic programs, including those that offered doctoral degrees.

The quantitative changes were related to the growth in enrollment and the corresponding increase in size of faculty and staff. In 1970, ECU had a student population of 10,000 and enrollment increases in the previous decades were modest. By 1980, enrollment had jumped to 13,165, and for the next two decades the university experienced a major growth, reaching an enrollment of 18,750 in 2000. ECU in 2005 had a student population of over 23,000 and over 4,500 faculty and staff.

The academic transformation of ECU began to have a major impact on the city in which it resides. In many ways the ECU campus is the center of life in Greenville, as the university has become the hub of activities —sports, music, dance, theatre, lectures, and art shows—that serve a large population of the town and region. The Brody School of Medicine and the Pitt County Memorial Hospital proved to be major additions to Greenville's landscape. In the local economy, ECU is a major economic engine that contributed significantly to the growth of the city. In short, the growth of Greenville is intimately tied to the growth of ECU and its potential to develop into a major educational institution in the state.

ECU AS AN ECONOMIC ANCHOR

In an article on the role of colleges and universities in local economic development, a joint study by the Initiative for a Competitive Inner City (ICIC), a nonprofit organization dedicated to the promotion of economic development in inner cities and the chief executive officers for cities (a bipartisan alliance of mayors, corporate executives, university presidents, and other nonprofit leaders), stated that academic institutions are increasingly becoming engines of economic growth including centers of science and technology, incubators of companies, major employers, creators of housing, and purchasers of goods and services. The article also noted that "in many respects, the bell-tower of academic institutions had replaced smoke-stacks as the drivers of the American economy." The U.S. Department of Housing and Urban Development (HUD), Office of University Partnership, expressed a similar view that few institutions can contribute more to rebuilding America's communities than its colleges and universities.

The ICIC/CEO report outlined a framework and a strategic approach through which universities may provide meaningful service as economic anchors in communities. These services are related to the role of a university as employer, purchaser, workforce educator, real estate developer, incubator, and adviser/network builder. ECU has become an engine of economic growth and a center of cultural activities for Greenville and the surrounding regions. This chapter examines ECU's contribution to local economic development, with a specific focus on the roles outlined in the ICIC/CEO report.

In March 2000, the ECU Regional Development Institute (RDI) conducted a study on the economic impact of ECU to the local economy. According to the RDI report, ECU in 2000 had 3,964 employees and a total budget of $368 million. An analysis of the university's impact showed that the total annual financial contribution (including direct, indirect, and induced impact) of the university was $1.4 billion. To give a comparative picture, the total revenue for Pitt County for the same year was $151 million.

The same study indicated that ECU's direct employment of 3,964 in 2000 translated into a total employment impact of 21,424 jobs (direct, 3,964; indirect, 9,555; and induced, 7,905). This trend showed that the financial as well as the employment impact of the university had a multiplier effect of

3.8 and 5.4 respectively, much higher than the average for the agriculture or the manufacturing sectors.

In 2004–5, ECU employed 4,525 people. Occupational distribution of employees represented about 34 percent faculty, 24 percent administrators and professionals, and the remaining 42 percent secretarial/clerical, technical, craft workers, and maintenance staff (figure 12.1). The total operating budget of the university was $474 million in 2004–5. To give a comparative perspective, the total budget of the city of Greenville for 2004 was $54 million. Based on the multiplier developed by RDI, the total employment and income impact of ECU would be 24,435 jobs and $1.8 billion in 2004–5. This level of economic impact demonstrated that ECU formed the major asset in the changing economic base of Greenville and surrounding communities.

ECU's employment growth rate for the last three decades increased to twice that of Pitt County. For instance, employment at ECU increased at an average annual rate of 2.2 percent between 1999 and 2003 (figure 12.2). The corresponding growth rate for Pitt County was 1.3 percent. The national employment trend shows that education and knowledge creation marked the second-fastest-growing industry in the country, and ECU's employment record matched this trend.

ECU does not have a locally focused employment strategy. As a state institution, it sought an open and competitive employment policy that at-

FIGURE 12.1   ECU Employment by Occupational Category, 2003–4

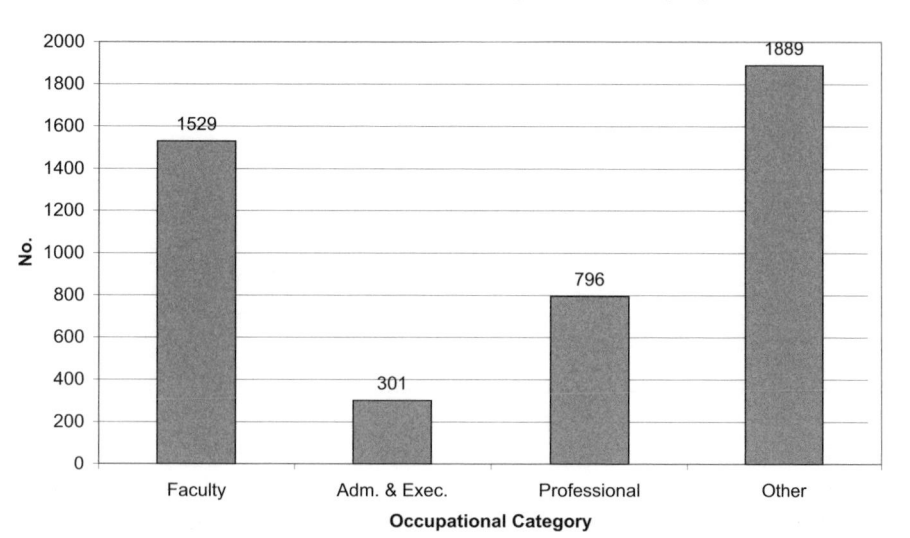

Source: 2004–2005 Fact Book, ECU.

FIGURE 12.2   Employment at ECU and Greenville, 1970–2003

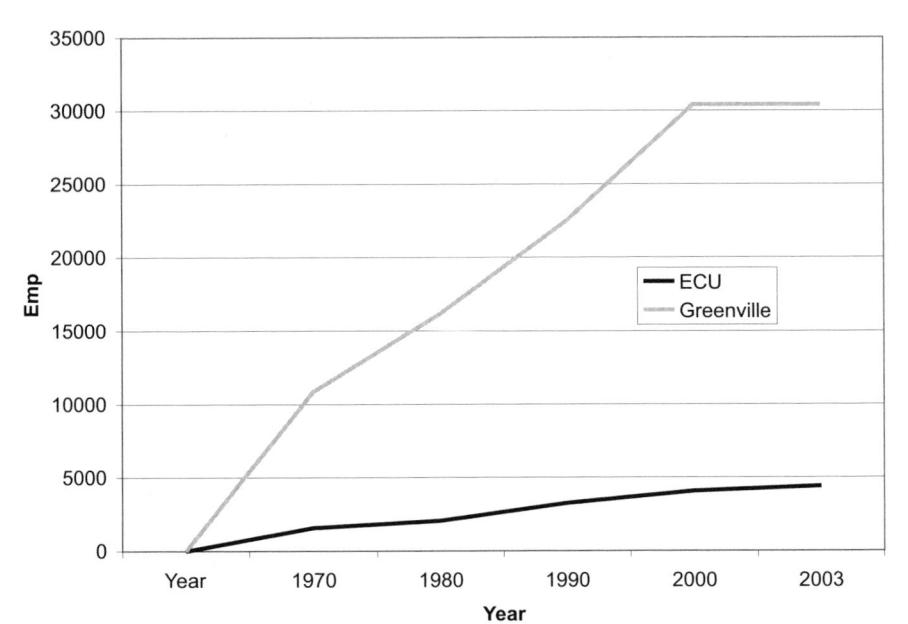

Source: 2004–2005 Fact Book, ECU; Employment Security Commission.
Note: 2003 employment data for Greenville are estimates.

tracted the best and most qualified people to its workforce. Since ECU
recruited both faculty and students nationally and internationally, Greenville became more diverse in the makeup of its population than did the
surrounding towns. Historically dependent on agricultural and industrial
employment, the labor force in the region needed high-level training to
qualify for the specialized positions that ECU often advertised. A training program aimed at honing the skill level of the labor force in the region would be an appropriate strategy and within the major goals of ECU—
promoting economic development in eastern North Carolina. Moreover,
a locally focused training program aimed at improving the quality of the
labor force from the region would help ECU garner political support and
local pride.

Local purchasing composes a very important strategy used by many universities to support their neighbors. University departments incorporate
local purchasing as one of the evaluative criteria of the staff to demonstrate
their commitment. ECU's 2003–4 operating expenses totaled $474 million.
While 66 percent of the total expenses ($311 million) were for wages and
salaries, about a quarter of the expenses ($124 million) were used for the

FIGURE 12.3   ECU Operating Expenses, 2003–4

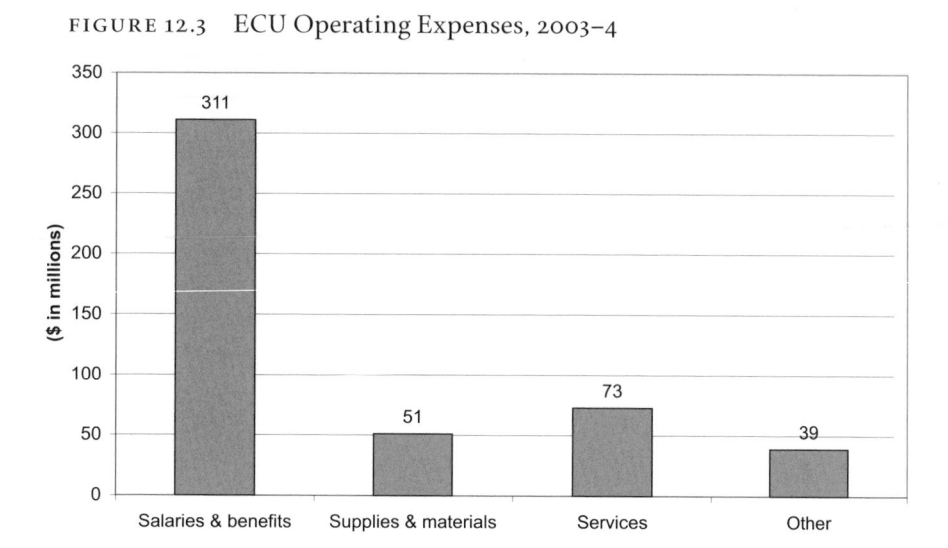

purchase of goods and services (figure 12.3). Although it is difficult to trace the proportion used for the purchase of goods and services locally, it is obvious that even a small percentage of this budget used to purchase from local vendors would have a major impact on the local economy. Wages and salaries composed the other aspect of the operating expense. The $311 million spent on wages and salaries are received by employees, who spend a significant proportion of the revenue to purchase goods and services from local businesses.

Universities shape the physical characteristics of communities. As a major property owner and developer, a university's real estate ownership, construction, and expansion activities strongly affect neighboring land uses. ECU is no exception. With a total campus area of 482 acres, ECU became the largest real estate holder in Greenville. About two-thirds of this area is in the east campus, with the remaining one-third in the west campus and the research campus. In the last ten years, ECU undertook a significant capital improvement program ranging from the expansion of Joyner Library to the construction of a new science and technology building, the addition and renovation of the Dowdy-Ficklen Stadium, and the addition and renovation of the Rivers Building and the Flanagan Building, to name a few. As ECU expands its real estate development program, it will continue to serve as a major economic anchor to local and regional revitalization programs.

ECU's partnership with the city of Greenville to promote downtown revitalization will play a significant role in priming the pump for private sector development and the transformation of housing, public spaces, and infrastructure in the downtown area. In 2003, ECU agreed to commit $2 million to help develop the strategic east-west thoroughfare, also known as the Tenth Street Connector. This gesture to partnership with the city is in addition to the funds the university allocated for the purchase of property along Tenth Street. It also demonstrated the level of commitment of the university in the redevelopment of the communities around the campus.

The national economic change from an agriculture-based to manufacturing and knowledge-based economy, particularly in the area of technical innovation and commercialization, made universities major players in enhancing the economic base and competitiveness of many communities. The inventions and commercialization of inventions can become the catalyst for job growth. In some cases, universities are able to combine scientific discovery, capital, and management to help initiate local economic development. While universities are not the primary owners and operators of business incubators, they often affiliate with technology-based incubators at a local level. Two examples illustrate the excellent partnership between ECU and its communities in promoting local economic development.

The first example is the relationship between East Carolina University and the Pitt County Development Commission (PCDC). In 1996, the PCDC purchased the old Prepshirt (Hampton Industries) building on North Green Street, with 60,000 square feet of space, and converted it into a technology and business incubator facility. The decision to purchase the facility was part of the county's strategy to attract high-tech industries and retain high-tech start-ups by enterprising investors. It was also partly influenced by the desire to entice some of ECU's academic and research departments to translate their research success into start-up industrial enterprises. The facility was designed for multitenant occupancy with start-up industries leasing space for up to three years, after which they would be expected to establish themselves independently. The facility was targeting biotech start-ups and other medical service and information technology industries, largely encouraged by the success of the ECU Medical School and its research facilities.

On December 18, 1997, Regional Development Services (RDS) of ECU entered into an agreement with PCDC for RDS to act as an operational management agent for Pitt County's incubator facility. RDS was to be responsible for day-to-day operation of the facility, including administrative and management duties. Some of the specific tasks included marketing of the facility, maintenance of facility and equipment, identifying tenant problems and providing recommendations, and providing technical services. Albert Delia, associate vice chancellor, representing the RDS, and John Chaffee, executive director of the Pitt County Development Commission, signed the agreement. In return, RDS would receive an annual fee of $1.00 for its services and provide office space in the facility. The management agreement has now been dissolved following the reorganization that moved the Center for Applied Technology, the agency that directly managed the facility, from RDS to another unit.

A second example of ECU's collaboration with neighbors is Pitt County's effort to attract foreign investment. Pitt County's success in attracting ASMO Company, Ltd., a Japanese firm specializing in the production of a variety of small electric motors for automobiles, can be traced to the dedication and excellent partnership role played by the director of the Japan Center East of ECU, the late Dr. Don Spence. According to Chaffee, Spence used his linguistic skills and cultural expertise to steer Japanese investment on the right path, and he was instrumental in securing the ASMO plant for Pitt County. In 1994, ASMO decided to locate in Greenville. The company made an initial investment of $35 million and planned to employ close to 260 workers within a period of three years. It started operations in 1995, and, in 2005, ASMO had an investment of more than $70 million and employed over 500 workers. ASMO was Pitt County's first Japanese industry. However, because of the tendency of the Japanese to "cluster" in areas where they feel welcome and where schools, health services, and other amenities are of good quality, four new Japanese industries located in Pitt County, with a combined investment of over $100 million and employment of 750 workers. Additionally, another three Japanese companies have located within a 45-mile radius of Greenville and ECU. Thus, the region's success in attracting these industries is a testimony to the productive relationship that existed between ECU and its communities.

Programs that channel student and faculty know-how to business owners are one of the major university/community engagement activities that have become popular in the last few years. Universities often set up programs to work closely with companies or businesses to improve their operation. Small business center services include one-on-one counseling, business training and education, start-up assistance, market research, information technology transfer, and other business operation enhancement services. Many students at ECU participate in programs such as internships, career development activities, and short-term assigned operations to receive real-world experience. These programs are also valued by businesses. In some cases, specialized centers offer educational or training programs in addition to consulting and research. Two programs at ECU exemplify this trend.

In the School of Business, the Office of Professional Programs, under the

BB&T Executive Leadership Development Program, performs a major role in training executives as well as students. Through its outreach program, the office organized workshops and other short-term training programs to expose small businesses to new developments and ideas in business management. Similarly, the Center for Applied Technology in the College of Technology and Computer Science incorporated faculty expertise to advise businesses and industries on technology-related issues and problems.

The primary mission of a university is to develop a well-trained and effective workforce. ECU has graduated over 2,500 people in each of the last ten years. It has also made a major effort to develop programs in the form of continuing education, short-term conferences and workshops, and attachment of individual faculty to businesses or institutions. The Office of Continuing Education and the Office of Career Development are two offices responsible for coordinating various types of training programs on campus.

Few programs at ECU have contributed as significantly to the local economy by providing health services and by attracting health-related businesses as the School of Medicine. The Brody School developed into one of the leading programs in the state. The school and Pitt County Memorial Hospital work in concert. City officials take initiatives to help the two institutions flourish and minimize any adverse effects that may result from uncontrolled growth of the city. The medical district plan is one example that demonstrates the level of commitment of the city to ensure that the growth and development of the medical school is not hampered by uncontrolled growth resulting from rapid urbanization.

The tax-exempt status of universities is an area of tension that has affected relationships between universities and the communities in which they are located. Universities are significant real estate owners in many cities, which means that there is a substantial loss of tax revenue to the local treasury. This issue is particularly difficult for small cities whose major source of revenue depends on property taxes. Fortunately, this issue has not affected relationships between ECU and the city of Greenville. ECU has used some of the creative measures used by other universities to avert tensions emanating from its tax-exempt status. Two of the most recognized methods used by many universities include payments in lieu of taxes (PILOTs) and services in lieu of taxes (SILOTs). These arrangements are often made by negotiations undertaken between the city and the university. Two examples used by ECU include the university's willingness to commit $2 million toward the Tenth Street Connection project and the $225,000 it allocated toward the purchase of a high-rise ladder truck for the Greenville Fire Department.

A major consequence of the qualitative and quantitative transformation of ECU centered on the impact that these changes had on campus facilities such as housing, parking, classroom space, and office space. The capacity of many of these facilities simply could not cope with the demand. Over 50 percent of the students in the mid-1980s lived off campus, and, by 2003, this figure had jumped to 75 percent. In fall 2004, out of the total enrollment of 23,000, only 5,113 students lived on campus. Parking and office spaces on campus are also limited. These circumstances forced the university to search for additional space close to campus. At the same time, the conversion of many homes into student residences became a major concern for the city of Greenville as well as the neighborhoods next to the campus. The neighborhoods in the Fifth Street and the Tar River area, which have organized themselves into neighborhood associations, voiced their concerns to city officials and the university administration about the changes. Residents worried about the pace of change as more and more houses converted into duplexes to make them attractive to students. The neighborhoods believed that at the rate things were changing, the community's identity would be in jeopardy. Meanwhile, students continued to move into the area, looking for rental space.

This search for more space next to campus was not limited to students. The university also actively looked for additional office space, a matter that concerned many property owners. For instance, in early 1990, ECU secured the building on 1001 East Fourth Street for office space. The Tar River Neighborhood Association (TRNA) voiced its concern about noise, traffic, congestion, and other nuisances resulting from the university's use of the property. To help address the organization's concern, ECU entered into an agreement with TRNA on the university's use of the property. According to the agreement, executed in February 1990, the university agreed to restrict its use of the building to offices only. There was to be no plan for expansion of the building, no signs, no construction of storage facilities or use of the premise for parking state vehicles. The university also agreed to have no more than sixteen staff members working in the building.

In 1992, ECU initiated a long-term planning process to map strategies on future growth of the campus. The university retained O'Brien/Atkins Associates of the Research Triangle Park to develop a campus master plan. The plan recommended that the university's long-term development process should consider the acquisition of property next to the campus. For instance, two of the areas the plan identified included land in the southwest corner of Cotanche Street, between Ninth and Tenth Streets (which is now used as a parking lot) and the area east of Fletcher Music Building extending to Elm, Tenth Street, and Fifth Street. Other areas identified included the old Rose High School property and the Elmhurst Elementary School site.

With the university's decision to initiate a long-term planning process, many of the latent concerns shared by the neighborhood associations and the city began to surface. Three cases illustrate how delicate relationships among the university, the city, and the neighborhood associations were handled. The cases deal with the establishment of a historic district in the College Hill area, the development of the Medical Park, and ECU's eastward expansion plan.

The College View Historic District

The Tar River Neighborhood Association (TRNA) and the University Neighborhood Association (TUNA) were established in 1980 and 1985 respectively as a result of the residents' concern on how to maintain the character of their neighborhood. Their primary objective was to preserve the character of their neighborhood and to protect the value of their property. In the early 1980s, as they began to see changes, the associations started to search for strategies that could help protect their neighborhood. They embarked on a major initiative to get their neighborhood designated as a historic district, a decision that had several benefits. First, it helped maintain the character of the neighborhood by controlling architectural and other structural changes of the buildings. A second advantage lay in the tax benefits: property owners can take advantage of state as well as federal tax benefits granted to historic sites.

In 1982, the City Council, acting on the recommendation of the Environmental Advisory Council, authorized Kate B. Ohno, a private consultant, to conduct a survey of historic buildings in the area. Ohno recommended to the council the nomination of the College View area for listing in the National Register of Historic Places. However, under North Carolina law (NCGS 160A-400), a local historic zoning district could not be established without the approval of the City Council. Also, the council must establish a historic commission to provide a zoning certificate (Certificate of Appropriateness) and to issue a zoning permit before approving the establishment of a historic district.

The TRNA and TUNA lobbied the Greenville City Council to establish a Historic Commission for Greenville. In 1988, the council unanimously approved the establishment of a Historic Preservation Commission. The responsibility of the commission was to work with state, federal, and local governments and to recommend the selection and preservation of historic buildings as well as historic neighborhoods to the City Council. Beginning in early 1989, the commission met regularly to develop guidelines and map strategies on how to identify potential grants. Meanwhile, TRNA coordinated its efforts with TUNA, including actively lobbying the city to designate their neighborhood as a historic district. Between 1989 and 1990, the two organizations held several meetings to discuss the requirements and guidelines for a historic district. According to the Greenville City Ordinance, for a structure to be included as a part of a historic district, the proposed building must be at least fifty years old and possess some historic and architectural significance. The designation process included surveying and the preparation of a document that included historical material relevant to the structure under review. A neighborhood can be designated as a historic district if 70 percent or more of the structures in the area qualify to be included as part of the historic district. At the time College View was being considered for a historic district, there were about three hundred buildings with the potential to qualify as historic structures.

In 1990, the Historic Commission applied for a grant from the N.C. Division of Archives and History to inventory and prepare for nomination by the National Register of Historic Places. The commission selected Historic Preservation Consulting Inc., of Greenville, to conduct the survey and prepare the nomination form. The city also assigned a staff member to coordinate the project with the division, the consultant, and the neighborhood associations. The consultant recommended the designation of the College View area as a historic district and subsequently prepared the nomination form. The area extended from First Street in the north to East Carolina University in the south to Holly Street in the west and Eastern Street to the east. Figure 12.4 depicts the geographic location of the district. The district includes 246 properties on 57 acres of land, including 13 properties that constitute the historic area of the ECU campus. On March 22, 1991, Mrs. Melinda Coleman Wall, chairperson of the Historic Preservation Commission, advised the university of the designation of the College View area as a historic district. On November 19, 1992, the College View area was officially listed on the National Register of Historic Places, but approval at the local level did not occur until 1994.

The Historic Preservation Commission and the Greenville Planning and Zoning Commission (P&Z) held several meetings to review the proposal developed by the consultant. They heard from various groups, pro and con, on the designation of the College View area. On January 18, 1994, the P&Z recommended the approval of the proposal to the City Council. James L. Smith, executive assistant to Chancellor Eakin, appeared before the Greenville P&Z Commission and presented the university's position, reiterating that the university was opposed to including its properties as part of the historic district. ECU owned six properties, the Chancellor's

FIGURE 12.4   College View, Historic District

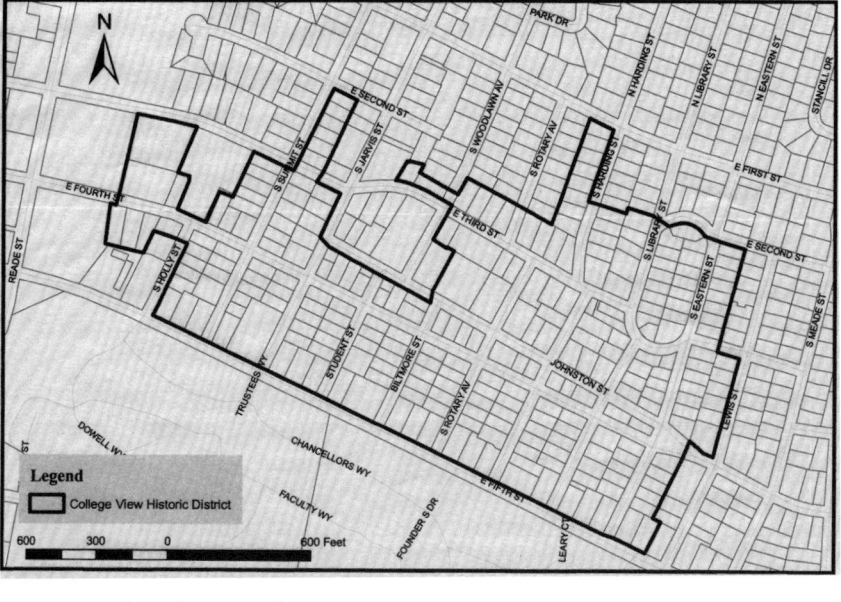

Source: Daily Reflector, February, 6, 1994, B-1.

House (William Dail House), Career Services Building (the original president's house), Taylor-Slaughter Alumni Center, Howard House, Facilities
Services Office, and Ward Guest House. Historic district guidelines require
that any repair work or architectural change on properties in the historic
district must be cleared by the Historic Preservation Commission to ensure
that the changes meet the guidelines set by the commission. Such a process, the university believed, would be restrictive and full of red tape. ECU
was not opposed to the establishment of a historic district; it only wanted
its properties to be excluded from the district or a written agreement to be
included that would exempt the university from having to comply with historic district guidelines. In short, the university did not want any restrictions on use of its properties.

At the time that the proposal was being reviewed by the Historic Preservation Commission, university officials had expressed their disapproval
of the inclusion of university properties. On March 6, 1991, at a meeting of
city officials and representatives of the Historic Preservation Commission
and the chancellor, the university expressed its concern about the inclusion
of university properties in the historic district. On March 26, 1991, in a letter to Ron Kimble, City Manager Dick Edwards, assistant to the chancellor,
reaffirmed the university's objection to the inclusion of university proper-

ties within the historic district. On April 13, the university received a draft copy of the nomination form. Preliminary discussions between the city and the university seemed to suggest that the city was willing to exclude university properties from its list if the university would give up its objection to having its properties listed in the National Register. But as events unfolded, the city continued to pursue its objective of developing a historic district. On April 14, 1991, an editorial in the *Daily Reflector* endorsed the inclusion of the College View district but warned against creating a situation that would inhibit the growth of the university.

The university's objection was based on concerns of limiting future plans for expansion or alterations. If the university properties are included in the Historic Register, then the university would have to comply with the regulations to protect the architectural and structural integrity of the properties listed before it could use state funds to alter, demolish, or repair any of its properties listed in the register. The determination whether the university is complying for any changes would have to be made by the state Historic Preservation Office. The university felt that the procedure would create an undue burden regarding its decisions on future development plans of university properties. Experiences in other areas, notably Raleigh and Chapel Hill, indicated that memoranda of agreements are often executed between state agencies and the Historic Commission to set up a consultative process to work out an acceptable course of action. In Chapel Hill, the consultative process has proven to be helpful to accomplish UNC's plans without any impediments from the Historic Properties Commission.

On June 3, 1991, in a letter to Ron Kimble, Chancellor Eakin reaffirmed the university's position by requesting the city to delete university properties included in the proposed National Register nomination. A week before the hearing by the City Council, ECU filed a protest petition. In October 1991, Eakin sent another letter to Mayor Nancy Jenkins and other city officials reaffirming the university's opposition to the proposal. The ECU Board of Trustees also expressed its position through a unanimous vote opposing the proposal.

At the City Council's meeting on February 10, 1994, Dr. James L. Smith made a plea either to exclude ECU properties from the district or to include a written agreement that would exempt the university from having to comply with the historic guidelines. Earlier, in a letter to the editor, Smith had affirmed the university's position when he noted that the university believed that complying with external regulations would place an unnecessary and heavy burden on the time and resources of the university. Smith went on to state that while ECU upholds the proud traditions of its campus and its neighborhood, it is opposed to adding another layer of bureaucracy and burdensome regulation to its environment.

There were close to 100 area residents supporting the proposal at the City Council meeting. As for the university, despite the efforts by the chancellor and the last minute plea by Dr. Smith, the council was not swayed by the reasons offered. The council unanimously approved the proposal to designate the College View area as a historic district, the first in the city's history. The council's decision was the culmination of a ten-year effort on the part of the TRNA and TUNA to get the College View area designated a historic district. Many of the residents in the neighborhood were ready to have their neighborhood designated, and they had waited for the action of the City Council. After extensive discussion among the staff and administrators of the university, the matter was left to rest without any further actions. The university had to take into account the importance of maintaining a good relationship with the city as well as its neighbors.

The College View Historic District designation has provided a mechanism to insure that the neighborhood maintained its historic character. Many of ECU's students reside in this neighborhood. Property owners preserve the architectural quality of the neighborhood, which, in turn, helped to create a safe and peaceful environment for residents, many of whom are students.

The ECU Medical Park

The idea of developing a medical district in Greenville goes back to 1974, when the Greenville City Council designated 2,300 acres of land around the old Pitt County Hospital area (currently occupied by the Pitt County Office) to be developed as a medical arts and health care district. About 300 of the 2,300 acres were zoned office and institutional. In 1975, the state legislature approved the ECU Medical School, and, in 1977, the first class was enrolled.

As the area surrounding the medical school and the Pitt County Memorial Hospital began to grow, the Greenville city planning department continued to receive more and more requests for rezoning of property in the area. Concerned with the increasing development pressure, the Greenville City Council in 1984 adopted Resolution No. 689, suspending rezoning requests involving the medical arts and health care district areas until further studies determined the impact of land-use changes on the medical school and the hospital. In 1985, the council appointed a nine-member Medical District Land Use Study Committee, charged with the responsibility of developing a comprehensive plan for a medical park. The membership of the committee included prominent individuals from the university, the city, and the county as well as some property owners: Richard I. Flye (chairman emeritus), Janice Faulkner (successor), D. Wayne Adams, Thomas O. Baines, Charles M. Berkey, Phillip R. Dixon, Wes Hankins, Richard J. McKee, and Daniel Worthington. In December 1985, the committee presented the proposed medical park comprehensive plan to the Greenville City Council.

The plan proposed that by the year 2000, the East Carolina Medical Park would develop into a campuslike environment covering 5,300 acres where 10,000 employees could work in medical and medical-related activities. The commission also envisioned that over six hundred doctors would provide specialized care to patients from the eastern part of the state. The report recommended that the City Council should adopt a long-range planning process that would (a) acquire land for the proposed medical park in advance of need and (b) appoint a permanent East Carolina Medical Park Advisory Committee with the power to conduct regular studies on the development of the park. Other recommendations included the development of an appropriate zoning ordinance to regulate land use, traffic flow, and other development standards that would govern lot dimensions, signage, and landscaping.

In 1986, the proposed plan was adopted by the City Council after a review by various committees including the Planning and Zoning Commission, the Pitt County Development Commission, and the Pitt County Board of Adjustment. Traffic flow was a major concern of the commission, which recommended that the City Council give priority to the development of Arlington Boulevard in its thoroughfare plans and upgrade the east-west access road to Highway 264. It also recommended the adoption of measures to protect environmentally sensitive areas and to acquire recreational space.

No sooner was the proposal adopted than issues regarding the commitment of both the city and the county to protect the proposed medical park surfaced. Complaints of "turf battle," eroding the very concept of a medical zone, and "ignoring the medical park plan in urging zoning passages" started to erupt. A major zoning case prompted the Greenville *Daily Reflector* to voice its concerns through a series of articles. The case involved a request by John's Flowers in July 1987 for a special use permit to operate a flower shop in the medical district (MD-2) area. Special use permits have to be granted by the Board of Adjustments, a quasi-judiciary body appointed to review special cases. The board denied the special use request for the flower shop.

In August 1987, John's Flowers requested the Greenville P&Z Commission for an amendment of the zoning ordinance to allow the location of a flower shop in the MD-2 area. The P&Z denied the request and sent its recommendations to the City Council. In March 1988, the City Council, against the recommendations of the P&Z, amended the zoning ordinance to include flower shops in a medical district area. This decision prompted the *Daily Reflector* to issue a blistering editorial that expressed its disap-

FIGURE 12.5   Medical District Area

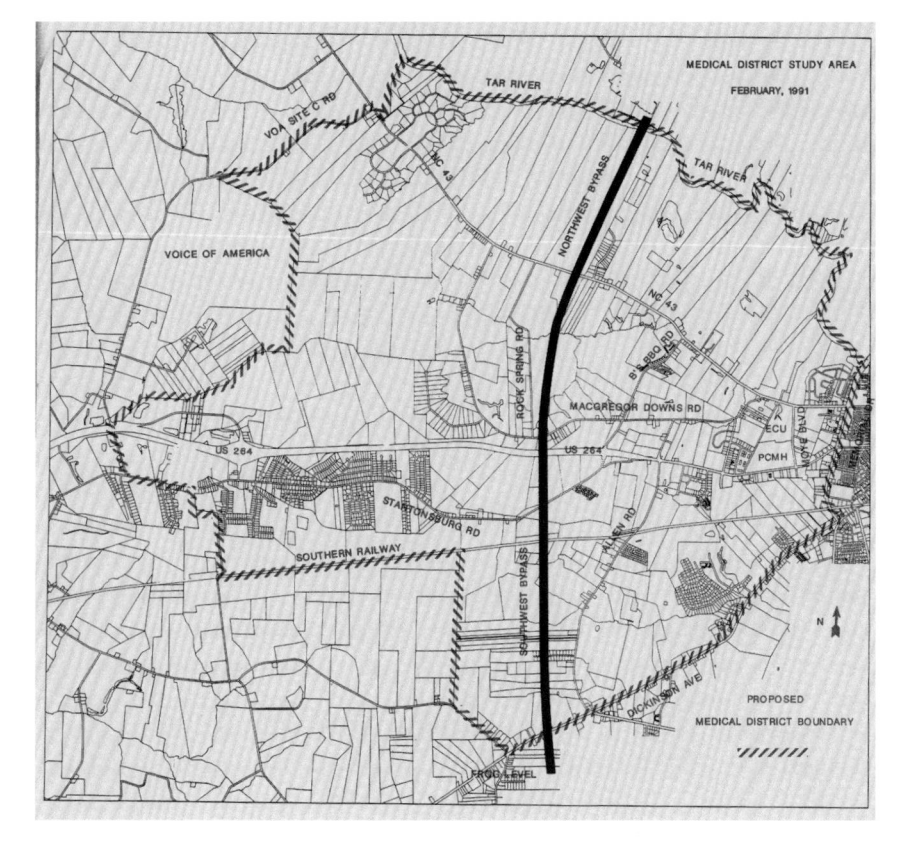

pointment with the council and urged voters to question the wisdom of the
council's decision. It characterized the council's decision to disregard the
effort to protect the integrity of the medical district zoning as ill advised
and a regressive position.

In April 1988, Mayor Ed Carter requested the P&Z to review the medical district (MD-1, MD-2, MD-3) areas. A subcommittee of the P&Z made up
of Ric Miller, Steve Blades, and Wallace Wooles was appointed. The P&Z
subcommittee presented its recommendations to the council in July 1988.
Meanwhile, in June 1988, the Pitt County Medical Society had presented the
council with a resolution requesting the establishment of a Medical Park
Advisory Commission, the adoption of a moratorium for three years on the
granting of variance in the medical district area, city and county cooperation in determining the growth of the medical park area, and supporting
the P&Z Commission's position in keeping a flower shop as a special use request, which would require the approval of the Board of Adjustments.

At the July 1988 meeting, the council reviewed the recommendations from its subcommittee as well as the resolutions from the Pitt County Medical Society and decided to appoint a council subcommittee to further study the resolution. Mayor Carter appointed two council members (Nancy Jenkins and Lorraine Shinn) and two P&Z members (Wally Wooles and Wes Hankins) to study the recommendations. The council subcommittee presented its recommendations in September 1988. The recommendations included a rezoning amendment of selected sites for areas south of Stantonsburg Road (MD-2 and MD-3). The council requested the input of the P&Z, which was granted in February 1989. In March 1989, the council held public hearings to seek input on the proposed amendments. There was a strong public reaction in favor of rejecting the amendments. In April, the council decided to table the proposed amendments, and Mayor Carter requested Janice Faulkner to reconvene the original Medical District Land Use Study Committee to review the case. Faulkner's response was a resounding no to the request for convening the original Medical District Land Use Study Committee. She believed that the need to reconsider the plan was not motivated by problems related to the original document but due to inconsistencies of the city's commitment to full implementation of the plan. Furthermore, Faulkner believed that any change that deviates from the original plan would be viewed as caving in to political pressure rather than upholding the basic principles of sound planning.

Meanwhile, property owners made several rezoning requests for areas designated within the medical district area. In March 1990, a joint meeting of the city and the county appointed a task force to review the plan. The task force was supposed to be broad-based, representing the county, the city, and the university. Members of the task force included Bruce Flye, Jr., director of facilities planning at ECU (chairman); Philip Flowers, a developer (vice chairman); and members Andrew Best, Dorothy Dail, Deborah Davis, Kenneth Hite, Tom Irons, J. D. Lawrence, Kim Ramseur, and Larry Seigler. Staff members from the city, the county, the Greenville Utilities Commission, and the Pitt County Development Commission were assigned to provide support to the task force. The main charge of the task force was to "review and assess past efforts and recommend future steps to (be taken) to develop an updated plan of action for implementing the East Carolina Medical Park Concept."

The task force proposed a 12,000-acre medical district whose boundary included Tar River to the north, Memorial Drive to the east, US 264A (Dickinson Avenue) and the Southern Railway to the south, and Voice of America to the west. The committee also recommended that the following steps be taken to implement the plan:

- Develop a 1,200–2,000 acre research and development park within the larger medical district area.
- Appoint a Medical District Advisory Commission. This group should serve as the special planning and zoning advisory body. Final decision making authority on city and county properties rests with the City Council and the County Commissioners. The size of the Commission should be large enough to have good representation from various groups of the community.
- Increase the Medical District area to the proposed 10,000 acres. Land that is currently in the Greenville ETJ (Extraterritorial Jurisdiction) would be given a "holding" designation, that is, area zoning would remain unchanged until the medical district boundary is clearly defined.
- Establish a nonprofit corporation to acquire land and oversee development and management of the district. This body would include members from the city, county, East Carolina University, Pitt County Memorial Hospital and corporate sponsors.
- Prepare a medical district land use plan for adoption by the city and the County. The Plan should be developed by the Medical District Advisory Commission.
- Develop a nonprofit park corporation to initiate a marketing strategy for further development of the district.

Both the city and the county officials welcomed the establishment of a medical district with the necessary plans and regulatory measures in place. But there were concerns about the size of the area to be designated as part of the district. Some property owners as well as city and county officials felt that the size of the district was too large. There were also concerns about zoning being too restrictive. Pitt County had not adopted zoning, and property owners were afraid that zoning would take away their right to control their land. This concern was made clear by Tom Johnson Sr., chair of the County Commission. Part of the problem stemmed from the fact that the city of Greenville had a zoning ordinance that has been in operation since the late 1940s, but the county lacked one. Another problem came because the city had created its own medical district in the mid-1980s, while the concept was quite new to the county.

In late January 1992, the size of the proposed district was reduced from the original 12,000 acres to 6,000 acres (with 60 percent from the county and 40 percent from the city). County Manager Kramer Jackson and City Manager Ron Kimble made a recommendation to reduce the size to 6,000 acres. Public discussion of the proposal during preliminary hearings was heated, and many landowners opposed the idea of introducing zoning. Zoning, in their view, would be too restrictive and remove their control over use of their property. After a long debate, the medical district boundary was finally defined. It was to be bounded by Tar River on the north, Southern Railway train tracks to the south, secondary road 1202 (McGregor Downs Road) to the east, and a line 300 feet west of the bypass to the west. The district would include 3,400 acres in the county and 2,600 acres in the city. Jackson and Kimble also agreed that a land-use study should be conducted before any zoning takes place. The proposal was submitted to a joint meeting of the city and the county, which together decided to undertake a land-use study.

At the end of January 1992, the city and the county governing board hired an outside consultant for $25,000 to study the feasibility of the 6,000 acres of land close to the hospital and the medical school for a medical district. The study was to provide an "expert opinion" on the proper use of land in the area and the impact of zoning. Although there was opposition from some county commissioners on the idea of spending taxpayers' money to hire a consultant when the study could be done in-house by the county staff, the contract to undertake the study was given to Edward D. Stone Jr. and Associates of Durham.

Edward D. Stone and Associates made a comprehensive land-use study of the area in the county to the west of Greenville and presented its recommendations, which endorsed the designation of a medical district covering an area of 6,000 acres to be set aside for future development, the establishment of a Medical District Development Commission to serve in an advisory capacity, the initiation of a management entity for the technology park, and the establishment of a corporation to start purchasing land within the area for development. It also included other land use and planning recommendations such as allowing mixed land use, establishing a master land-use plan review process, promoting cluster development, and initiating greenway areas.

Many of the recommendations from the Medical District Task Force were later included in the Medical District Plan prepared by Edward D. Stone, but they have yet to be implemented. Neither a Medical District Advisory Commission nor a nonprofit corporation, as recommended by the task force, has been created to acquire properties and market the medical area. The development process was pretty much left to market forces. However, despite the failure to implement some of the recommendations of Edward D. Stone and those offered by the various task forces going back to 1985, the medical district plan was instrumental in establishing a rational land-use process that helped the city to regulate development around the hospital and the ECU Medical School. The Medical District Plan was subsequently incorporated as an addendum to Horizon, the comprehensive plan for the city of Greenville, and later into the revised Horizon Plan of 2004.

The Eastward Expansion Plan

In spring 2000, ECU's Office of Institutional Planning was in the process of developing the 2000–2005 strategic plan. Enrollment projections indicated that ECU would attract over 8,000 new students to reach an enrollment of 27,000 by 2008. University officials indicated that there would be a need for more space to accommodate the projected growth. They estimated that ECU would need an additional 100 acres of land and about 3 million square feet of building space to accommodate the projected students and additional 1,000 faculty and staff.

As part of the main campus master plan, the university planning office's proposal included the incorporation of neighborhoods bordering the eastern part of the campus, specifically the neighborhood bordering Elm, Fifth, and Tenth Streets, which included about three dozen houses and several downtown businesses. In June 2000, they presented the expansion plan to a meeting of community leaders and residents, but the reaction of the community to the proposal was strongly negative. Many of the residents maintained that the plan would destroy their stable neighborhood that has been part of Greenville's history. The targeted neighborhoods organized themselves under the University Neighborhood Association (TUNA) and initiated an extensive campaign to oppose the university's plan through letter writing, placing posters on front lawns, and attending meetings and actively opposing the plan. "Save our neighborhood" and "Not in my backyard" were some of the slogans used by the neighborhood to oppose the plan. There were also signs on lawns in the Elmhurst Elementary School and Forest Hills areas carrying the same message.

University officials also had to deal with the opposition of Uptown Greenville, Inc., a group of merchants and businesspeople representing the downtown area. ECU's expansion plan indicated that the university would be interested in acquiring property in the downtown area for offices and parking spaces. The university plan also included modifications of the zoning ordinance to allow mixed land uses, so that buildings in the second and higher floors could be used for residential purposes while first floors could remain for business use. Members of Uptown Greenville, Inc., expressed their disapproval of the proposal by signing a resolution opposing ECU's expansion plan into their area. Uptown Greenville, Inc., was founded in the 1990s to help revitalize the downtown area as the heart of Greenville. The major objective of the group is to revitalize downtown Greenville while preserving its role as the cultural, social, and business hub of the city oriented toward pedestrians and bicyclists. In May 2000, the ECU Board of Trustees decided to strike the eastward expansion plan of the campus, and the plan was subsequently removed from the campus master plan by university officials.

The Town-Gown Committee

Before the 1990s, ECU and the city of Greenville had no formal administrative structure that met regularly to discuss matters of mutual concern. Meetings to address issues of interest on both sides were held on an ad hoc basis. For instance, during Halloween, officials from both sides would get together, usually about a week before Halloween, to review safety, traffic, and other issues related to the event. Downtown Greenville has developed a reputation as the place to be on Halloween night. Many people from surrounding communities converge downtown to participate in a street party. The area often gets overcrowded, and safety becomes a concern. To avoid problems, university and city officials would meet to strategize on how they would manage the crowd without dampening the festive atmosphere.

The town-gown relationship was limited to such ad hoc meetings. Relations between ECU and Greenville have always been very good, as the city views ECU with pride. For instance, in the 1970s, Barrus Construction Company donated about 15 acres of land north of Tar River and east of Green Street to the East Carolina Foundation. This open tract of land had three small lakes that were remnants of a sand mining operation. The city of Greenville was interested in developing a park north of the Tar River, and the Parks and Recreation Department approached the ECU Foundation expressing the city's interest. The foundation sold the land to the city for $75,000. River Park North has a number of facilities including a picnic shelter, fishing and boating, nature trails, camping, and a museum of natural history. It is one of the most visited parks in the city and has become a favorite destination for many organizations, school-group activities, and corporate picnic outings.

Beginning in the early 1990s, there was more and more need for interaction between the city and the university. Three factors contributed to this change. First, with the increase in student population and faculty and staff employment, the university had to deal with a number of problems, such as the need for more office and classroom space and parking, which affected the city and the surrounding communities. A second reason deals with parking, traffic, noise, and crime. As the number of students residing off campus increased, problems related to parking, traffic, noise, and crime began to rise, and many residents, particularly those close to campus, began to complain about these problems. By early 1990, it was clear that unless university and city officials established a mechanism by which they could address many of these issues, the problem would escalate to a crisis.

A third factor is the university's decision to initiate a long-term planning process that envisaged the physical growth of the university beyond the traditional core campus to the surrounding neighborhoods. Before the early 1990s, although the university had short-term plans, there were limited funds available to implement the plans. In 1994, a new budgetary process gave the university the opportunity to acquire new property. The new budgetary process granted the university a flexible budget management authority that allowed it to carry over unused funds—up to 2.5 percent of the budget—to the following year. Some of these funds could be used to purchase property. Before 1994, any surplus fund had to be returned to the state. Thus, the new budgetary system facilitated the university's plan to expand to neighboring areas by acquiring property. By the same token, it forced the university to deal with a number of issues affecting its neighbors as well as the city.

In 1989, Mayor Nancy Jenkins proposed the idea of establishing a Town-Gown Committee that would meet regularly to discuss matters of mutual concern. Ron Kimble, city manager, contacted Dick Edwards, executive assistant to Chancellor Eakin, to discuss the mayor's idea and the advantage of establishing a high-level policy review committee. On December 5, 1989, Chancellor Eakin notified Kimble the university would endorse Mayor Jenkins's idea. He also identified university members who would represent it on the committee.

On January 17, 1990, Mayor Jenkins responded positively to Chancellor Eakin's proposed membership, and the first meeting was held on January 16, 1990, at the River Park North. The city of Greenville served as the host. The meeting discussed the importance of establishing a high-level administrative review committee that would meet regularly to discuss issues affecting both the city and the university. For the purpose of illustration, a sample of the range of issues covered at the various meetings is included below.

> Campus master plan
> Halloween planning
> Public safety communications
> Historic preservation and the Tar River Neighborhood Association
> One-way street patterns, status report
> Noise ordinance review
> Parking
> Greenway dedication
> Convention center
> Efforts to curb illegal and underage drinking
> Dormitory sprinkler system
> International festival

Speakers and car radio blasters in Tar River neighborhood
Public transportation
Downtown bar—occupancy limits, complaints by black ECU students

Table 12.1 presents a chronological order of the dates and conveners of the meetings.

For the last fourteen years, the Town-Gown Committee has met at least once a year. Many of the members have characterized the committee as an

TABLE 12.1   Chronology of Town-Gown Meetings, 1990–2003

Date	Convener	Place
February 16, 1990	City	River Park North
May 4, 1990	ECU	Mendenhall Student Center (MSC)
August 22, 1990	City	City Hall-Conference Room
October 11, 1990	ECU	MSC
June 25, 1991	City	Parks and Rec, Cedar Lane
September 17, 1991	ECU	MSC
June 26, 1992	City	Public Works Facility
August 25, 1992	ECU	MSC
October 28, 1992	ECU	MSC
February 22, 1993	City	Greenville Teen Center
September 13, 1993	ECU	MSC
June 14, 1994	City	Public Works Facility
September 19, 1994	City	River Park North
August 8, 1995	ECU	MSC, Trustee Suite
August 13, 1996	City	PFR Building
February 11, 1997	ECU	Sweethearts
July 30, 1997	City	City Hall, 1st Floor
August 18, 1998	ECU	MSC, Trustee Suite
January 22, 1999	City	Fire Rescue Building
August 26, 1999	ECU	MSC, Trustee Suite
March 9, 2000	City	Bradford Creek Golf
August 7, 2000	ECU	MSC, Trustee Suite
March 20, 2001	City	City Tennis Center
September 20, 2001	ECU	MSC, Trustee Suite
June 18, 2002	City	Public Works Administration Building
September 18, 2002	ECU	Edwin W. Monroe
July 21, 2003	City	River Birch Center at Evans Park

effective body responsible for the smooth and productive relationship between the city and the university. While the discussions were frank and at times blunt, members handled themselves in a professional manner. The success of the committee in dealing with many of the complicated issues affecting both the university and the city is attributable to the leadership quality and the dedication of the members from both sides. Although the committee has not met in the last couple of years, both city and university officials believe that the meetings will resume once the new administrative structure of the university is in place.

The Good Neighborhood Initiative

Largely pressed by concerns expressed by property owners residing close to the university campus regarding the violation of city codes, the city of Greenville in 2000 approached the university administration to develop a plan on how the neighborhoods affected by violation of city codes could be protected. Some of the concerns expressed by the property owners included parking on unimproved surfaces such as front yards; more than three unrelated people occupying a dwelling unit; overgrown grass or weeds taller than 12 inches; litter in yards, especially alcoholic beverage containers; loud noise, especially music from stereos or live bands; and public intoxication and urination.

The university agreed to meet with city staff to develop a program that would minimize the negative effects of some of the above concerns. The two groups came up with a concept known as the Zero Tolerance Neighborhood Initiative. The objective of the initiative is to "maintain and improve the safety, appearance and quality of life in the affected neighborhoods." According to the initiative, Zero Tolerance would allow the city, through its Police Department and the Planning and Community Development Office, to strictly enforce the regulations pertaining to violations of the city code. In July 2000, the city's director of planning and community development invited the property owners in the area for a meeting to discuss the proposed concept. He indicated that the team made up of university and city staff had come up with a concept that emphasizes the principle of good neighborliness while it is also willing to use the concept of Zero Tolerance as a last resort. The property owners endorsed the initiative.

While the concept of Zero Tolerance was basically premised on strict enforcement of the law, there were some concerns on how to communicate the underlying objectives of the initiative to the community. Both the university and city officials believed that communication was key to help residents understand why the Zero Tolerance initiative was introduced. They focused on strategies on how to disseminate information to property owners and tenants, who are mostly students, about the new policy. After extensive consultation, both the city and the university officials agreed to adopt the following procedures for effective implementation of the policy.

First, at the beginning of each academic year, officials from the university and the city would meet with property owners and student representatives to discuss the objectives and purposes of the policy. Second, a letter outlining the concept of being a good neighbor and the consequences of violating city codes would be sent to all property owners in the area. Third, a door hanger prepared in the form of a poster with relevant information on Zero Tolerance and on how to be a good neighbor would be distributed to residents in the area. Fourth, both city and university officials would seize every opportunity, including neighborhood and organization meetings (e.g., meetings of fraternities and sororities) to convey the message of how to be a good neighbor. The views from both sides are that the system has been helpful in maintaining good neighborhood relations. Students appreciate the effort city officials are making to inform them about good neighborliness. Similarly, city officials believe that the procedure has helped in minimizing violations of city codes. Although both sides are trying to create a good environment, many problems, particularly those related to parking, are far from being addressed. Students complain about their cars being towed away (in the first three weeks of the fall semester in 2005, 197 vehicles were towed away for parking violations near the campus), while residents insist that they are being blocked by cars parked in their driveways. In 2004, the university created the Office of Student-Neighborhood Relations to help address some of the problems both students and neighborhoods near the campus face. The office has an outreach program that informs students about city ordinances, safety issues, and how to address neighborhood concerns.

ECU-City-County Development Committees

Since 1994, administrators from ECU, the city, and the county have regularly met for open discussions on development issues. The meetings, designed to forge working relationships among officials of the city, county, and university, have been informal. Most of them focus on the same issues discussed in the Town-Gown Committee meetings, with the only difference that these meetings were for department heads dealing with development issues. They include individuals from the city manager's office and department heads of police, fire/rescue, planning, and public works. University representatives include the special assistant to the chancellor, department heads of economic development and community engagement, budgeting, institutional planning, and student services. The county sends the deputy county manager and planning director. By contrast, the Town-

Gown meetings include department heads as well as high-level officials including the chancellor and the mayor or their designees.

In November 2002, the Greenville City Council appointed members to a newly established Redevelopment Commission. The purpose of the commission is to rebuild blighted areas of the city, particularly the central part of the city, which includes the western edge of the university campus. One of the major objectives of the commission is to coordinate the expansion plans of ECU into downtown and the preservation of neighboring communities. This commission will also coordinate the activities for the acquisition of property for the Tenth Street Connector project, which will link ECU's east and west campuses. The membership includes prominent individuals from the university, Uptown Greenville, Inc., and neighborhoods in the central city area.

The commission is in the process of developing a city center redevelopment plan. Some of the components of the redevelopment plan will include new housing, commercial in-fill development, a hotel, and an alumni/welcome center for ECU. Once the plan is approved, it is expected to play a major role in shaping the redevelopment of the central city of Greenville as well as the western edge of the campus.

Chancellor's Community Advisory Council

The idea of establishing a Community Advisory Council goes back to 1999, when Chancellor Eakin announced at the October 22, 1999, trustees meeting his plan to establish a Sustainable Economic Recovery and Growth Center at ECU that will serve as a model for how universities engage, reach out, and provide public services to improve their constituent regions. Eakin's plan was precipitated by the devastating flood following Hurricane Floyd that affected much of eastern North Carolina in 1999. Eakin set up a task force of university administrators and experts to meet with community leaders to help develop a better understanding of the needs of the region and identify the resources that ECU may be able to make available to affected communities.

In 2001, Chancellor Muse, soon after his arrival on campus, initiated a major community development program that included visits to several communities as part of his Hometown Tour to understand the concerns of neighboring communities. In 2003, Muse directed his staff to hold focus group discussions to further identify the major issues and problems affecting eastern North Carolina. University staff held three major focus group discussions with the African American and the Hispanic/Latino communities locally. The focus groups generated a lot of information related to:

- The need to establish better communication between ECU and various community organizations in the area
- Concerns about ECU's expansion plans into West Greenville
- How ECU can help community organizations to secure funding from outside organizations
- How ECU students and faculty can help communities in setting priorities
- How ECU can help in job training and in enhancing educational opportunities, particularly for the chronically unemployed
- Appreciation of values of diversity to create better understanding.

In 2003, Chancellor Muse created the Chancellor's Community Advisory Council to help facilitate his community engagement program. In 2004, Chancellor Ballard recommended the creation of a standing advisory council and the adoption of bylaws. At his inaugural address, Ballard reaffirmed the university's commitment to playing a major role in transforming the economy of our region; partnering with public, private, and civic organizations; valuing diversity and openness in building a conducive and robust learning environment; and serving as a vital educational steward of the state as ECU strives to become the leadership university of the twenty-first century.

REFERENCES

City of Greenville. Papers. Greenville, North Carolina.
Daily Reflector, 1987–2004, Greenville, NC: Cox North Carolina Publications, Inc.
ECU News & Communications Services. *East: The Magazine of East Carolina University*, East Carolina University Archives.
ECU News & Communications Services. Press Releases. East Carolina University Archives.
ECU Institutional Planning, Research & Effectiveness Office. *Fact Book*, Greenville, NC: East Carolina University.
ECU Public Safety Office. Papers. East Carolina University Archives.
ECU Regional Development Institute. *ECU Impact*, East Carolina University.
Harris, Andy, personal interview by author, 2006.
Pitt County Development Commission. Papers. Greenville, North Carolina.
Initiative for a Competitive Inner City and Chief Executive Officers for Cities. *Leveraging Colleges and Universities for Urban Economic Revitalization: An Agenda, Greater Philadelphia Regional Review*, Spring 2003.
U.S. Housing and Urban Development. *An Alliance for Community Building*, Rockville, MD, 2003.

ACKNOWLEDGMENTS

I would like to thank Mr. Andy Harris of the city of Greenville and Mr. Wes Hankins of ECU for providing me with information and reviewing drafts of this chapter. Mr. John Chaffee of the Pitt County Development Commission, Drs. James L. Smith and Bob Thompson, and Mr. Bruce Flye were also helpful in providing information.

Index

D.D.S. in Seven program, 128
"Dean's Office Operational Plan," 25
Debnam Resource Center for Family Literacy, 137
Degree in Three Program, 127
degree programs, 20
Delia, Albert, 346
Denkler, Mary, 310
Department of Athletics, 221–222
Department of Drama and Speech, 314
Department of English
  operational planning report, 36
Department of Family Medicine, 268, 277–278
Department of Industrial Technology
  operational planning report, 36. See also School of Industry and Technology
Department of Internal Medicine, 273, 276
Department of Intramural Recreational Services, 310
Department of Materials Management, 336
Department of Philosophy
  operational planning report, 1996, 37t
  progressive narrative, 1996, 38t
"Department of Physics Operational Plan, 1990–1993," 25, 26
Department of Recreational Services, 311, 312, 313
Department of Theatre and Dance, 314, 315
departments, reorganization, 197–198
Designers Associates, 319
development, expansion efforts, 222–223
Dews, Kenneth, 292, 294, 295, 296, 297–298
Dews, Mamie, 292
Dhan, Robert, 194
Dickey, James, 318
Disney National Teacher of Year, 335
distance learning, 129–131
Distinguished Educator Awards, 328
Distinguished Professsorship of International Studies, 329
diversity goal, 53–55
diversity officer, 118
"Diversity Yes!" brochures, 117
Division of Academic Affairs, 103
Division of Student Life, 72, 77, 87
Dixon, James, 321
Dixon, Phillip R., 216, 328, 330, 353–354
doctoral degree programs, 124

doctoral status, 229–230, 330, 340
Dooley, Joe, 308
Doris Duke Innovation in Clinical Research Award, 333
Dowd, Caleb, 190
Dowdy, Mary Ellen, 326
Dowdy, Ronald, 303–304, 324, 326–327
Dowdy–Ficklen Stadium, 110, 303–304, 326, 344. See also Ficklen Stadium
Dowdy Student Stores, 111, 125, 192, 337, 338. See also Student Stores
Downing, Dr. Clinton, 102
Dragicevich, Nicholas A., 193
Dukakis, Michael, 176
Duke, Christy, 119
Duke University, 255, 284, 288, 289, 301
Duncan, Fitzhugh D., 115
Durham, John, 243

Eakin, Richard R., 20, 21, 22, 29, 30, 33, 34, 35, 38–39, 48, 70, 72, 82, 93, 105, 110, 115–116, 117, 135, 175, 200, 205–206, 211, 213, 215, 223, 224–226, 227, 229, 268, 269–269, 305, 306, 307, 311, 324–325, 326, 329, 331, 333, 334–335, 350, 352, 361, 365
  campus renovation and landscaping, 226–229
  commencement December 2000, 236–237
  comprehensive campaigns, 231–232
  Conference USA, 230–231
  doctoral II status, 229–230
  faculty governance, 226
  goals for 1995–2005, 36–37
  Hurricane Floyd, 233–236, 365
  information technology, 232–233
  science and technology advances, 228
  student recreation, 228–229, 302
  university planning and regional accreditation, 224–225
Eakin, Jo Ann, 70, 110, 113, 224–225, 226, 237
Early Assurance Awards, 128
Eason, Frances, 330
East, John, 321
East Carolina Art Society, 319
East Carolina Bank, 327
East Carolina College, 8
East Carolina Foundation, 360
East Carolina Friends, 174
East Carolina Medical Park, 354, 356

374 INDEX

University of Chicago, 284
University of Kentucky, 144, 330
University of Maine, 243
University of Miami, 306, 330
University of Michigan, 299
University of Minnesota, 243
University of North Carolina, 3, 11, 77, 78, 109, 117, 284, 301
  intercollegiate athletics policy, 211
  School of Medicine at Chapel Hill, 254–255
  system appropriations, 151, *151*
University of North Carolina Board of Governors, 258
  Code (UNC Code), 201, 208
  strategic planning directions, 61–62
University of North Carolina School of Law, 2
University of North Carolina system, strategic directions (2006–2011), 60–61
University of Notre Dame, 299
University of Pittsburgh, 284, 307
University of Tennessee, 299, 307
university organization, Long-Range Planning Commission (1982–1992), 18
University Scholars Awards, 222, 323, 324
university status, 11
Uptown Greenville, Inc., 359, 365
Urals Academy of Public Administration, 336
U.S. Civil Rights Commission, 93–94
U.S. Department of Education, 87, 337
U.S. Department of Health, Education, and Welfare (HEW), 309
U.S. Department of Housing and Urban Development (HUD), 341
U.S.S. *Monitor*, 322, 323
Utah Jazz, 308

Vainright, Julian, 115
Van Fleet, James, 103
Varner, Carroll, 134, 141, 334
Village Green apartments, explosion, 169
Villella, Edward, 314
Villorente, Catalina Maria, 184
Virginia-Pilot/Ledger Star, 324
vision statements (2005), 58
Visual Arts Forum, 319
Voice of America site (west research campus), 87–88
Volpe, Angelo, 203, 224

Wachovia Corporation, 326, 338
Wake Forest College, 2
Wake Forest University, 76, 255, 301
Walas, Joseph, 101–102
Walker, LeRoy T., 317, 329
Walker, Jimmy, 167
Walker Cup International Women's Wheelchair Basketball Tournament, 317
Walker International Human Performance Center, 317. *See also* International Human Performance Center
Wall, Melinda Coleman, 350
Walter, Robbs, Callahan, and Pierce, 135
Ward, Margaret, 334
Ward, Michelle, 310
Ward, Robert A., 231, 326, 330
Ward Guest House, 351
Ward Sports Medicine Building, 67, 74
Ward Sports Medicine Building, 304
Warner, Alex, 328
Warren, Ed, 266–267, 328
Washington Post, 324
Washington State University, 224
Watkins, Greg, 170
Watson, Lawrence, 95
Waugh, William, 272–273
Weaver, Ann R., 328
Webb, Robert C., 70
Wechter, Nell Wise, 321
West End Dining Hall, 77, 87
West Virginia University, 76
Western Carolina University, 307
Westmoreland, Jim, 91
Wetherington, Kitty, 243
Whatley, Ralph, *272*, 275
Whichard, David J. II, 6, 332
Whichard, Jack, 328
Whichard Building, 132, 178
Whichard family, 325
White, Ruth Allen, 10
White Residence Hall, 179, 182
Whitehurst, Grover, 332
Whitehurst, William "Bill," 110
William E. Laupus Health Science Library, 145. *See also* Laupus Library
Williams, Lynwood, 273
Williams, Esther Spencer, 321
Williams, Robert, 254–255
Williams, Theresa, 318
Williams, Walter, 327
Williams, Wayne, 254–255
Williams Arena, 114, 304, 327

Contributors

GEORGE BAILEY received his Ph.D. in philosophy from the University of Miami, Coral Gables, Florida. A faculty member at East Carolina University since 1980, he became chair of the philosophy department in 1992. He has written a variety of articles and a monograph. Since 1988, with the initiation of the strategic planning process, he has participated actively on both administrative and faculty planning committees.

ROGER BILES obtained his Ph.D. at the University of Illinois, Chicago. He is chair of the history department at Illinois State University. He has taught at the University of Memphis, Oklahoma State University, East Carolina University, and Northern Illinois University. He is a specialist in urban history and twentieth-century America and has published extensively in those fields.

PAT BIZZARO is director of the University Writing Programs and professor of English at East Carolina University. Recipient of a Ph.D. from Miami University of Ohio, he is the author of twenty-seven books, including works of poetry, literary criticism, and pedagogical scholarship as well as textbooks. His many awards include being named the 2002 University of North Carolina Board of Governors Distinguished Professor for Teaching.

HENRY C. FERRELL JR. is university historian at East Carolina. He holds a Ph.D. from the University of Virginia. He has taught, researched, and published on the South since 1877 and on the twentieth-century United States. Active in faculty governance organizations from the local to the national level, he is a former chair of the faculty.

BRUCE L. FLYE JR. was university architect at East Carolina from 1992 to 2002. He has a B.A. from North Carolina State University in environmental design in architecture. In addition to responsibility for many expansion projects, he contributed significant effort to the planning of the Higher

Education Facilities Bond Bill passed in 2000. Before joining the university, he was a practicing architect in eastern North Carolina, of which he is a native.

BRETT HURSEY, who earned a Ph.D. in English from Oklahoma State University, has published three full-length collections of poetry, two chapbooks, and work in over a hundred literary journals across the United States and Canada. Additionally, his comedy *Figment* was performed off-Broadway in Manhattan. Hursey presently teaches English at Longwood University.

BRENDA KILLINGSWORTH is an associate professor in the College of Business. Lead academic researcher and coordinator in the college's Labor Market Information Institute, she teaches systems analysis and design. She has given oversight to several university planning projects and has been active in academic shared governance committees. A former chair of the faculty, she currently chairs the University of North Carolina Faculty Assembly.

JIM KIRKLAND teaches courses in folklore, American literature, and rhetoric and composition in East Carolina's English department. His articles and reviews on subjects ranging from Herman Melville's literary uses of tall-tale tradition to composition pedagogy and magico-religious healing traditions have appeared in many journals. Holding a Ph.D. from the University of Tennessee, he has coauthored or coedited seven books.

BOB MORRISON obtained the Ph.D. with a concentration in theoretical chemistry from the University of Nebraska. His principal field of interest is the quantum theory of atoms and molecules with particular interest in the one-particle nature of many-electron systems. He has been active in shared governance for many years, serving on Faculty Senate and administrative committees since the early 1970s. He is a former chair of the faculty.

FREDERICK NISWANDER, PH.D., C.P.A., is the dean of the College of Business and W. Howard Rooks Distinguished Professor. He gained a Ph.D. in accounting from Texas A&M University, and, before joining the ECU accounting faculty in 1993, he held various executive positions in industry and public accounting over a thirteen-year period. A C.P.A. since 1981, he is a former chair of the East Carolina faculty.

WALTER J. PORIES, F.A.C.S., received with honors his M.D. from the University of Rochester School of Medicine and Dentistry. He is the founding chairperson of the Department of Surgery at the Brody School of Medicine, which he led from 1977 to 1996. He continues to serve as chief of the Metabolic Institute. In addition to his teaching and research contributions, he is well known for his cartoons about medicine and academia.

MARY ANN ROSE was assistant to the chancellor under Chancellors Brewer, Howell, Eakin, Muse, and Shelton. She holds the bachelor of science in nursing degree from Georgetown, the master of science in nursing from Case Western Reserve, and the doctorate in education from North Carolina State University. She is currently professor of nursing and leads a research team studying the care of morbidly obese patients.

RALPH SCOTT is professor and curator of rare books in the special collections department of East Carolina University's Joyner Library. He holds a master's degree in history from East Carolina. Currently he is president of the North Carolina Association of Historians and editor of the North Carolina Library Association's *North Carolina Libraries*.

JIM SMITH studied aerospace engineering and philosophy at Pennsylvania State University. He received a doctoral degree in philosophy from Tulane University and joined the East Carolina University faculty in 1969. He has served the university in many academic, faculty governance, and administrative capacities. A former faculty chair, Smith currently is university provost and vice chancellor for academic affairs.

ROBERT J. THOMPSON is an associate professor of political science. Holding a Ph.D. from the University of Oklahoma, between 1988 and 2005 he served in a variety of administrative roles as chair of political science, director of planning and institutional research, chief of staff to Chancellor Eakin, interim vice chancellor for academic affairs under Chancellors Eakin and Muse, and director of institutional planning, research, and institutional effectiveness.

MULATU WUBNEH is chair and professor of the Department of Planning. Holding a Ph.D. from Florida State University, he has been a professor at East Carolina for over twenty-five years. He has served on various committees of the city of Greenville, including work as chair of the board of adjustment. He conducts research on a wide range of development issues including economic development, infrastructure investment, and planning.